Illustrated Framework III

Deborah L. Stone

Wordware Publishing, Inc.

1506 Capital Ave.
Plano, Texas 75074

Printed in the United States of America

ISBN 1-55622-114-2

10 9 8 7 6 5 4 3 2 1

All inquiries for volume purchases of this book should be addressed to Wordware Publishing, Inc. at the above address. Telephone inquiries may be made by calling:

(214) 423-0090

Preface

ABOUT FRAMEWORK III There have been several books written about the different integrated products currently on the market. This book is about Ashton-Tate's Framework III, one of the most popular multi-function products.

Framework III can be used to manipulate ideas, words, numbers and information. *Illustrated Framework III* is meant to supplement the Framework III manuals, not replace them. It restructures the information into a more palpable form, which contains simplified descriptions, several forms of quick reference information, and lots of illustrations.

ABOUT ILLUSTRATED BOOKS As a microcomputer consultant, I am constantly looking for good, authoritative sources of information. This includes books that can help me learn, and that are in a format I can use to teach others.

That's how the Illustrated series began; it was devised to provide quick, easy-to-understand, well illustrated information about an often complicated application. This series is the brainchild of Russell A. Stultz, the author of the first *Illustrated* books.

The alphabetized, modular format lets you find the area of interest quickly. A description, applications, and step-by-step illustrations are provided. This combination gets results. It provides quick answers to questions, and includes examples to help solve real problems.

I hope readers enjoy using this book as much as I've enjoyed writing it.

DEBORAH L. STONE

Contents

Contents (Cont.)

Contents (Cont.)

Recommended Learning Sequence

Recommended Learning Sequence (Cont.)

	Sequence	Description	Module	Page
□	48	Open All, Close All, Size All, Blank All	60	244
□	49	Contents Included	18	77
□	50	Labels Included	50	208
□	51	Notes Included	58	237
□	52	Hide Borders	44	184
□	53	Control Options	19	80
□	54	Database	20	86
□	55	Ascending Sort	9	38
□	56	Spreadsheet	81	327
□	57	Height (# Rows/Records) { }	43	180
□	58	Width (# Cols/Fields) { }	88	359
□	59	Columns/Fields: Add { }	16	66
□	60	Columns/Fields: Remove	17	72
□	61	Rows/Records: Add { }	76	305
□	62	Rows/Records: Remove	77	309
□	63	Decimal Places { }, General, Integer, Fixed Decimal, Currency, Business, Percent, Scientific	22	99
□	64	Descending Sort	23	103
□	65	Go to { }	42	177
□	66	Lock Columns/Rows	52	214
□	67	Words Left/#s Right, Left, Right, Middle	91	369
□	68	Protect from Editing	68	279
□	69	Allow Editing	6	26
□	70	Formulas Included	38	161
□	71	Output Options	64	263
□	72	Entry Format for Data	31	135
□	73	Options for Recalc	62	254
□	74	Draw New Graph	28	122
□	75	Bar, Stacked Bar, Pie, Line, Unmarked Line, Marked Points, X-Y, High-Low-Close	10	43
□	76	Column Has X-axis Labels	15	62
□	77	Row Has X-axis Labels	75	302
□	78	Options (for Graph)	61	249
□	79	Add to Existing Graph	4	18
□	80	Mailmerge Using { }	54	223
□	81	Print Labels Using { }	67	274
□	82	Template { }	84	346
□	83	Macro/Abbreviation	53	218
□	84	DOS Access	25	111
□	85	dBASE	21	95
□	86	Import	47	197
□	87	Export	32	139
□	88	Telecommunications	83	340
□	89	Apps Add-in	8	34
□	90	Network File	55	227
□	91	Network Mail	56	229

Module 1

ABOUT THIS BOOK

INTRODUCTION

Illustrated Framework III describes Ashton-Tate's Framework III. It presents information about the many different operations available in one software package.

This book is designed for beginning users who wish to learn how to "get around" without getting lost. It is also for intermediate and advanced users who need a quick reference which contains examples and explains the rules.

In this book, you will find detailed descriptions of each of the menu options as well as examples which show you how to use them. The menu is across the top of the screen in the following display.

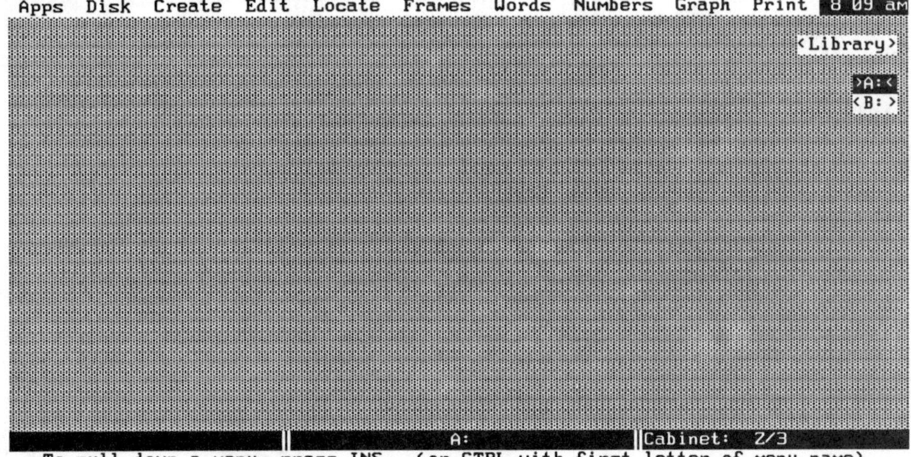

Each menu selection is described in a separate module. The modules are organized alphabetically by option name.

A table in the front of this book lists the recommended order for learning to use Framework III. Each topic listed has a *recommended learning sequence number* to guide you during your learning activity. The actual module number where the topic is covered is also listed for your convenience.

The checklist is ordered for the beginning user in a step-by-step approach. As you complete each module, place a check in the box next to the topic. The checklist begins with the basic requirements and progresses through more advanced topics.

ORGANIZATION

To fit the broad range of users this book addresses, it is organized into small, easy-to-read modules. The modules include descriptions, applications, and illustrations that provide insight into how Framework III can be used to solve practical, everyday problems.

Many examples are presented in the Description, Applications, and Typical Operation sections of the modules. These examples are helpful to users at all skill levels.

The examples in this book can be used as models to design your own application solutions. They bring to light details that are otherwise buried in the material presented in the Framework III manual. With the exception of Modules 1 through 3, each of the modules in this book contains information that pertains to one specific Framework III option.

Module 2 is an introduction to the Framework III package. This module covers Framework III guidelines, terms, and techniques.

Module 3 presents an overview of the Framework rules and keys which tell Framework III what to do.

HARDWARE AND SOFTWARE REQUIREMENTS

Framework III operates on the IBM PC, XT, AT, 3270 PC or a 100% compatible computer. It must use the PC-DOS (version 2.0 or higher) operating system. A minimum of 640K of memory is also required. Your system should be equipped with disk drives and a printer if you want to print documents.

WHAT YOU SHOULD KNOW

You should be familiar with your computer, its keyboard, and some of the commands available on your operating system which allow you to:

- list a directory of your diskettes (or hard disk),
- format a disk (if you have floppy disk drives on your system),
- copy, rename, and delete files.

If you can do these things, you're ready to use Framework III.

Module 2

AN OVERVIEW OF FRAMEWORK III

INTRODUCTION

With the computer hardware explosion experienced during the last few years, "personal computers" are now able to handle more sophisticated software. This opened the door for Framework and now the more powerful Framework III.

Framework III is a software package which is capable of doing many things. Use it as a word processor, an outline processor, a spreadsheet, a database handler, a graphing tool, or a communications link.

Since Framework III is "menu driven," you can use it without having to know a lot about the computer operating system, files, or programming languages. All you have to know to use Framework III is how to position the cursor, read the messages at the bottom of the screen, and press Enter. This book helps you get more acquainted with your many choices and how to use them.

WHY FRAMEWORK III?

Versatility, ease, and power are good reasons.

Framework III combines several different operations in one package. It is a word and outline processor with which you can write letters, a database manager to handle business information, a spreadsheet to do "what if" analysis, a graphing tool to convert numbers to pictures, and a communications link to transfer files to and from other packages.

Operations are done quickly since Framework III doesn't use color or do a lot of drawing on the screen. It is a business tool to be used to make your life easier by helping with your work.

Framework III has several menus from which you select the operations you need to perform. If you make a mistake (short of deleting a file), it can often be "undone" or corrected easily.

A few "play" sessions can get you to a very productive, comfortable relationship with your computer as well as Framework III's power.

Once you discover that "trial and error" is not usually disastrous, your collection of other software packages could get dusty.

Module 3

GAME RULES

DESCRIPTION

Learning to use Framework III is like learning a game. You read the rules, play a few practice games, and then you play for real.

The rules for Framework III are easy to follow. Although there are several of them, you'll get the hang of it as you experience your first few sessions.

Be sure to use the Framework III Setup disk and run SETUPFW to configure the program to match your computer hardware. You only need to do this once.

Before beginning a Framework III session, make sure that your Framework III system disk is in drive A (or on your hard disk). Place a blank, formatted disk in drive B (or drive A). Type FW and press Enter to begin your Framework III session.

When Framework III draws its introduction and presents the license agreement to the screen, insert the System 2 disk and press Enter. A Framework III screen called the "desktop" (similar to the following one) appears on your screen.

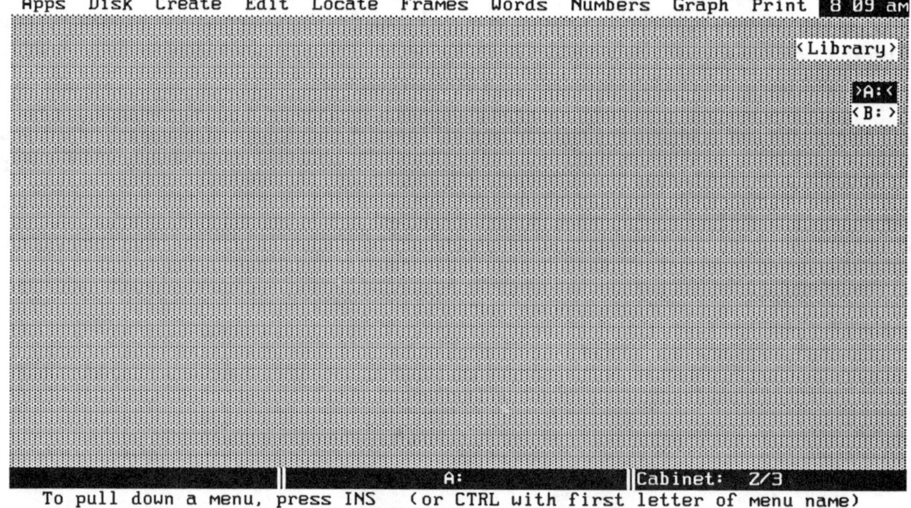

The <A:> and <B:> are disk drive indicators. By positioning the cursor (using the arrow keys) on <A:> and pressing Enter, a frame containing the disk's directory of files is opened on the desktop. The following display shows a desktop with an open frame containing the directory of the disk in drive A.

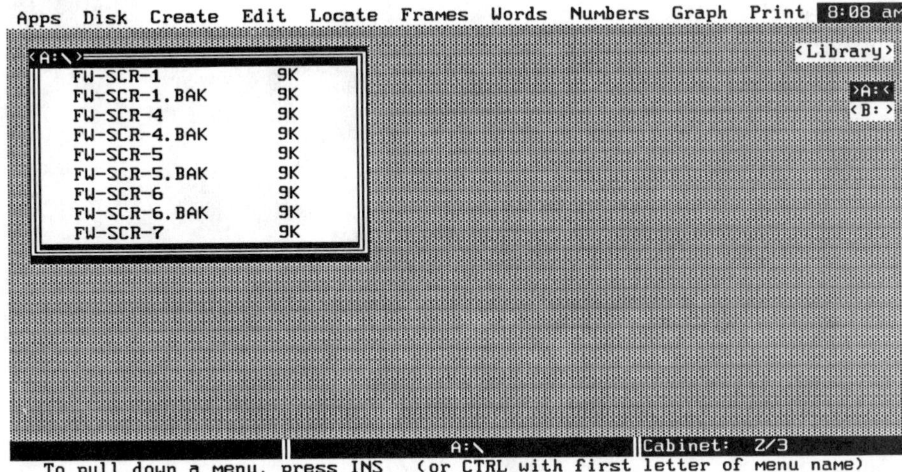

Press Enter to remove the disk directory frame from the desktop. The cursor returns to the drive A indicator.

Each of the words along the top of your desktop is a Main Menu option. Press Ins to position the cursor on the Main Menu line. Next, use the arrow (cursor) keys to highlight the word for the menu frame you need. Framework III displays a "pull-down" menu of options for your selection.

The <Library> on your desktop is used to create and keep special information. For example, your name, special abbreviations, and printer codes to change typefaces can be made available to you at all times. By pressing the arrow (cursor) keys, position the cursor on the <Library> option and press Enter. A frame similar to the one on the following desktop appears on your screen.

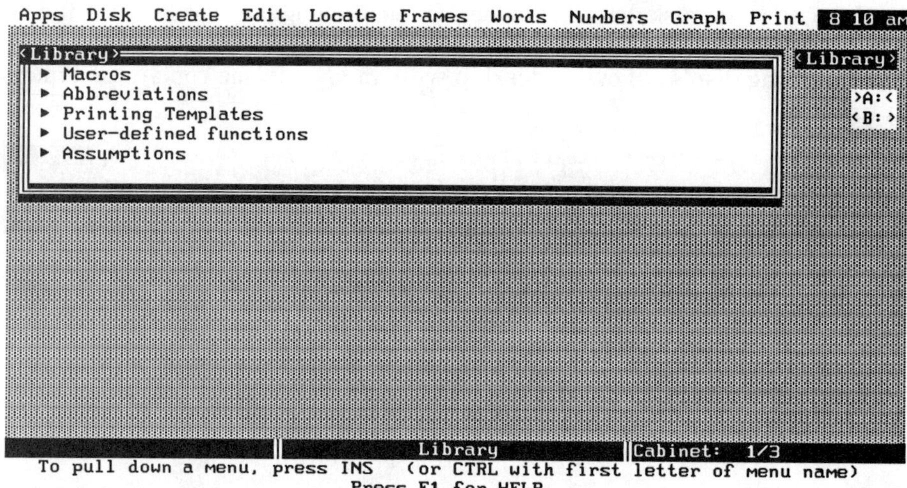

Press Enter to erase the frame. The cursor returns to the <Library> indicator.

The current time (if you have a clock in your computer) is displayed in the top right-hand corner of your desktop. If your computer lacks a clock, Framework III displays the default DOS time or the one you typed when you began your computer session.

The Apps Main Menu option is for the Applications Menu frame. It provides telecommunications (using a phone modem), checks a frame for proper spelling, as well as provides custom applications. Press Ins and Left Arrow twice. The following display shows the Apps Menu frame.

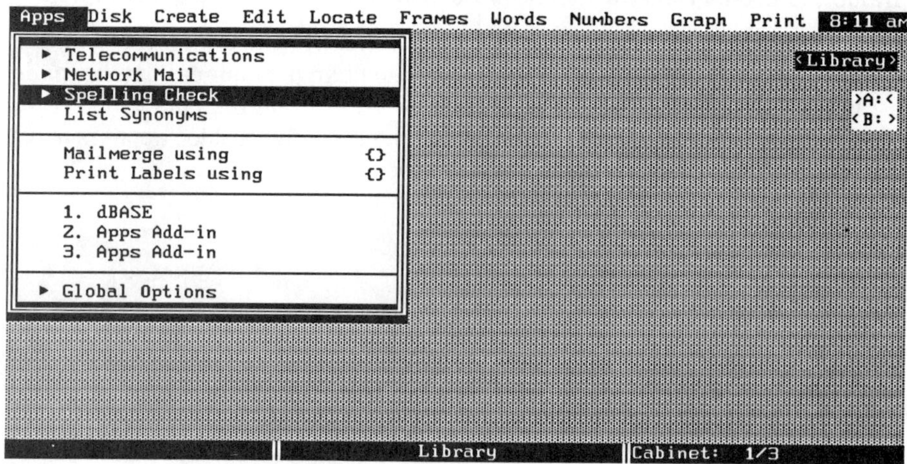

Notice the pointers (►) on the left side of the menu frame. These arrows identify the option as another menu frame. This second menu is called a submenu frame. For example, when you position the cursor on "Telecommunications" and press Enter, the desktop resembles the following display.

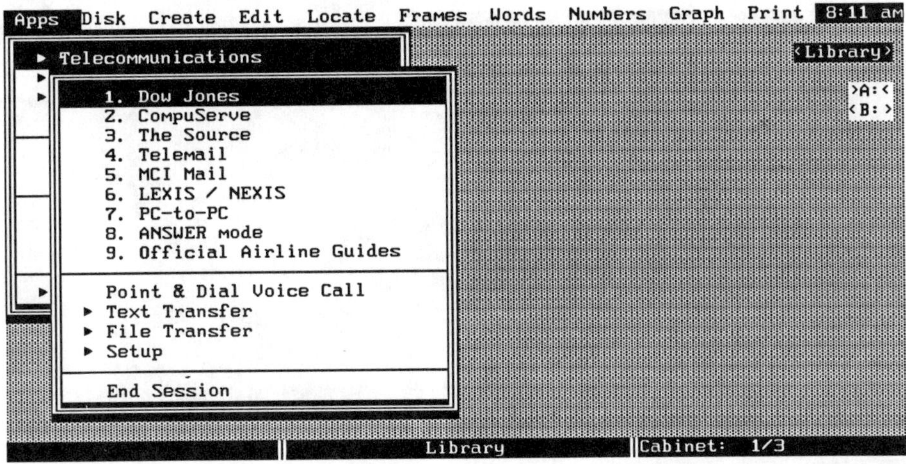

Dial first service for quick access (install your own service in Setup program)

To return the cursor to the Apps Main Menu frame, press Left Arrow. The Esc key is also used to avoid selecting a submenu or main menu option.

Next, highlight the word Disk at the top of the screen by pressing Right Arrow. Selecting the Disk Menu provides the following frame. This menu is used to read from or write to a disk as well as to end your Framework III session.

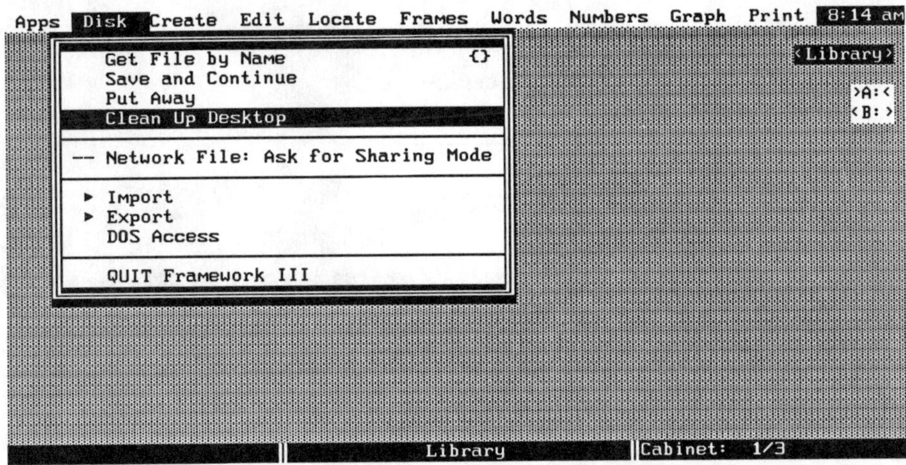

Close and stack all documents and cabinets

Press Right Arrow. The Create Menu frame resembles the following display. You open frames and create files by using this set of menu options.

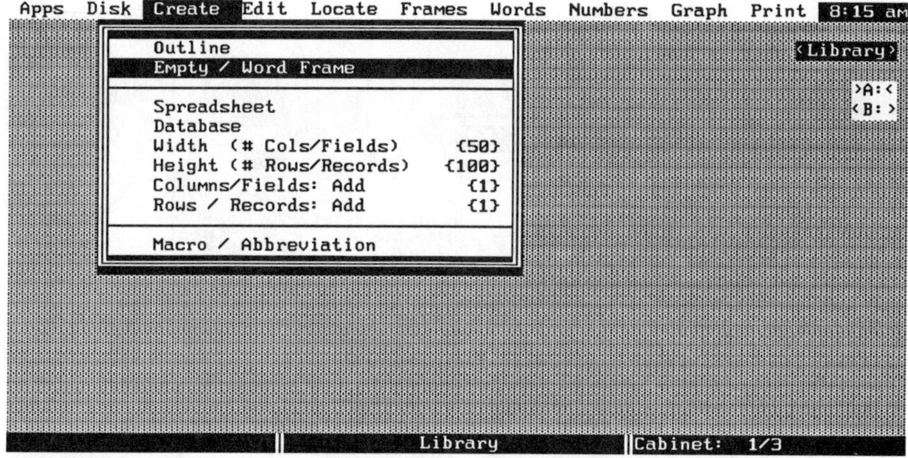

Create a frame for word processing or for containing other frames

Press Right Arrow. The Edit Menu frame helps you make changes (and sometimes undo a mistake) to a frame's contents. This menu frame appears as follows.

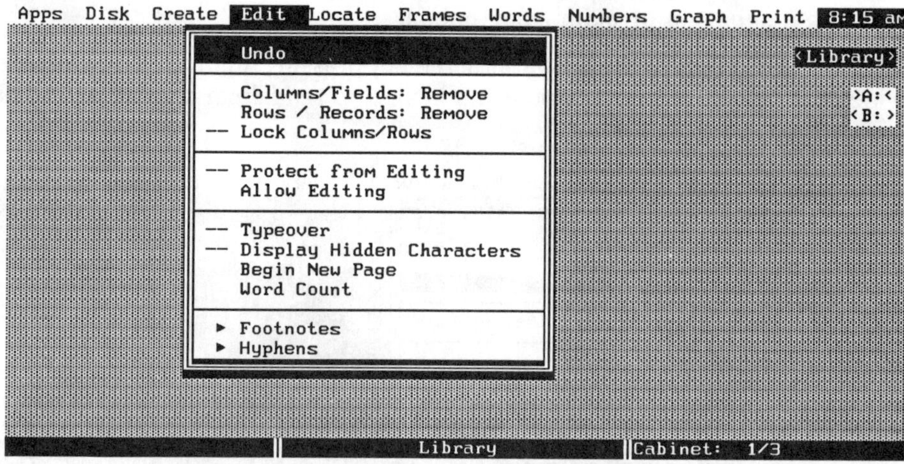

Undo the last action taken that can be undone

Press Right Arrow. The Locate Menu frame lets you find and/or replace a character, word, or phrase. It resembles the following display.

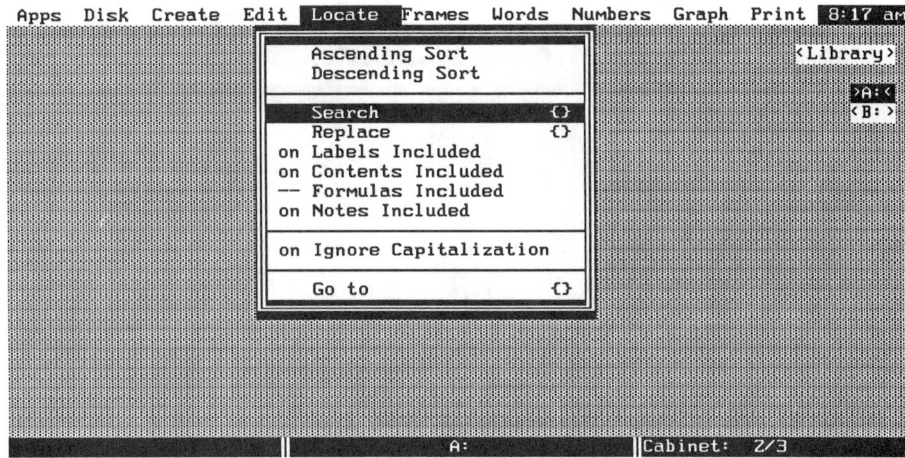

Find any specified word or phrase -- in any type of frame

Press Right Arrow. The Frames Menu helps you change the characteristics of all your frames during your current Framework III session. For example, you can tell Framework III you want all your frame windows to be larger than the preset (default) size. The Frames Menu follows.

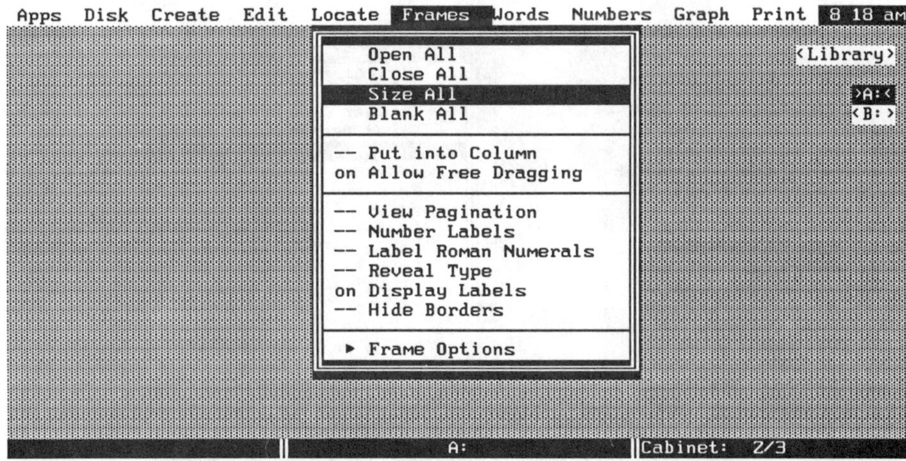

Size column-arranged frames within selection to fit just inside containing frame

Press Right Arrow. The Words Menu is probably the one which is most often used. You can change typefaces and position text within an open frame and see the results on the screen. This menu resembles the following display.

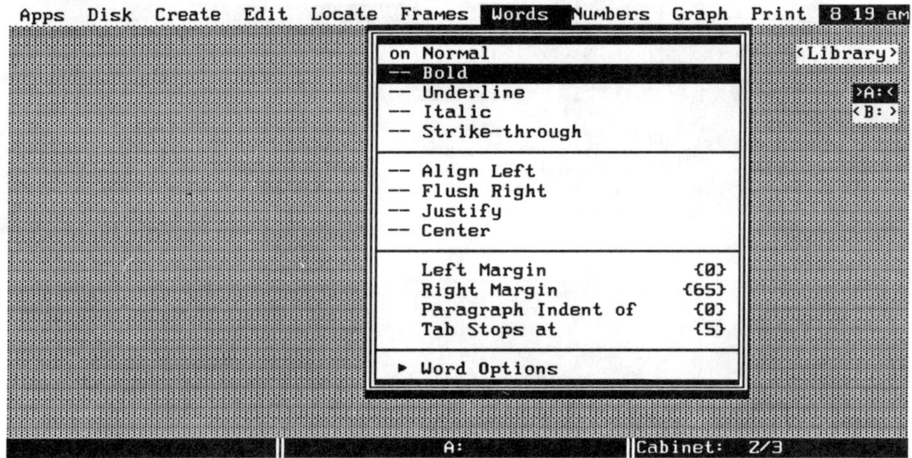

Boldface selected text -- in any type of frame

Press Right Arrow. The next Main Menu on the menu line is the Numbers Menu frame. It is used to change the style and position of your numeric information within your open frames. The Numbers Menu frame follows.

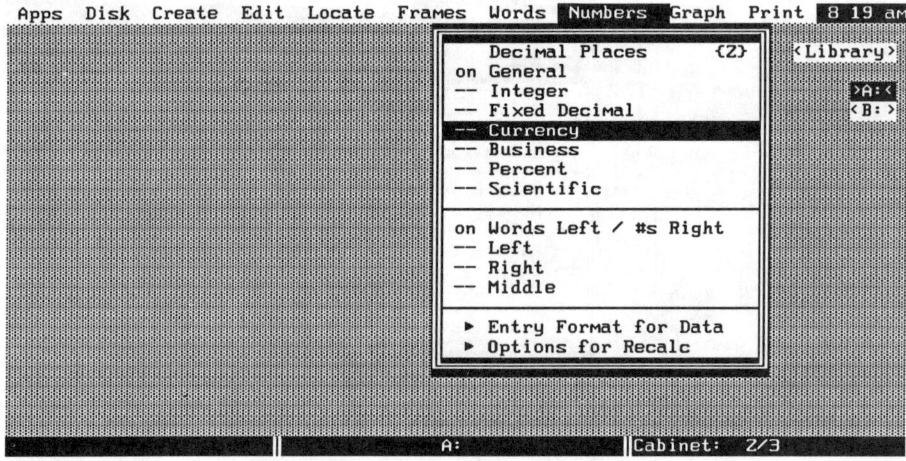

Display numbers in selected cells/fields with currency symbol or name and commas

Press Right Arrow. The Graph Menu frame allows you to draw a graph for numeric information you highlight within an open frame. This menu follows.

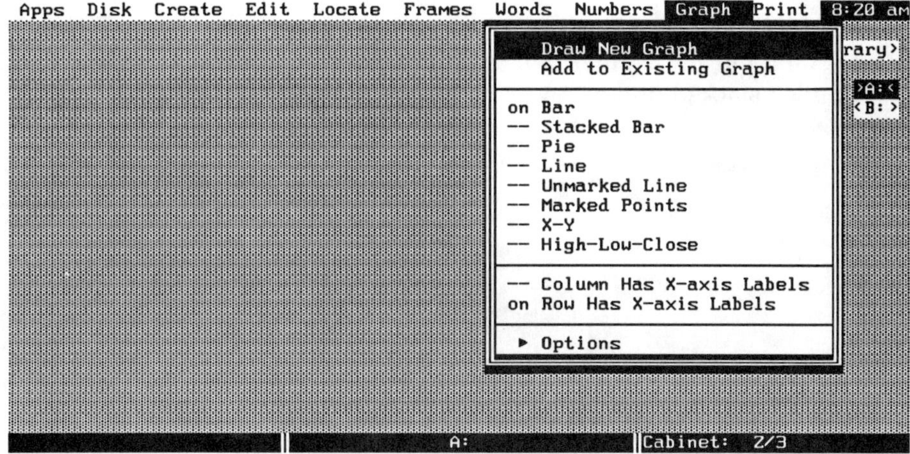

Draw graph of chosen type, using values in selected cells/fields

Press Right Arrow. The Print Menu frame sends the open document (whole or part) to the printer. Remember that it prints one or more pages, not just what appears within the open frame on the screen.

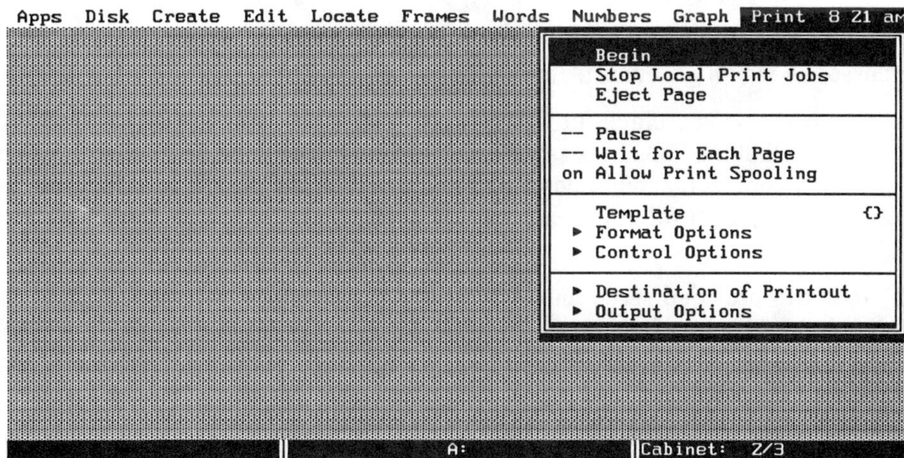

Begin printing selected frames

The highlighted line at the bottom of the desktop keeps you informed. It is called the status line. It is divided into three parts. The left-hand side sometimes displays Framework III information. The center part displays the name of the most recently opened frame. Finally, the right-hand part identifies the cursor status.

For example, when the cursor is positioned on the <Library>, the status line displays "Cabinet: 1/3." When positioned on the <A:> or <B:>, the cursor status displays "Cabinet: 2/3" or "Cabinet: 3/3," respectively.

Like any good desktop, you have a tray located on the lower right side of your screen. When you finish your work on a file, press Enter to close it and put it in your desktop tray. The following display has two files stacked in the tray.

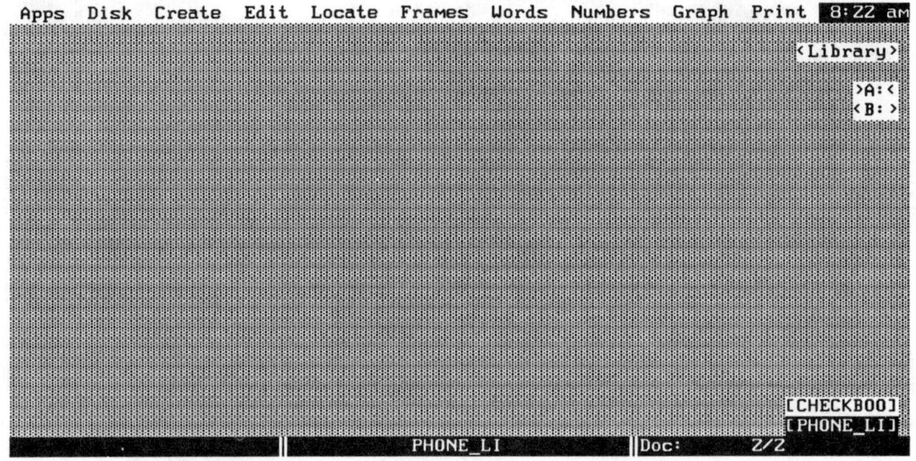

If the cursor is positioned on a filename in the desktop tray, the status line displays "Doc: 1/1." When the cursor is inside an open frame, "Char: 1/1" appears on the status line.

Next to the cursor status is a place for CAPS and NUM. When you see CAPS displayed on the status line, you know that the Caps Lock key is turned on so that each letter you type is in uppercase. The same situation applies for the appearance of NUM on the status line. When it is displayed, using the numeric keypad results in numbers, not cursor movement and the other nonnumeric results.

These two areas are provided since many computer keyboards do not have lighted Caps Lock and Num Lock keys. This way, you know how the keyboard is set and what the press of a key produces. The following desktop shows that Caps Lock and Num Lock have been pressed.

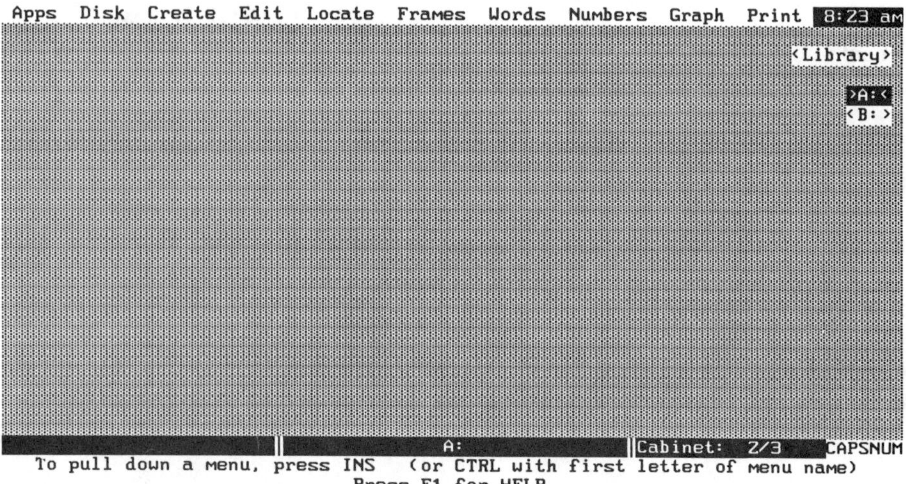

Under the status line, Framework III displays messages or little reminders for you. To get to main menu, press Ins and Left Arrow. As the cursor moves from one menu option to another, the Message line briefly describes the highlighted option. For example, the cursor in the following display is positioned on the Telecommunications option of the Apps Main Menu. Notice the message at the bottom of the display.

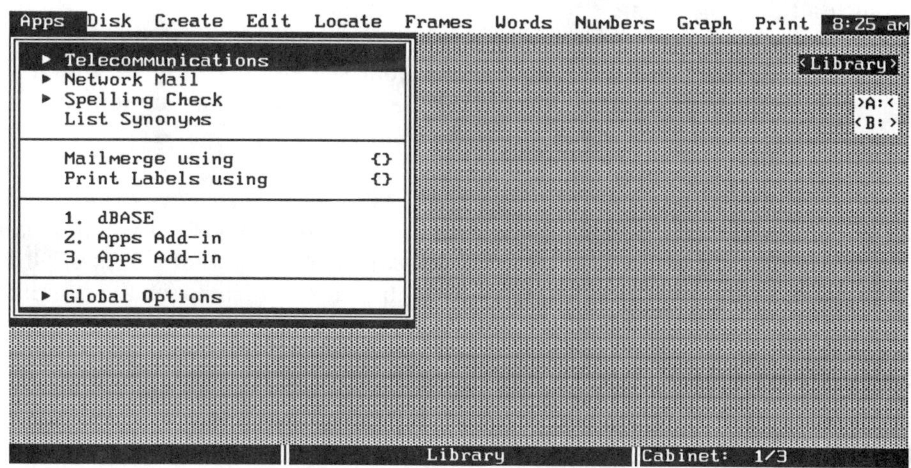

Now that you are more familiar with the Framework III desktop, it's time to learn how to use the special keys on the keyboard.

THE MAGIC KEYS

Of course, most of the keys on your computer keyboard are important, but some of them are special. These keys are used to tell Framework III what you want to do.

ENTER This key is used when the cursor is positioned on the option you want to select. It tells Framework III to "do it."

ESC When you open a menu frame but change your mind, pressing this key makes the menu frame disappear. Neither your open frame nor any of its information is altered when this key is pressed.

DEL The Del key removes (deletes) the open frame from your desktop or desktop tray. The file is *not* saved before removing it from your desktop. If it has been changed and you want to save it on disk (using the Disk Main Menu option), you must do so *before* pressing this key.

INS Pressing this key opens a Main Menu frame. If the menu frame opened is not the one you want, just move the cursor left or right on the menu line using the cursor (arrow) keys until you get the Main Menu you need.

GRAY + It is located on the far right side of your keyboard (gray color with a + symbol on it). When a frame is opened on your desktop, the cursor sits on the top, left corner of the frame border. This key is used to move the cursor inside the open frame so you can work on the information inside the open frame.

GRAY – This key is located on the far right side of your keyboard (gray color with a – symbol on it). When you are finished working inside the open frame, use this key to move the cursor to the frame border.

UP ARROW, DOWN ARROW, LEFT ARROW, RIGHT ARROW These keys are located on your numeric keypad on the far right of your keyboard. They are marked with the appropriate arrow. Remember to watch for "Num" in the status line of your desktop so that you can tell when the arrows can be used — otherwise, a number appears in your open frame (or the computer beeps at you).

NUM LOCK The Num Lock key is at the top of the numeric keypad. Some computers combine the arrow keys with numbers on the numeric keypad. For example, the same key is pressed for a 4 or a Right Arrow. This key lets you designate which one you want the key press to produce. Press this key to change the arrow keys to numbers. Press it again to change them from numbers to arrow keys again.

SCROLL LOCK This key is located on the top, right-hand corner of the keyboard. It moves the cursor between the desktop tray and the drive identifiers.

BACKSPACE This key is located to the left of the Num Lock key. Press it to delete the character identified by the cursor position within your open frame.

HOME This key is the 7 on your numeric keypad. It is used like the arrow keys. As you type within an open frame, the information moves up so that eventually you can't see some of what you typed. The Home key tells Framework III to position the cursor on the beginning of the current line in the open window.

END This key is the 1 on your numeric keypad. It is used like the arrow keys. It tells Framework III to position the cursor on the end of the current line in the open window.

PGUP This key is the 9 on your numeric keypad. It is used like the arrow keys. It is called page up. Press this key to move the cursor to the top of the current page in the open window.

PGDN This key is the 3 on your numeric keypad. It is used like the arrow keys. It is called page down. Press this key to move the cursor to the bottom of the current page in the open window.

F (FUNCTION) KEYS These keys are located on the far left or top of your keyboard. They are labeled F1, F2, etc. Each has a special function for Framework III.

F1 - Help

This key presents information on the screen to help you understand what Framework III expects from you. It is like a book on your computer when you need help.

F2 - Edit

This key tells Framework III that you want to change the status of a cell in a spreadsheet or a field in a database. It is called the Edit key.

F3 - Drag

Use this key when you want to rearrange the frames on your desktop. It's like moving sheets of paper on your desk. It is called the Drag key.

F4 - Size

The Size key is used to change the size of the current open frame. It makes the window larger or smaller than the preset (default) size.

F5 - Recalculate

The Recalc key must be pressed when you are using a spreadsheet or database frame and you have turned off automatic recalc of cells or database fields. By pressing this key, you force Framework III to recalculate the cells where mathematics are specified.

F6 - Extend Select

This key makes the cursor bigger for a special operation. For example, if you want a word or phrase to be changed to boldface type, use this key to highlight the information. Then open the Words Menu frame and select the Bold option. The word or phrase is then displayed in bold typeface.

F7 - Move

The Move key moves the information within the highlighted cursor area to another area in the open frame. This is used to reorganize a document.

F8 - Copy

The Copy key copies the information within the highlighted cursor area to another area in the open frame.

F9 - Zoom

This key changes your open frame to desktop size. In other words, you don't have to look through a small window all the time.

F10 - View

The View key changes the way information is displayed in the open frame. For example, a database can be seen in table-like form or as a series of mini-frames.

F11 - Out

Same as Gray – (move cursor out of frame).

F12 - In

Same as Gray + (move cursor into frame).

SHORTCUTS Moving the cursor to the menu line is done by pressing the Ins key and then using the arrows to move to the next Main Menu option. Once the Main Menu frame is open, move the cursor to an option within the menu and press Enter. This method of option selection is great for beginners but tedious for experienced users.

There is a shortcut to select a specific Main Menu frame and then select the option within the open menu frame. This is done by using the Ctrl key and the first letter or number of the option you need to use.

Press the Ctrl key like you would press the Shift key for an uppercase letter, then type the letter for the selected option. Remember, Ctrl-A means press and hold down the Ctrl key (like using the Shift key) and then type A.

For example, by pressing Ctrl-A, the Apps Main Menu frame opens on your desktop. Then pressing Ctrl-T opens the Telecommunications submenu. Your desktop resembles the following display.

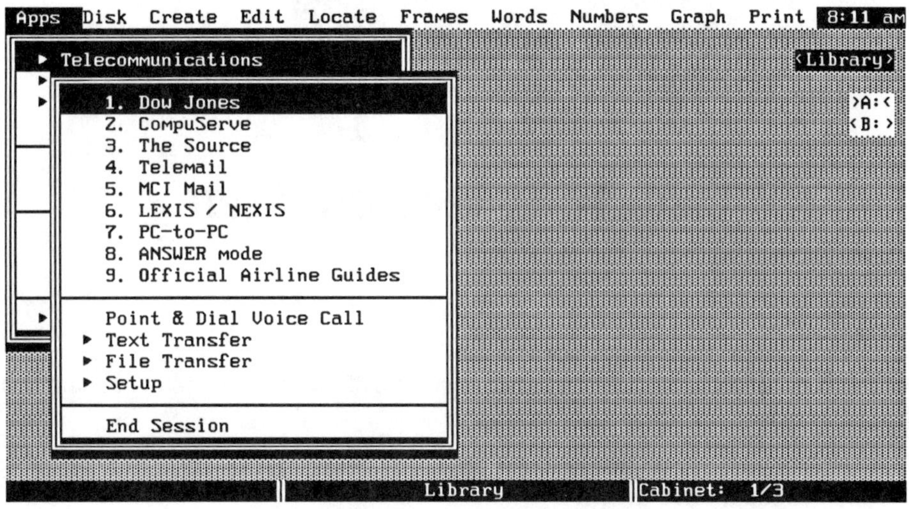

Dial first service for quick access (install your own service in Setup program)

From this submenu, you could call Dow Jones by pressing Ctrl-1. (Do not do this now.) Framework III would then dial the Dow Jones phone number. It is not necessary to move the cursor to the option you want and then press Enter to select that option.

Use this shortcut for any option you want done by Framework III. A list of the Ctrl key combinations for Main Menu frames follows.

Ctrl-A Applications
Ctrl-D Disk
Ctrl-C Create
Ctrl-E Edit
Ctrl-L Locate
Ctrl-F Frames
Ctrl-W Words
Ctrl-N Numbers
Ctrl-G Graph
Ctrl-P Print

For your convenience, all the "magic keys" are listed in the Appendices. After a few Framework III sessions, these key combinations become second nature. Just be patient. Practice is the secret to this game.

Turn to Module 41 to begin the learning sequence.

Module 4

ADD TO EXISTING GRAPH

DESCRIPTION

Sometimes you need to show the relationship of two sets of numbers. Instead of using two separate graphs, just put them both on one.

For example, the following graph shows the relationship between two sets of numbers. The monthly sales for two salespeople are drawn in one picture.

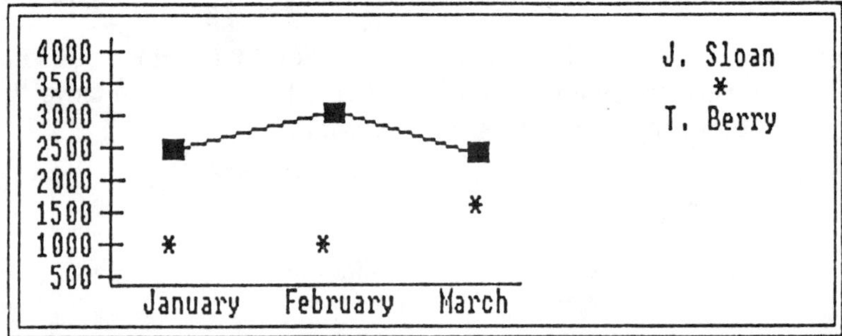

The Add to Existing Graph option is available through the Graph Menu frame.

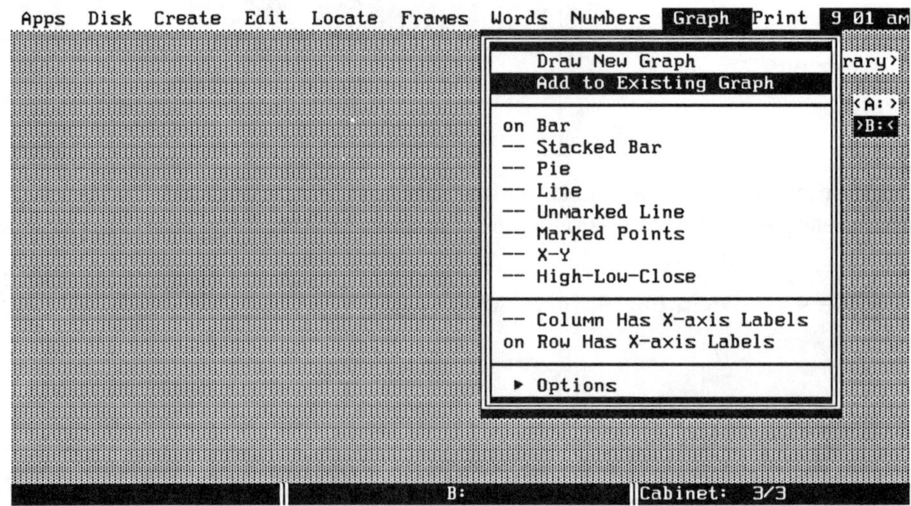

When overlaying two or more graphs, use any of the graph types except the pie or X-Y options. Make sure, however, that the scale used is one that covers each number to be included in the graph when completed.

Draw the first graph with the Draw New Graph option. Press Up Arrow to return to the spreadsheet. Then press Gray + to move the cursor into the spreadsheet or database frame. Identify the numbers for the next graph overlay and open the Graph Menu frame. Change the type of graph to another option and then select the Add to Existing Graph option.

APPLICATIONS

Use graphs to interpret the relationship of numbers within a spreadsheet or database. Include several graphs on one picture by using the Add to Existing Graph option.

To do this, however, the scale created by the first graph needs to handle each number you intend to include in the one picture. Use the Options submenu of the Graph Menu frame to set the Manual Y-axis Scaling, Lowest Y-axis Value { }, Highest Y-axis Value { }, and Scale in Increments of { } options.

TYPICAL OPERATION

This example shows you how to open a spreadsheet, select numbers, and draw two overlays on one graph. Close any open frames on your desktop and position the cursor on your data drive indicator. The shortcut key combinations, if applicable, are enclosed by braces.

1. {Press **Ctrl-D**}. Press **Ins** to move the cursor to the Main Menu line. Press the arrow (cursor) keys until the Disk Menu frame is open on your desktop.

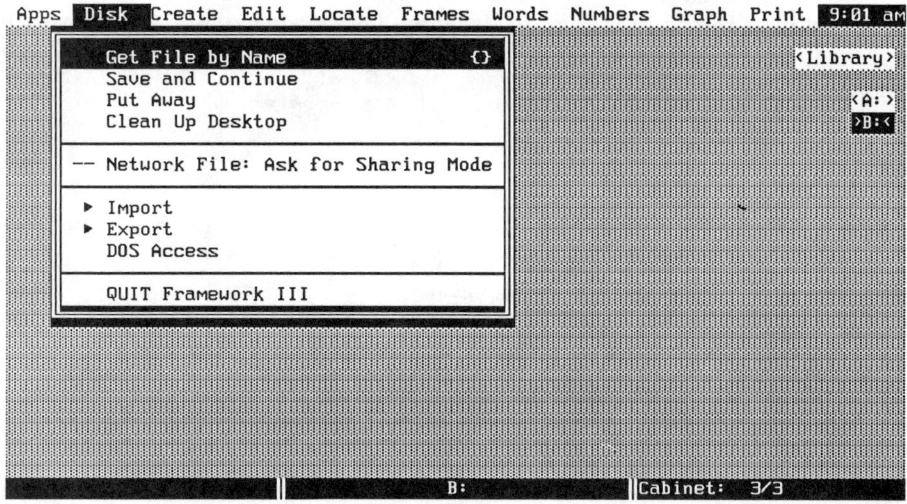

2. {Press **Ctrl-G**}. Press **Up Arrow** until the cursor is positioned on the Get File by Name option and press **Enter**. The cursor then moves to the Message line at the bottom of your desktop. Type **SALES** and press **Enter**. The spreadsheet opens on your desktop.

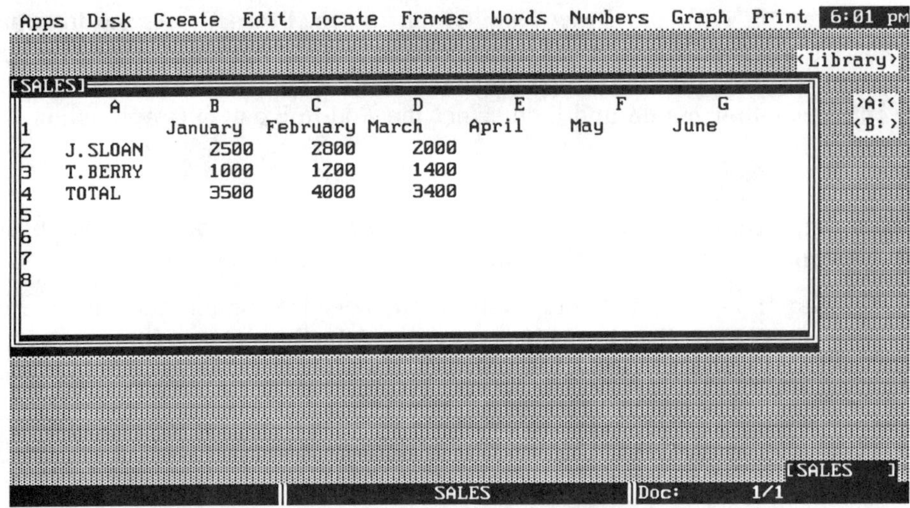

3. Press **Gray +** to move the cursor inside the open frame.
4. Press **Esc** to change the cursor size. Press **Up Arrow** until the cursor is positioned on cell B2. Press **F6** (Extend). Press **Right Arrow** twice until cells B2, C2, and D2 are highlighted. Press **Enter**.
5. {Press **Ctrl-G** and then **Ctrl-O**}. Press **Ins** to move the cursor to the Main Menu line. Press **Right Arrow** until the Graph Menu is also open on your desktop. Press **Down Arrow** until the cursor is positioned on the Options option and press **Enter**. The submenu also opens on your desktop.

6. Select each of the submenu options until your desktop resembles the following display.

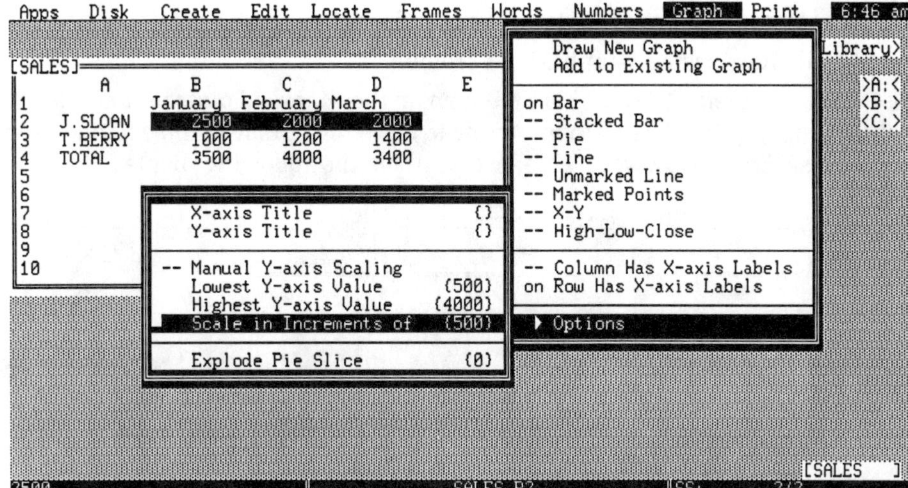

7. Press **Esc** to close the open menus.
8. {Press **Ctrl-G**}. Press **Ins** to move the cursor to the Main Menu line. Press **Right Arrow** until the Graph Menu frame is again open on your desktop.
9. {Press **Ctrl-L** and then **Ctrl-D**}. Select the Line graph option to turn it on. Then select the Draw New Graph option. Framework III asks if you want to draw it in the open frame or a new one. Just press **Enter** to use a new frame. The graph resembles the following display.

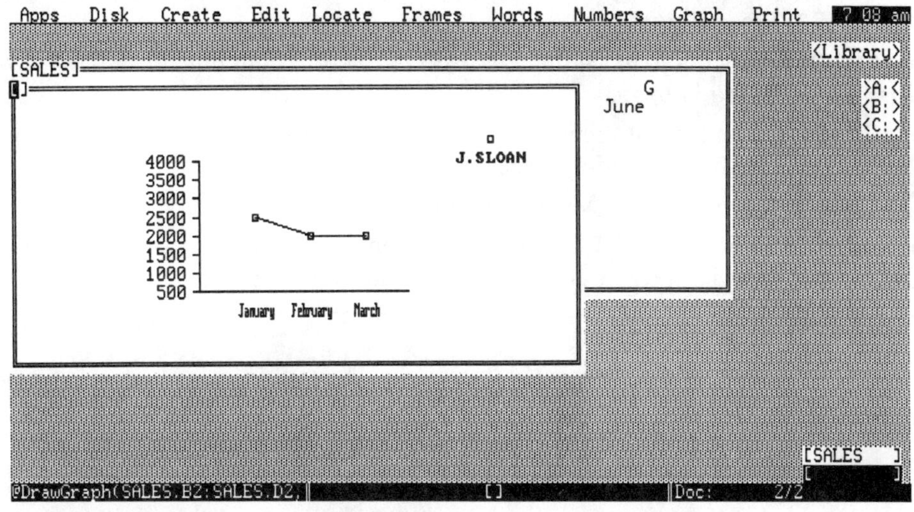

10. Press **Down Arrow** to move the cursor to the spreadsheet frame and press **Gray +** so that it is again inside the open frame.
11. Press **Down Arrow** to move the cursor across B3, C3, and D3.
12. {Press **Ctrl-G**}. Reopen the Graph Menu frame.
13. {Press **Ctrl-M** and then **Ctrl-A**}. This time turn on the Marked Points option. Select the Add to Existing Graph option. Press **Down Arrow** to move the cursor to the existing graph frame and then press **Enter**. Now your screen resembles the following display.

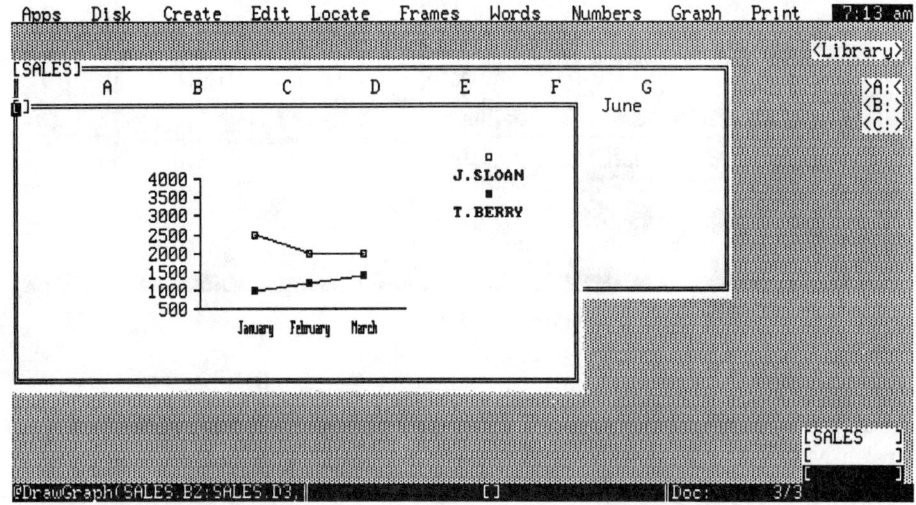

Graph: Add to Existing Graph

14. Type **GRAPH2** within the brackets so that when it's saved on disk, the filename is GRAPH2.FW3. Press **Enter**.
15. {Press **Ctrl-D**}. Press **Ins** to move the cursor to the Main Menu line. Press **Left Arrow** until the Disk Menu frame is open.
16. {Press **Ctrl-P**}. Select the Put Away option to save the graph frame on disk. With the cursor on the spreadsheet frame border, press **Del** to remove the frame from the desktop.
17. {Press **Ctrl-D**}. Open the Disk Menu frame again.
18. {Press **Ctrl-Q**}. Select the QUIT Framework option. When asked if you are sure you want to quit, type **Y**. This is the end of your Framework III session.
19. Turn to Module 54 to continue the learning sequence.

Module 5

ALIGN LEFT

DESCRIPTION

When you begin each Framework III session, word processing frames are set so that every line typed begins on the left side of the open frame. If the left margin is set to 10, each line begins ten spaces from the left side of the open frame.

The Align Left option is available for word processing frames. Access it through the Words Menu frame.

Framework III begins each new word processing frame with the Align Left option turned on. Once you turn it off, it stays off until you select the Center, Flush Right, or Justify option for your open frame.

The cursor positions itself at the left of each new line. As each line is filled, or Enter is pressed, the cursor returns to the left margin of the next line.

As soon as one of the positioning options is selected, Framework III displays a message at the bottom of your screen. When you press Enter, the message disappears.

APPLICATIONS

This option is available for word processing frames only. Select this option when you want each new line to begin at the left margin of your open frame.

Once the Align Left option is selected, cursor positioning on new lines is automatic. You must select one of the other positioning options in the Words Menu frame to turn it off. As soon as the current frame is closed, Framework III turns on the Align Left option regardless of which positioning option was last chosen.

TYPICAL OPERATION

This example shows you how to use the Align Left option of the Words Menu frame. Close any open frames on your desktop and position the cursor on your data drive indicator (drive B in this example). The shortcut key combinations, if applicable, are enclosed by braces.

1. {Press **Ctrl-D**}. Press **Ins** to move the cursor to the Main Menu line. Press **Left Arrow** or **Right Arrow**, if necessary, until the Disk Menu frame is open on your desktop.
2. {Press **Ctrl-G**}. Press **Up Arrow** to move the cursor to the Get File by Name option and then press **Enter**. The cursor moves to the Message line at the bottom of your desktop.

3. Type **B:BIRTHDAY**. As you type, notice that the braces next to the Get File by Name option fill. Press **Enter**. The disk is read and the frame you specified is opened on your desktop as follows.

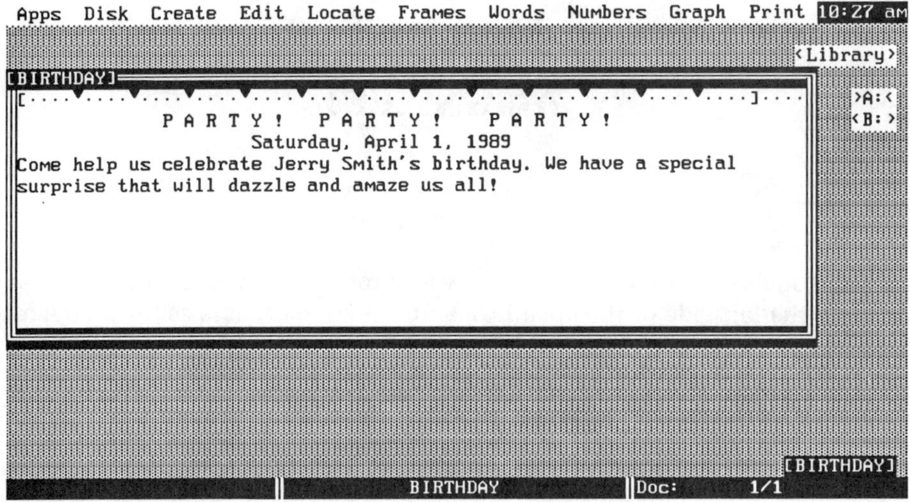

4. Press **Gray +** to move the cursor inside your open frame. Your cursor is positioned after the last change of the document. Press **Up Arrow** until the cursor is positioned on the top line.
5. {Press **Ctrl-W**}. Press **Ins** to move the cursor to the Main Menu line. Press **Right Arrow** until the Words Menu frame is also open on your desktop. Notice that the Center option is currently turned on in the following Words Menu frame.

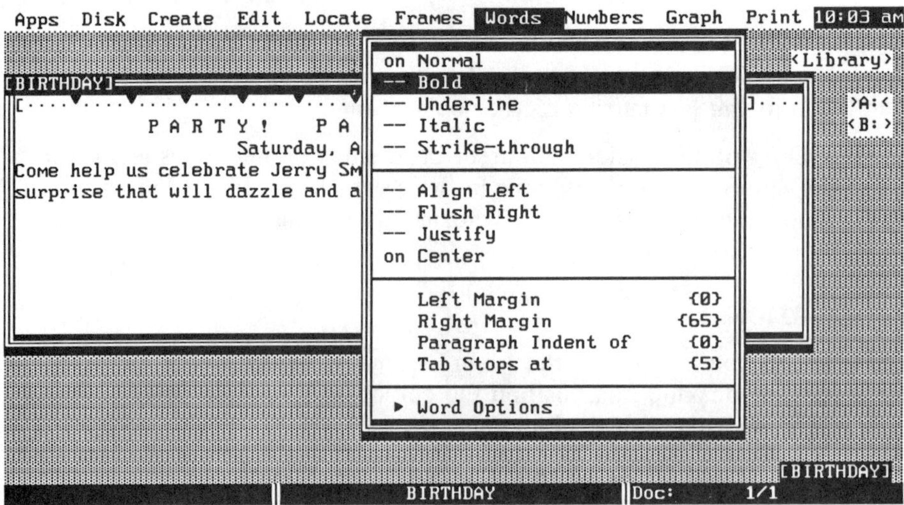

Boldface selected text -- in any type of frame

6. {Press **Ctrl-A**}. Press **Down Arrow** until the cursor is positioned on the Align Left option. Press **Enter**. The Words Menu frame disappears from your desktop. The first line now begins at the left margin of your open frame.
7. Move the cursor to the end of the line if it is not already there and press **Enter**. A blank line is inserted between the first and second lines. Notice that the cursor is positioned on the left of this blank line. Each new line begins at this point until you turn the Align Left option off.
8. Press **Gray –** to move the cursor to the frame border and then press **Del**. Type **Y** to accept the prompt "Do you really want to delete frame(s)? (y/n). By doing this, the changed invitation is not saved on disk but is removed from your desktop.
9. Turn to Module 33 to continue the learning sequence.

Module 6

ALLOW EDITING

DESCRIPTION

If you try to edit (change) a spreadsheet cell or database field which has been protected, Framework III won't let you make the change. Use the Allow Editing option to unprotect the cell or field.

Protection is accomplished by using the Protect from Editing option of the Edit Menu frame. It causes a beep for each keystroke upon a protected area. Use this option to unprotect the spreadsheet cell or database field you need to change.

This option is available for any type of frame. Access it through the Edit Menu frame.

To unprotect spreadsheet cells or database fields, position the cursor on the cell you want to unprotect. Then open the Edit Menu frame and select the Allow Editing option. If you need to unprotect several consecutive cells, press F6 (Extend) to expand the cursor highlighted area before selecting the option.

Unprotect a whole frame by positioning the cursor on the frame border. Then select this option and save the frame on the disk.

APPLICATIONS

The Allow Editing option is available for any type of frame. For example, unprotect a cell or field which has been protected by using the Protect from Editing option. Doing this causes Framework III to allow changes to the frame, cell, or field.

If you try to change a protected cell or field, Framework III beeps with each keystroke. Also, a message is displayed at the bottom of the screen telling you that the frame is protected (though it may only be the cell or field). Using this option reverses the protection effects.

TYPICAL OPERATION

This example shows you how to use the Allow Editing option of the Edit Menu frame. Close any open frames on your desktop and position the cursor on your data drive indicator (drive B in this example). The shortcut key combinations, if applicable, are enclosed by braces.

1. {Press **Ctrl-D**}. Press **Ins** to move the cursor to the Main Menu line. Press **Left Arrow** or **Right Arrow**, if necessary, until the Disk Menu frame is open on your desktop.

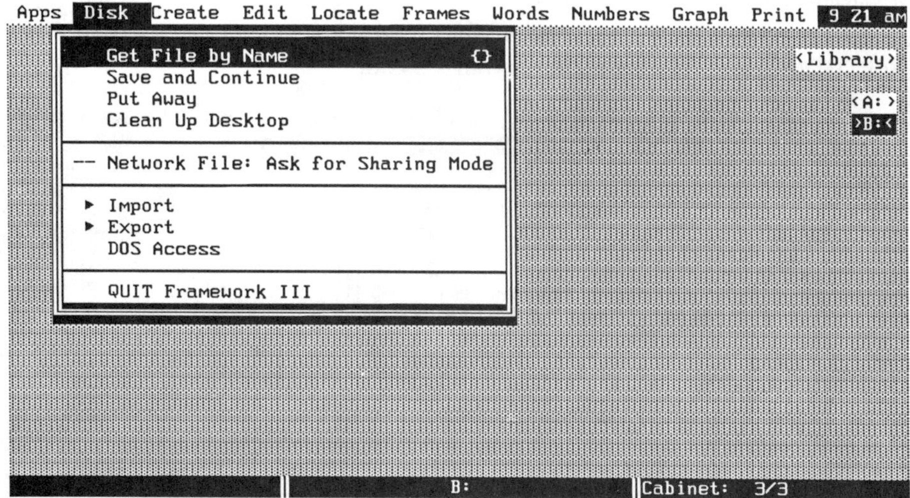

Bring specified file from disk and place beneath selected frame

2. {Press **Ctrl-G**}. Press **Up Arrow** to move the cursor to the Get File by Name option and then press **Enter**. The cursor moves to the Message line at the bottom of your desktop.
3. Type **B:CHECKBK**. As you type, notice that the braces next to the Get File by Name option fill. Press **Enter**. The disk is read and the frame you specified is opened on your desktop as follows.

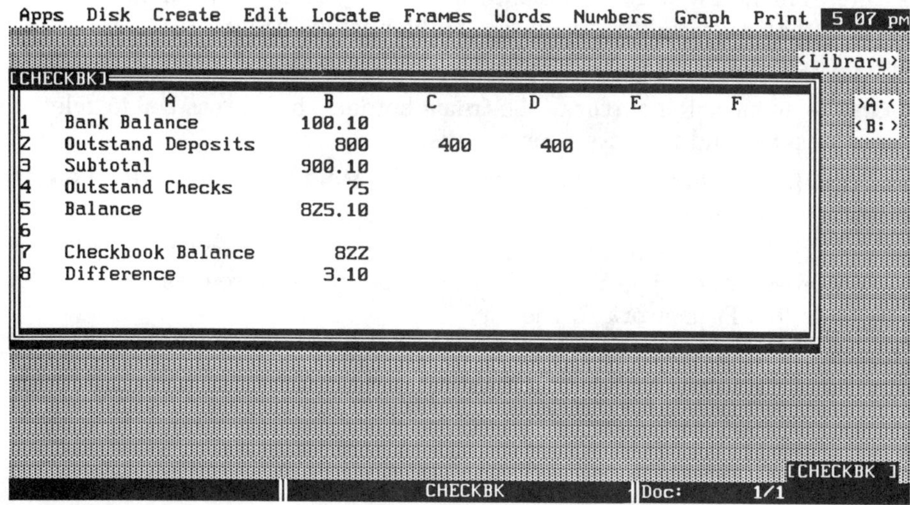

4. Press **Gray +** to move the cursor inside your open frame. Your cursor is positioned after the last change of the document. Use the arrow (cursor) keys until the cursor is positioned on cell B3.

5. Type **393** and notice that with each keystroke, the computer beeps. Also, a message is displayed at the bottom of the screen. It tells you that the frame is protected; however, in this case, only the cell is protected.
6. {Press **Ctrl-E**}. Press **Ins** to move the cursor to the Main Menu line. Press **Right Arrow** until the Edit Menu frame is also open on your desktop.

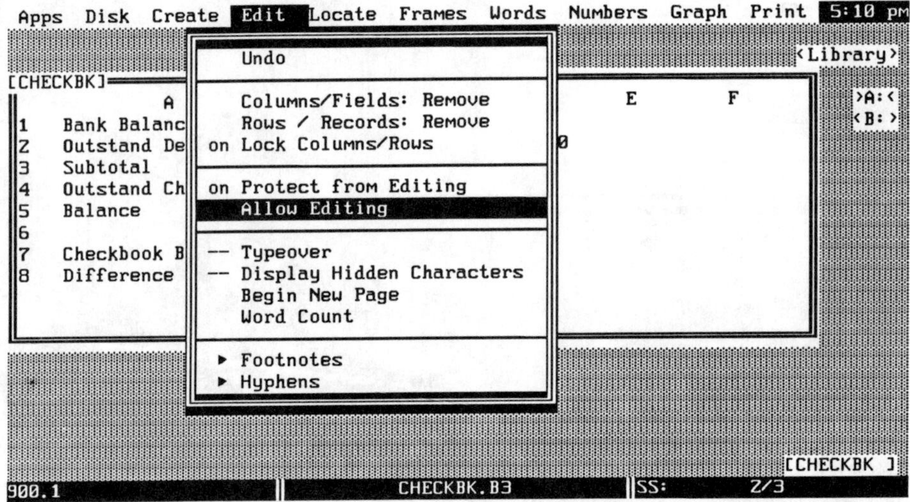

Allow changes to selected frames/cells/fields

7. {Press **Ctrl-A**}. Press **Down Arrow** until the cursor is positioned on the Allow Editing option. Press **Enter**. The Edit Menu frame disappears from your desktop. Notice that the message line reports that Allow Editing is on for the highlighted areas.
8. Again type **393** and press **Enter**. The cell is changed to 393.
9. Press **Gray –** to move the cursor to the frame border. Then, press **Del** to delete the frame from your desktop and not save it on the disk.
10. {Press **Ctrl-D**}. Press **Ins** to move the cursor to the Main Menu line. Press **Left Arrow** until the Disk Menu frame is open on your desktop.
11. {Press **Ctrl-Q**}. Using the arrow keys again, position the cursor on the QUIT Framework option and press **Enter**. Type **Y** when asked if you are sure you want to quit Framework III. This ends this Framework III session.
12. Turn to Module 38 to continue the learning sequence.

Module 7

ALLOW FREE DRAGGING

DESCRIPTION

This option lets you move a subframe by pressing F3 (Drag). For example, a frame you want to use for reference is outside the open window. Just drag it to the frame on which you want to work. This makes both frames accessible at the same time.

Select this option through the Frames Menu frame.

The Allow Free Dragging option is turned on and off when selected. If it is turned on, Put into Column is turned off. When the Put into Column option is on, Allow Free Dragging is turned off.

The Allow Free Dragging option must be turned on before pressing F3 (Drag). Otherwise, you are reminded to turn on the Allow Free Dragging option.

APPLICATIONS

Use this option with any frame which contains subframes. It lets you move a frame which is out of sight to an area you can see.

For example, subtopic 1.1 needs several pieces of the information from subtopic 1.6. Instead of moving the cursor back and forth between the two subframes, just drag subframe 1.6 to an area on your desktop where both are visible.

If they overlap, however, only one subframe is visible at a time. When you use the arrow (cursor) keys to move from one subframe to the other, remember the subframes are still in order. To move from subframe 1.1 to 1.6, you must press Down Arrow five times even though they are both on the same area of your desktop.

TYPICAL OPERATION

This illustration shows you how to use the Allow Free Dragging capabilities of Framework III. Make sure that your desktop is clear and the cursor is positioned on one of the drive indicators. The shortcut key combinations, if applicable, are enclosed by braces.

1. {Press **Ctrl-D**}. Press **Ins** to move the cursor to the Main Menu line. Press **Left Arrow** or **Right Arrow**, if necessary, until the Disk Menu frame is open on your desktop.

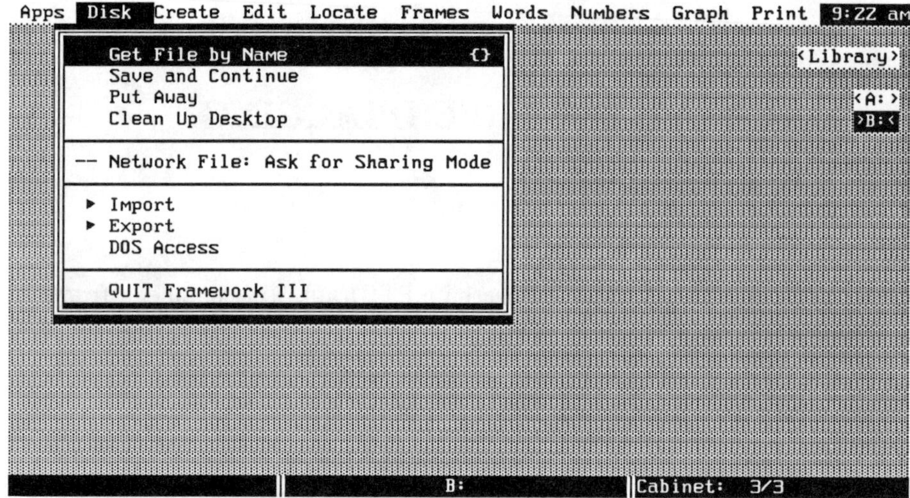

Bring specified file from disk and place beneath selected frame

2. {Press **Ctrl-G**}. Press **Up Arrow** to move the cursor to the Get File by Name { } option and then press **Enter**. The cursor moves to the Message line at the bottom of your desktop.
3. Type **EXERCISE**. As you type, notice that the braces next to the Get File by Name { } option fill. Press **Enter**. The disk is read and the frame you specified is opened on your desktop. If it appears only in the desktop tray with the cursor, press **Enter** to open it on your desktop.

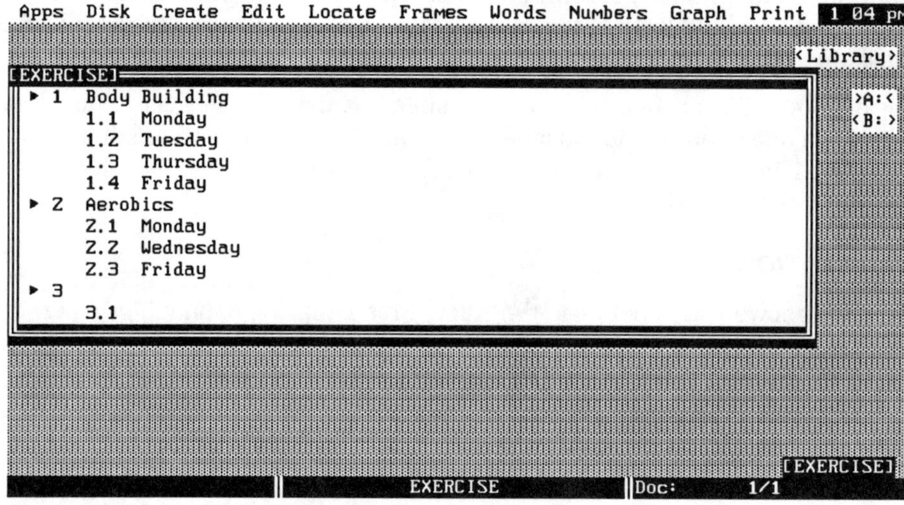

4. Press **Gray +** to move the cursor to the inside of your open frame. Notice that the cursor is positioned on the first major topic of your outline.
5. {Press **Ctrl-F**}. Press **Ins** to move the cursor to the Main Menu line. Press **Right Arrow** until the Frames Menu frame is also open on your desktop.

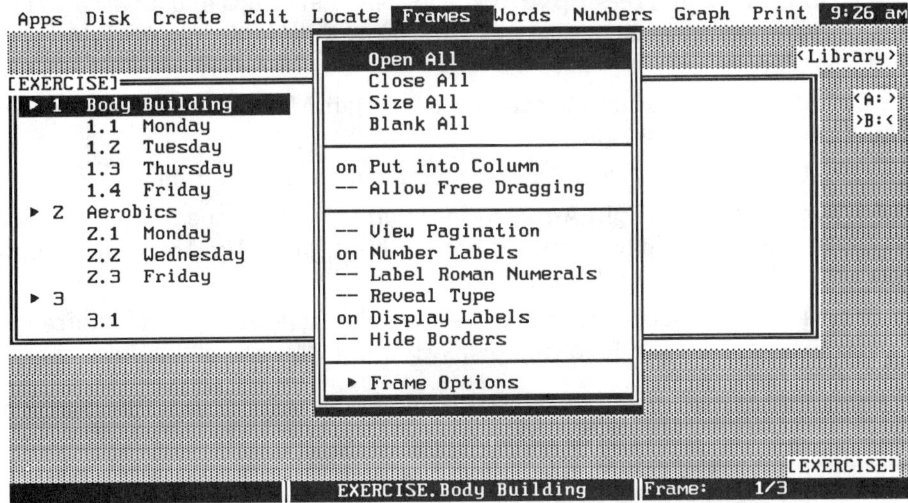

6. {Press **Ctrl-O**}. Press **Up Arrow** until the cursor is positioned on the Open All option and press **Enter**. This tells Framework III that you want to see the contents of all subframes.
7. Position the cursor on the major topic line of Body Building. Press **F10** (View) to open the subframes. Then press **F9** (Zoom) to see the following display.

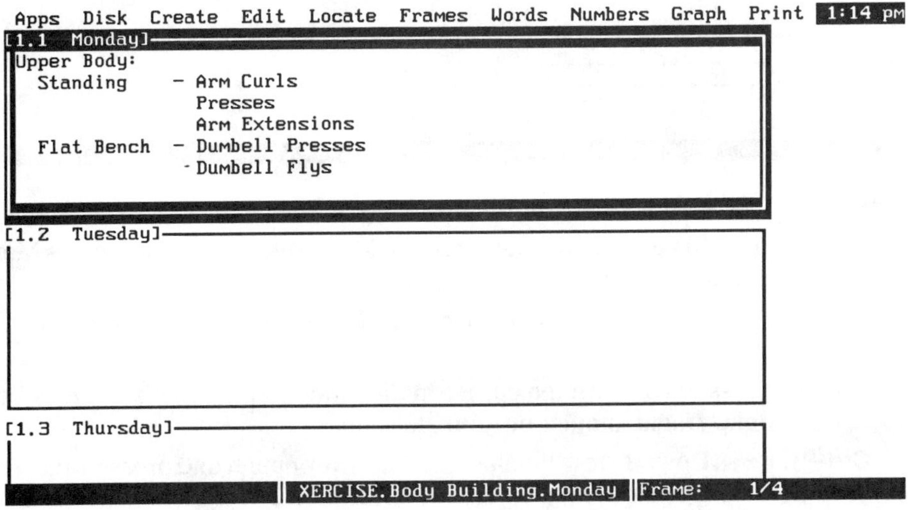

8. Press **F6** (Extend). Press **Down Arrow** three times until all four subframes are highlighted. Press **Enter**.
9. Press **F4** (Size). Press **Left Arrow** 30 times to make the frame sizes smaller. Press **Enter**. Then position the cursor on subframe number 1.4.
10. Press **F3** (Drag) and then press **Up Arrow**. The computer beeps and advises you that if you want to drag a frame vertically, you must first select the Allow Free Dragging option of the Frames Menu frame.
11. {Press **Ctrl-F**}. Press **Ins** to move the cursor to the Main Menu line. The Frames Menu frame is again open on your desktop.
12. {Press **Ctrl-A**}. Select the Allow Free Dragging option to turn it on.
13. Press **F3** (Drag) and press **Right Arrow** to see another border appear and move to the right. Continue this until it is clear of the old border. Next, press **Up Arrow** until subframe 1.4 is even with subframe 1.1 and press **Enter**.
14. Press **Gray +** to move inside subframe 1.4. Type the first four lines of subframe 1.1 until your desktop resembles the following display.

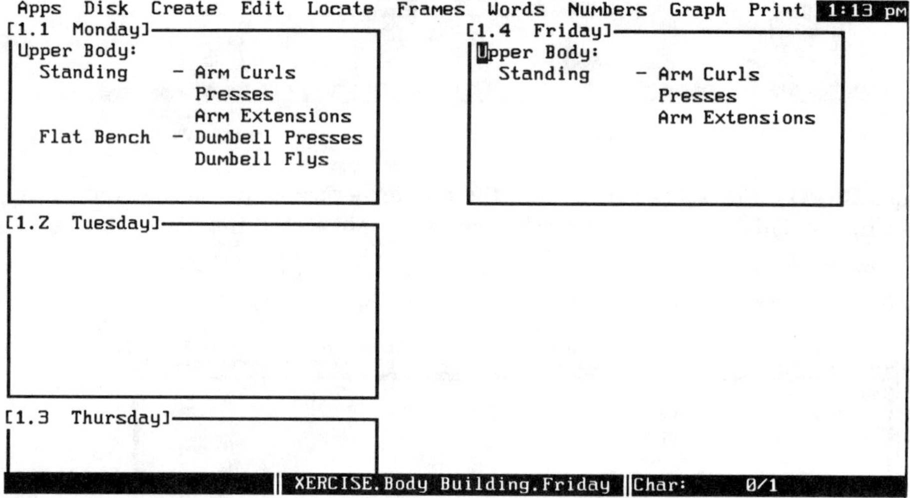

15. Press **Gray –** to move the cursor to the subframe border.
16. {Press **Ctrl-F**}. Press **Ins** to move the cursor to the Main Menu line. The Frames Menu frame is again open on your desktop.
17. Press **F10** (View) to return to the outline format. Then press **Gray –** twice to move the cursor to the EXERCISE frame border.
18. {Press **Ctrl-D**}. Press **Ins** to move the cursor to the Main Menu line. Next, press **Left Arrow** until the Disk Menu frame is open on your desktop.
19. {Press **Ctrl-P**}. Press **Down Arrow** to select the Put Away option and press **Enter**. This option clears your desktop and saves the file called EXERCISE.FW3 on the data disk.

20. {Press **Ctrl-D**}. Press **Ins** to move the cursor to the Main Menu line. The Disk Menu frame is again open on your desktop.
21. {Press **Ctrl-Q**}. Using the arrow (cursor) keys, position the cursor on the QUIT Framework option and press **Enter**. Type **Y** when Framework III asks if you're sure you want to quit Framework III. The system prompt appears on your screen. This ends this Framework III session.
22. Turn to Module 70 to continue the learning sequence.

Module 8

APPS ADD-IN

DESCRIPTION

Running other programs through Framework III is often useful. For example, run dBASE without quitting Framework III. Or, include a Basic program you wrote to accomplish a certain task as another Add-in option.

There are three Add-in options in the Apps Menu frame, although the first is preset to run dBASE. They are the numbered options 1 through 3 in the following display.

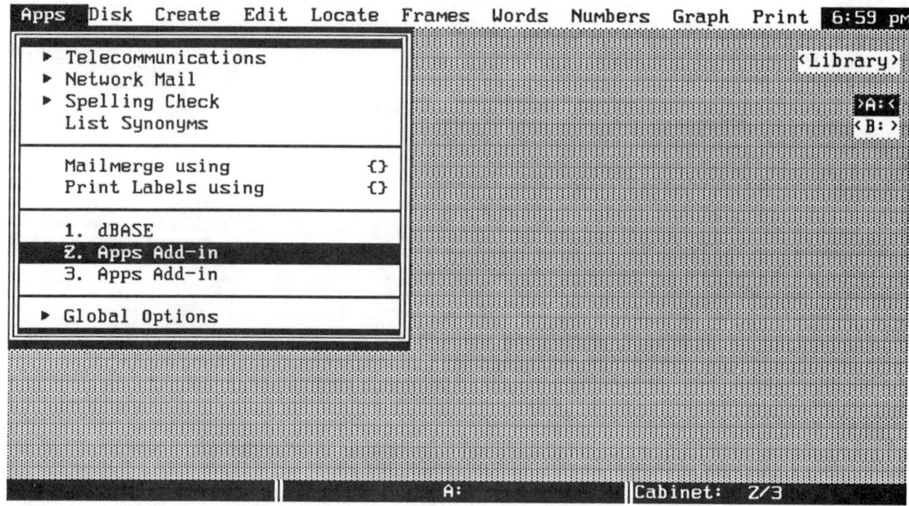

Use Setup to add your application here

The first Add-in (dBASE) is preinstalled. Use it as an example for setting up your own Add-ins. Change the first one to something else if dBASE is not a program you intend to use with Framework III.

To change or copy the dBASE Add-in, open the frame called RUNDBASE.FW3 and use it as a model. This frame contains a small FRED program which runs dBASE and a subframe which provides a help message if the program you want to run is not available.

Change the name of the frame to one that is meaningful to you. Press F2 (Edit) and then press F9 (Zoom) to change the FRED program. The @display and @run FRED commands are the only ones you must change; however, the program has several references to dBASE and its requirements. For example, dBASE III requires 256K, and dBASE IV requires 640K of available memory. If that amount is not available, the FRED program displays a message accordingly.

When the FRED program changes are complete, press Esc to return to the frame view. Then press Gray + to move to the Helpmsg subframe. Pressing F10 (View) opens the subframe on your desktop. By pressing Gray +, move the cursor inside the open frame and type the help message you want to display if the program is not available.

After all changes have been made, press Gray – twice to move the cursor to the frame border. Open the Disk Menu frame and save your work with the Put Away option.

Quit your Framework III session and insert the Setup disk which is included in your package. Run it to assign the Add-in option on the Apps Menu frame to the FRED program just saved. The next time you open the Apps Menu frame, your program is available in the Framework III Apps Menu frame.

APPLICATIONS

The Add-in options of the Apps Menu frame let you run programs without quitting your Framework III session.

Run any DOS or FRED program you have written by setting up the Add-in options of the Apps Menu frame. Framework III is preset so that the first Add-in option runs dBASE.

Use the dBASE installation as a model to set up programs of your choice. When the setup is complete, run the program you wrote by selecting the appropriate Add-in option.

TYPICAL OPERATION

This exercise shows you how to change an Add-in option of the Apps Menu frame. In this illustration, an Apps Add-in option is set to run BASIC like dBASE. If your machine requires another version of BASIC (e.g., GWBASIC), replace all the references to BASIC with the proper program name.

Make sure that your desktop is clear and the cursor is positioned on one of the drive indicators. The shortcut key combinations, if applicable, are enclosed by braces.

1. {Press **Ctrl-D**}. Press **Ins** to move the cursor to the Main Menu line. Press **Left Arrow** or **Right Arrow**, if necessary, until the Disk Menu frame is open on your desktop.
2. {Press **Ctrl-G**}. Press **Up Arrow** to move the cursor to the Get File by Name option and then press **Enter**. The cursor moves to the Message line at the bottom of your desktop.

3. Type **RUNDBASE.FW3**. As you type, notice that the braces next to the Get File by Name option fill. Press **Enter**. The disk is read and the frame you specified is opened on your desktop as follows.

```
Apps  Disk  Create  Edit  Locate  Frames  Words  Numbers  Graph  Print  9:33 am

@local(ch, msg1, msg2, msg3, msg4, msg5, msg6, msg7, msg8, msg),
@local(drive, directory, filename, mac, olddirectory, olddrive, err1, err2),
@local(foo, original directory, floppy),

msg1 := "Not enough memory to run dBASE",
msg3 := "Loading dBASE...",
msg4 := "Run dBASE from which drive?",
msg5 := "Run dBASE from which directory?",
msg6 := "dBASE wasn't found in the specified directory or drive",
msg7 := "Either the specified drive or directory was invalid",
msg8 := "  --- Press any key.",
floppy := #FALSE,
original directory := @setdirectory,
@pk("{Menu#DC}"),
@display(RundBASE.Helpmsg),
@eraseprompt,
ch := @nextkey,
@echo(#OFF),
@if(ch <> {Return},
   @echo(#ON),
                    RUNDBASE          Char:     0/1

         Full-screen formula/number editing:  ESC finishes
```

4. Press **Spacebar**. Type **RUNBASIC** and press **Enter**. This changes the frame name so that when it is saved on disk, a new file is created.

5. Press **F2** (Edit) and then **F9** (Zoom) to change the FRED program. Your desktop should resemble the following.

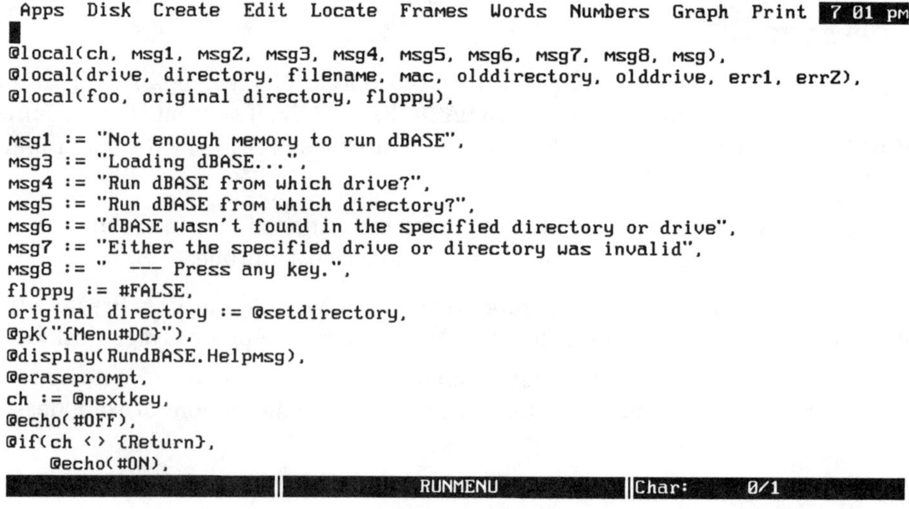

```
Apps  Disk  Create  Edit  Locate  Frames  Words  Numbers  Graph  Print  7 01 pm

@local(ch, msg1, msg2, msg3, msg4, msg5, msg6, msg7, msg8, msg),
@local(drive, directory, filename, mac, olddirectory, olddrive, err1, err2),
@local(foo, original directory, floppy),

msg1 := "Not enough memory to run dBASE",
msg3 := "Loading dBASE...",
msg4 := "Run dBASE from which drive?",
msg5 := "Run dBASE from which directory?",
msg6 := "dBASE wasn't found in the specified directory or drive",
msg7 := "Either the specified drive or directory was invalid",
msg8 := "  --- Press any key.",
floppy := #FALSE,
original directory := @setdirectory,
@pk("{Menu#DC}"),
@display(RundBASE.Helpmsg),
@eraseprompt,
ch := @nextkey,
@echo(#OFF),
@if(ch <> {Return},
   @echo(#ON),
                    RUNMENU           Char:     0/1

         Full-screen formula/number editing:  ESC finishes
```

6. Press **Ctrl-L** and **Ctrl-R**. When asked for the search value, type **dBASE** and press **Enter**. When asked what to replace, type **BASIC** and press **Enter**.

7. When you finish making the changes you want, press **Esc**. The frame view returns to your desktop.
8. Press **Gray +** to move the cursor inside the RUNBASIC frame. This is the subframe which contains the help message. Press **F10** (View) to open the subframe.
9. Press **Gray +** to move the cursor from the frame border into the frame. Open the Helpmsg frame. This is just a word processing frame which advises you to put the proper disk in drive A. Change the references from "dBASE" to "BASIC" so that your frame resembles the one in the following display.

```
Apps  Disk  Create  Edit  Locate  Frames  Words  Numbers  Graph  Print  7 04 pm
    Basic Menu is not included with Framework III.   If you have access to
    a copy  of  Basic Menu,  answer the questions  following  this display
    screen to let Framework III know where to find it.

    If you started Framework III from a floppy disk,  you will not be able
    to run Basic Menu from within Framework III.    Press ESC at this time,
    quit Framework III, and run Basic Menu from DOS.

    If  you are running Framework III from  a hard  disk  and wish  to run
    Basic Menu from a floppy disk,  insert its System  Disk #1  in drive A
    and follow the on-screen directions.

                     Press RETURN to run BASIC menu
                        or press ESC to Quit.

    If you have  other DOS programs  you  want  to  run  frequently within
    Framework III,  use the Change Add-ins branch of the  Setup program to
    include them in the Apps menu.
```

10. Press **Gray –** twice to move the cursor to the RUNBASIC frame border. If you want to change the default drive or directory, move to those subframes and make the necessary changes.
11. {Press **Ctrl-D** and then **Ctrl-P**}. Open the Disk Menu frame and select the Put Away option.
12. Reopen the Disk Menu frame and select the QUIT Framework III option. End this Framework III session so that you have the system prompt on the screen.
13. Get your Setup disk from your Framework III package and put it in drive A. Type **A:** and press **Enter** to make drive A your logged disk drive. Type **SETUPFW** and press **Enter** to begin the setup program. Follow the menu options to change the second option from "Apps Add-in" to "BASIC."
14. When completed, exit the Setup program and re-enter Framework III. Open the Apps Menu frame and select the option you just made available through Framework III.
15. Turn to Module 55 to continue the learning sequence.

Module 9

ASCENDING SORT

DESCRIPTION

When looking for a person's name in a phone directory, you know the directory is in alphabetical order. That fact makes the search easy.

This option lets you order the information in your spreadsheets and databases from low to high. Access the Ascending Sort option through the Locate Menu frame.

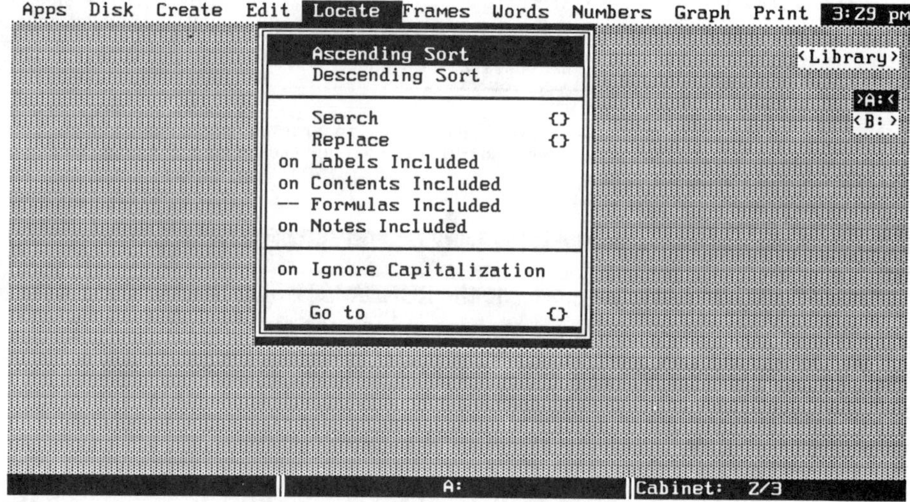

Arrange selected frames/rows/records from A to Z, low to high, early to late

First, open the frame you need to sort. Position the cursor on the cell or field you need sequenced from low to high. Open the Locate Menu frame and select the Ascending Sort option. The menu frame disappears and all your information is sorted.

If you only want a certain number of rows or records sorted, press F6 (Extend) to specify the information. Otherwise, Framework III sorts all rows or records.

Before selecting this option, however, verify the Ignore Capitalization option. If it is turned off before the sort occurs, all lowercase letters (a through z) appear before uppercase letters (A through Z). Review the following Ascending sorted list.

Ignore Capitalization on	*Ignore Capitalization off*
4-H of Denton	4-H of Denton
A A A Company	adams & weaver
A+ Hardware	zane 'n sane
Adams, Inc.	A A A Company
adams & weaver	A+ Hardware
zane 'n sane	Adams, Inc.
Zoro Entertainment	Zoro Entertainment

The computer always sorts in the following order: 1.) blank spaces; 2.) special characters (e.g., #, !); 3.) Numbers; 4.) letters. The Ignore Capitalization option affects sequencing since the case of the letter is considered when this option is turned off.

When you need to sort on more than one field, list the cells or fields on a sheet of paper. Then identify which is the most important down to the least important. Once you have done this, begin your sort with the least important cell or field. Then sort the next most important cell or field.

For example, to sort a database of names so that all the last names of "Smith" are together, the last name field is the most important. To have "Amy Smith" before "John Smith," the first name is the least important.

Position the cursor on the first name field and select the Ascending Sort option. Then position the cursor on the last name field and sort it. When complete, your database is sorted just like the telephone directory.

APPLICATIONS

Use this option for spreadsheet and database frames to sequence the information. This is helpful if you need to print the spreadsheet or database as a report.

For example, sort numeric cells or fields so that the row or record with 0.00 appears before 99.99. Sort a character cell or field so that the rows and records are in alphabetical order. Specific information is more easily found when there is order to the list.

TYPICAL OPERATION

This example shows you how to sort information in a database by using the Ascending Sort option of the Locate Menu frame. Close any open frames on your desktop and position the cursor on your data drive indicator (drive B in this example). The shortcut key combinations, if applicable, are enclosed by braces.

1. With the cursor positioned on the data drive indicator, press **Enter**. A frame similar to the following display appears on your desktop.

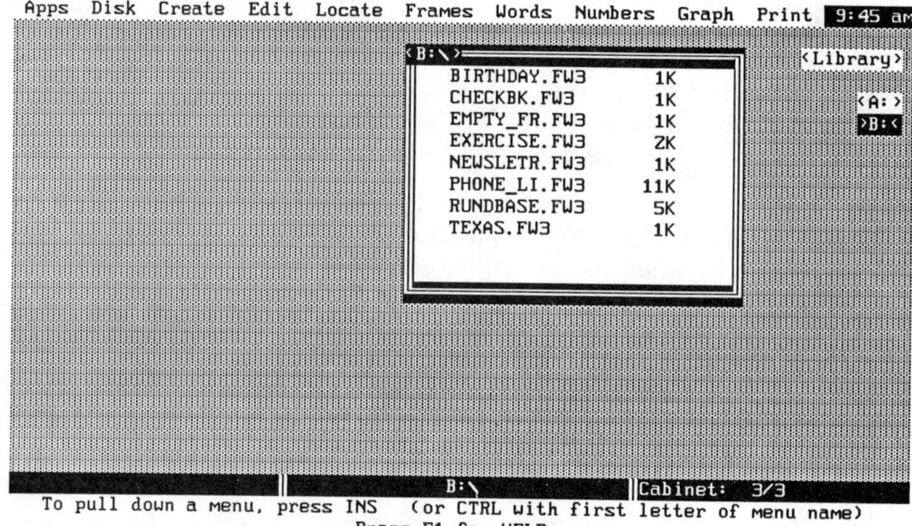

2. Since the cursor is positioned on the border of the open frame, press **Gray +**. Now you're inside the open frame. Press **Down Arrow**, if necessary, until the cursor is positioned on the filename PHONE_LI.FW3 and then press **Enter**. Another frame is opened on your desktop as in the following display.

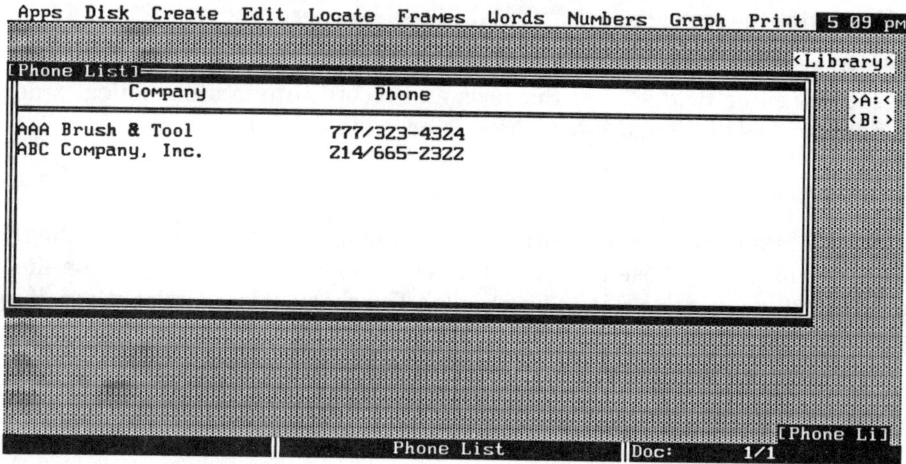

3. Press **Gray +** to move the cursor from the frame border to the inside of your open frame. Using the arrow (cursor) keys, position the cursor on the phone fieldname.
4. {Press **Ctrl-L**}. Press **Ins** to move the cursor to the Main Menu line. Press **Left Arrow** or **Right Arrow** until the Locate Menu frame is also open on your desktop.

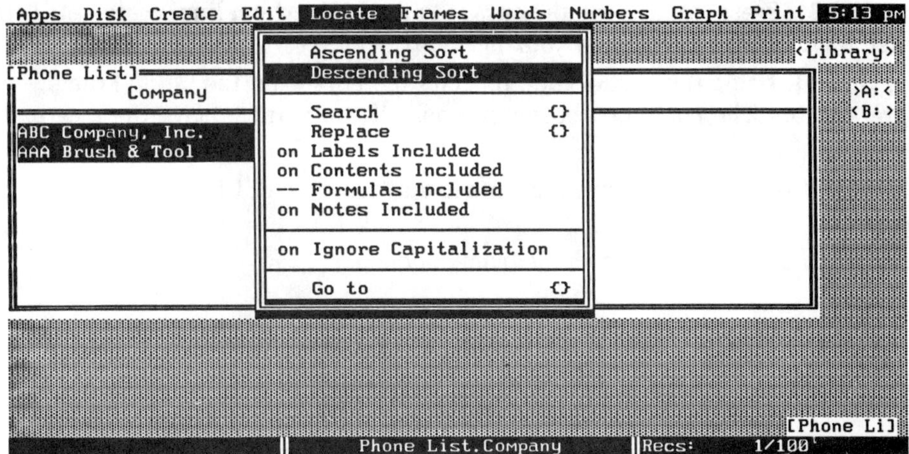

5. {Press **Ctrl-A**}. Press **Down Arrow** or **Up Arrow** until the cursor is positioned on the Ascending Sort option and press **Enter**. The Locate Menu frame disappears from your desktop. The Message line reports that Framework III is sorting the file. When complete, the order of your records is changed.

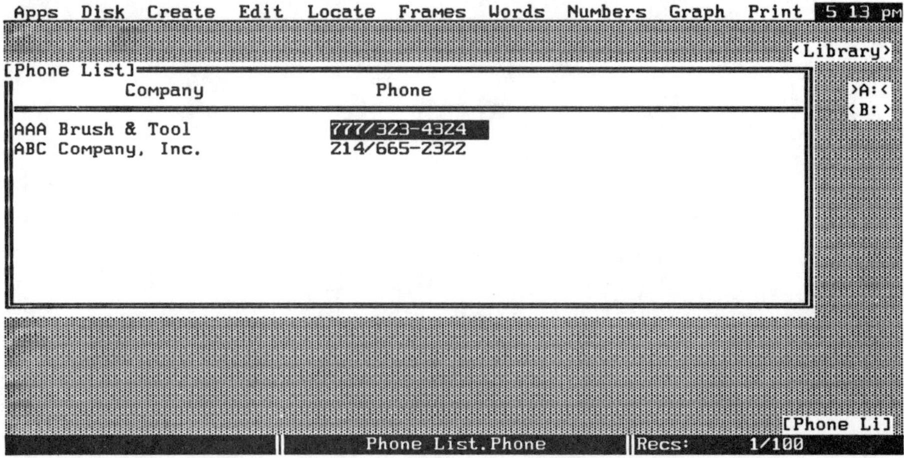

6. Now, sort the database again by fieldname Company.
7. Press **Gray –** to move the cursor to the frame border. Then press **Enter** to close the frame to the desktop tray.
8. Press **Scroll Lock** to move the cursor to the directory frame. Press **Gray –** and then press **Enter** to close the directory frame.
9. {Press **Ctrl-D**}. Press **Ins** to move the cursor to the Main Menu line. Press **Left Arrow** until the Disk Menu frame is open on your desktop.
10. {Press **Ctrl-Q**}. Using the arrow keys, position the cursor on the QUIT Framework option and press **Enter**. The computer beeps and asks if you want to save the new or modified frames. Type **N**.
11. Type **Y** when asked if you are sure you want to quit Framework III. This ends this Framework III session.
12. Turn to Module 81 to continue the learning sequence.

Module 10

BAR, STACKED BAR, PIE, LINE, UNMARKED LINE, MARKED POINTS, X-Y, HIGH-LOW-CLOSE

DESCRIPTION

Use any one of several graph forms to draw your picture. Each graph form has an impact of its own. The effect you want helps you choose which graph form to use.

The graph form selections are available through the Graph Menu frame.

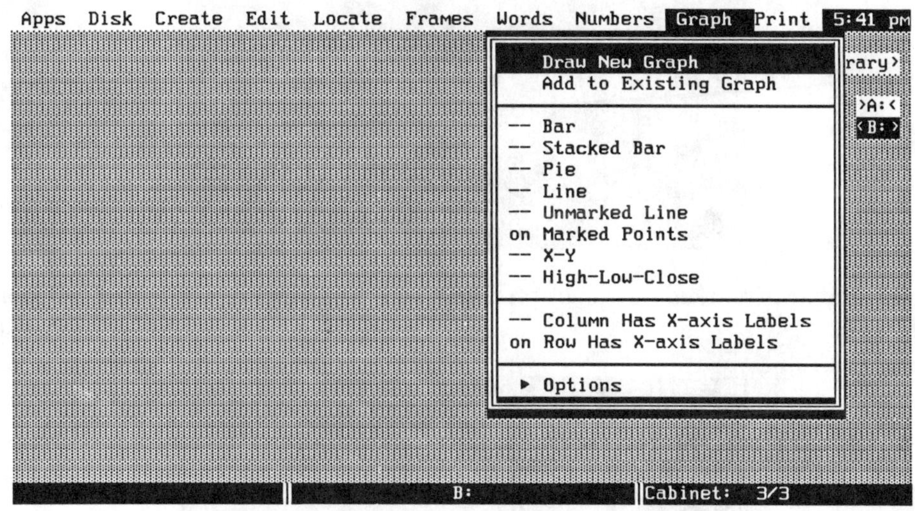

Bar This graph form presents each number you selected from your spreadsheet or database as a vertical bar. The larger the number, the higher the bar on your graph. The following graph is a Bar graph.

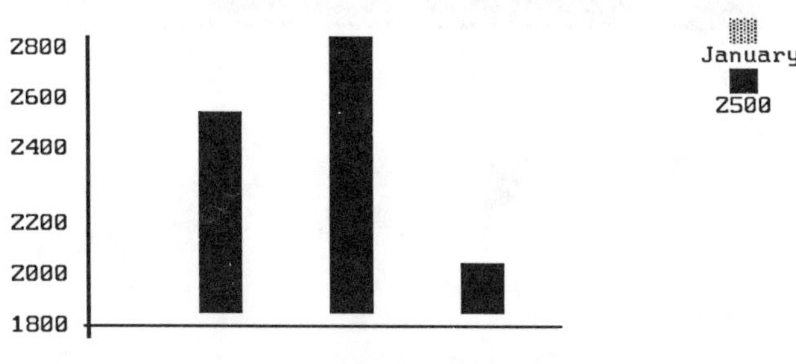

Stacked Bar Each number you select is presented as a piece of one vertical bar. The bar changes symbols as each number is represented.

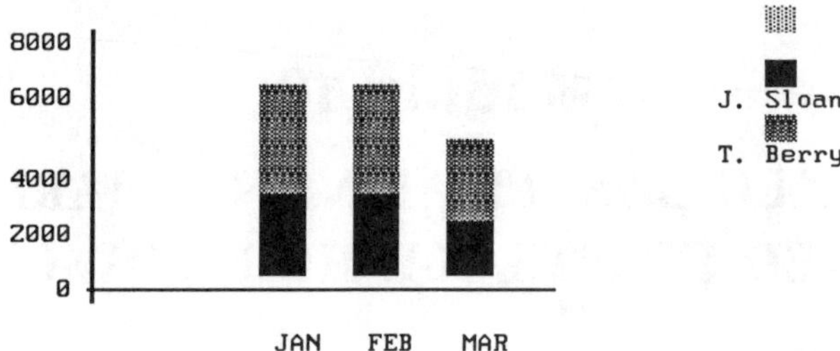

Pie This graph form is a pie which is cut into slices to represent the numbers selected. Each slice is a different size and symbol. Emphasize this graph form by choosing the Explode Pie Slices option. Pull one or several slices away from the circle to attract more attention to that part of the graph.

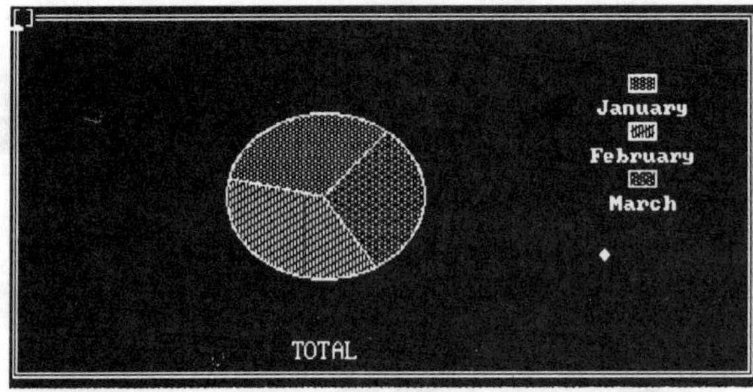

Line Each number is marked on the graph frame by a small empty box with a line connecting each position.

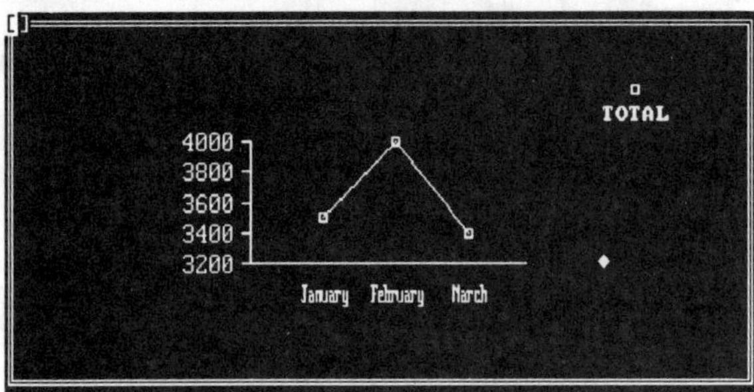

Unmarked Line Each number is charted on a line in the graph without any marked points.

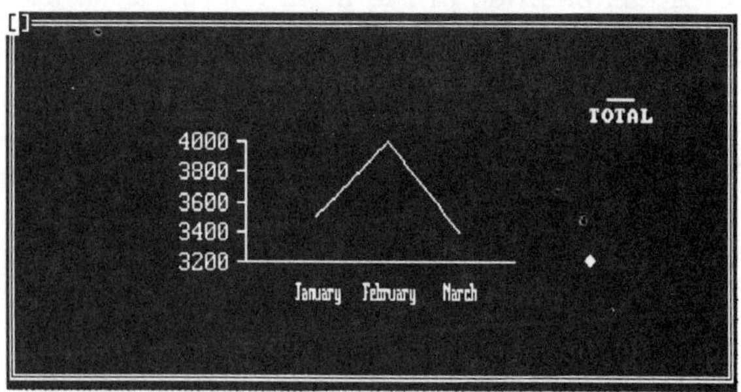

Marked Points This graph form displays a small empty box for each number you select from the spreadsheet or database.

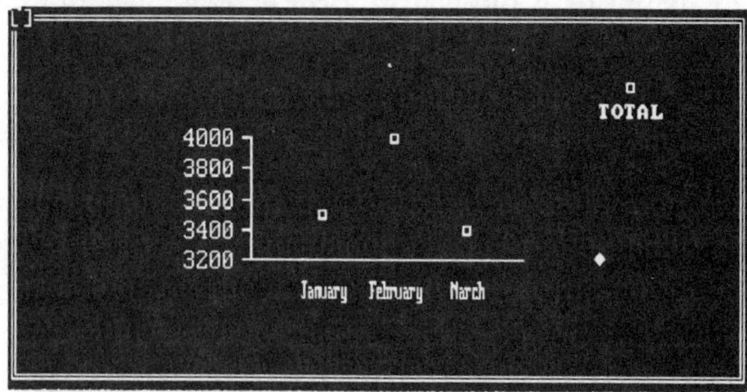

X-Y At least two rows or columns must be selected from the spreadsheet or database when using this graph form. The first set is used to establish the X-axis. The second set is the Y-axis. A small box is displayed at each place where the two numbers intersect. Otherwise, it resembles the Marked Points graph form.

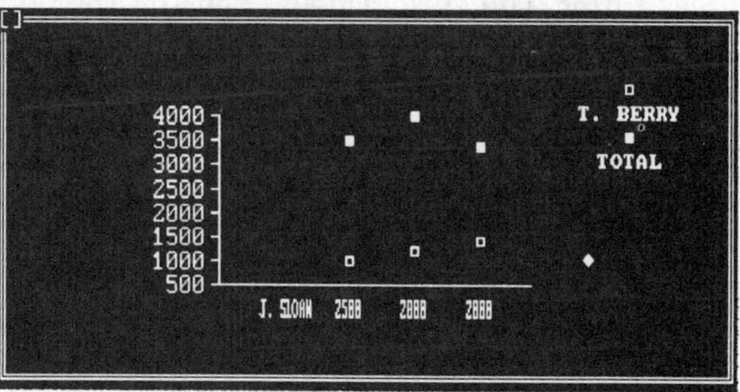

High-Low-Close Use this graph form to show the activity range of a stock's quotes for a time period. Graph any one or a combination of the high, low, or close numbers.

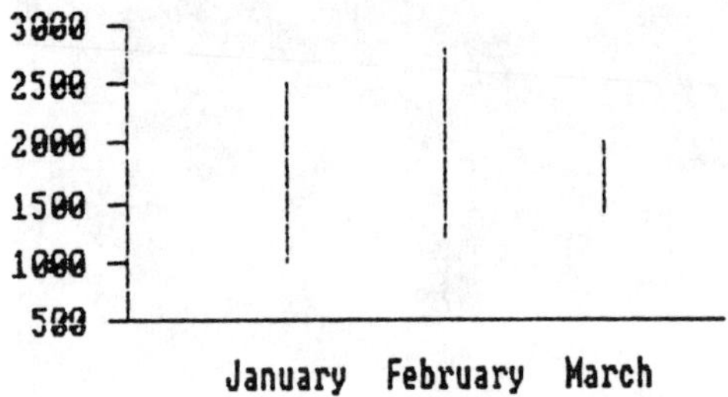

APPLICATIONS

The graph form used is often decided by the information to be shown as well as the impact you want for your picture. For example, a pie graph form shows percentages better than a marked points graph. An X-Y graph form is best for showing the relationship of numbers.

Just choose the form which meets your needs. When it is turned on, just select the Draw New Graph or Add to Existing Graph option.

TYPICAL OPERATION

This example shows you how to open a spreadsheet, select numbers, choose a graph form, and draw it. Close any open frames on your desktop and position the cursor on your data drive indicator. The shortcut key combinations, if applicable, are enclosed by braces.

1. {Press **Ctrl-D**}. Press **Ins** to move the cursor to the Main Menu line. Press the arrow (cursor) keys until the Disk Menu frame is open on your desktop.
2. {Press **Ctrl-G**}. Press **Up Arrow** until the cursor is positioned on the Get File by Name option and press **Enter.** The cursor then moves to the Message line at the bottom of your desktop. Type **SALES** and press **Enter.** The spreadsheet opens on your desktop.

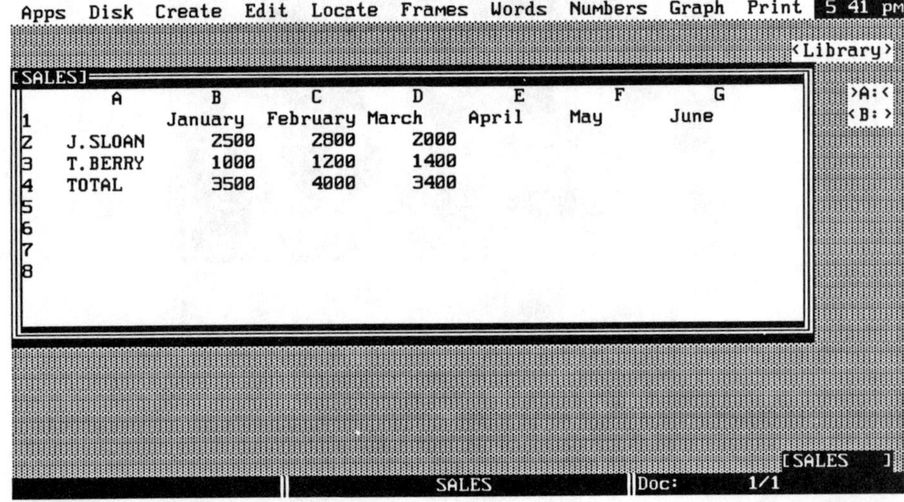

3. Press **Gray +** to move the cursor inside the open frame. Press **Esc** to return the cursor to normal size.
4. Press **Up Arrow** until the cursor is positioned on cell B2. Press **F6** (Extend). Press **Right Arrow** twice until cells B2, C2, and D2 are highlighted. Press **Down Arrow** one time so that the sales for both salespeople are highlighted. Press **Enter** to stop extending the cursor.
5. {Press **Ctrl-G**}. Press **Ins** to move the cursor to the Main Menu line. Press **Right Arrow** until the Graph Menu frame is open on your desktop.

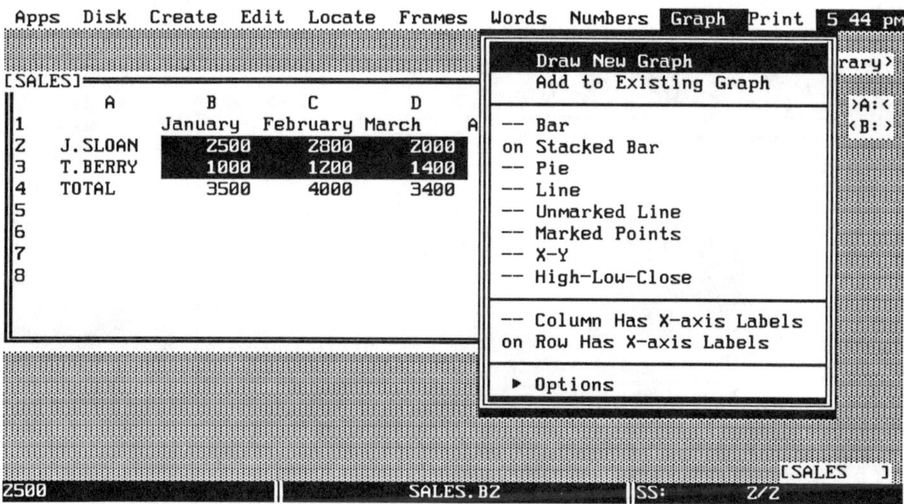

6. {Press **Ctrl-S** and then **Ctrl-D**}. Select the Stacked Bar option so that it is turned on. Then select the Draw New Graph option. Framework III asks if you want to draw it in the open frame or a new one. Just press **Enter** to use a new frame. The graph resembles the following display.

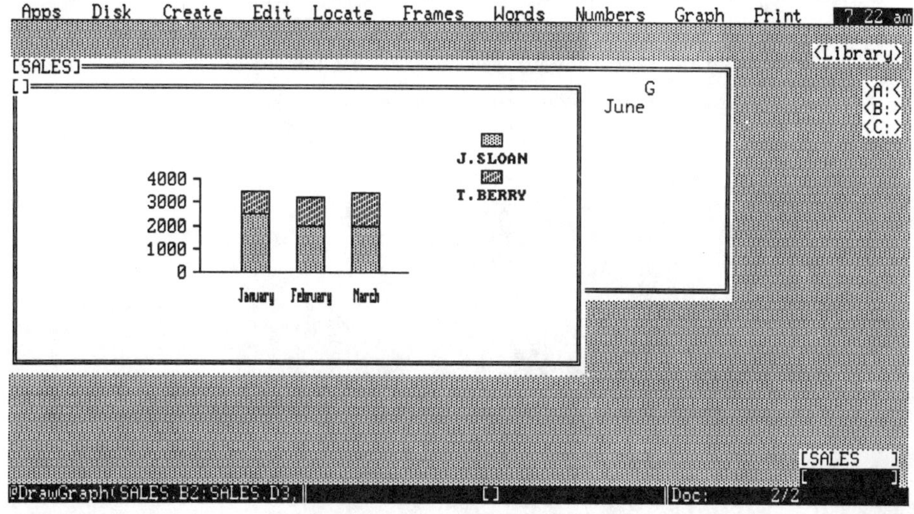

7. Press **Del** to remove the open graph frame from your desktop.
8. Press **Gray +** so that the two rows are highlighted again.
9. {Press **Ctrl-G**}. Press **Ins** to move the cursor to the Main Menu line. Press **Right Arrow** until the Graph Menu frame is again open on your desktop.
10. {Press **Ctrl-P** and then **Ctrl-D**}. Select the Pie Graph option so that it is turned on. Then select the Draw New Graph option. Framework III asks if you want to draw it in the open frame or a new one. Just press **Enter** to use a new frame. The graph resembles the following display.

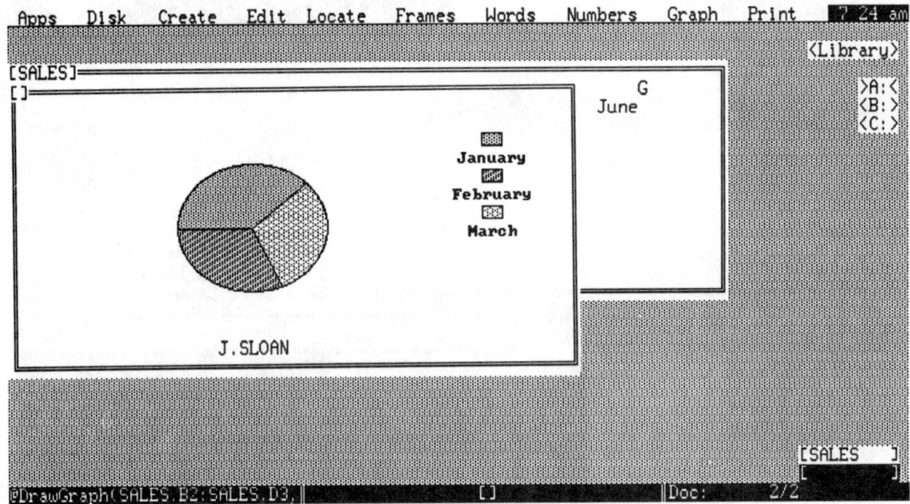

Graph: Draw New Graph

11. Press **Del** to remove the open graph frame from your desktop. The cursor returns to the spreadsheet frame. Press **Del** again so that your desktop is clean.
12. {Press **Ctrl-D**}. Open the Disk Menu frame on your desktop.
13. {Press **Ctrl-Q**}. Select the QUIT Framework option. When asked if you are sure you want to quit, type **Y**. This is the end of your Framework III session.
14. Turn to Module 15 to continue the learning sequence.

Module 11

BEGIN, STOP LOCAL PRINT JOBS

DESCRIPTION

If you have a printer for your computer, you obviously plan to print a few, if not all, of your documents. The Begin option lets you start the printing of your document while the Stop Local Print Jobs option halts printing. Remember, the document must be on your desktop before sending it to the printer.

The Begin and Stop Local Print Jobs options are in the Print Menu frame displayed below.

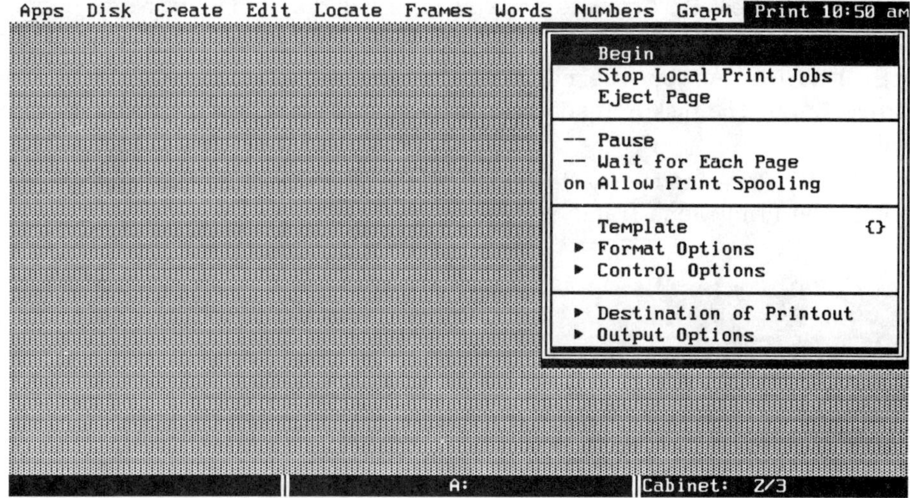

Begin printing selected frames

The document you want to print does not have to be open on your desktop. If it is in the desktop tray with the cursor positioned on it, open the Print Menu and select the Begin option. Just remember, the cursor identifies the document to be printed when the Print Menu frame is opened.

If you change your mind after printing has begun, open the Print Menu frame and select the Stop Local Print Jobs option. This cancels the printing of your document. The printer may not stop immediately if it has memory in it so don't panic. The printer stops as soon as the information in its memory is printed.

APPLICATIONS

Use the Begin option of the Print Menu frame to start printing the selected document on the printer.

Use the Stop Local Print Jobs option to cancel the printing activity. This can be done at any time, but if the printer has memory in it (called a buffer), it must finish printing the buffer.

When the printer stops, Framework III reminds you to reset the printer and move the paper to the top of the next page of paper. The reminder appears on the Message line at the bottom of your screen.

TYPICAL OPERATION

This example shows you how to use the Begin and Stop Local Print Jobs options of the Print Menu frame. Turn on your printer. Make sure that your desktop is clean and the cursor is positioned on a drive indicator on the right side of your desktop. The shortcut key combinations, if applicable, are enclosed by braces.

1. {Press **Ctrl-D**}. Press **Ins** to move the cursor to the Main Menu line. Press **Left Arrow** or **Right Arrow**, if necessary, until the Disk Menu frame is open on your desktop.
2. {Press **Ctrl-G**}. Press **Up Arrow** to move the cursor to the Get File by Name option and then press **Enter**. The cursor moves to the Message line at the bottom of your desktop.
3. Type **B:BIRTHDAY**. As you type, notice that the braces next to the Get File by Name option fill. Press **Enter**. The disk is read and the frame you specified is opened on your desktop as follows.
4. {Press **Ctrl-P**}. Press **Ins** to move the cursor to the Main Menu line. Press the arrow (cursor) keys until the Print Menu frame is open on your desktop.

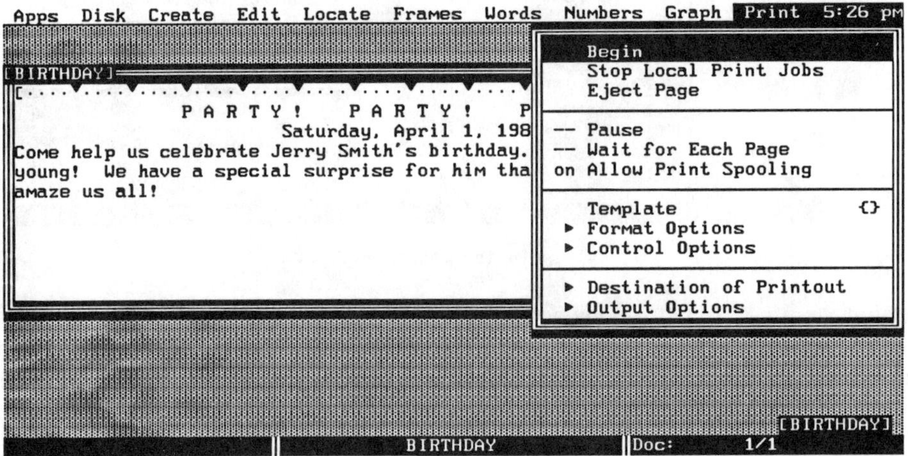

5. {Press **Ctrl-B**}. Using the arrow (cursor) keys, position the cursor on the Begin option and press **Enter**. The printer starts printing the document on paper.
6. {Press **Ctrl-P**}. Press **Ins** to move the cursor to the Main Menu line again. The Print Menu frame is open on your desktop.
7. {Press **Ctrl-B**, then quickly press **Ctrl-P** and **Ctrl-S**}. With the cursor still positioned on the Begin option, press **Enter**. This time cancel the print. Press **Ins** to move the cursor to the Main Menu line again. The Print Menu frame is open on your desktop. Using the arrow (cursor) keys, position the cursor on the Stop Local Print Jobs option and press **Enter**. The printer stops printing the document.
8. Press **Del** to remove the document from the desktop.
9. Turn to Module 66 to continue the learning sequence.

Module 12

BEGIN NEW PAGE

DESCRIPTION

Use this option in frames you are going to print. It is available through the Edit Menu frame shown in the following display.

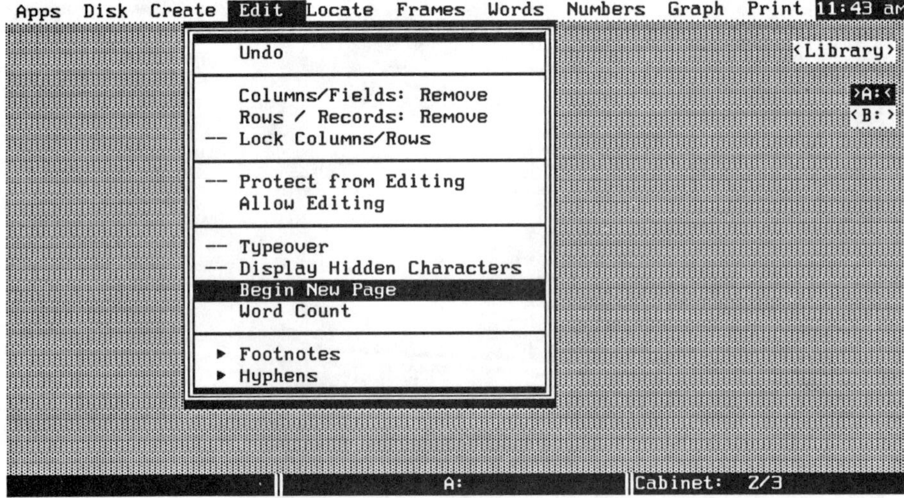

In a word frame, begin a new page at current cursor position

Every time you select this option within an open document, Framework III puts a large dashed line where the cursor was positioned. This dashed line is your way of telling Framework III to begin the next line on a new page of paper when the document is printed. You are forcing a page break.

APPLICATIONS

When you print a frame, Framework III handles all the positioning of the document on the page of paper. It uses the top and bottom margins to determine how many lines can be printed on a piece of paper.

There are times when you need to force Framework III to go to a new page even though the proper number of lines have not filled the previous page. The Begin New Page option gives you that control.

TYPICAL OPERATION

This illustration opens a word processing frame to show you how to use the Begin New Page option. Close any open frames on your desktop and position the cursor on one of the drive indicators. The shortcut key combinations, if applicable, are enclosed by braces.

1. {Press **Ctrl-D**}. Press **Ins** to move the cursor to the Main Menu line. Press **Left Arrow** or **Right Arrow**, if necessary, until the Disk Menu frame is open on your desktop.
2. {Press **Ctrl-G**}. Press **Up Arrow** to move the cursor to the Get File by Name option and then press **Enter**. The cursor moves to the Message line at the bottom of your desktop.
3. Type **BIRTHDAY**. As you type, notice that the braces next to the Get File by Name option fill. Press **Enter** twice. The disk is read and the frame you specified is opened on your desktop.
4. The cursor is positioned within the brackets at the top border of the frame. Press **Gray +** to move the cursor inside the open frame.
5. Press **Down Arrow** five times to position the cursor after the main paragraph.

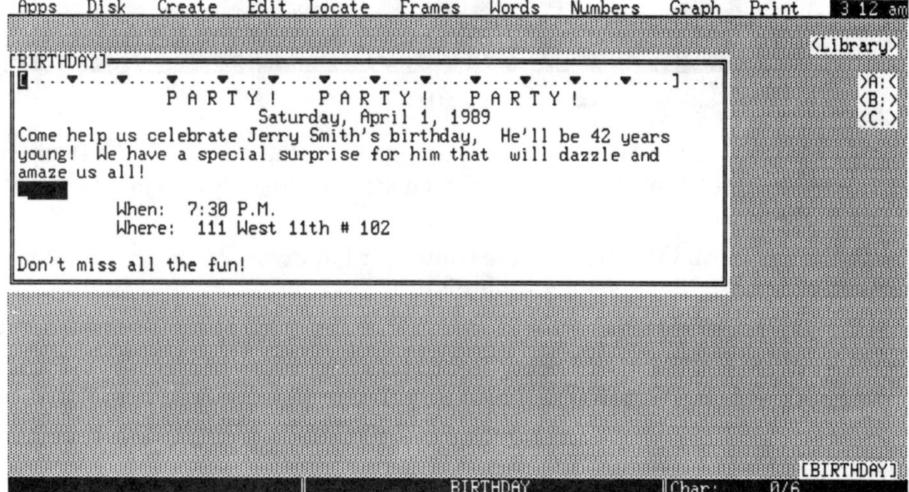

6. {Press **Ctrl-E**}. Press **Ins** to move the cursor to the Main Menu line. Next, press **Right Arrow** until the Edit Menu frame is open on your desktop.
7. {Press **Ctrl-B**}. Press **Down Arrow** to move the cursor to the Begin New Page option and then press **Enter**. Notice that a dashed line has appeared within the text and the lines after the cursor position have been moved down.

8. {Press **Ctrl-P**}. Press **Ins** to move the cursor to the Main Menu line. Press the arrow (cursor) keys until the Print Menu frame is open on your desktop.

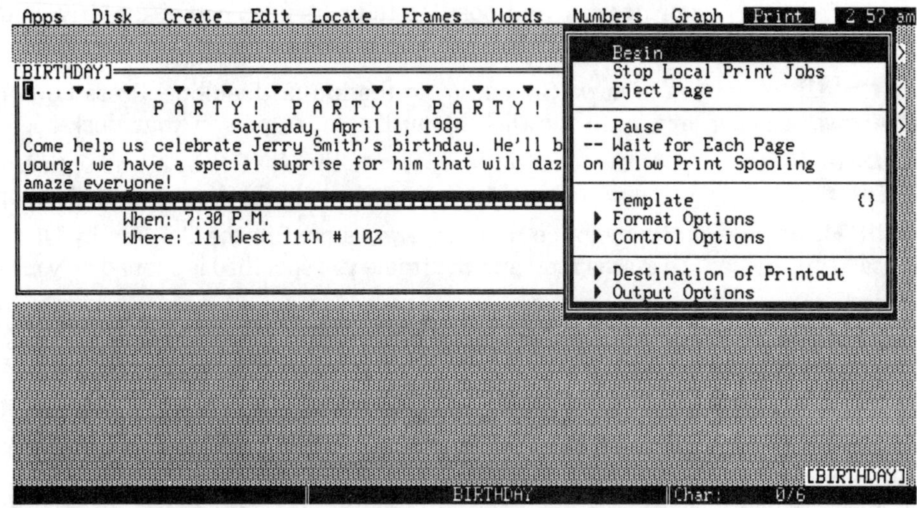

Begin printing selected frames

9. {Press **Ctrl-B**}. Using the arrow (cursor) keys, position the cursor on the Begin option and press **Enter**. The printer starts printing the document on paper. Notice that the table is printed on a separate page.

10. Press **Gray –** to move the cursor to the frame border. Press **Del** to remove the open frame from your desktop without saving it on disk.

11. {Press **Ctrl-D**}. Press **Ins** to move the cursor to the Main Menu line. Press the arrow (cursor) keys until the Disk Menu frame is open on your desktop.

12. {Press **Ctrl-Q**}. Using the arrow keys again, position the cursor on the QUIT Framework option and press **Enter**. Type **Y** when asked if you are sure you want to quit Framework III. This ends this Framework III session.

13. Turn to Module 79 to continue the learning sequence.

Module 13

CENTER

DESCRIPTION

In the old days, centering information on a sheet of paper was a chore. Smart typewriters and word processing software on computers handle centering, justification, spelling, and many other time-consuming typing activities.

This option is available for word processing frames. Access it through the Words Menu frame.

Framework III begins each new word processing frame with the Center option turned off. Once you turn it on, it stays on until you select the Align Left, Flush Right, or Justify options for your open frame.

The cursor positions itself in the center of each new line. As you type, the Center option immediately repositions the text.

As soon as one of the positioning options is selected, Framework III displays a message at the bottom of your screen. When you press Enter, the message disappears.

APPLICATIONS

This option is available for word processing frames only. Select this option when you want to center the text on the current and/or following lines.

Once the Center option is selected, centering text is automatic. You must select one of the other positioning options in the Words Menu frame to turn it off. As soon as the current frame is closed, Framework III automatically turns on the Align Left option.

TYPICAL OPERATION

This example shows you how to use the Center option of the Words Menu frame. Close any open frames on your desktop and position the cursor on your data drive indicator (drive B in this example). The shortcut key combinations, if applicable, are enclosed by braces.

1. Type **FW** to load Framework III. {Press **Ctrl-D**}. Press **Ins** to move the cursor to the Main Menu line. Press **Left Arrow** or **Right Arrow**, if necessary, until the Disk Menu frame is open on your desktop.
2. {Press **Ctrl-G**}. Press **Up Arrow** to move the cursor to the Get File by Name option and then press **Enter**. The cursor moves to the Message line at the bottom of your desktop.

3. Type **B:BIRTHDAY.FW3**. As you type, notice that the braces next to the Get File by Name option fill. Press **Enter**. The disk is read and the frame you specified is stacked in your desktop tray. Press **Enter** to open the frame.

4. Press **Gray +** to move the cursor inside the open frame. Your cursor is positioned after the last word of the document. Press **Up Arrow** until the cursor is positioned on the top line.

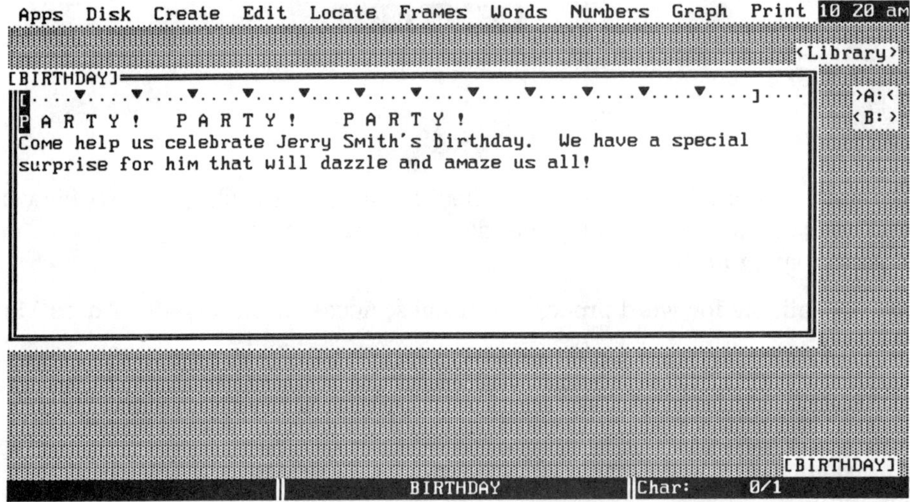

5. {Press **Ctrl-W**}. Press **Ins** to move the cursor to the Main Menu line. Press **Left Arrow** or **Right Arrow** until the Words Menu frame is also open on your desktop. Notice that the Align Left option is currently turned on.

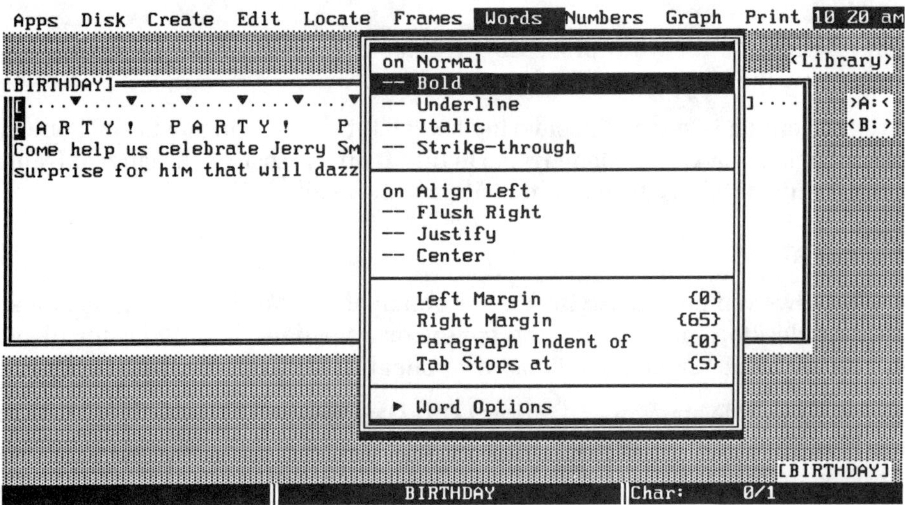

Boldface selected text -- in any type of frame

6. {Press **Ctrl-C**}. Press **Down Arrow** until the cursor is positioned on the Center option. Press **Enter**. The Words Menu frame disappears from your desktop. Notice that the first line of text is now centered within your open frame.

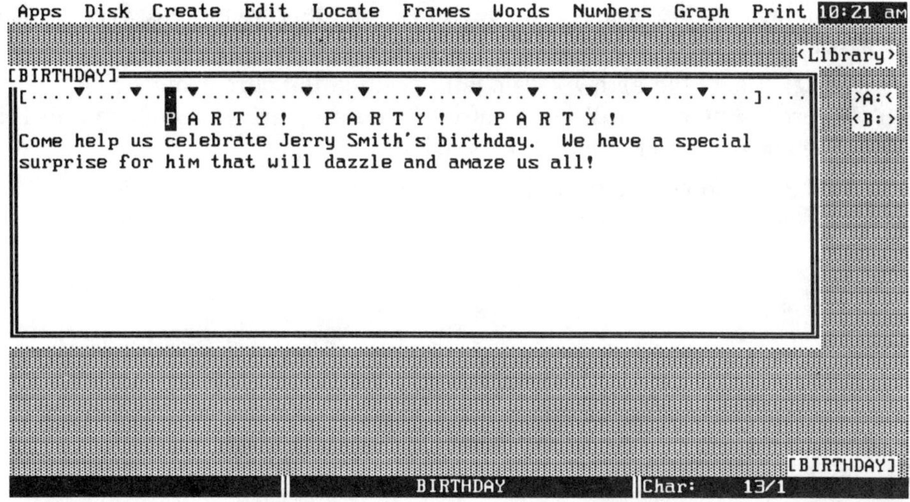

Words: Center on

7. Press **Right Arrow** to move the cursor to the end of the first line and press **Enter**. A blank line is inserted between the first and second lines. The cursor is positioned in the center of this blank line.
8. Type **Saturday, April 11, 1989**, and notice that each new letter is automatically centered. This continues until you turn the Center option off.
9. {Press **Ctrl-D**}. Press **Ins** to move the cursor to the Main Menu line. Press **Left Arrow** until the Disk Menu frame is also open on your desktop.

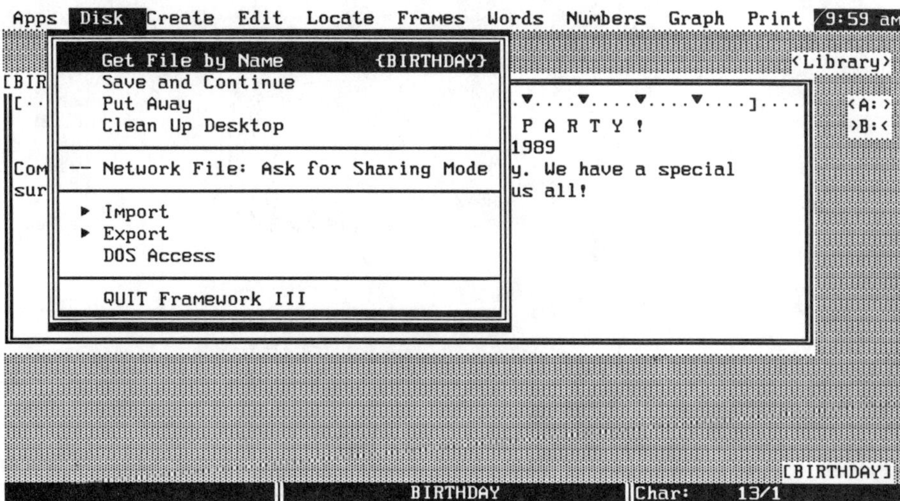

Bring specified file from disk and place beneath selected frame

10. {Press **Ctrl-P**}. Using the arrow (cursor) keys, position the cursor on the Put Away option and then press **Enter**. The Message line displays the word "SAVING" and the disk drive lights. When complete, the frame name is no longer on your desktop.
11. {Press **Ctrl-D**}. Press **Ins** to move the cursor to the Main Menu line. Press **Left Arrow** or **Right Arrow** until the Disk Menu frame is again open on your desktop.
12. {Press **Ctrl-Q**}. Using the arrow keys again, position the cursor on the QUIT Framework option and press **Enter**. Type **Y** when asked if you are sure you want to quit Framework III. You have ended this Framework III session.
13. Turn to Module 69 to continue the learning sequence.

Module 14

CLEAN UP DESKTOP

DESCRIPTION

Just like your desk, Framework III's desktop can get pretty cluttered. When you have a desktop of open frames, there comes a time when you need to clean it off. This option only closes open frames and stacks them in the desktop tray — it does not save them on the data disk.

By always saving each frame before continuing to another, you know that all of them have been saved on disk. Use the Clean Up Desktop option to close and stack the open frames.

This option is available through the Disk Menu frame as in the following display.

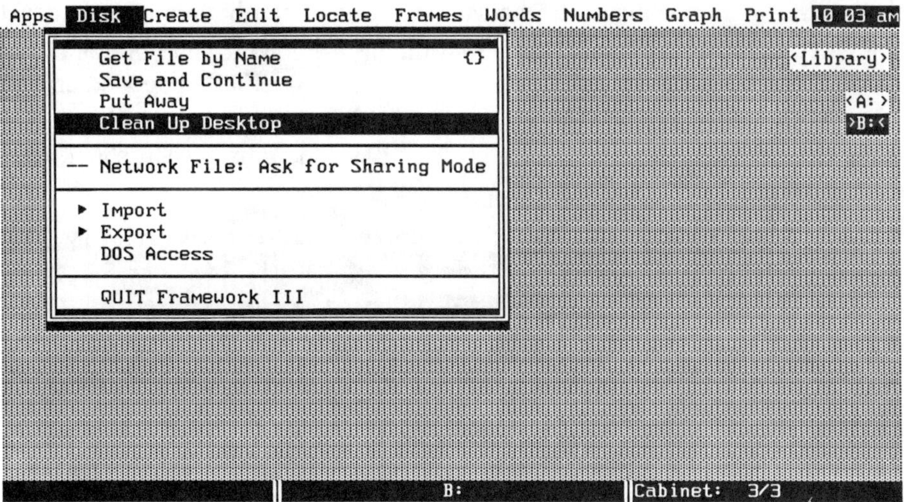

Close and stack all documents and cabinets

Remember, the Clean Up Desktop option *does not* save the frame on disk. It simply closes the *file* from your desktop and stacks it in the desktop tray. If you need the frame again, move the cursor to the name of the file in the tray and press Enter.

APPLICATIONS

While you work on an open frame, use the Save and Continue option. This saves the open frame on disk and lets you resume your work on that same frame.

When you are ready to open another frame, save it using the Put Away option. This saves the frame on disk and removes it from your desktop. However, if you intend to reopen the frame during the current Framework III session, just move it to your desktop tray and then use the Save and Continue option.

As you open more frames, you can get quite a mess on your desktop. Eventually, you need to clean it off if you plan to continue the current Framework III session.

Remember, your computer memory limits the number of files allowed on your desktop or tray. Make a habit of saving them regularly. If you run out of computer memory, you only have yourself to blame when you lose some of your work!

TYPICAL OPERATION

This exercise shows you how to tell Framework III to use the Clean Up Desktop option of the Disk Menu frame. Make sure that your desktop is clear and the cursor is positioned on one of the drive indicators. The shortcut key combinations, if applicable, are enclosed by braces.

1. {Press **Ctrl-D**}. Press **Ins** to move the cursor to the Main Menu line. Press **Left Arrow** or **Right Arrow**, if necessary, until the Disk Menu frame is open on your desktop.
2. {Press **Ctrl-G**}. Press **Up Arrow** to move the cursor to the Get File by Name option and then press **Enter**. The cursor moves to the Message line at the bottom of your desktop.
3. Type **B:BIRTHDAY**. As you type, notice that the braces next to the Get File by Name option fill. Press **Enter**. The disk is read and the frame you specified is opened on your desktop.
4. {Press **Ctrl-C**}. Press **Ins** to move the cursor to the Main Menu line. Press **Right Arrow** until the Create Menu frame is open on your desktop. Your screen should resemble the following display.

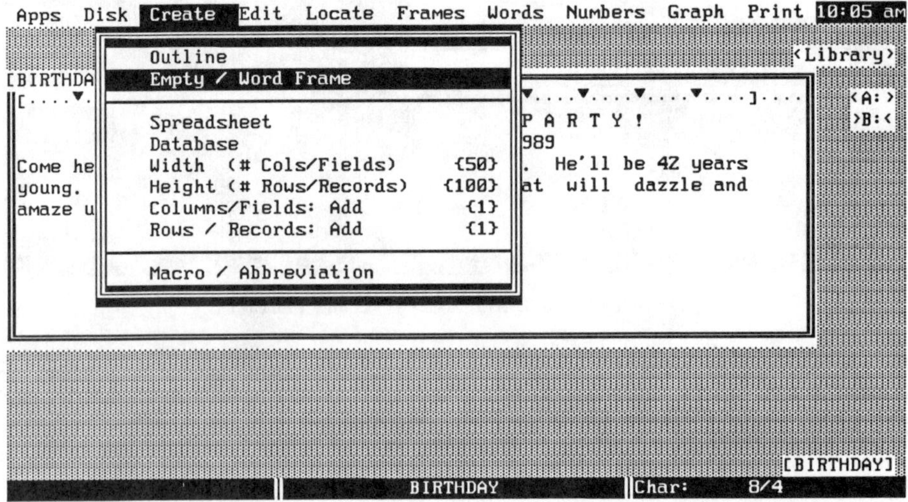

Create a frame for word processing or for containing other frames

5. {Press **Ctrl-E**}. Press **Down Arrow**, if necessary, to move the cursor to the Empty/Word Frame option of the Create Menu frame. Press **Enter** to select the option. An empty frame appears on your screen with the birthday invitation.
6. The cursor is positioned within the brackets at the top border of the frame. Type **EMPTY FRAME** and press **Enter**.
7. Press **Up Arrow** to see the birthday frame move into view.
8. Press **Down Arrow** for the empty frame again. This is like referring to one document to help you write another.
9. {Press **Ctrl-D**}. Press **Ins** to move the cursor to the Main Menu line. Press **Left Arrow** until the Disk Menu frame is also open on your desktop.
10. {Press **Ctrl-C**}. Using the arrow (cursor) keys, position the cursor on the Clean Up Desktop option and then press **Enter**. Both open frames are closed and stacked in the desktop tray. The saving message isn't displayed since this option does not save the open frames on the data disk.
11. {Press **Ctrl-D**}. Press **Ins** to move the cursor to the Main Menu line. The Disk Menu frame is again open on your desktop.
12. {Press **Ctrl-Q**}. Using the arrow keys again, position the cursor on the QUIT Framework option and press **Enter**. Type **N** when asked if you want to save the new or modified frames.
13. Turn to Module 51 to continue the learning sequence.

Module 15

COLUMN HAS X-AXIS LABELS

DESCRIPTION

Since a spreadsheet is usually a collection of numbers, it helps to provide labels. Just reserve the first column to describe the information in each row. Also, describe the information in each column by reserving the first row.

Select this option to display the first column of the spreadsheet (descriptions) on the horizontal line (X-axis) of your graph. It is available through the Graph Menu frame displayed below.

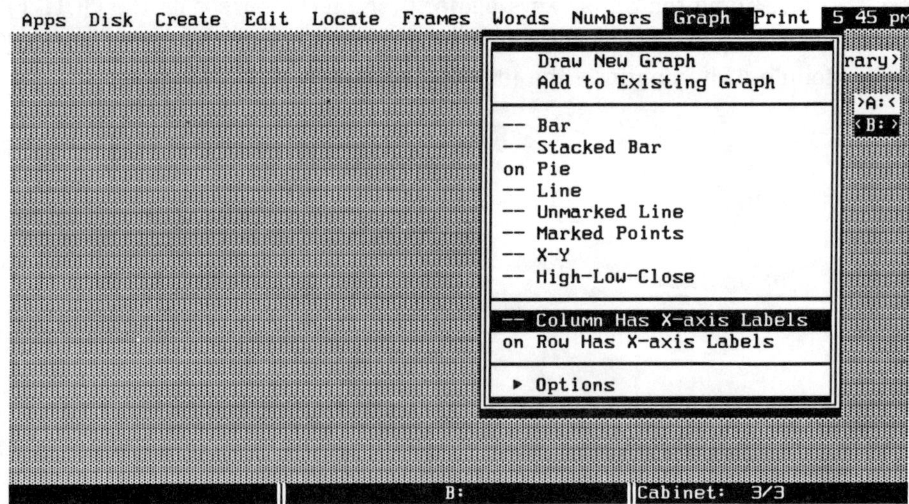

If ON, x-axis labels are taken from frame's first column, legends from first row

When you begin your Framework III session, this option may be on or off. When off, descriptions in the first *row* are used when the graph is drawn. By opening the Graph Menu and selecting this option, the labels in the first column are used to describe the X-axis of your graph.

For example, notice the following spreadsheet labels.

```
Apps  Disk  Create  Edit  Locate  Frames  Words  Numbers  Graph  Print  5:49 pm
                                                                      <Library>
[SALES]
        A           B         C        D        E        F        G        >A:<
1               January  February March    April    May      June          <B:>
2   J.SLOAN        2500      2800     2000
3   T.BERRY        1000      1200     1400
4   TOTAL          3500      4000     3400
5
6
7
8
                                                                    [SALES    ]
                                SALES                   Doc:      1/1
```

By pressing F6 (Extend) to highlight the numbers in rows 2 and 3, column B, you identify the information for your graph. Open the Graph Menu frame, select Column Has X-axis Labels, and then select the Draw New Graph option. Notice that the names of the salespersons appear on the X-axis.

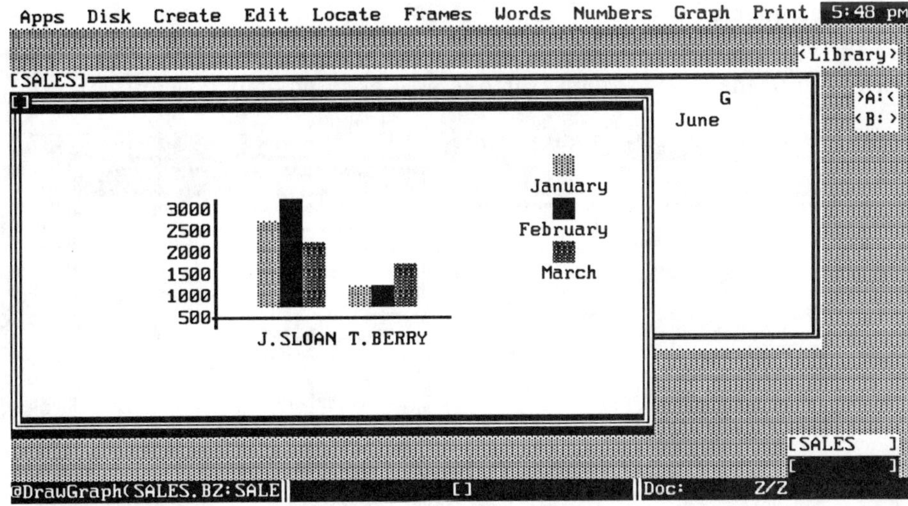

Graph: Draw New Graph

If the Columns Has X-axis Labels is off, the graph is drawn so that the months appear on the X-axis. Choose the way you prefer and then tell Framework III to draw it.

APPLICATIONS

Use the X-axis (horizontal line) of your graph to describe the information drawn. By selecting the Column Has X-axis Labels option, you're telling Framework III to draw the graph so that the labels in column A appear under the graph's X-axis.

Be sure that you notice whether this option is on or off before selecting the Draw New Graph option. You might not notice the labels until the graph is drawn and copies are distributed.

TYPICAL OPERATION

This example shows you how to open a spreadsheet, select numbers, and draw a graph so that the column's labels appear on the X-axis. Close any open frames on your desktop and position the cursor on your data drive indicator (drive B in this example). The shortcut key combinations, if applicable, are enclosed by braces.

1. With the cursor positioned on the data drive indicator, press **Enter.**
2. Since the cursor is positioned on the border of the open frame, press **Gray +**. Now you're inside the open frame. Press **Down Arrow** until the cursor is positioned on the filename SALES.FW3 and then press **Enter**. A spreadsheet is opened on your desktop.
3. Press **Gray +** to move the cursor from the frame border to the inside of your open frame.
4. The cursor is positioned on cell B4 through B6. Press **Esc** to change the cursor size. Press **Up Arrow** to move the cursor to cell B2.
5. Press **F6** (Extend) to tell Framework III you want to extend the cursor. Press **Down Arrow** to see the highlighted area expand to cell B3.
6. {Press **Ctrl-G**}. Press **Ins** to move the cursor to the Main Menu line. Press **Right Arrow**, if necessary, until the Graph Menu frame is also open on your desktop.

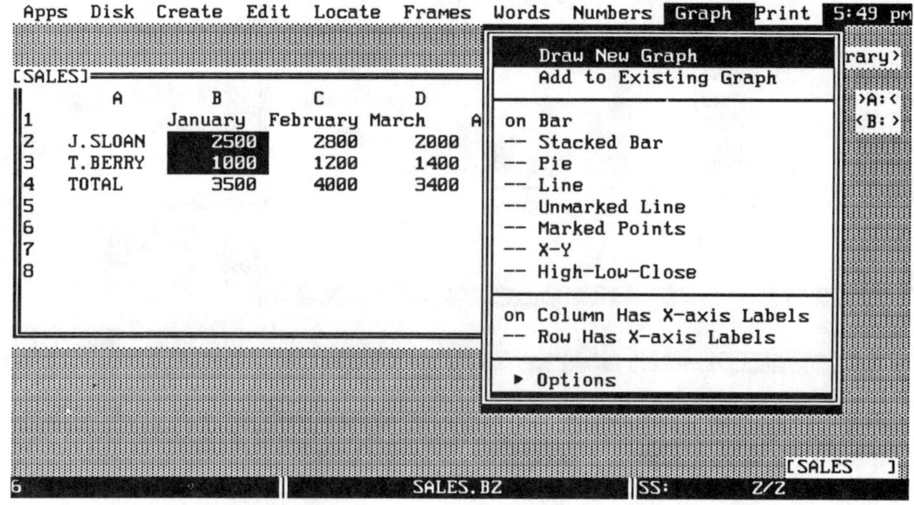

Draw graph of chosen type, using values in selected cells/fields

7. Notice whether or not the Column Has X-axis Labels is on. If on, skip this step. {Press **Ctrl-C**}. By pressing **Down Arrow**, move the cursor to the Column Has X-axis Labels option and press **Enter**.
8. {Press **Ctrl-D**}. Press **Up Arrow** until the cursor highlights the Draw New Graph option and press **Enter**. Framework III asks if you want to draw it in the open frame or a new one. Just press **Enter** to use the open frame. The graph should resemble the following display.

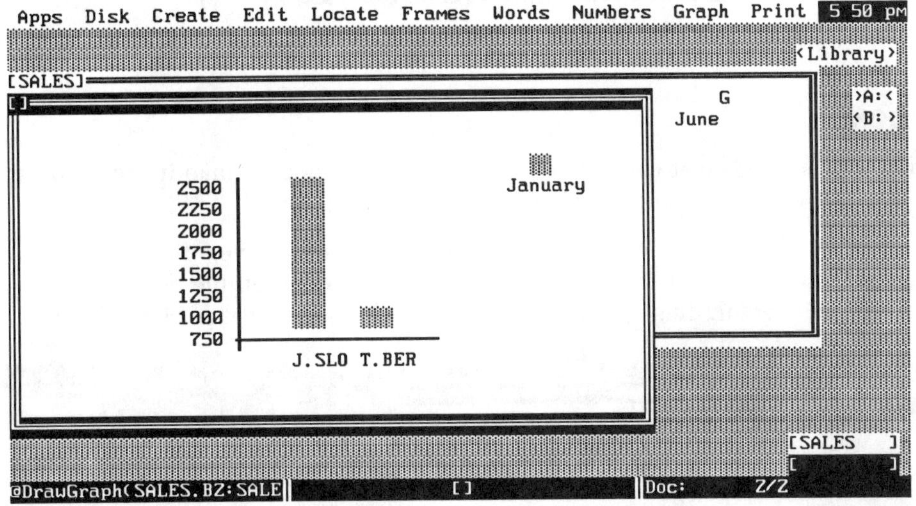

Graph: Draw New Graph

9. Press **Del** to delete the new graph from your desktop without saving it on disk. Press **Del** again to remove the open spreadsheet. Press **Enter** to close the directory frame.
10. {Press **Ctrl-D**}. Press **Ins** to move the cursor to the Main Menu line. Next, press the arrow (cursor) keys until the Disk Menu frame is again open on your desktop.
11. {Press **Ctrl-Q**}. Position the cursor on the QUIT Framework option and press **Enter**. Type **Y** when asked if you are sure you want to quit Framework III. This ends this Framework III session.
12. Turn to Module 75 to continue the learning sequence.

Module 16

COLUMNS/FIELDS: ADD { }

DESCRIPTION

A Framework III spreadsheet or database is never cut in stone. Make it bigger or smaller — anytime. To make it larger, use the Columns/Fields: Add option.

Use this option to add or insert columns across a spreadsheet or new fields within a database file. Remember, the spreadsheet or database file must be open on the desktop and the cursor positioned before selecting this option. It is available from the Create Menu frame as follows.

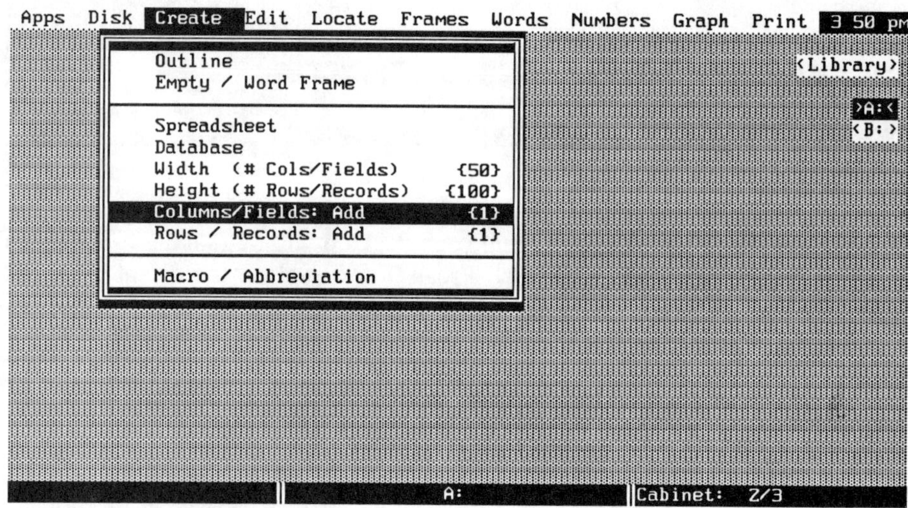

Add specified number of columns/fields after the selected one

Notice the Columns/Fields: Add option. The "1" contained within the braces specifies how many new columns or fields are added to the open file. It is currently set to add only one column or field when this option is selected. Before Framework III increases the size of the open spreadsheet or database, you are given the opportunity to change this number.

For example, the following spreadsheet frame has five rows and four columns (A, B, C, and D). Notice that column D is currently empty.

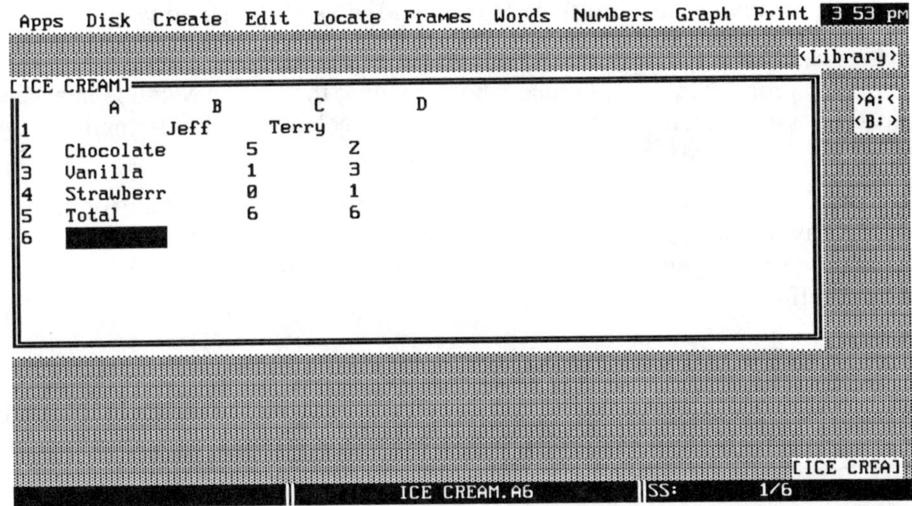

To keep the column names (Jeff and Terry) in alphabetical order, new columns are inserted with the Columns/Fields: Add option. The following spreadsheet has three new columns *inserted between* the existing columns. In the following display, Framework III inserted three new columns between those labeled Jeff and Terry. Notice the Message line at the bottom of the screen.

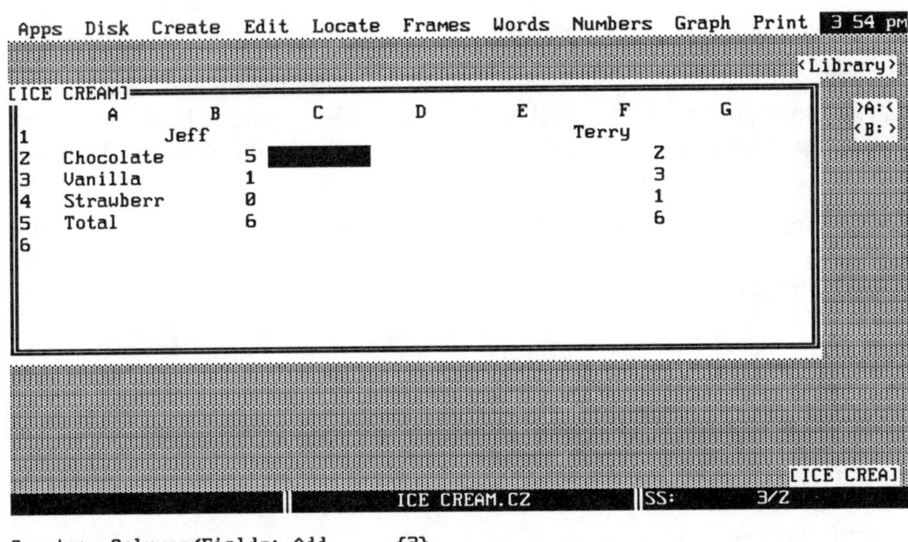

Create: Columns/Fields: Add {3}

Notice that columns C, D, and E are the new columns. Terry was on column C before the Columns/Fields: Add option was performed. It was automatically moved across the spreadsheet to column F when the three new columns were inserted.

The new columns or fields are always inserted to the right of the column where the cursor is positioned. This gives you the choice of where the additional columns are added.

This option is also available for database frames and is used the same way.

Remember that you can add the new columns or fields *anywhere* within the file. Position the cursor within the spreadsheet or database before opening the Create Menu frame. Then select the Columns/Fields: Add option, type the number of new columns or fields you need, and press Enter. Framework III changes the file within the frame.

If the change meets your needs, save it on disk by using the Save and Continue option of the Disk Menu frame. By saving your open frames at regular intervals (e.g., after you review and approve a major change), power failures and other such catastrophies are only bothersome — not a major loss of time and effort.

APPLICATIONS

Needs and situations change from day to day. When you create a spreadsheet or database, it's comforting to know that the size is not "set in concrete." You can easily change the file as often as necessary to keep it up-to-date.

Being restricted to the original format of a spreadsheet or database would certainly slow new development. Framework III provides the flexibility needed to get your work computerized quickly. If, and when, your needs change, the file size can change too. In other words, a "quick and dirty" job can be done for the short-term. Then, when time allows, the spreadsheet or database can be enhanced to accommodate your long-term needs.

TYPICAL OPERATION

The following illustration shows you how to create a small spreadsheet and then insert new columns into it. Make sure that your desktop is clean and the cursor is positioned on the data drive indicator. If you have two drives, the data drive is drive B. The shortcut key combinations, if applicable, are enclosed by braces.

1. Press **Ctrl-C** to cause the Create Menu frame to open on your desktop. Notice the Width and Height options in the following menu. Framework III is set to create a spreadsheet with 50 columns across and 100 rows down.

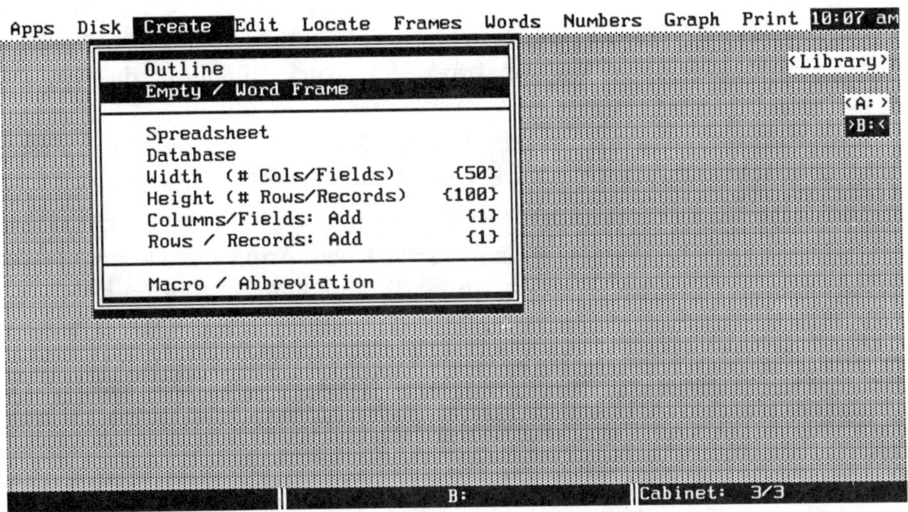

Create a frame for word processing or for containing other frames

2. {Press **Ctrl-W**}. Since the width and height settings are so large, they must be changed before creating your spreadsheet. (When a file is saved on disk, more disk space is used for a large spreadsheet — even though you don't use it all.) Press **Down Arrow** to move the cursor to the Width (# Cols/Fields) option and press **Enter**. Type **4** and press **Enter**. Notice that the Width (# Cols/Fields) option has 4 within the braces.
3. {Press **Ctrl-H**}. Press **Down Arrow** to move the cursor to the Height (# Rows/Records) option and press **Enter**. Type **5** and press **Enter**. Notice that the Height (# Rows/Records) option has 5 within the braces.
4. {Press **Ctrl-S**}. Now, it's time to create your spreadsheet. Using the arrow (cursor) keys, position the cursor on the Spreadsheet option, then press **Enter**. An empty spreadsheet frame appears on your desktop. Notice that there are only four columns and five rows in your spreadsheet.

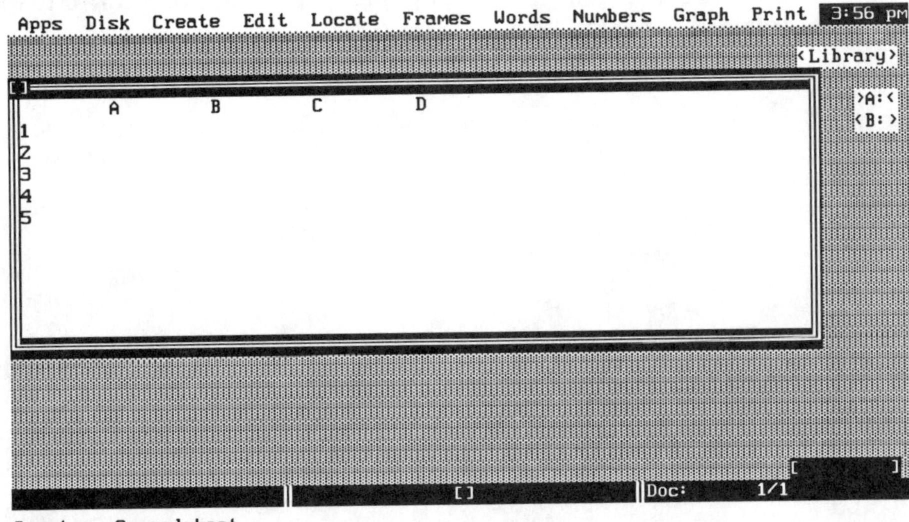

Create: Spreadsheet

5. The blinking cursor is positioned within the brackets at the top of the frame. Type **Flavors** and press **Enter**. Notice the desktop tray. Framework III knows this frame (file) as FLAVORS.FW3.
6. Press **Gray +** to move the cursor inside the open frame. It is positioned on row 1, column A. Press **Right Arrow** to move the cursor to column B, type **Jeff**, and press **Enter**.
7. Press **Right Arrow** to move the cursor to column C, type **Terry**, and press **Enter**.
8. Since columns B and C now have headings, press **Down Arrow** once and **Left Arrow** twice to position the cursor on row 2, column A. Type **Chocolate** and press **Enter**.
9. Press **Right Arrow** once, type **5**, and press **Enter**. Press **Right Arrow** again to move the cursor to column C. Type **2** and press **Enter**. Notice the following display.

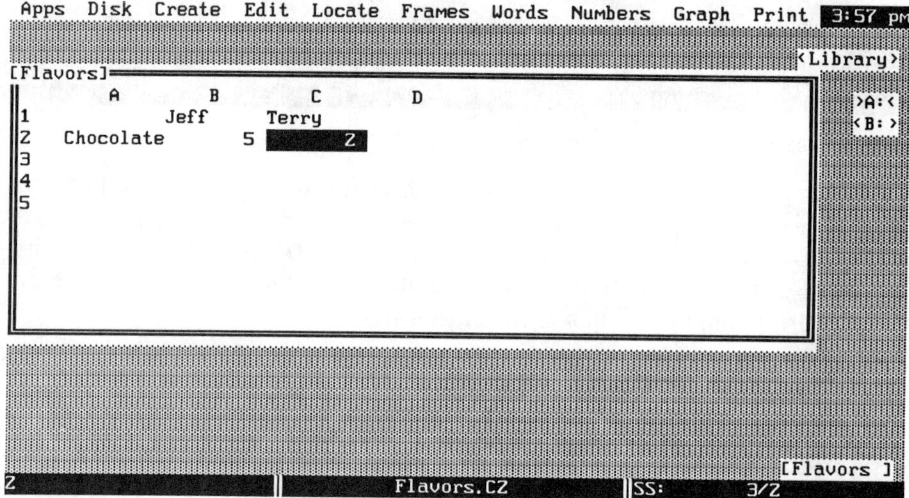

10. Now, it's time to insert three new columns between the columns labeled "Jeff" and "Terry." Position the cursor on row 2, column B, by pressing **Left Arrow**. Press **Ctrl-C** to reopen the Create Menu frame.

11. Position the cursor on the Columns/Fields: Add option and press **Enter** (or use the shortcut **Ctrl-C**). The cursor moves to the bottom of the desktop (the Message line). Type **3** and press **Enter**. The Create Menu disappears and your spreadsheet has three empty columns between Jeff and Terry as follows.

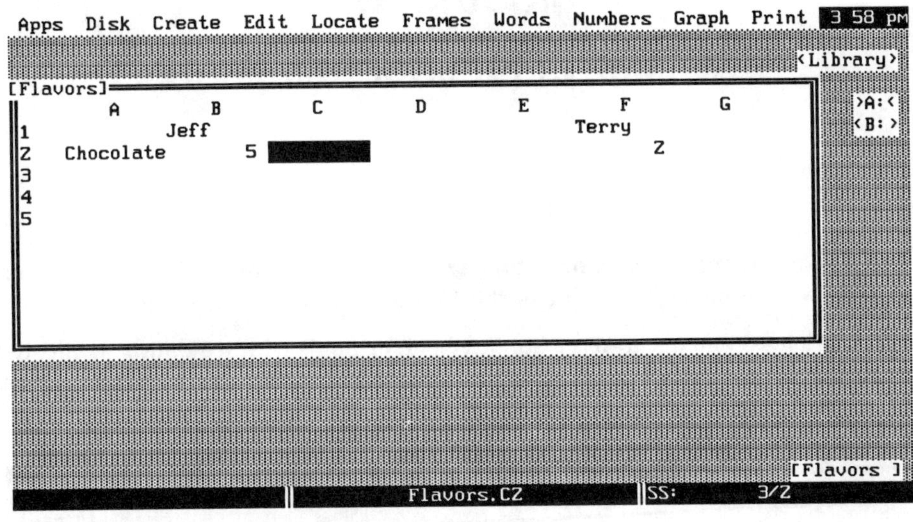

12. Press **Gray –** to move the cursor to the top of the frame border. Then press **Enter** to close the open frame. Framework III closes the frame and moves the cursor to the desktop tray.

13. Press **Ctrl-D** to open the Disk Menu frame and move the cursor to the Put Away option. Then press **Enter** to select the option (or use the shortcut **Ctrl-P**). The Message line reports that the B:FLAVORS.FW3 document is saved. Framework III saves your spreadsheet on drive B (or your data drive) and names it FLAVORS.FW3. Also, the desktop tray is removed from your screen since it is empty. Your file has been "Put Away" for later use.

14. {Press **Ctrl-D** and then **Ctrl-Q**}. Reopen the Disk Menu frame and move the cursor to the QUIT Framework option. Press **Enter** to select the option. When asked if you really want to quit Framework III, type **Y**. Your Framework III session is complete.

15. Turn to Module 17 to continue the learning sequence.

Module 17

COLUMNS/FIELDS: REMOVE

DESCRIPTION

Change a Framework III spreadsheet or database whenever you want. Make it bigger or smaller — anytime. One way to make it smaller is the Columns/Fields: Remove option.

Use this option to delete columns across a spreadsheet, or fields within a database file. Remember, the spreadsheet or database file must be open on the desktop and the cursor positioned before selecting this option. It is available from the Edit Menu frame as follows.

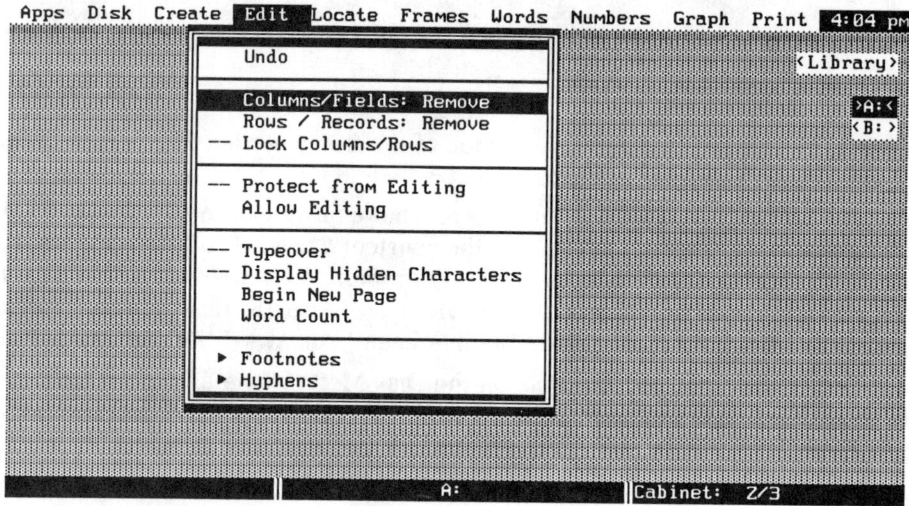

Remove selected columns/fields from a spreadsheet/database

Notice the Columns/Fields: Remove option. Each time this option is selected, the column currently selected is deleted. For example, the following spreadsheet frame has five rows and seven columns (A, B, C, D, E, F, and G). Notice that columns C, D, E, and G are currently empty.

```
Apps  Disk  Create  Edit  Locate  Frames  Words  Numbers  Graph  Print  4 03 pm
                                                                  <Library>
[Flavors]
        A       B          C        D         E        F        G       >A:<
1            Jeff                                   Terry               <B:>
2   Chocolate          5                                      2
3   Vanilla            1                                      3
4   Strawberr          0                                      1
5   Total              6                                      6

                                                                  [Flavors ]
                                   Flavors.D1            SS:       4/1
```

Since these empty columns are not used, they can be deleted from the spreadsheet with the Columns/Fields: Remove option. In the following display, two empty columns have been removed. Notice the Message line at the bottom of the screen.

```
Apps  Disk  Create  Edit  Locate  Frames  Words  Numbers  Graph  Print  4:03 pm
                                                                  <Library>
[Flavors]
        A       B          C        D         E                         >A:<
1            Jeff                 Terry                                 <B:>
2   Chocolate          5                2
3   Vanilla            1                3
4   Strawberr          0                1
5   Total              6                6

                                                                  [Flavors ]
                                   Flavors.D1            SS:       4/1
Edit:  Columns/Fields: Remove
```

Columns B and D now have the information that was in columns B and F. Terry was in column F before the Columns/Fields: Remove option was performed. It was automatically shifted to column D when the two empty columns were removed.

Columns or fields are always deleted from the cursor position (inclusive) to the right of the column where the cursor is positioned. This gives you the choice of where the columns are deleted.

This option is also available for database frames and is used the same way.

Remove as many columns or fields from the open frame as you want. Position the cursor within the spreadsheet or database before opening the Create Menu frame. Then, open the Edit Menu frame, and select the Columns/Fields: Remove option for each column to be deleted. Framework III shifts the information within the frame.

If the change meets your needs, save it on disk by using the Save and Continue option of the Disk Menu frame. By saving your open frames at regular intervals (e.g., after you review and approve a major change), power failures and other such "catastrophies" are only bothersome — not a major loss of time and effort.

APPLICATIONS

Needs and situations change from day to day. When you create a spreadsheet or database, it's comforting to know that the size is not "set in concrete." You can easily change the file as often as necessary to keep it up-to-date.

Framework III provides the flexibility needed to get your work computerized quickly. If and when your needs change, the file size can change too.

In other words, a quick job can be done for the short-term. Then, when time allows, it can be enhanced to accommodate your long-term needs.

TYPICAL OPERATION

The following illustration shows you how to remove columns from an existing spreadsheet. Make sure that your desktop is clean and the cursor is positioned on the data drive indicator. If you have two drives, the data drive is drive B. The shortcut key combinations, if applicable, are enclosed by braces.

1. {Press **Ctrl-D**}. Press **Ins** to move the cursor to the Main Menu line. Press the arrow (cursor) keys, if necessary, until the Disk Menu frame is open on your desktop.
2. {Press **Ctrl-G**}. Press **Up Arrow** until the cursor is positioned on the Get File by Name option and press **Enter**. The cursor then moves to the Message line at the bottom of your desktop. Type **FLAVORS** and press **Enter**. The spreadsheet opens on your desktop.
3. Press **Gray +** to move the cursor inside the open frame.
4. Now, it's time to delete columns D and E. Position the cursor on row 2, column C.

5. {Press **Ctrl-E**}. Press **Ins** to move the cursor to the Main Menu line. Press **Right Arrow** until the Edit Menu frame is open on your desktop.

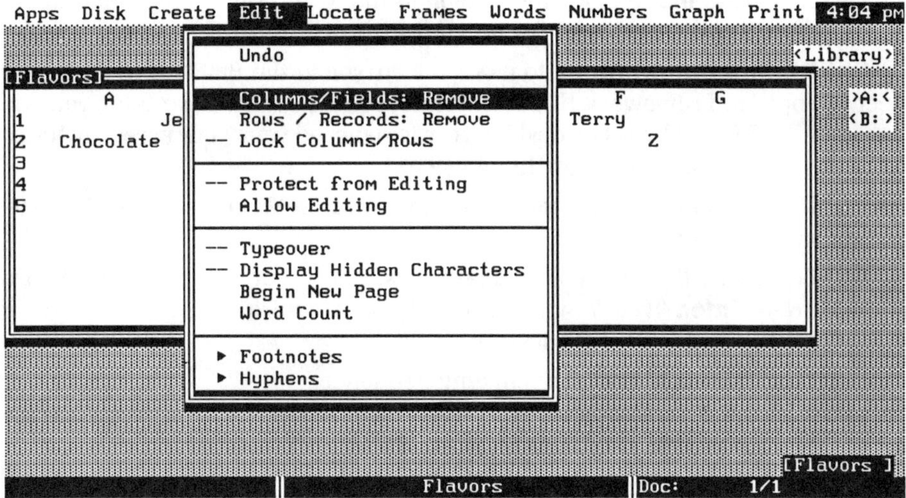

Remove selected columns/fields from a spreadsheet/database

6. {Press **Ctrl-C**}. Using the arrow (cursor) keys, position the cursor on the Columns/Fields: Remove option and press **Enter**. The computer beeps and tells you that this operation is not "Undoable." Type **Y** to continue the operation. Reopen the Edit Menu and select the Columns/Fields: Remove option again. When the Edit Menu frame disappears, your spreadsheet is changed.

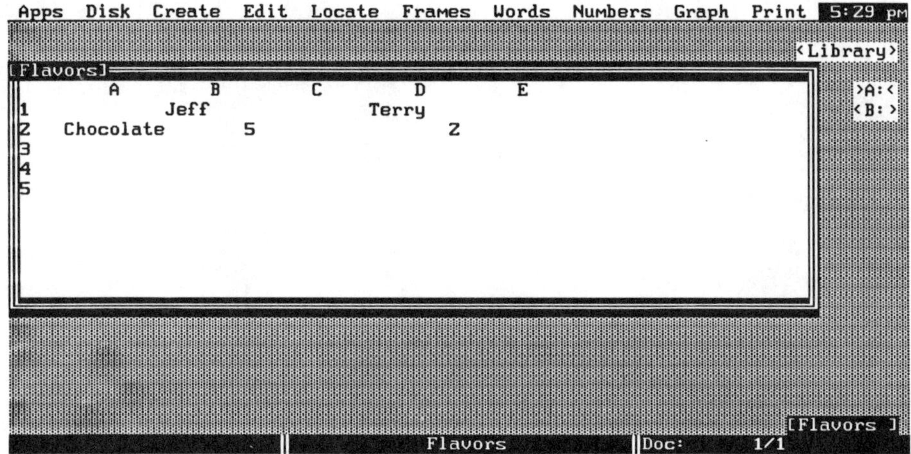

7. Press **Gray –** to move the cursor to the top of the frame border. Press **Enter** to close the open frame. Framework III closes the frame and moves the cursor to the desktop tray.
8. {Press **Ctrl-D**}. Press **Ins** to move the cursor to the Main Menu line. Next, use the arrow (cursor) keys until the Disk Menu frame opens.
9. {Press **Ctrl-P**}. Press **Down Arrow** to move the cursor to the Put Away option. Press **Enter** to select the option. Framework III saves your spreadsheet on drive B (or your data drive) and names it FLAVORS.FW3. The desktop tray is removed from your screen since it is empty. Your file has been "Put Away" for later use.
10. {Press **Ctrl-D**}. Press **Ins** to move the cursor to the Main Menu line. The Disk Menu frame is open on your desktop.
11. {Press **Ctrl-Q**}. Using the arrow keys again, position the cursor on the QUIT Framework option and press **Enter**. Type **Y** when asked if you are sure you want to quit Framework III. This ends this Framework III session.
12. Turn to Module 76 to continue the learning sequence.

Module 18

CONTENTS INCLUDED

DESCRIPTION

When using the Search { } or Replace { } options, only the frame labels are reviewed unless this option is turned on. It causes Framework III to include or ignore what is inside the open frame during the search or replace activity.

The Contents Included option is available through the Locate Menu frame.

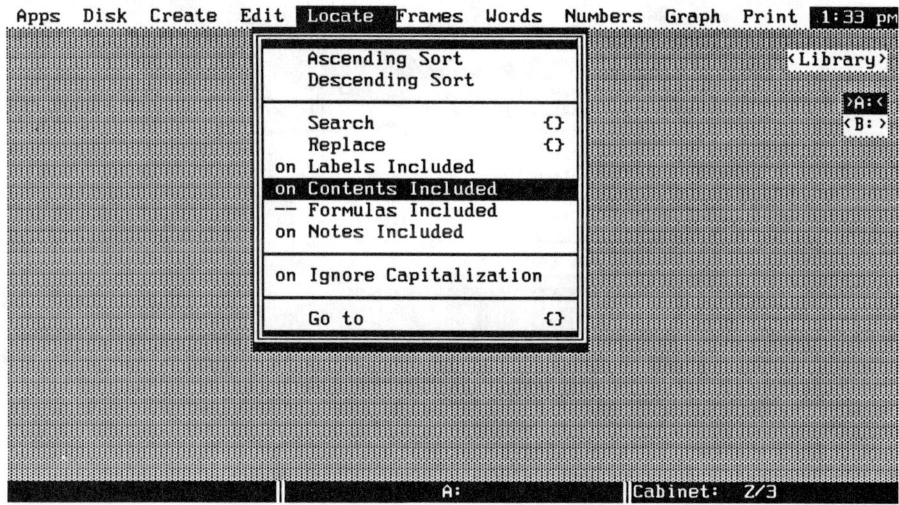

If ON, include frame contents in Search/Replace

APPLICATIONS

The Contents Included option is useful for any type of frame. Select this option before doing a search or replace operation when you want to control what is evaluated by Framework III.

Selecting this option turns it on and off. This option is automatically turned on when you begin your Framework III session.

If it is turned off, position the cursor on the Contents Included option and press Enter. Then move the cursor to the Search { } or Replace { } option and press Enter. When Framework III looks through the document for the specified text, the contents are included in the review.

TYPICAL OPERATION

Use this illustration to learn how to use the Contents Included option of the Locate Menu frame. Close any open frames on your desktop and position the cursor on your data drive indicator (drive B in this example). The shortcut key combinations, if applicable, are enclosed by braces.

1. {Press **Ctrl-D**}. Press **Ins** to move the cursor to the Main Menu line. Press **Left Arrow** or **Right Arrow**, if necessary, until the Disk Menu frame is open on your desktop.
2. {Press **Ctrl-G**}. Press **Up Arrow** to move the cursor to the Get File by Name option and then press **Enter**. The cursor moves to the Message line at the bottom of your desktop.
3. Type **B:EXERCISE**. As you type, notice that the braces next to the Get File by Name option fill. Press **Enter** twice. The disk is read and the frame you specified is opened on your desktop.
4. {Press **Ctrl-L**}. Press **Ins** to move the cursor to the Main Menu line. Press **Right Arrow** until the Locate Menu frame is also open on your desktop. Notice that the Contents Included option is turned on. (If not, press **Ctrl-C** to turn it on.)

Find any specified word or phrase — in any type of frame

5. {Press **Ctrl-S**}. Press **Up Arrow** until the cursor is positioned on the Search { } option and press **Enter**. Type **Body** and press **Enter**. The Locate Menu frame disappears from your desktop. Notice that the cursor is positioned on Body Building within the EXERCISE frame border.

6. Press **Down Arrow** to see the cursor positioned within the subframe on the word you specified in the Search option. Your frame resembles the following display.

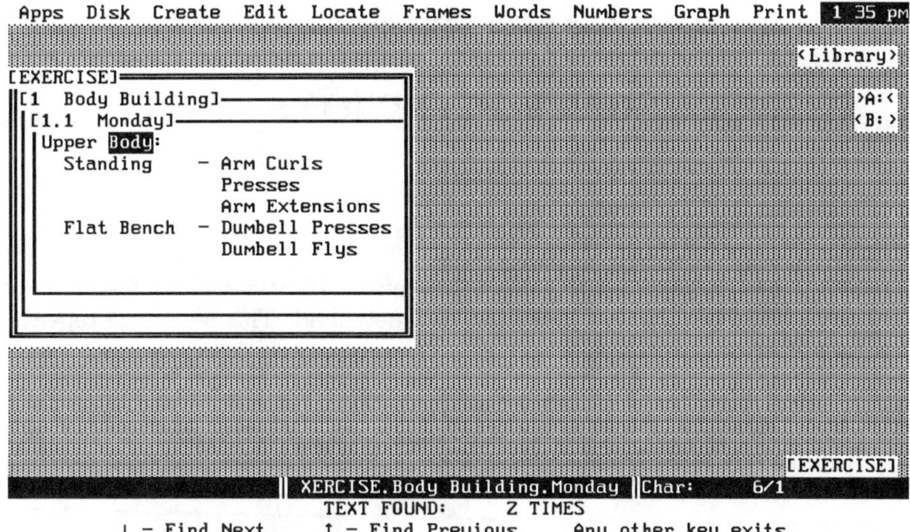

7. Press **Gray –** three times to move the cursor to the EXERCISE frame border.
8. {Press **Ctrl-L**}. Press **Ins** to move the cursor to the Main Menu line. The Locate Menu frame is again open on your desktop.
9. {Press **Ctrl-C**}. Press **Down Arrow** until the cursor is positioned on the Contents Included option. Press **Enter** to turn it off.
10. {Press **Ctrl-S**}. Press **Up Arrow** until the cursor is positioned on the Search { } option and press **Enter**. Since the word "Body" is already enclosed by the braces, press **Enter**. Notice that the cursor positioned on the Body Building frame border.
11. Press **Down Arrow** to find the next occurrence of the search word. Framework III reports that no other exists. This is because the second occurrence is within the frame contents. When the Contents Included option is turned off, Framework III ignores everything within a frame.
12. Press **F10** (View) to return to the Outline view.
13. Press **Gray –** to move the cursor to the EXERCISE frame border. Since the outline has not been changed, press **Del** to remove it from the desktop without saving it again on disk.
14. {Press **Ctrl-D**}. Press **Ins** to move the cursor to the Main Menu line. Press **Right Arrow** until the Disk Menu frame is open on your desktop.
15. {Press **Ctrl-Q**}. Using the arrow keys again, position the cursor on the QUIT Framework option and press **Enter**. Type **Y** when asked if you are sure you want to quit Framework III. This ends this Framework III session.
16. Turn to Module 50 to continue the learning sequence.

Module 19
CONTROL OPTIONS

DESCRIPTION

When you print a frame containing subframes, Framework III prints all subframes continuously until it fills a page. Then it advances the paper to a new page. This sequence repeats until the current page is full or the printing is complete.

Use the Control Options submenu to force page breaks for any subframe you choose. When a subframe for which you specified a page break is encountered, Framework III advances the paper to the next page. Printing is continued until the next subframe with a page break is supposed to print.

This submenu also allows you to control page numbers, print fonts, and recalculate formulas before printing. These options are available through the Control Options submenu of the Print Menu frame.

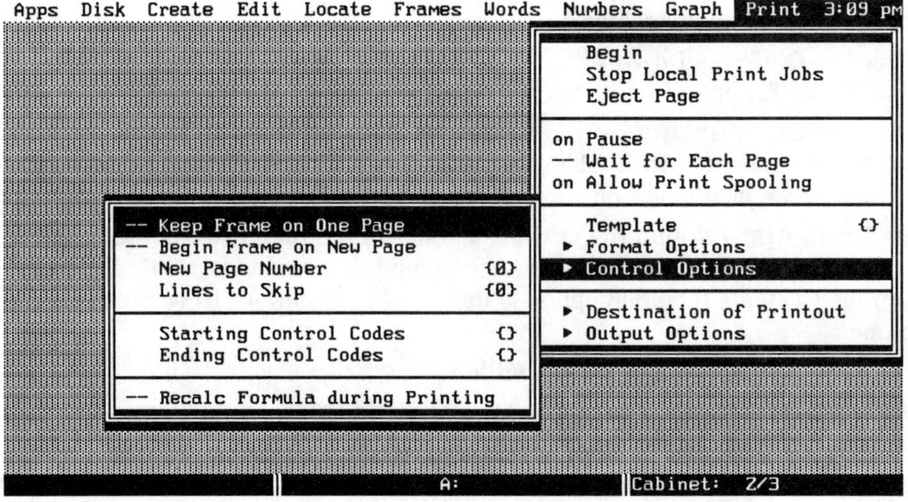

First, position the cursor on the frame or subframe for which you want to change options. The frame the cursor identifies is the selected frame. Then, open the Print Menu frame. Press Down Arrow to move the cursor to Control Options and press Enter.

The submenu also opens on your desktop. Press Down Arrow or Up Arrow to move the cursor to the option in the submenu. When all changes have been made, press Esc to close the open menu frames.

The options in the Control Options submenu frame are assigned to each frame or subframe. As you make changes to the submenu, the changes apply only to the frame selected by cursor position before opening the menu and its submenu.

Keep Frame on One Page Position the cursor on this option and press Enter. The word "on" or dashes appear to the left of the option. When turned on, this option forces the frame to the next page if necessary.

Begin Frame on New Page This option is changed like the Keep Frame on One Page option. Use it to tell Framework III that you want the paper advanced to a new page before printing the selected frame. When this option is turned off, the selected frame and its subframes continue printing on the current page.

New Page Number { } When you select this option, the cursor moves to the edit line at the bottom of the screen. Type the page number you want assigned to the selected frame and press Enter. The number appears within the braces for the option. If you skip a number, the printer skips a page of paper.

Lines to Skip { } Use this option to set the additional number of lines to advance the paper before printing the selected frame. Framework III automatically advances one line so this number is only for additional lines. It is preset to 0.

Starting Control Codes { } Select this option when you want the selected frame to use special printer codes. For example, use it when the selected frame contains a title page that is to be printed in large print. Type the decimal codes your printer requires for the special font. When the frame is sent to the printer, the codes are activated before printing the contents of the frame. Remember that these codes remain in effect until a frame with the Ending Control Codes { } option set is printed.

Ending Control Codes { } This option is selected like the Starting Control Codes { } option. After the frame is printed, the codes for the printer are sent. For example, the Starting Control Codes { } option might set the printer to a large print font. Use this option to change the print font from large print to normal size.

Recalc Formula during Printing This option is turned on and off when selected. Turn it on for subframes which contain cells or fields that perform calculations. Each formula is recalculated before the frame is printed.

APPLICATIONS

Use the Control Options submenu for frames which have subframes. Each frame and subframe has control options automatically assigned by Framework III. Change these options for any frame or subframe when you need something other than Framework III's preset values. Each option helps you print your document the way you want — frame by frame, if necessary.

Change any of these options until the document prints properly. When it is saved on disk, all changed options are also saved. The next time you print the document, all options remain as they were when you saved the frame.

TYPICAL OPERATION

This example shows you how to use the Control Options submenu. Turn on your printer. Make sure that your desktop is clean and the cursor is positioned on a drive indicator on the right side of your desktop. The shortcut key combinations, if applicable, are enclosed by braces.

1. {Press **Ctrl-D**}. Press **Ins** to move the cursor to the Main Menu line. Press **Left Arrow** or **Right Arrow**, if necessary, until the Disk Menu frame is open on your desktop.
2. {Press **Ctrl-G**}. Press **Up Arrow** to move the cursor to the Get File by Name option and then press **Enter**. The cursor moves to the Message line at the bottom of your desktop.
3. Type **B:EXERCISE**. As you type, notice that the braces next to the Get File by Name option fill. Press **Enter**. The disk is read and the frame you specified is opened on your desktop. If it just appears in your desktop tray, press **Enter** to open it.

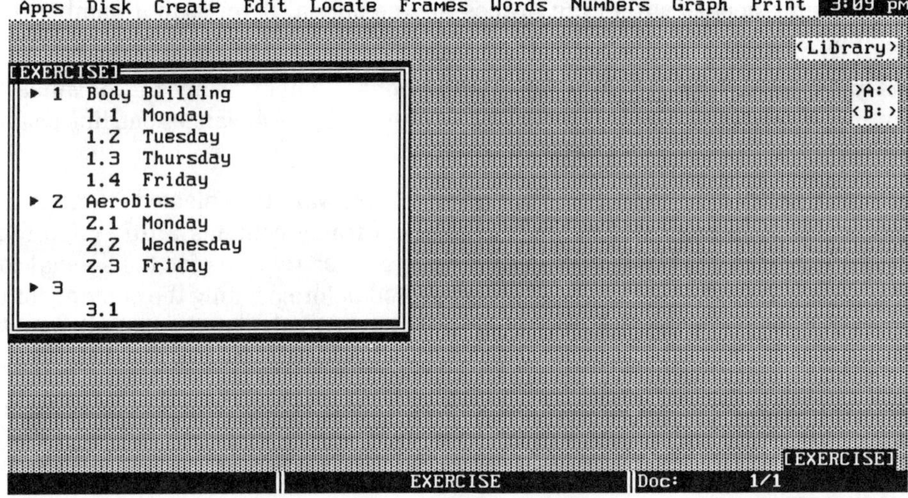

4. {Press **Ctrl-F** and then **Ctrl-V**}. Press **Ins** to move the cursor to the Main Menu line. Press the arrow (cursor) keys until the Frames Menu frame is open on your desktop. Press **Up Arrow** or **Down Arrow** until the cursor is positioned on the View Pagination option and press **Enter**. Now, your desktop resembles the following display.

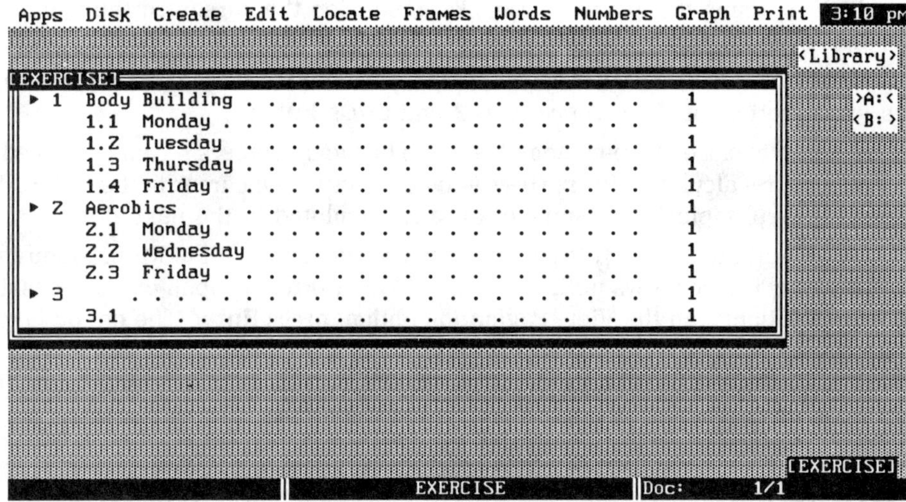

5. Press **Gray +** to move inside the frame. Press **Down Arrow** until the cursor is positioned on subtopic 1.2.
6. {Press **Ctrl-P** and then **Ctrl-C**}. Press **Ins** to move the cursor to the Main Menu line again. Next, press the arrow (cursor) keys until the Print Menu frame is open on your desktop. Position the cursor on the Control Options submenu and press **Enter**. The subframe is now open on your desktop.

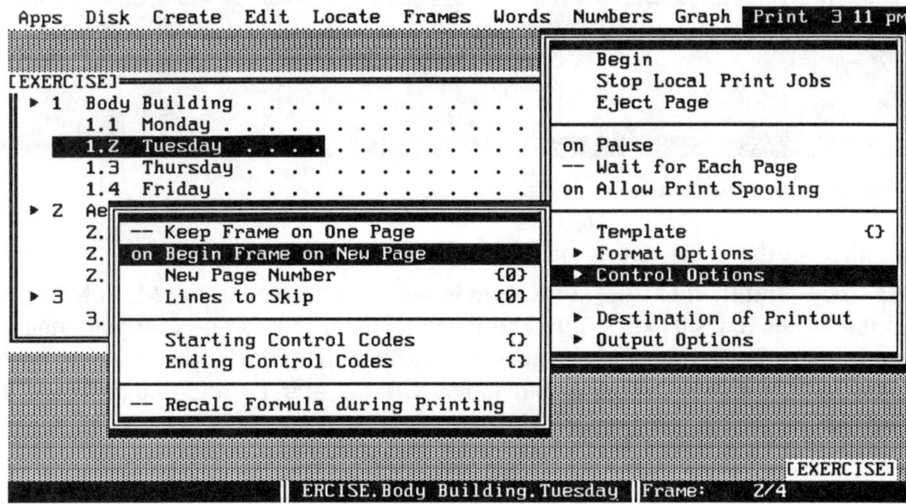

Print: Control Options: Begin Frame on New Page on

7. {Press **Ctrl-B**}. Using the arrow (cursor) keys, position the cursor on the Begin Frame on New Page option and press **Enter**. This option is now turned on.
8. {Press **Ctrl-N**}. Select the New Page Number { } option. When you press **Enter**, the cursor moves to the bottom of the screen. Type **2** and press **Enter**.
9. Now, press **Esc** to close all open menu frames. The page numbers haven't changed because they need to be recalculated. Press **Gray –** twice to move the cursor to the EXERCISE frame border so that all topics' page numbers are recalculated in the next step.
10. {Press **Ctrl-F** and then **Ctrl-V**}. Press **Ins** to move the cursor to the Main Menu line. Next, press the arrow (cursor) keys until the Frames Menu frame is open on your desktop. With the cursor positioned on the View Pagination option, press **Enter**. The option is turned off and the menu disappears. Now, reopen the Frames Menu and select the View Pagination option. The pages are recalculated and your desktop resembles the following display.

```
Apps  Disk  Create  Edit  Locate  Frames  Words  Numbers  Graph  Print 10 22 am
                                                                   <Library>
[EXERCISE]
 ▸ 1   Body Building . . . . . . . . . . . . . . . . . . .   1        <A: >
       1.1  Monday . . . . . . . . . . . . . . . . . . . .   1        >B:<
       1.2  Tuesday . . . . . . . . . . . . . . . . . . . .   2
       1.3  Thursday . . . . . . . . . . . . . . . . . . .   2
       1.4  Friday . . . . . . . . . . . . . . . . . . . .   2
 ▸ 2   Aerobics . . . . . . . . . . . . . . . . . . . . .   2
       2.1  Monday . . . . . . . . . . . . . . . . . . . .   2
       2.2  Wednesday . . . . . . . . . . . . . . . . . . .   2
       2.3  Friday . . . . . . . . . . . . . . . . . . . .   2

                                                                  [EXERCISE]
                         EXERCISE                 Doc:      1/1

Frames:  View Pagination on
```

11. Now, perform the same operations for subtopic 1.3.
12. {Press **Ctrl-P** and then **Ctrl-B**}. Press **Ins** to move the cursor to the Main Menu line. Next, press the arrow (cursor) keys until the Print Menu frame is open on your desktop. Press **Down Arrow** or **Up Arrow** until the cursor is positioned on the Begin option and press **Enter**. The document is printed. Notice that topics 1.1, 1.2, and 1.3 each begins on a new page.
13. Press **Gray –** twice and then press **Enter** to close the open frame and put it in your desktop tray.
14. {Press **Ctrl-D**}. Press **Ins** to move the cursor to the Main Menu line. Press the arrow (cursor) keys until the Disk Menu frame is open on your desktop.

15. {Press **Ctrl-P**}. Press **Down Arrow** until the cursor is positioned on the Put Away option and press **Enter**. The document is removed from the desktop and saved on disk.
16. {Press **Ctrl-D**}. Press **Ins** to move the cursor to the Main Menu line. The Disk Menu frame is again open on your desktop.
17. {Press **Ctrl-Q**}. Using the arrow keys again, position the cursor on the QUIT Framework option and press **Enter**. Type **Y** when asked if you are sure you want to quit Framework II. This ends this Framework II session.
18. Turn to Module 20 to continue the learning sequence.

Module 20
DATABASE

DESCRIPTION

Information which is organized and saved on the computer for later retrieval is called a *database*. The type and amount of information you keep, as well as the way it is organized, is up to you.

For example, a set of company names and their phone numbers could be kept in a database. Review the following list of names and phone numbers.

Name	Phone
AAA Brush & Tool	777/323-4324
ABC Company, Inc.	214/665-2322
XYZ Steel, Inc.	331/555-2121

Each line, the combination of the company name and its phone number, is called a *record*. Each of the columns is called a *field*. In other words, the company name is one field, and the phone number is a second field.

The first field of the second record contains "ABC Company, Inc." The second field of the third record contains "331/555-2121."

To create a database frame, the Create Menu frame must be opened. The Create Menu frame appears below.

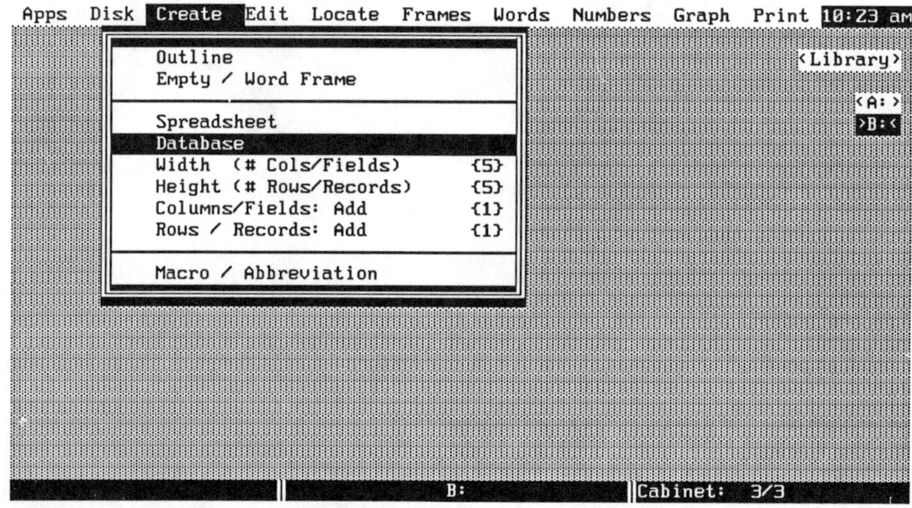

Create a database of specified Width and Height

Notice the Width and Height options which are available in this menu. These options tell Framework III how big to make each new database.

The Width option specifies the number of fields to be made available across the database. The 50, which is enclosed in braces, is the number of fields Framework III makes available across each new database created. This is a preset (default) number which can be changed before creating your new database frame.

The Height option specifies the number of lines or records down the database. As in the Width option, Framework III allocates a preset (default) number of records. The Height option is preset to create new databases with 100 records.

The size of your database is important for two reasons. First, the size depends on the amount of computer memory you have in your machine. It must be large enough to hold the database you create. Second, the size is affected by the amount of disk space you have available. If you create a database which is 50 fields across but only use 5 of the 50 fields, you are wasting disk space. Framework III reserves the space for all 50 fields — used or not! The same is true for unused database records.

Customize the database before creating it by selecting the Width and Height options and changing the numbers. If you don't know how large a database you need, use numbers that meet your best guess.

As you fill the database with your information, add fields and records using the Columns/Fields: Add option or the Rows/Records: Add option of the Create Menu frame. Delete fields and records by using the Columns/Fields: Remove option or the Rows/Records: Remove option of the Edit Menu frame.

With the Create Menu frame open, press Ctrl-D (or move the cursor to the Database option and press Enter). The following database frame is opened on your desktop.

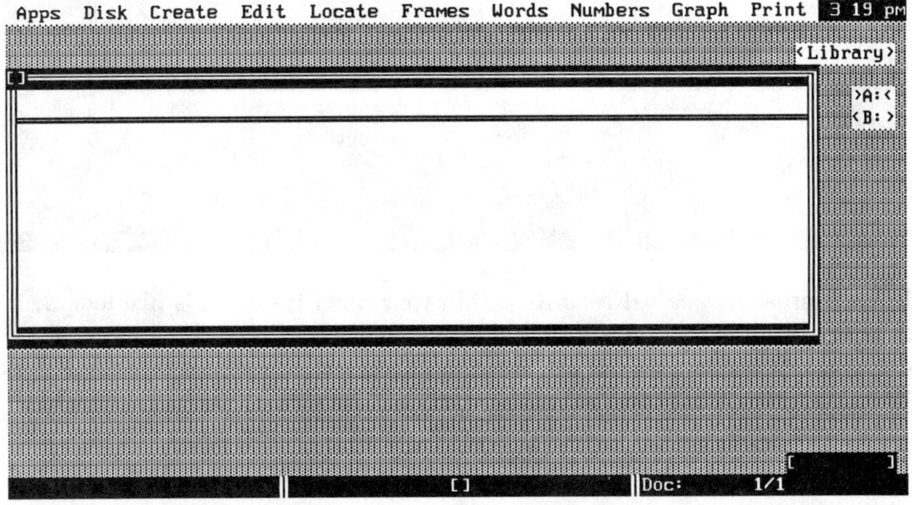

Create: Database

The cursor is positioned on the top border of the database frame between the left and right brackets. This is where you assign a name to the database. The name which you type can be anything you choose.

Framework III uses the first eight positions of the name to create the name of the file which is saved on the disk. The first eight positions, or whatever you type if less than eight, are provided a suffix of .FW3 to develop a filename.

For example, when you type Phone List within the brackets, Framework III saves the database as Phone_Li.FW3. The underline replaces any blank spaces which exist within the name.

Once the database is saved on the disk, it is read from there to your desktop by using the Disk Menu frame. All information and formulas which are saved on disk are available as though the document had never left your desktop.

A database can be viewed in any of three ways on your desktop. By pressing F10 (View) once, the database is in Table View form. A second press of F10 (View) displays it in Forms View. A third press of F10 (View) changes the display to dBASE View. Each press of F10 (View) repeats the sequence just described. Remember, the database is the same, it is just displayed on the desktop differently.

The database of company names and phone numbers is displayed below in Table View form.

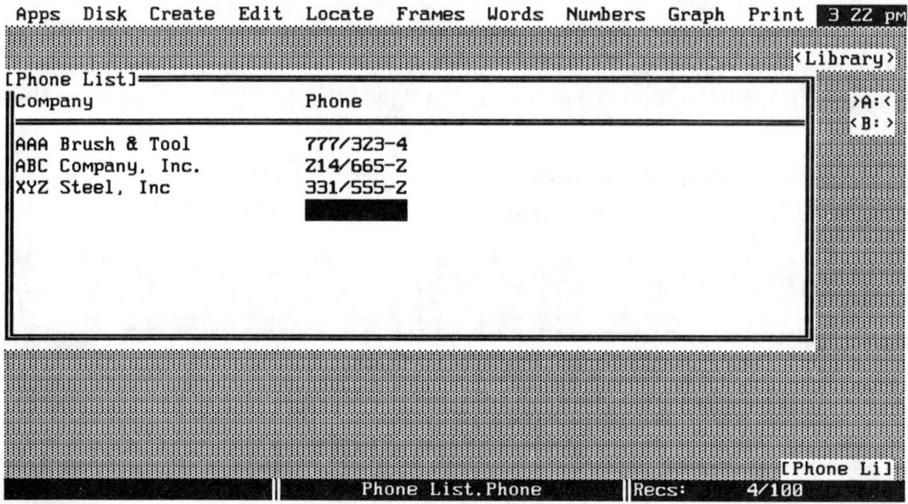

The Table View presents several records within your open frame. It is like looking at a list on a sheet of paper. If you have several fields of data and/or many records, some may not be visible on the screen. To view other portions of the database, move the cursor toward a frame border so the information moves within your frame so that you can see what you need.

The second way to view a database is the Forms View display. As already mentioned, the database is the same as in the Table View. This type of display, however, allows only one record at a time to be seen in the open frame. The first record of the database is shown in the following frame display.

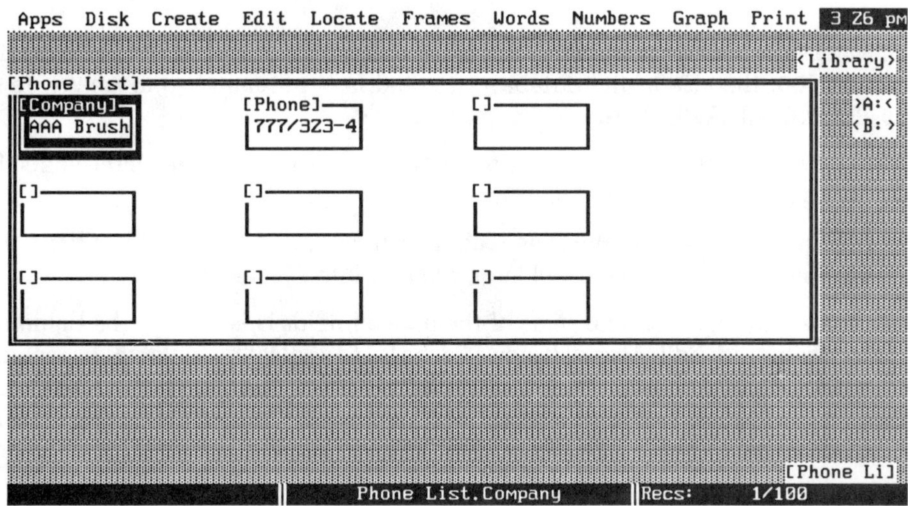

The Forms View makes each field look like a small frame within your database frame. The database is not different, nor has it been changed. It only *looks* different.

Finally, the dBASE View, like the Forms View, shows only one record at a time. Each fieldname appears in brackets and the contents of the field is displayed to the right of the fieldname. The following desktop display shows only the first record in the database.

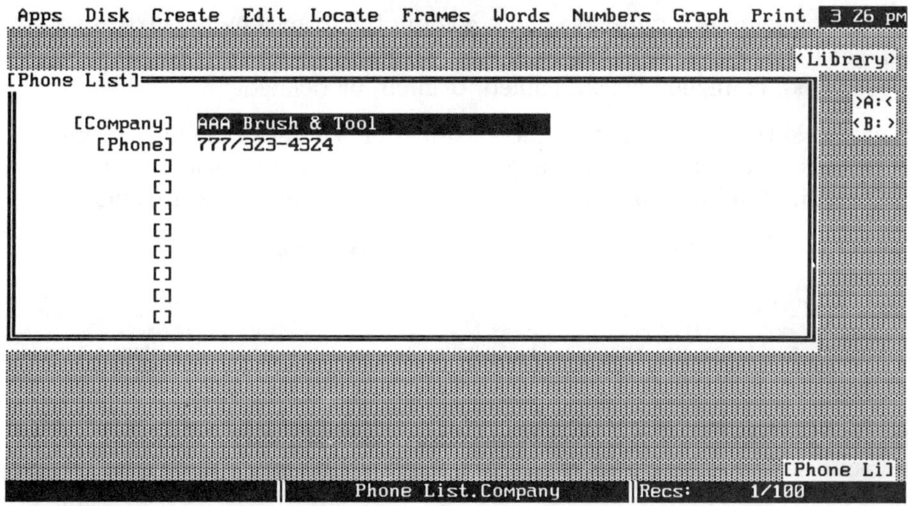

The Forms View and the dBASE View show you that only two of the record's 50 fields are being used. Other fields can be seen within the frame by pressing Up Arrow and Down Arrow. The next record can be seen by pressing PgDn. To see the previous record, press PgUp. Pressing Home moves the first record into the frame; pressing End moves the last record in the database file into view.

Since Framework III presets the number of fields per record to 50 and the number of records per database to 100, the size of the database created may not match your needs. In the case of filename PHONE_LI.FW3, there are too many fields.

Even though you don't use the extra fields or records, Framework III reserves the space for them. That means that your disk space is being wasted!

Remember, when creating a new database, change the Width and Height options to a more appropriate number. Insert or delete fields or records later, if necessary.

If the database already exists, delete some of the unused fields by selecting the Columns/Fields: Remove option from the Edit Menu frame. Records can also be deleted by selecting the Rows/Records: Remove option from the Edit Menu frame. If you think you might need to add more records to your database, leave a few extra records in the file. Planned expansion is worth using a little more disk space!

APPLICATIONS

A database can be used for many things. Keep a phone list, a check register, a list of antiques, or any other set of information which you want to maintain and use. A database is simply a collection of information.

The fields within a database record are not just numbers which are to be used in calculations like in a spreadsheet. They are a mixture of numbers and text (words).

For example, each record of a database might contain fields for a name (text), an address (text), a phone number (text), a total sales figure (number), and a credit limit (number). Each field can be sorted, searched, changed, moved, copied, printed, or deleted.

New fields are added or inserted among the existing fields by selecting the Columns/Fields: Add option in the Create Menu frame. Additional records are added or inserted among the existing records by selecting the Rows/Records: Add option in the Create Menu frame.

In short, you can customize the database as your needs change.

TYPICAL OPERATION

A small database is created in this illustration. It keeps company names and phone numbers for a phone list.

Make sure that your desktop is clean and the cursor is positioned on a drive indicator on the right side of your desktop. The shortcut key combinations, if applicable, are enclosed by braces.

1. {Press **Ctrl-C**}. Press **Ins** to move the cursor to the Main Menu line. Press **Left Arrow** or **Right Arrow**, if necessary, until the Create Menu frame is open on your desktop.

2. {Press **Ctrl-D**}. By pressing **Down Arrow**, position the cursor on the Database option and press **Enter**. An empty database frame opens on your desktop.
3. The blinking cursor is positioned within the brackets on the top border of the open frame. Type **Phone List** and press **Enter**. When saved on the disk, PHONE_LI.FW3 is assigned as the name of this database file.
4. Press **Gray +** to move the cursor into the frame. It is automatically positioned at the far left of the top line. This area is where you assign names to your database fields.
5. Type **Company** and press **Enter**. The first field (column) is now called Company.
6. Press **Right Arrow** to move the cursor to the right (next field), type **Phone**, and press **Enter**. The second field is named Phone. Your desktop should resemble the following display.

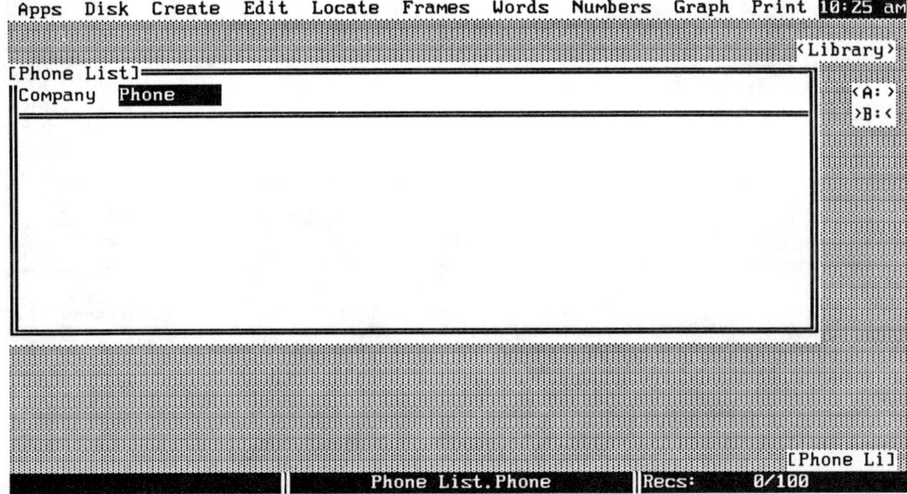

7. Press **Down Arrow** once, and then press **Left Arrow** to move the cursor to the first field (Company) of the first record in the database.
8. This field is not large enough to hold the company names. To enlarge it, first press **F4** (Size). Notice the "SIZE: stretch frame size with cursor keys; RETURN finishes" message at the bottom of the screen. Press **Right Arrow** 10 times and watch the cursor expand and the Phone fieldname move to the right. When finished, press **Enter**.
9. Type **AAA Brush & Tool** and press **Enter**.

10. By pressing **Right Arrow**, move the cursor to the Phone field. Since this is a phone number, you must be careful that Framework III knows it is a text field. Press the **Spacebar** once. Notice that the message at the bottom of the screen says that this field is a text field. Otherwise, as a numeric field, Framework III performs division and subtraction — that's not what you want to happen. Next, type **777/323-4324** and press **Enter**. Your desktop resembles the following display.

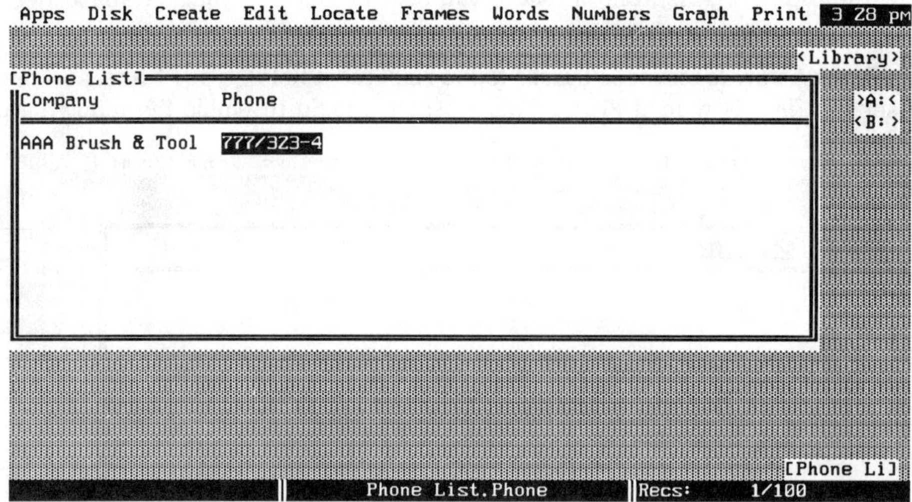

11. Notice that the Phone field is not long enough for the full number to be displayed. Although Framework III knows the whole phone number, it should be displayed too. Press **F4** (Size) once and then press **Right Arrow** three times. Notice that the whole phone number is displayed. Press **Enter**.

12. Press **Down Arrow** once and then press **Left Arrow** to move the cursor to the Company field. Type **ABC Company, Inc.** and press **Enter**.

13. Press **Right Arrow** to move the cursor to the phone field of the second record. Press **Spacebar** once, type **214/665-2322**, and then press **Enter** as you did for the first record.

14. {Press **Ctrl-D**}. Press **Ins** to move the cursor to the Main Menu line. Using the arrow (cursor) keys, move the cursor to the Disk Menu option.

15. {Press **Ctrl-S**}. Press **Down Arrow** or **Up Arrow** to position the cursor on the Save and Continue option and then press **Enter**. Notice that the message at the bottom of the screen says that the file is being saved on disk.

16. Press **F10** (View) once and notice the frame has changed to the Forms View as displayed in the following desktop.

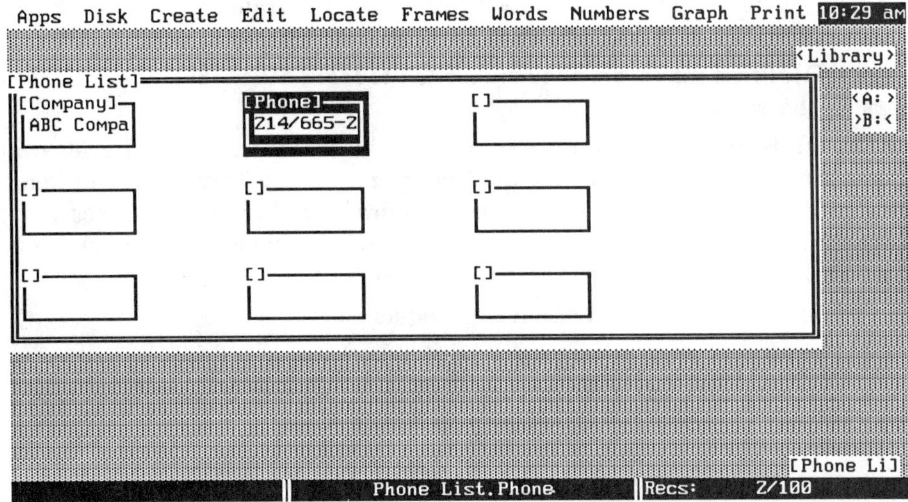

17. Press **F10** (View) again and notice the frame has changed to the dBASE View as displayed in the following desktop.

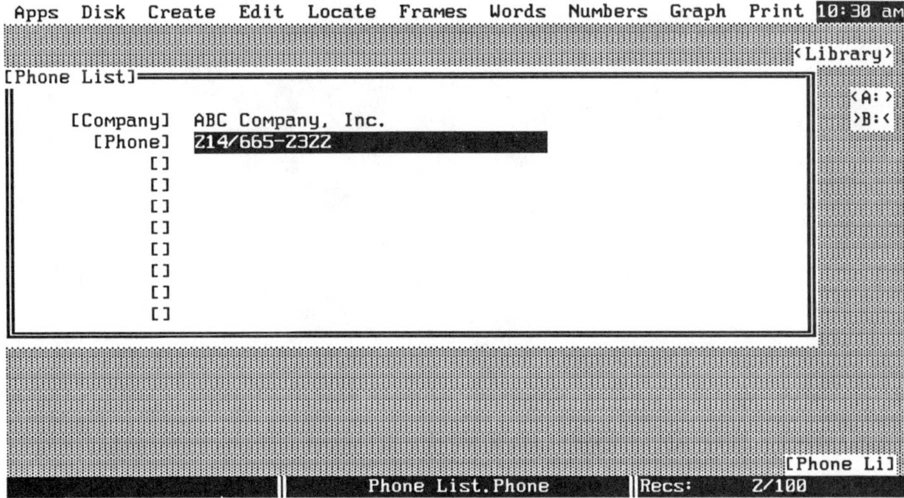

18. Press **PgUp** to move the first record into the open frame. Press **PgDn** to return to the second record in the file. Press **PgDn** again when you want to add another record.
19. Press **Gray –** to move the cursor to the top border of the frame. Then press **Enter** to close the open frame. The cursor is positioned on the frame name in your desktop tray.
20. {Press **Ctrl-D**}. Press **Ins** to move the cursor to the Main Menu line. The Disk Menu option appears on the screen.
21. {Press **Ctrl-Q**}. By pressing **Down Arrow**, position the cursor on the QUIT Framework option and press **Enter**. If you didn't save the documents in the tray since the last changes, Framework III asks if you want to save them before letting you end your session. Since all changes have been saved, Framework III asks if you're sure you want to end this session. Type **Y**. The DOS system prompt returns to the screen.
22. Turn to Module 9 to continue the learning sequence.

Module 21

dBASE

DESCRIPTION

Have you ever been working with a software package and needed to use dBASE? Usually, you must quit one to use another. Framework III, however, is preset to let you access dBASE through the Apps Menu frame.

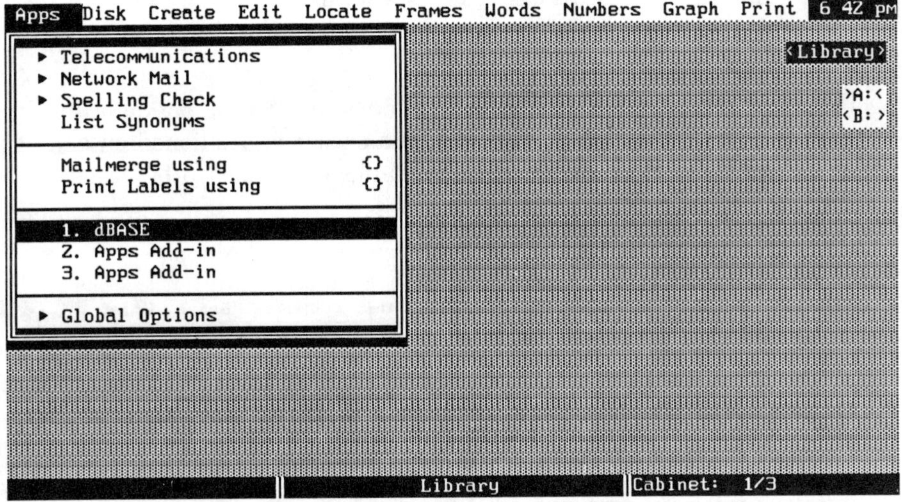

Run dBASE within Framework III

When you select this option, Framework III asks you for the drive and subdirectory used for dBASE. Next, the available memory is checked. Your computer needs 640K to run Framework III and any version of dBASE. If you change your mind, just press Esc and return to your Framework III desktop.

If everything is available to run dBASE, your Framework III desktop disappears. When dBASE begins, you see the license agreement and then the dBASE Assistant for dBASE III or the Control Center menu for dBASE IV. Do whatever dBASE work you need to perform. When you finish your dBASE work, just type QUIT and press Enter. You automatically return to your Framework III desktop session as though you had never left.

APPLICATIONS

Use this option when you need to access dBASE. If your computer has less than 640K, Framework III cannot run dBASE. When you select the dBASE option of the Apps Menu frame, the available memory is checked. If there is enough memory, dBASE appears on your screen instead of Framework III.

For example, use this option when you create a Framework III database which you want to make available to dBASE. Open the database frame on your desktop. Open the Disk Menu frame and select the Export submenu option. When the submenu opens, select the dBASE option.

Before selecting the dBASE option, move any open frames to your desktop tray. Before Framework III makes dBASE available, you are asked if the contents of the open frame are to be deleted. If this happens, just type N and Framework III continues to load dBASE.

It is a good idea to save on disk any unsaved frames prior to selecting this option. Losing power before you return to your Framework III desktop means a loss of any new or updated frames which were open before accessing dBASE. That is a lot of lost time and effort.

TYPICAL OPERATION

This exercise shows you how to tell Framework III to use the dBASE option of the Apps Menu frame. Make sure that your desktop is clear and the cursor is positioned on one of the drive indicators. The shortcut key combinations, if applicable, are enclosed by braces.

1. {Press **Ctrl-A**}. Press **Ins** to move the cursor to the Main Menu line. Press **Left Arrow** or **Right Arrow** until the Apps Menu frame is open on your desktop.

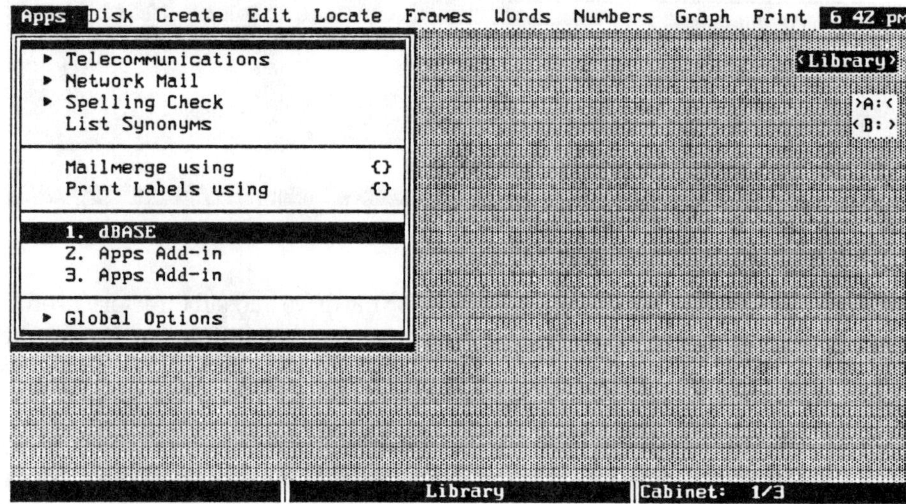

Run dBASE within Framework III

2. Using the arrow keys again, position the cursor on the dBASE option and press **Enter**. Your screen should resemble the following display.

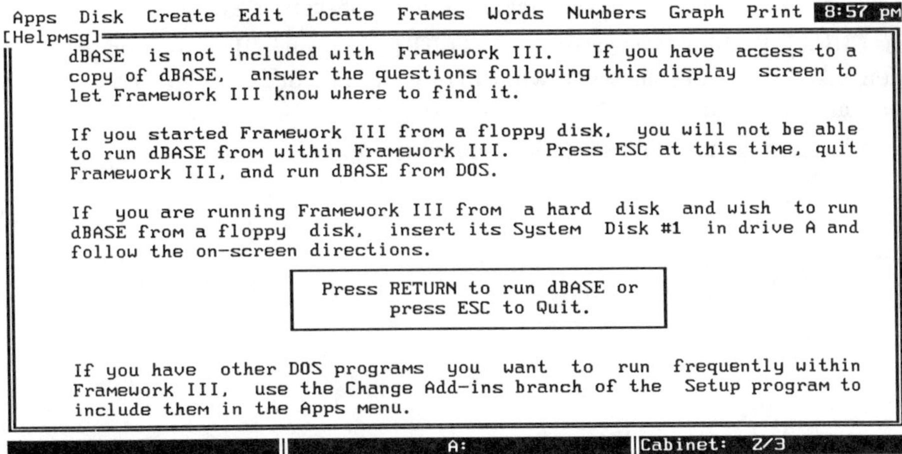

3. Press **Enter** to execute dBASE. Framework asks for the drive and subdirectory where dBASE resides.
4. If you do not have dBASE, press **Esc** to return to Framework. Otherwise, dBASE is loaded, and you can type any command.
5. Type **QUIT** and press **Enter**. Your Framework III desktop reappears.

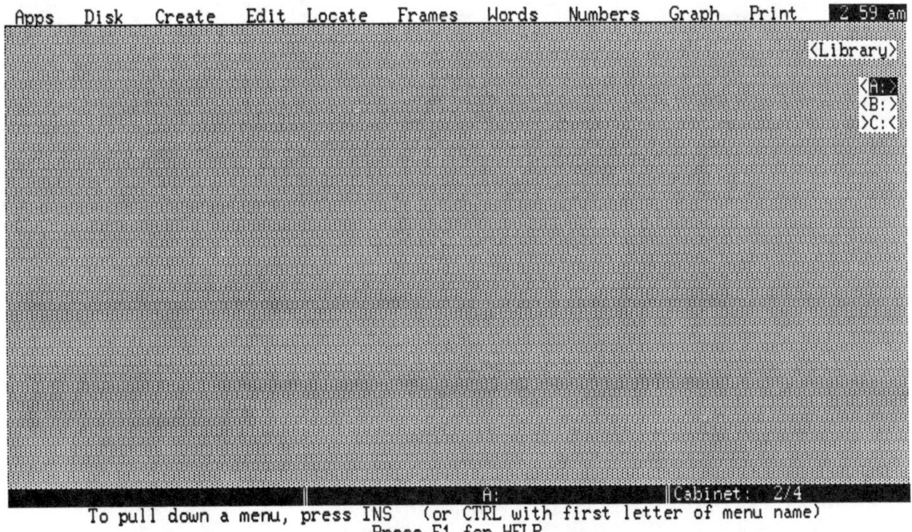

6. Press **Del** to remove it from your desktop.
7. {Press **Ctrl-D**}. Press **Ins** to move the cursor to the Main Menu line. Next, press the arrow (cursor) keys until the Disk Menu frame is open on your desktop.
8. {Press **Ctrl-Q**}. Position the cursor on the QUIT Framework III option and press **Enter**. Type **Y** when asked if you are sure you want to quit Framework III. This ends your Framework III session.
9. Turn to Module 47 to continue the learning sequence.

Module 22

DECIMAL PLACES { }, GENERAL, INTEGER, FIXED DECIMAL, CURRENCY, BUSINESS, PERCENT, SCIENTIFIC

DESCRIPTION

Spreadsheets and databases usually include cells and fields which contain numbers. Use these numeric format options to specify the form in which the number in that cell or field must appear. Change the form of the number within the cell or field at any time by selecting another format option.

These options are available through the Numbers Menu frame.

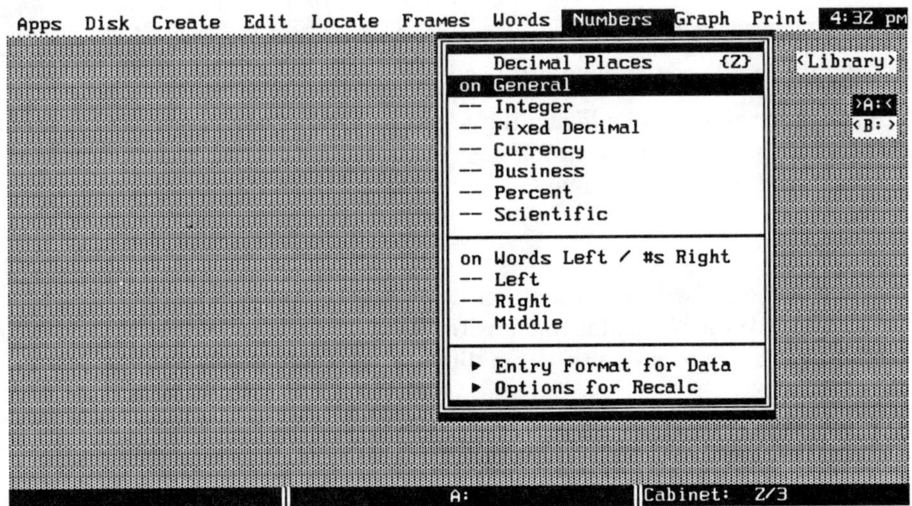

Display numbers in selected cells/fields with fullest possible precision

Only one of these options (excluding Decimal Places) is active for a cell or field at a time. Framework III automatically turns the General format option on. When any format option is selected, that option is turned on and all others are turned off. The selected option remains on until another option is chosen.

Framework III automatically sets the Decimal Places option to 2. Change the number of places to the right of the decimal point by selecting this option, typing the number of places you want, and then selecting the format option for the cell. Use the Decimal Places option with any other format option except the Integer option.

The following examples show numeric formats with the Decimal Places option set to 3.

Numbers Typed	33.333	22.000	18.230
General	33.333	22	18.230
Integer	33	22	18
Fixed Decimal	33.333	22.000	18.230
Currency	$33.333	$22.000	$18.230
Business	33.333	22.000	18.230
Percent	3333.300%	2200.000%	1823.000%
Scientific	3.333E+1	2.200E+1	1.823+1

Notice that three numbers to the right of the decimal point are typed; however, they are not displayed for all of the format options. Any numbers which are typed to the right of the decimal place are included if the cell or field is used in a calculation. Before using a cell or field in a formula, check the status line for the number that is really involved.

For example, multiplying the above integer numbers 33 by 22 results in 733.33 instead of 726.00. The numbers only look like they are whole numbers (integers). Framework III displays them as you specified but uses the number which was entered.

APPLICATIONS

Framework III lets you decide how you want to display numbers in the cells of spreadsheets or the fields of databases. These options are used only for spreadsheet and database frames.

Use these numeric formats for displaying the numbers in your open frame. The number which is actually typed is displayed on the status line. That number is used in any calculations — not the number displayed within the frame.

TYPICAL OPERATION

This example shows you how to use the numeric format options of the Numbers Menu frame. Close any open frames on your desktop and position the cursor on your data drive indicator (drive B in this example). The shortcut key combinations, if applicable, are enclosed by braces.

1. {Press **Ctrl-C**}. Press **Ins** to move the cursor to the Main Menu line. Next, press the arrow (cursor) keys, if necessary, until the Create Menu frame is open on your desktop.
2. {Press **Ctrl-S**}. Press **Up Arrow** or **Down Arrow** to position the cursor on the Spreadsheet option and press **Enter**. An empty spreadsheet frame opens on your desktop.
3. Press **Gray +** to move the cursor to the inside of your open spreadsheet frame. The cursor appears in cell A1.

4. Type **General** and press **Enter**. Press **Down Arrow** to cell A2, type **Integer**, and press **Enter**. Continue this process until your spreadsheet resembles the following display.

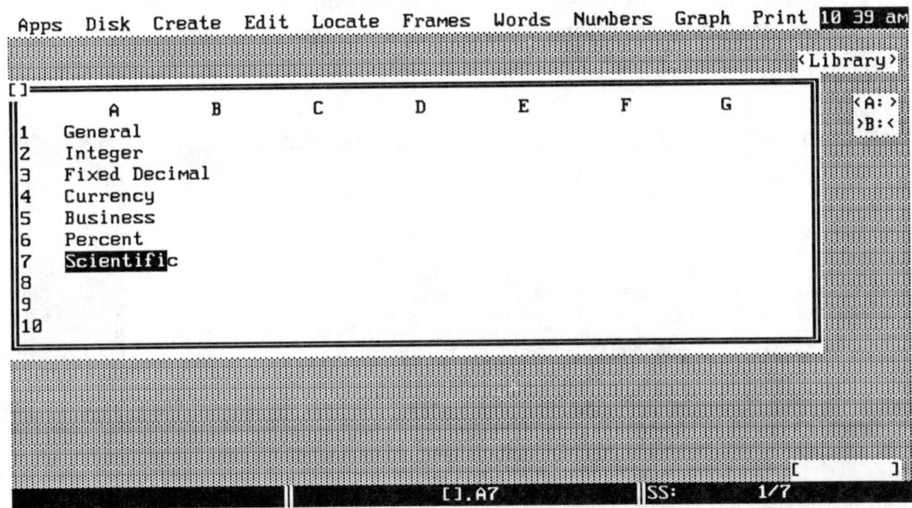

5. Press **Up Arrow** and **Right Arrow** until the cursor is positioned in cell C1.
6. {Press **Ctrl-N**}. Press **Ins** to move the cursor to the Main Menu line. Then press **Right Arrow** until the Numbers Menu frame is open.
7. {Press **Ctrl-D**}. Press **Up Arrow** until the cursor is positioned on the Decimal Places { } option and press **Enter**. The cursor moves to the Message line for you to type a new number for the braces. Type **3** and then press **Enter**.
8. {Press **Ctrl-N** and then **Ctrl-G**}. Open the Numbers Menu frame again and select the General format option for this cell (if it is not already turned on). It is now set to display numbers with three numbers to the right of the decimal point unless those numbers are zero. Type **33.333** and press **Enter**. Follow the same procedure to set cells D1 and E1 to General formats with three decimal places. Then type **22.000** and **18.230** in cells D1 and E1, respectively.

9. Set each cell in columns C, D, and E for the format option described in column A. Expand the size of the cursor across columns C, D, and E before selecting the format option. Be sure to change the Decimal Places option to the number 3 for each cell. Type the numbers 33.333, 22.000, and 18.230 in each column so that your spreadsheet resembles the following display.

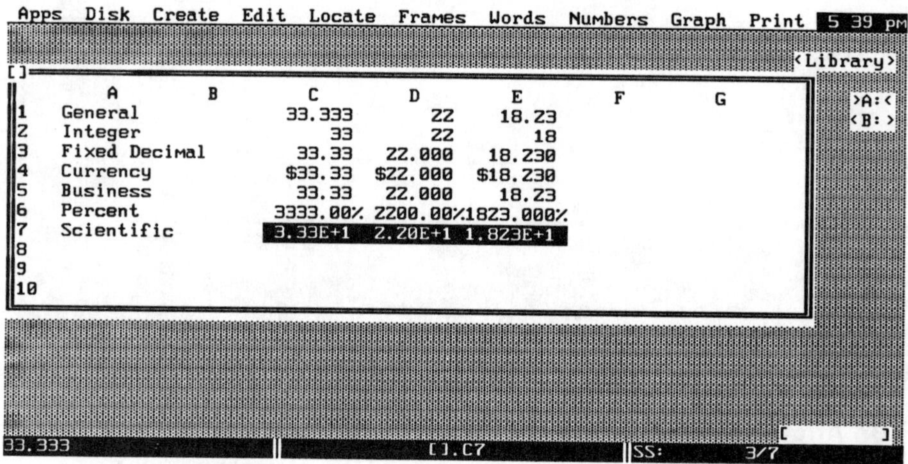

10. Press **Gray –** to move the cursor to the frame border. Since there is no reason to keep this spreadsheet, press **Del**.

11. {Press **Ctrl-D**}. Press **Ins** to move the cursor to the Main Menu line. Press **Left Arrow** until the Disk Menu frame is open on your desktop.

12. {Press **Ctrl-Q**}. By pressing **Down Arrow**, position the cursor on the QUIT Framework option and press **Enter**. When asked if you really want to quit Framework III, type **Y**. This Framework III session is complete.

13. Turn to Module 23 to continue the learning sequence.

Module 23

DESCENDING SORT

DESCRIPTION

There are times when you need information sequenced so that the highest values are at the top of the spreadsheet or database. This option lets you order the information in your spreadsheets and databases from high to low.

Access the Descending Sort option through the Locate Menu frame.

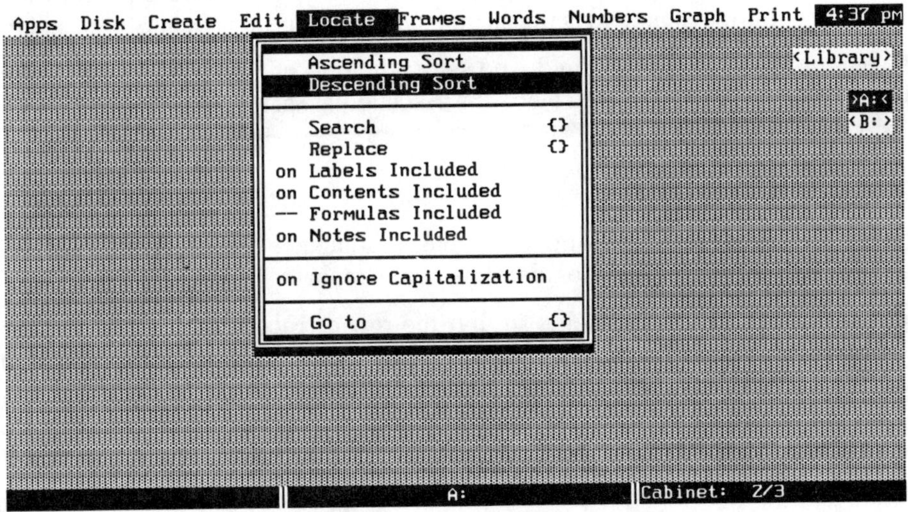

Arrange selected frames/rows/records from Z to A, high to low, late to early

First, open the frame you need to sort. Position the cursor on the cell or field you need sequenced from high to low. Open the Locate Menu frame and select the Descending Sort option. The menu frame disappears and all your information is sorted.

If you want only a certain number of rows or records sorted, press F6 (Extend) to specify the information. Otherwise, Framework III sorts all rows or records.

Before selecting this option, however, verify the Ignore Capitalization option. If it is turned off before the sort occurs, all uppercase letters (A through Z) appear before lowercase letters (a through z). Review the following sorted list.

Ignore Capitalization on	*Ignore Capitalization off*
Zoro Entertainment	Zoro Entertainment
zane 'n sane	Adams, Inc.
adams & weaver	A + Hardware
Adams, Inc.	A A A Company
A + Hardware	zane 'n sane
A A A Company	adams & weaver
4-H of Denton	4-H of Denton

The computer always sorts in the following order: 1.) blank spaces; 2.) special characters (e.g., #, !); 3.) Numbers; 4.) letters. The Ignore Capitalization option affects sequencing since the case of the letter is considered when this option is turned off.

When you need to sort on more than one field, list the cells or fields on a sheet of paper. Then identify which is the most important down to the least important. Once you have done this, begin your sort with the least important cell or field. Then sort the next most important cell or field.

For example, to sort a database of total dollar sales (descending) for each salesman within each division (ascending), the division field is the most important. The sales field is the least important.

Position the cursor on the total sales field, and select the Descending Sort option. Then, position the cursor on the division field and select the Ascending Sort option. When complete, your database is sorted just like you requested.

APPLICATIONS

Use this option for spreadsheet and database frames to sequence the information. This is helpful if you need to print the spreadsheet or database as a report.

For example, sort numeric cells or fields so that the row or record with 99.99 appears before 0.00. Sort a character cell or field so that the rows and records are in descending alphabetical order. Specific information is more easily found when there is order to the list.

TYPICAL OPERATION

This example shows you how to sort information in a database by using the Descending Sort option of the Locate Menu frame. Close any open frames on your desktop and position the cursor on your data drive indicator (drive B in this example). The shortcut key combinations, if applicable, are enclosed by braces.

1. {Press **Ctrl-C**}. Press **Ins** to move the cursor to the Main Menu line. Next, press the arrow (cursor) keys, if necessary, until the Create Menu frame is open on your desktop.
2. {Press **Ctrl-W**}. Press **Down Arrow** until the cursor is positioned on the Width option and press **Enter**. The cursor then moves to the Message line at the bottom of your desktop. Type **5** and press **Enter**.

3. {Press **Ctrl-H**}. Press **Down Arrow** until the cursor is positioned on the Height option and press **Enter**. The cursor then moves to the Message line at the bottom of your desktop. Type **8** and press **Enter**. Notice that the number within the braces is now 8 on your screen.
4. {Press **Ctrl-S**}. Press **Up Arrow** to position the cursor on the Spreadsheet option and press **Enter**. An empty spreadsheet frame opens on your desktop. Notice that only eight rows and five columns appear within your open frame.
5. The cursor is positioned at the top border of the frame within the brackets. Type **Sales 86** within the brackets and press **Enter**. The name of the file, when saved on the disk, is SALES_86.
6. Press **Gray +** to move the cursor to the inside of your open spreadsheet frame. The cursor appears in column A of row 1 (cell A1). Press **F4** (Size), then **Right Arrow** six times to increase the size of column A and then press **Enter**.
7. Type **Poole, Jerry** and press **Enter**. Press **Right Arrow** to move the cursor to the second column of the same row (cell B1). Type **1** and press **Enter**. Press **Right Arrow** again, type **100.10** and press **Enter**. Continue this activity until your spreadsheet resembles the following display.

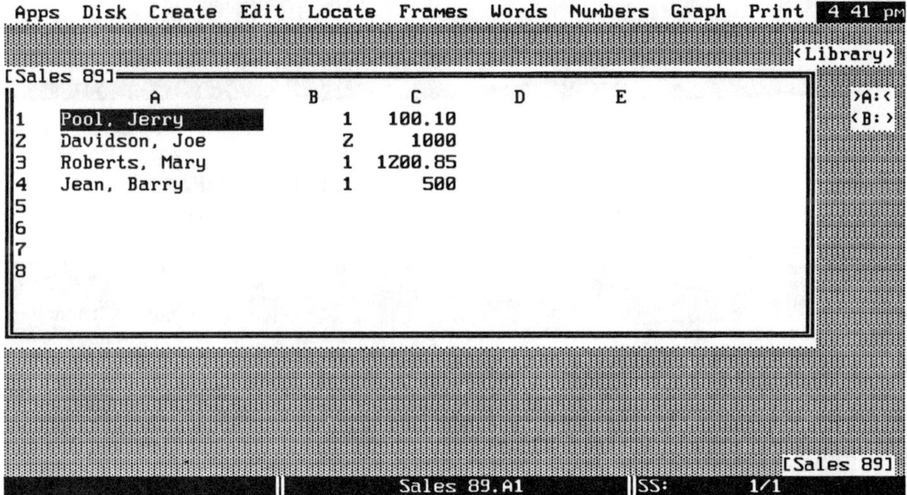

8. Position the cursor on cell C1 and press **F6** (Extend). Press **Down Arrow** until all numbers in column C are highlighted and then press **Enter**.
9. {Press **Ctrl-L**}. Press **Ins** to move the cursor to the Main Menu line. Next, press **Right Arrow** until the Locate Menu frame is also open on your desktop.

10. {Press **Ctrl-D**}. Press **Up Arrow** until the cursor is positioned on the Descending Sort option and press **Enter**. The Locate Menu frame disappears from your desktop. The Message line reports that Framework III is sorting the file. When complete, the order of your records is changed.

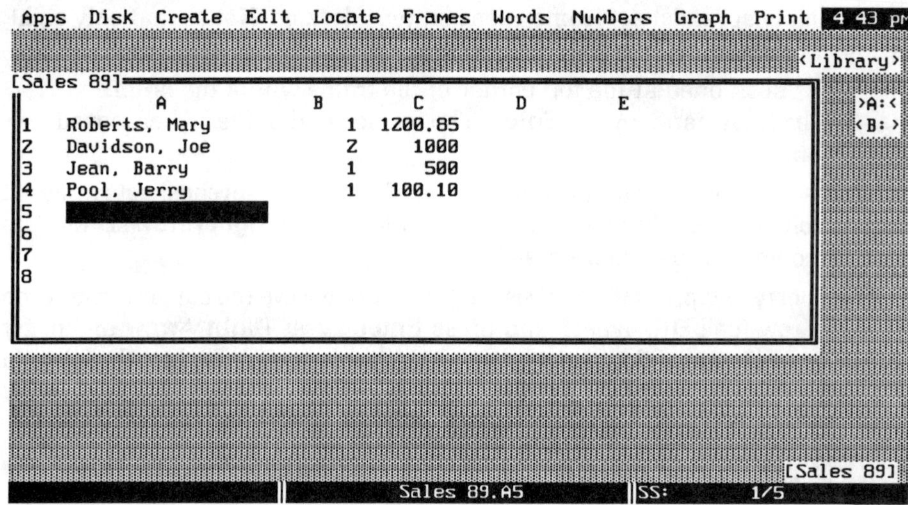

11. {Press **Ctrl-L** and then **Ctrl-A**}. Now, sort the spreadsheet again by positioning the cursor on cell B1. Open the Locate Menu frame and select the Ascending Sort option. Your spreadsheet now resembles the following display.

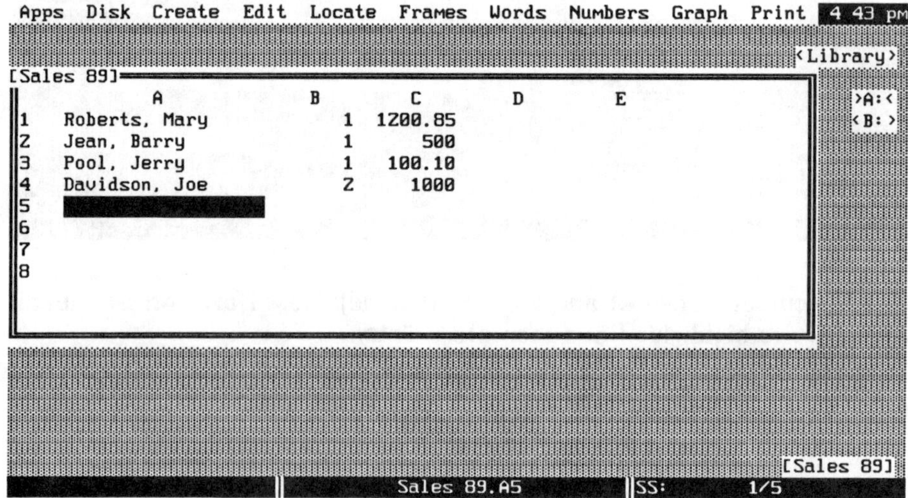

12. Press **Gray –** to move the cursor to the frame border. Then press **Enter** to close the frame to the desktop tray.
13. {Press **Ctrl-D**}. After all this work, you want to save the spreadsheet so it is available next month. Press **Ins** to move the cursor to the Main Menu line. Next, press the arrow (cursor) keys until the Disk Menu frame is open on your desktop.
14. {Press **Ctrl-P**}. By pressing the **Down Arrow** key, position the cursor on the Put Away option and press **Enter**. This saves the spreadsheet on the disk and removes it from your desktop.
15. {Press **Ctrl-D**}. Press **Ins** again to move the cursor to the Main Menu line. Press **Left Arrow** until the Disk Menu frame is open on your desktop.
16. {Press **Ctrl-Q**}. Position the cursor on the QUIT Framework option and press **Enter**. When asked if you really want to quit Framework III, type **Y**. This Framework III session is complete.
17. Turn to Module 42 to continue the learning sequence.

Module 24

DESTINATION OF PRINTOUT

DESCRIPTION

When you want a copy of your work to be put on paper or disk, Framework III lets you specify which device you want to use. The Printer 1 option is automatically selected unless you tell Framework III otherwise.

The Destination of Printout is an option of the Print Menu frame. When selected, a submenu of options opens on your desktop as in the following display.

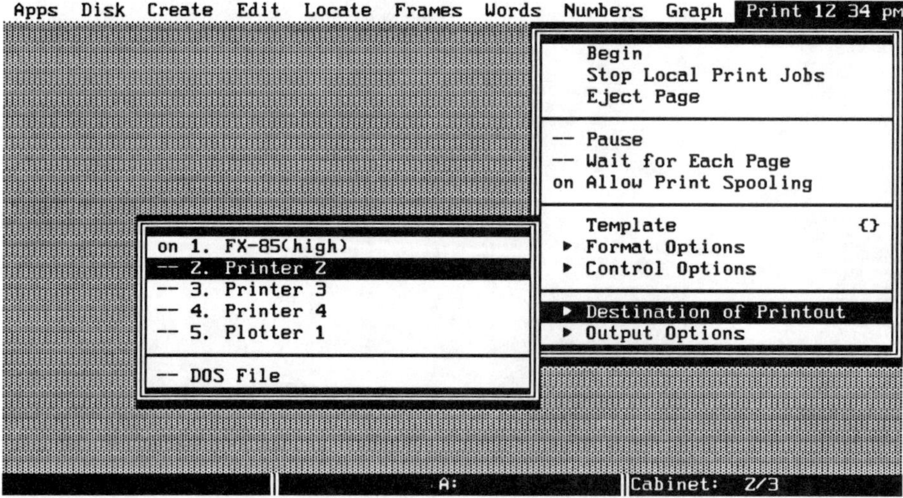

Each option is turned on or off. When one option is turned on, all others are turned off. Position the cursor on the option and press Enter. The option is turned on but nothing happens. Press Esc to close the open menu. Then reopen the Print Menu and select the Begin option.

Use the Framework III Setup program to tell Framework III about your printers and/or plotter. If you have a dot matrix printer, specify draft quality as Printer 1 and near letter-quality as Printer 2. You can configure from one to four printers and one plotter.

Framework III sends a copy of your open frame to the selected device. A printed copy is now available through any of the configured printer options (1-4).

A plotted copy (e.g., a graph) is available by selecting the Plotter option.

Use the DOS File option to copy a printable form of your open frame on disk. The file is saved with .PRT as the suffix. For example, the printable file of BIRTHDAY.FW3 is BIRTHDAY.PRT. Once saved on disk, print this copy directly from the DOS system prompt with the PRINT command.

APPLICATIONS

Use this submenu of options to send a document to one of your output devices. Framework III automatically routes output to the device described by the Setup program as Printer 1.

Remember, selecting the destination does not begin the print operation. Only the Begin option of the Print Menu frame actually causes the output activity.

TYPICAL OPERATION

This example shows you how to use the Destination of Printout submenu options of the Print Menu frame.

Turn on your printer. Make sure that your desktop is clean and the cursor is positioned on a drive indicator on the right side of your desktop. The shortcut key combinations, if applicable, are enclosed by braces.

1. {Press **Ctrl-D**}. Press **Ins** to move the cursor to the Main Menu line. Press **Left Arrow** or **Right Arrow**, if necessary, until the Disk Menu frame is open on your desktop.
2. {Press **Ctrl-G**}. Press **Up Arrow** to move the cursor to the Get File by Name option and then press **Enter**. The cursor moves to the Message line at the bottom of your desktop.
3. Type **B:BIRTHDAY**. As you type, notice that the braces next to the Get File by Name option fill. When finished, press **Enter** twice. The disk is read and the frame you specified is opened on your desktop as follows.

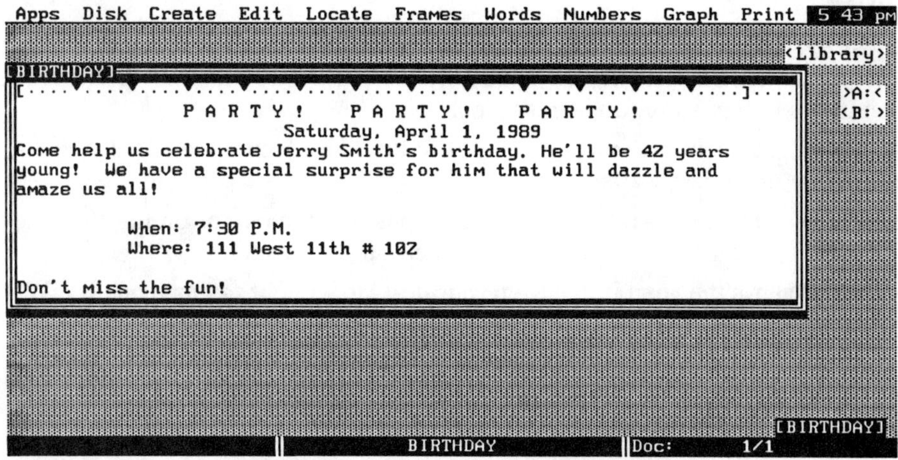

4. {Press **Ctrl-P**}. Press **Ins** to move the cursor to the Main Menu line. Next, press the arrow (cursor) keys until the Print Menu frame is open on your desktop.

5. {Press **Ctrl-D**}. Press **Down Arrow** until the cursor is positioned on the Destination of Printout option and press **Enter**. A submenu frame opens on your desktop.

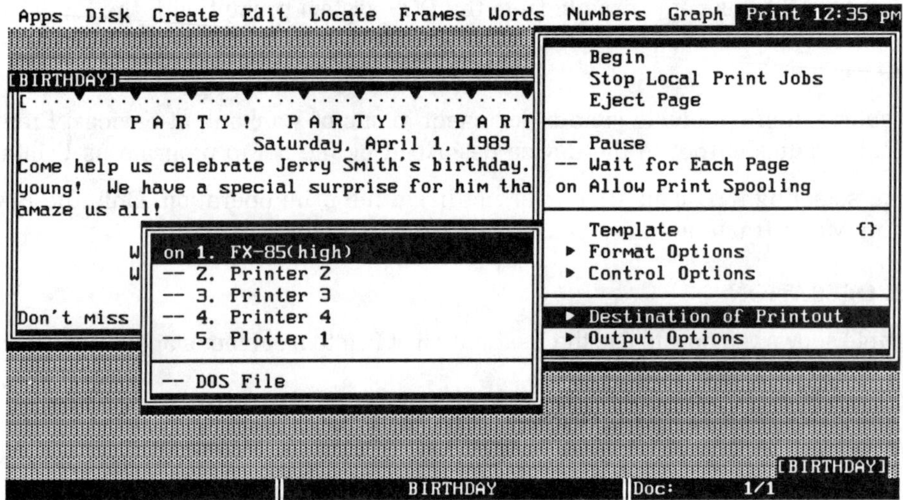

6. {Press **Ctrl-D**}. Press **Down Arrow** until the cursor is positioned on the DOS File option and press **Enter**. The option is turned on. Press **Esc** to remove the menu from your desktop.
7. {Press **Ctrl-P**}. Press **Ins** to move the cursor to the Main Menu line. The Print Menu frame is again open on your desktop.
8. {Press **Ctrl-B**}. Using the arrow (cursor) keys, position the cursor on the Begin option and press **Enter**. The Message line tells you that the file is being written on the data disk as BIRTHDAY.PRT.
9. {Press **Ctrl-P**, **Ctrl-D**, and then **Ctrl-D**}. Reopen the Print Menu and select the Destination of Printout submenu option. Turn off the DOS File option by selecting it again. Make sure that Printer 1 is turned on and press **Esc**.
10. {Press **Ctrl-P**}. Press **Ins** to move the cursor to the Main Menu line again. The Print Menu frame is open on your desktop.
11. {Press **Ctrl-B**}. Using the arrow (cursor) keys, position the cursor on the Begin option and press **Enter**. This time the document is printed on the printer.
12. Press **Del** to remove the open frame from your desktop without saving it on disk. When asked to confirm the deletion of the frame, type **Y**.
13. {Press **Ctrl-D**}. Press **Ins** to move the cursor to the Main Menu line. Next, press the arrow (cursor) keys until the Disk Menu frame is open on your desktop.
14. {Press **Ctrl-Q**}. Using the arrow keys again, position the cursor on the QUIT Framework option and press **Enter**. Type **Y** when asked if you are sure you want to quit Framework III. This ends your Framework III session.
15. Turn to Module 34 to continue the learning sequence.

Module 25

DOS ACCESS

DESCRIPTION

Have you ever been working with a software package and needed to format or copy a disk? Most software packages don't let you access the Disk Operating System (DOS) commands without quitting the program first.

This option lets you run DOS commands, type Exit, and return to your Framework III session as though you had never left. The DOS Access option is available through the Disk Menu frame.

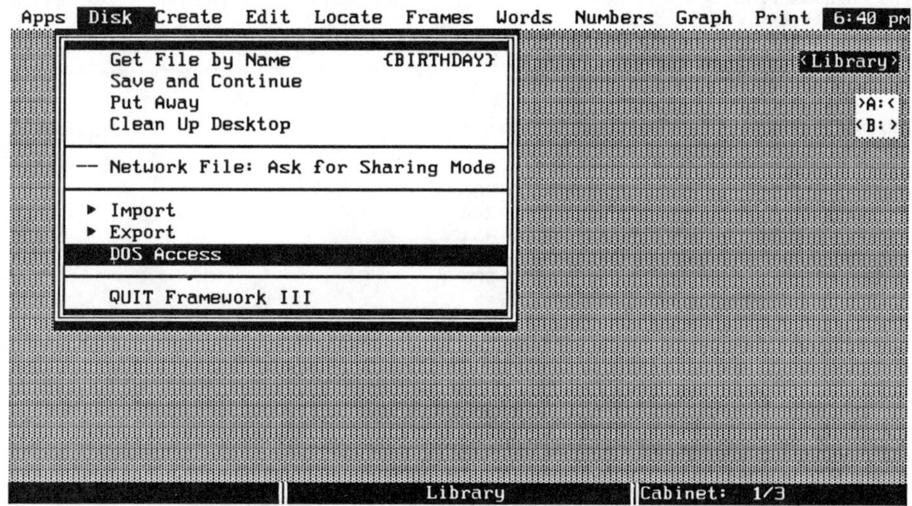

Execute DOS without leaving Framework III -- to format disks, etc.

When you select this option, your desktop disappears and you see the system prompt as though you had quit your Framework III session. Do whatever DOS work you need to do (e.g., FORMAT, COPY, DIR). When ready, type Exit at the next system prompt to return to your desktop.

APPLICATIONS

Before selecting the DOS Access option, move any open frames to your desktop tray. Before Framework III makes DOS available, you are asked if the contents of the open frame are to be deleted. If this happens, just type N and Framework III continues to the DOS prompt.

It is a good idea to save on disk any unsaved frames prior to selecting this option. Losing power before you return to your Framework III desktop means a loss of any new or updated frames which were open before accessing DOS. That is a lot of time and effort lost.

TYPICAL OPERATION

This exercise shows you how to tell Framework III to use the DOS Access option of the Disk Menu frame. Make sure that your desktop is clear and the cursor is positioned on one of the drive indicators. The shortcut key combinations, if applicable, are enclosed by braces.

1. {Press **Ctrl-D**}. Press **Ins** to move the cursor to the Main Menu line. Press **Left Arrow** or **Right Arrow**, if necessary, until the Disk Menu frame is open on your desktop.
2. {Press **Ctrl-D**}. Using the arrow keys again, position the cursor on the DOS Access option and press **Enter**. Your screen changes from the Framework III desktop to a normal DOS system prompt.
3. Type **DIR B*.FW3** and press **Enter**. Your screen resembles the following display.

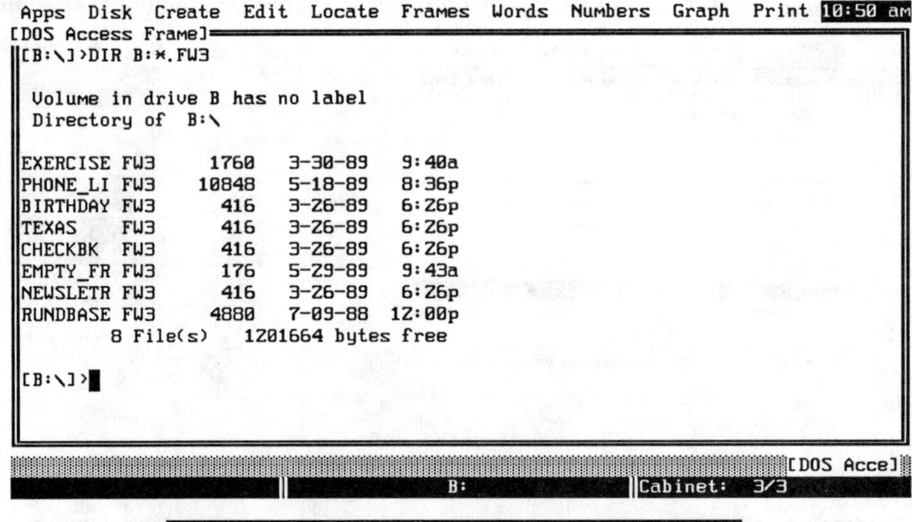

4. Type **EXIT** and press **Enter**. Your desktop reappears with an open DOS Access frame.

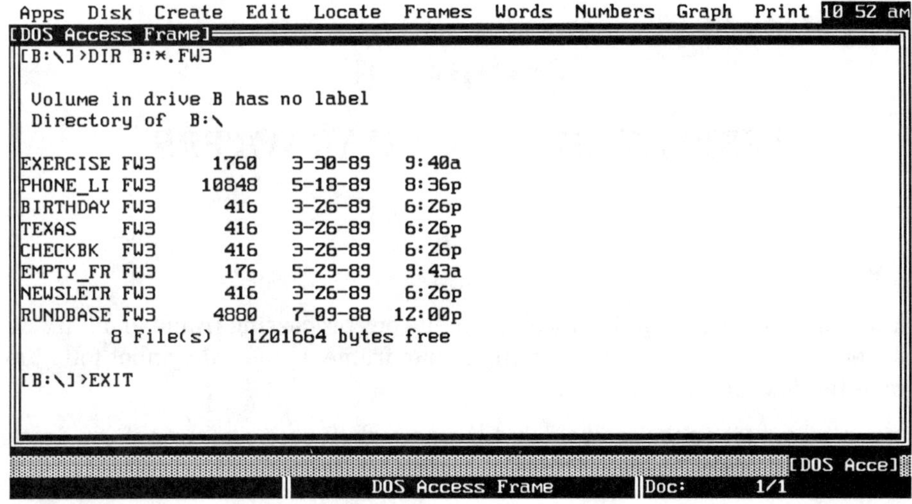
```
Apps  Disk  Create  Edit  Locate  Frames  Words  Numbers  Graph  Print 10 52 am
[DOS Access Frame]
[B:\]>DIR B:*.FW3

 Volume in drive B has no label
 Directory of  B:\

EXERCISE FW3      1760   3-30-89   9:40a
PHONE_LI FW3     10848   5-18-89   8:36p
BIRTHDAY FW3       416   3-26-89   6:26p
TEXAS    FW3       416   3-26-89   6:26p
CHECKBK  FW3       416   3-26-89   6:26p
EMPTY_FR FW3       176   5-29-89   9:43a
NEWSLETR FW3       416   3-26-89   6:26p
RUNDBASE FW3      4880   7-09-88  12:00p
        8 File(s)   1201664 bytes free

[B:\]>EXIT

[DOS Acce]
DOS Access Frame   Doc:   1/1
Disk:  DOS Access
```

5. Press **Del** to remove it from your desktop.
6. {Press **Ctrl-D**}. Press **Ins** to move the cursor to the Main Menu line. The Disk Menu frame is again open on your desktop.
7. {Press **Ctrl-Q**}. Position the cursor on the QUIT Framework option and press **Enter**. Type **Y** when asked if you are sure you want to quit Framework III. This ends your Framework III session.
8. Turn to Module 21 to continue the learning sequence.

Module 26

DISPLAY HIDDEN CHARACTERS

DESCRIPTION

Framework III embeds special symbols within each word processing frame to tell it how to look. For example, every time you press Enter within your frame, a special symbol tells Framework III to continue the text on the next line.

Usually, you don't want to see the symbols that Framework III uses. However, if you do, this option displays them for you.

The Display Hidden Characters option is available for any word processing frame. Access it through the Edit Menu frame.

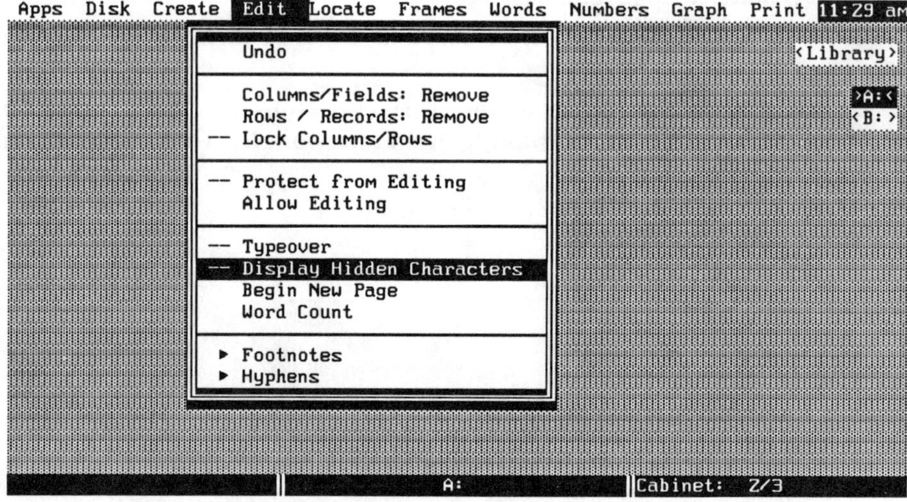

If ON, display end-of-paragraph, tab, soft hyphen, and space characters

This option is turned on or off when it is selected. When it is off, the text within your open frame looks normal to you. If turned on, special symbols appear within the text.

Open any word processing frame. It looks normal to you but you aren't seeing what Framework III sees.

Open the Edit Menu frame and select the Display Hidden Characters option. Each blank space is replaced by a dot. Each pressed Enter is replaced by the paragraph symbol. Select this option again to return your frame to normal.

APPLICATIONS

The option is available for word frames. Use it if you want to see the special symbols which are embedded within the text.

TYPICAL OPERATION

This example shows you how to use the Display Hidden Characters option of the Edit Menu frame. Close any open frames on your desktop and position the cursor on your data drive indicator (drive B in this example). The shortcut key combinations, if applicable, are enclosed by braces.

1. {Press **Ctrl-D**}. Press **Ins** to move the cursor to the Main Menu line. Press **Left Arrow** or **Right Arrow**, if necessary, until the Disk Menu frame is open on your desktop.
2. {Press **Ctrl-G**}. Press **Up Arrow** to move the cursor to the Get File by Name option and then press **Enter**. The cursor moves to the Message line at the bottom of your desktop.
3. Type **B:BIRTHDAY**. As you type, notice that the braces next to the Get File by Name option fill. Press **Enter**. The disk is read and the frame you specified is placed in the desktop tray. Press **Enter** again and it is opened on your desktop as follows.

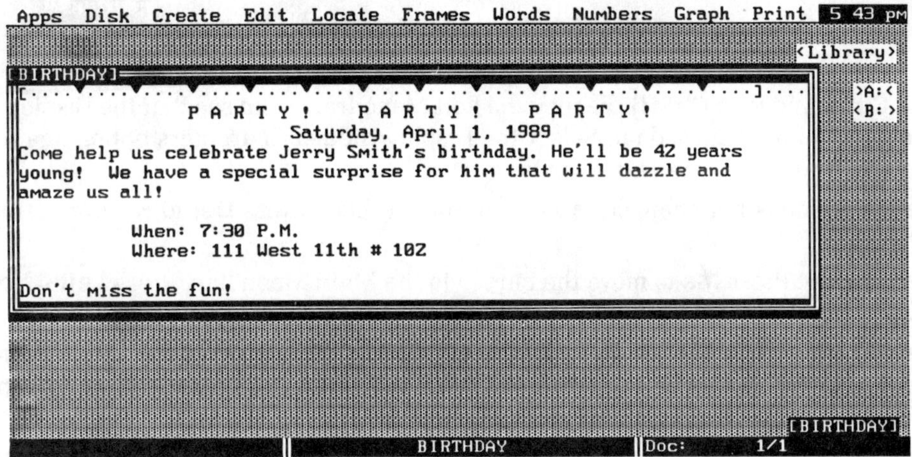

4. {Press **Ctrl-E**}. Press **Ins** to move the cursor to the Main Menu line. Next, press **Right Arrow** until the Edit Menu frame is also open on your desktop. Notice the dashes next to the Display Hidden Characters option.

5. {Press **Ctrl-D**}. Press **Down Arrow**, if necessary, until the cursor is positioned on the Display Hidden Characters option and then press **Enter**. The menu disappears and your open frame shows the special symbols used to indicate new lines (Enter), tabs, soft hyphens, and blank spaces.

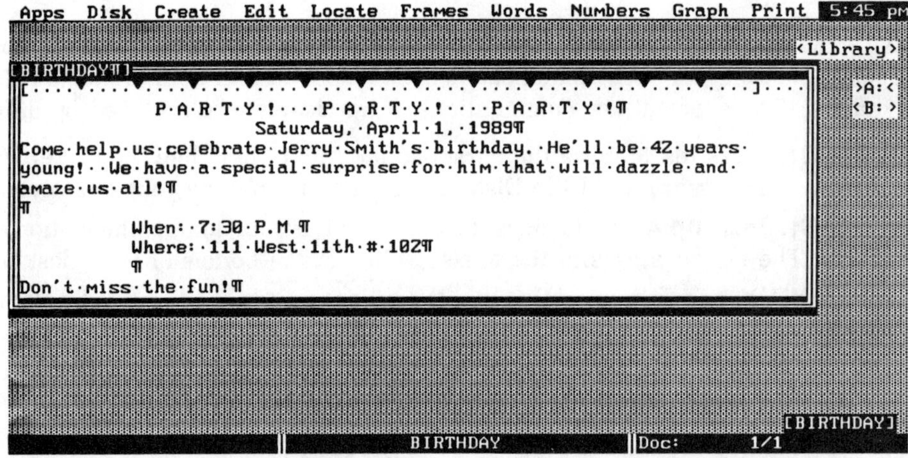

6. {Press **Ctrl-E** and then **Ctrl-R**}. Reopen the Edit Menu frame and see that the Display Hidden Characters option is turned on. Select the Display Hidden Characters option again. When the menu disappears, the text appears normal.
7. Since the frame is not changed (except in appearance), press **Del** to remove it from your desktop.
8. {Press **Ctrl-D**}. Press **Ins** to move the cursor to the Main Menu line. Press **Left Arrow** until the Disk Menu frame is open on your desktop.
9. {Press **Ctrl-Q**}. Using the arrow keys again, position the cursor on the QUIT Framework option and press **Enter**. Type **Y** when asked if you are sure you want to quit Framework III. You have ended this Framework III session.
10. Turn to Module 65 to continue the learning sequence.

Module 27

DISPLAY LABELS

DESCRIPTION

This option lets you remove or display frame headings. This is especially important when you want to print a document which contains subframes. Select this option through the Frames Menu frame.

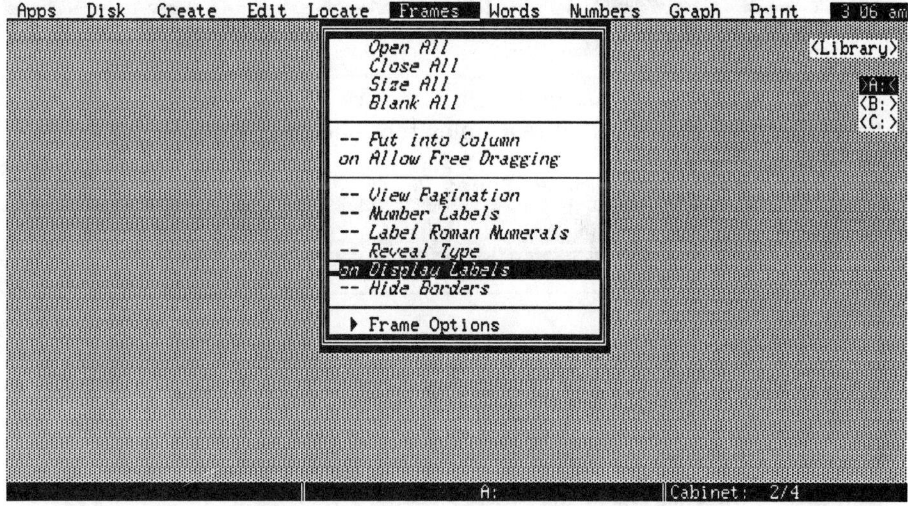

Display labels of frames within selection (in spreadsheet, display coordinates)

The Display Labels option is turned on and off when selected. If it is turned on, the selected frame label appears on the frame border as in the following display.

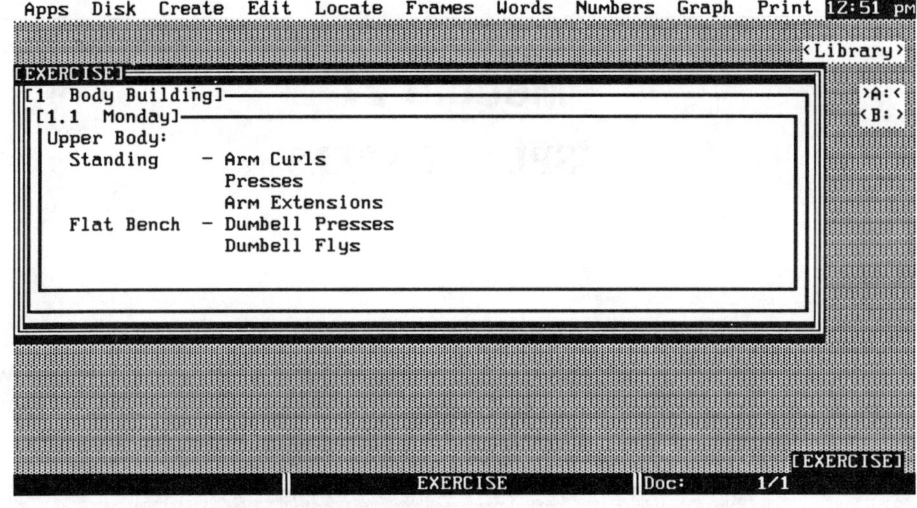

Disk: Get File by Name {exercise}

When turned off, this option suppresses the labels. It removes the labels from the currently selected frame and its subframes. Your desktop resembles the following display.

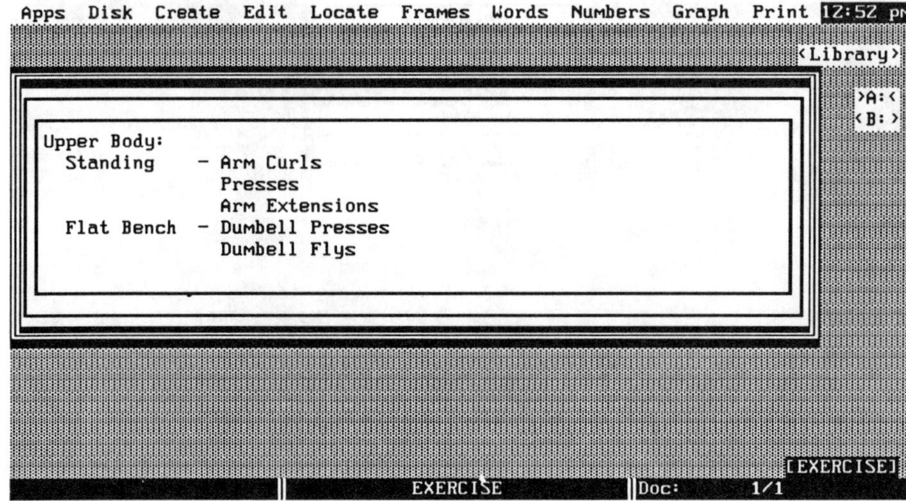

Frames: Display Labels off

This is especially important when you send the document to the printer. If it is used with the Hide Borders option turned on, the printed frame changes even more.

APPLICATIONS

Use this option with any frame which contains subframes. It lets you show or hide frame labels on the screen. By removing them from the screen, they are ignored when you print the open document.

TYPICAL OPERATION

This illustration shows you how to use the Display Labels option of the Frames Menu frame. Make sure that your desktop is clear and the cursor is positioned on one of the drive indicators. The shortcut key combinations, if applicable, are enclosed by braces.

1. {Press **Ctrl-D**}. Press **Ins** to move the cursor to the Main Menu line. Press **Left Arrow** or **Right Arrow**, if necessary, until the Disk Menu frame is open on your desktop.
2. {Press **Ctrl-G**}. Press **Up Arrow** to move the cursor to the Get File by Name { } option and then press **Enter**. The cursor moves to the Message line at the bottom of your desktop.
3. Type **EXERCISE**. As you type, notice that the braces next to the Get File by Name { } option fill. Press **Enter**. The disk is read and the frame you specified is opened on your desktop. If it appears only in the desktop tray with the cursor, just press **Enter** to open it on your desktop.

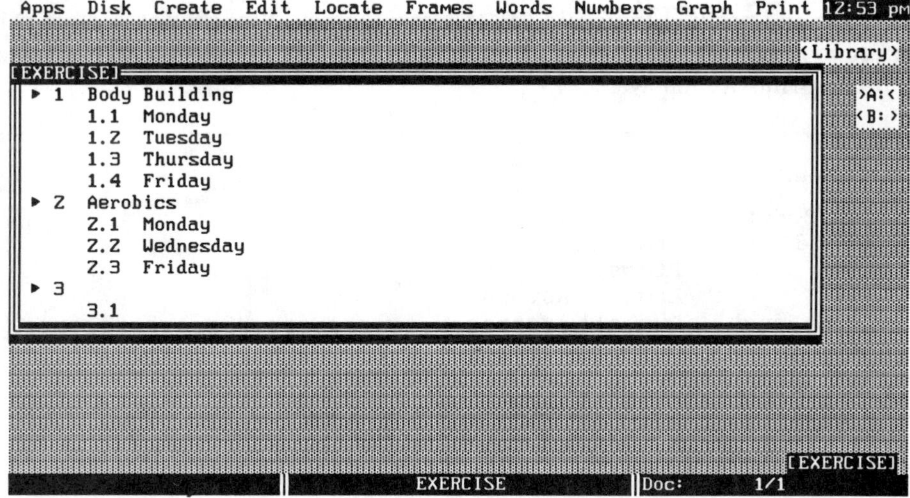

4. Press **Gray +** to move the cursor to the inside of your open frame. Notice that the cursor is positioned on the first major topic of your outline.

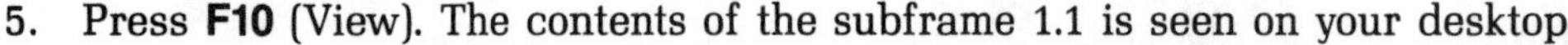

5. Press **F10** (View). The contents of the subframe 1.1 is seen on your desktop.

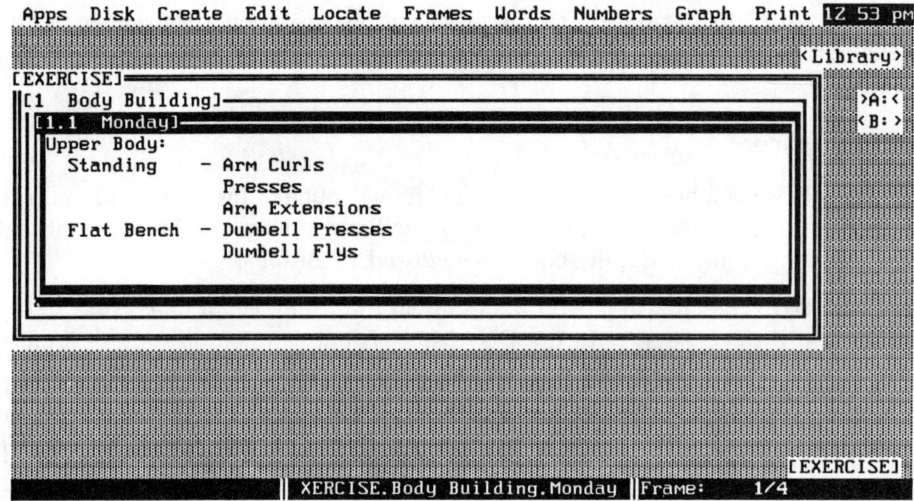

6. {Press **Ctrl-P** and **Ctrl-B**}. Press **Ins** to move the cursor to the Main Menu line again. Next, press the arrow (cursor) keys until the Print Menu frame is open on your desktop. Turn on your printer and position the cursor on the Begin option. Press **Enter** to start printing or press **Esc** to remove the Print Menu from your desktop. If the Begin option is selected, the open frame prints as follows.

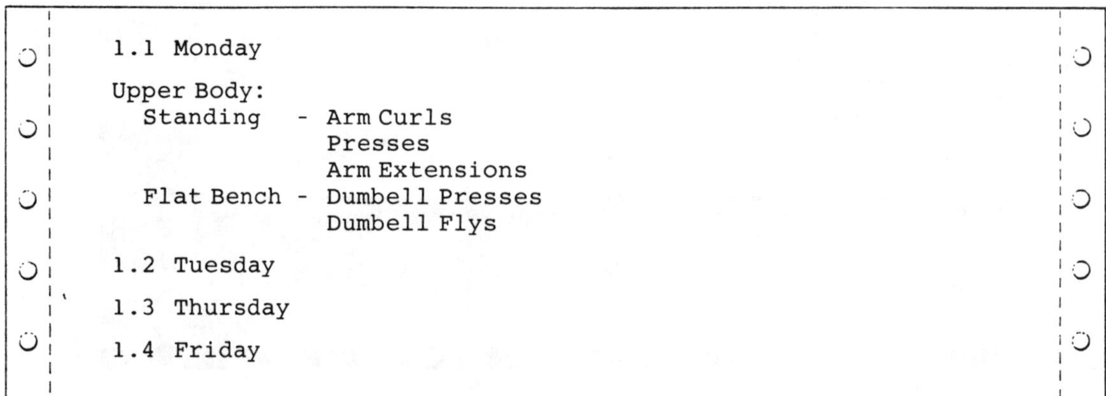

```
1.1 Monday

Upper Body:
  Standing    - Arm Curls
                Presses
                Arm Extensions
  Flat Bench  - Dumbell Presses
                Dumbell Flys

1.2 Tuesday

1.3 Thursday

1.4 Friday
```

7. {Press **Ctrl-F**}. Press **Ins** to move the cursor to the Main Menu line. Press **Left Arrow** until the Frames Menu frame is also open on your desktop. Notice that the Display Labels option is currently turned on.

8. {Press **Ctrl-D**}. Press **Up Arrow** or **Down Arrow** until the cursor is positioned on the Display Labels option and press **Enter**. This causes the subframe labels to disappear.

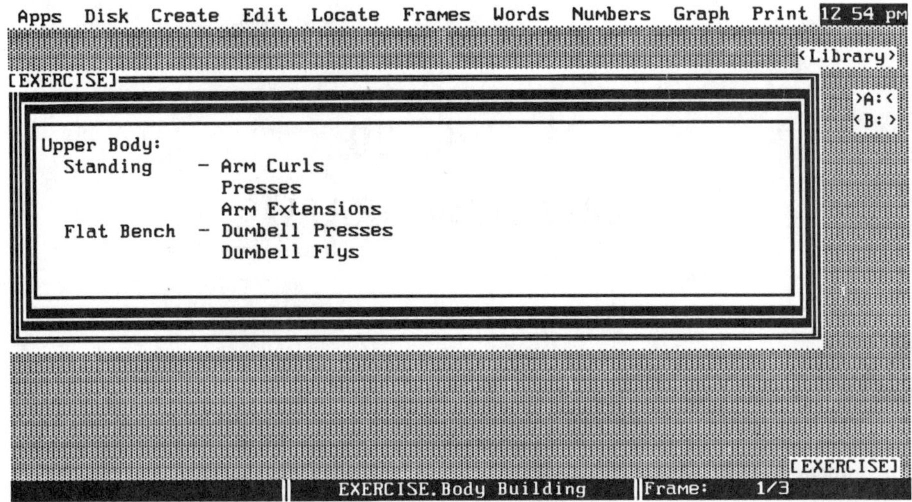

Frames: Display Labels off

9. {Press **Ctrl-P** and **Ctrl-B**}. Open the Print Menu frame again and select the Begin option. This time the printed frame resembles the following.

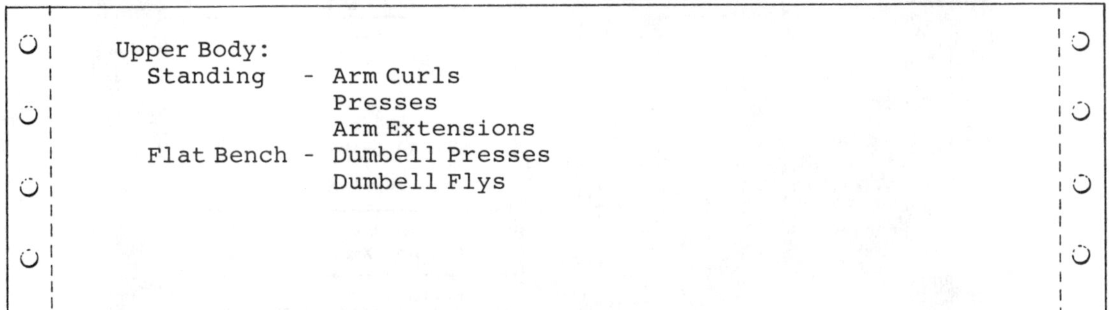

```
Upper Body:
  Standing   - Arm Curls
               Presses
               Arm Extensions
  Flat Bench - Dumbell Presses
               Dumbell Flys
```

10. {Press **Ctrl-F** and then **Ctrl-D**}. Reopen the Frames Menu frame and select the Display Labels option again. The labels return to the Body Building frame and its subframes.
11. Press **Gray –** to move the cursor to the EXERCISE frame border. Since the open frame has not been changed, press **Del** to remove the frame from you desktop without saving it on disk.
12. {Press **Ctrl-D**}. Press **Ins** to move the cursor to the Main Menu line. Press **Left Arrow** until the Disk Menu frame is open on your desktop.
13. {Press **Ctrl-Q**}. Using the arrow (cursor) keys, position the cursor on the QUIT Framework option and press **Enter**. Type **Y** when Framework III asks if you're sure you want to quit Framework III. The system prompt appears on your screen. This ends this Framework III session.
14. Turn to Module 49 to continue the learning sequence.

Module 28

DRAW NEW GRAPH

DESCRIPTION

Pictures always speak louder than words!

Spreadsheets are great for working with numbers, but it takes time to visualize the relationship between the numbers. The Draw New Graph option creates a new frame with a picture in it.

This option is available through the Graph Menu frame.

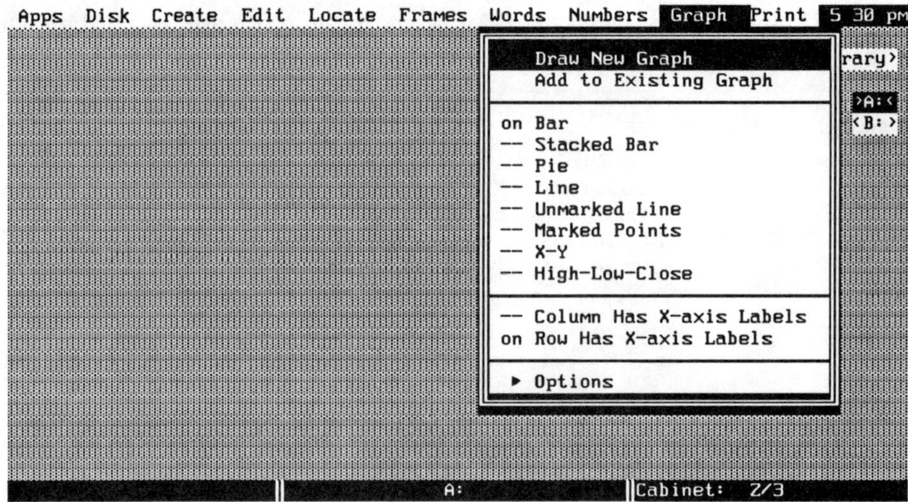

Draw graph of chosen type, using values in selected cells/fields

For example, the following spreadsheet shows first quarter sales for three sales people.

Apps Disk Create Edit Locate Frames Words Numbers Graph Print 5:34 pm

<Library>

[SALES]

	A	B	C	D	E	F	G
1		January	February	March	April	May	June
2	J.SLOAN	2500	2800	2000			
3	T.BERRY	1000	1200	1400			
4	TOTAL	3500	4000	3400			
5							
6							
7							
8							
9							

>A:< <B:>

[SALES]

SALES Doc: 1/1

By graphing the total sales for each month, notice how quickly you read the same information.

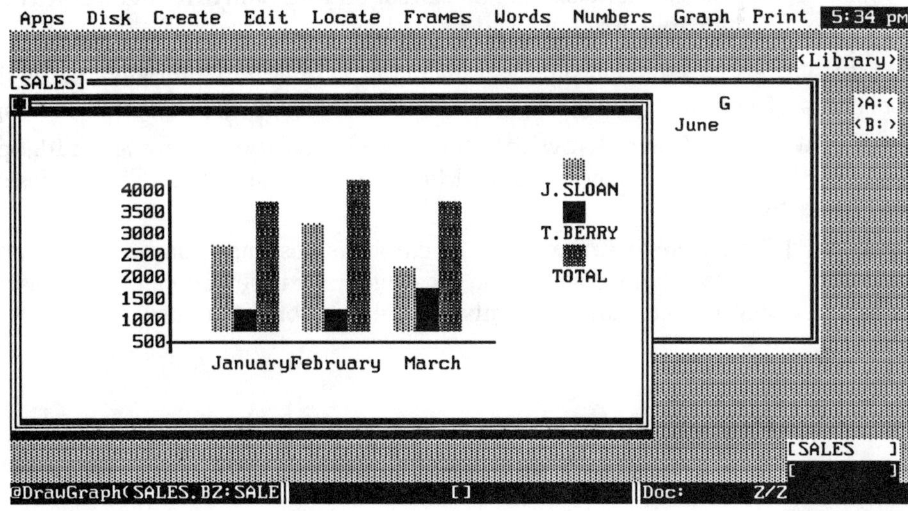

Graph: Draw New Graph

Although the graph shows the same information as the spreadsheet, it is a powerful visual tool. It shows the relationship of the numbers quickly.

Before opening the Graph Menu frame, you must specify the numbers for the graph. That means that a spreadsheet or database must be opened on your desktop first.

Press F6 (Extend) and the arrow (cursor) keys to highlight a series of cells or fields (down or across the frame). This identifies the numbers for your graph. When finished, open the Graph Menu frame.

Use the arrow keys to move the cursor to the options you want for your graph. For example, choose a pie instead of a bar graph. Framework III presets each option to an on or off condition when you begin your session. When ready, select the Draw New Graph option and let Framework III create it.

Once you've opened the Graph Menu, press Esc if you change your mind. This removes the Graph Menu from your desktop.

Remember that drawing a graph on the screen as an experiment does not change your open documents. Just play with the different options until you get the graph you want.

APPLICATIONS

Use graphs to interpret numbers within a spreadsheet or database. The information is quickly understood when it is in picture form.

Draw the graph as often as you want. The type of graph chosen often affects the impact of the picture. Try several options before deciding on one.

TYPICAL OPERATION

This example shows you how to open a spreadsheet, select numbers, and draw a graph. Close any open frames on your desktop and position the cursor on your data drive indicator. The shortcut key combinations, if applicable, are enclosed by braces.

1. {Press **Ctrl-C**}. Press **Ins** to move the cursor to the Main Menu line. Next, press the arrow (cursor) keys, if necessary, until the Create Menu frame is open on your desktop.
2. {Press **Ctrl-W**}. Press **Down Arrow** until the cursor is positioned on the Width option and press **Enter**. The cursor then moves to the Message line at the bottom of your desktop. Type **10** and press **Enter**.
3. {Press **Ctrl-H**}. Press **Down Arrow** until the cursor is positioned on the Height option and press **Enter**. The cursor then moves to the Message line at the bottom of your desktop. Type **8** and press **Enter**. Notice that the number within the braces is now 8.

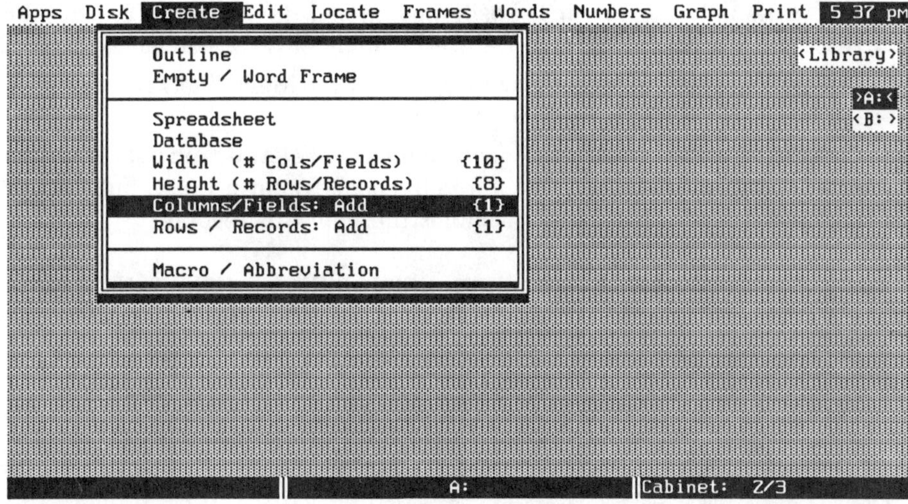

Add specified number of columns/fields after the selected one

4. {Press **Ctrl-S**}. Press **Up Arrow** to position the cursor on the Spreadsheet option and press **Enter**. An empty spreadsheet frame opens on your desktop.
5. The cursor is positioned at the top border of the frame within the brackets. Type **SALES** within the brackets and press **Enter**. The name of the file, when saved on the disk, is SALES.FW3.
6. Press **Gray +** to move the cursor to the inside of your open spreadsheet frame. Fill the cells so that your spreadsheet resembles the one in the following display.

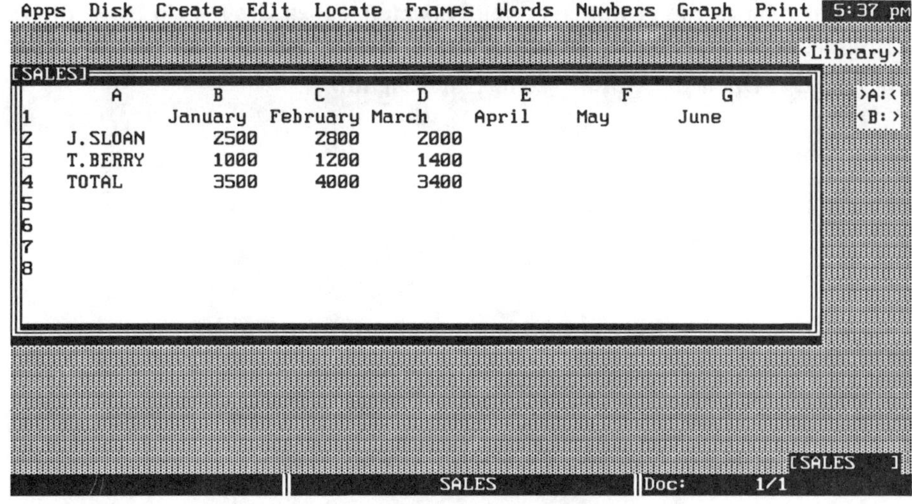

7. Press **Left Arrow** until the cursor is positioned on cell B4. Press **F6** (Extend). Press **Right Arrow** twice until cells B4, C4, and D4 are highlighted. When finished, press **Enter**.
8. {Press **Ctrl-G**}. Press **Ins** to move the cursor to the Main Menu line. Press **Right Arrow** until the Graph Menu is also open on your desktop.
9. {Press **Ctrl-D**}. With the cursor positioned on the Draw New Graph option and press **Enter**. Framework III asks if you want to draw it in the open frame or a new one. Just press **Enter** to use the open frame. The graph resembles the following display.

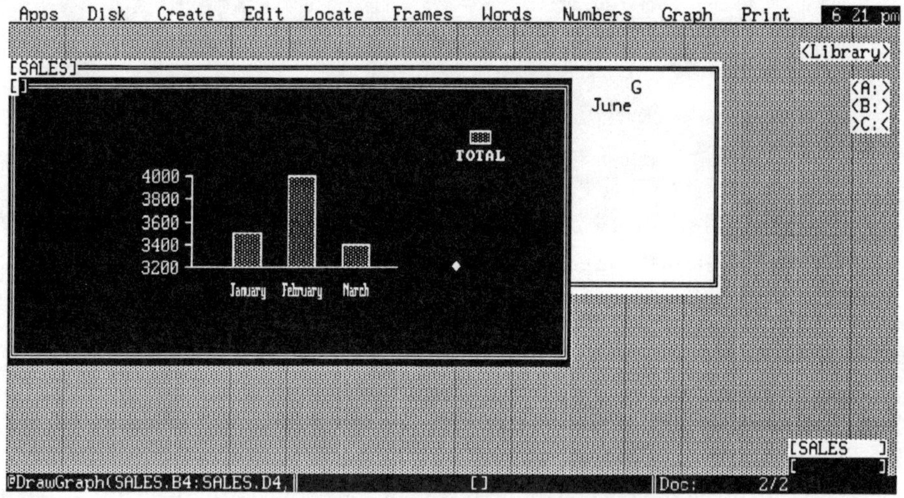

Graph: Draw New Graph

10. Press **Del** to remove the graph from your desktop. Press **Gray +** to move the cursor into the spreadsheet frame again. The numbers are still highlighted.
11. {Press **Ctrl-G**}. Open the Graph Menu frame again.

12. {Press **Ctrl-M** and then **Ctrl-D**}. Select the Marked Points option before drawing the graph. Now, your desktop resembles the following display.

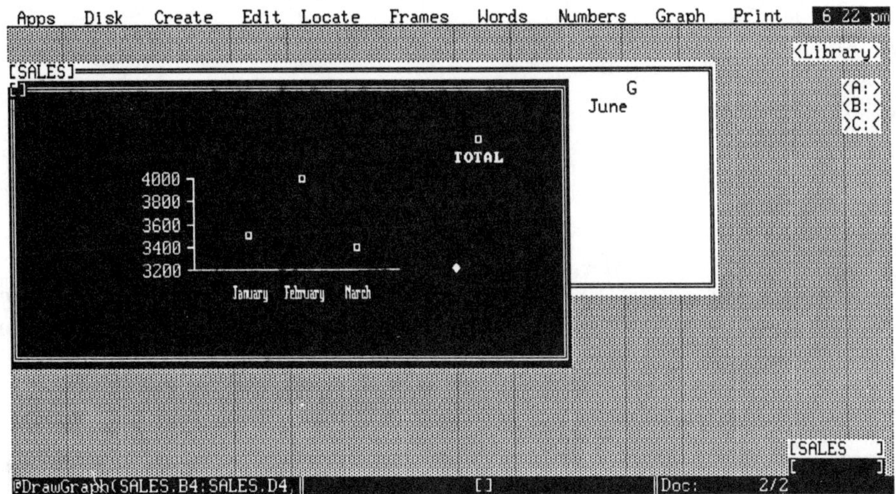

Graph: Draw New Graph

13. Type **Graph1** within the brackets of the graph frame and press **Enter**.
14. {Press **Ctrl-D**}. Press **Ins** to move the cursor to the Main Menu line. Press **Left Arrow** until the Disk Menu frame is open.
15. {Press **Ctrl-P**}. Select the Put Away option to save the graph frame on disk. Do the same for the SALES frame.
16. {Press **Ctrl-D**}. Open the Disk Menu frame again.
17. {Press **Ctrl-Q**}. Select the QUIT Framework option. When asked if you are sure you want to quit, type **Y**. This is the end of your Framework III session.
18. Turn to Module 10 to continue the learning sequence.

Module 29

EJECT PAGE

DESCRIPTION

If you use continuous paper, or an automatic form feed attachment, use this option to tell Framework III to move the paper in your printer to the top of the next page. This is very handy when you need to advance the paper without touching the printer.

The Eject Page option is in the Print Menu frame displayed below.

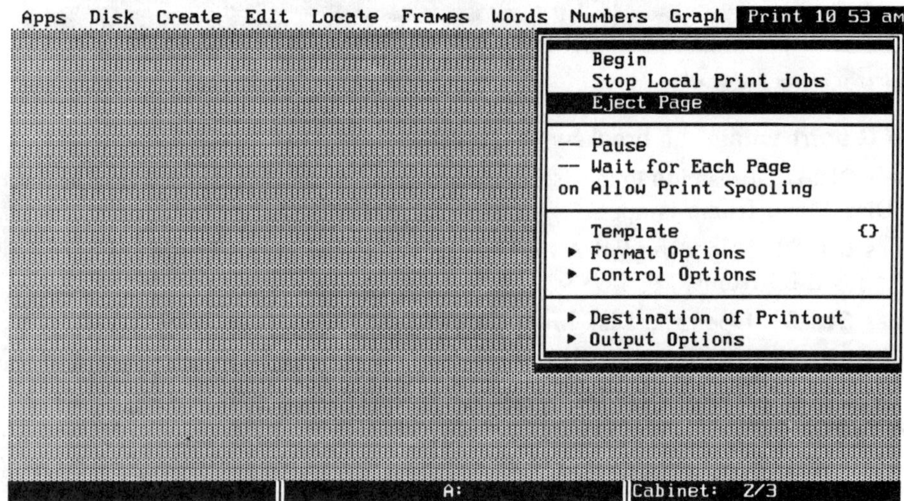

Use this option any time you want to move to another clean page of paper in the printer. The previous page is moved out, and a new one made available.

APPLICATIONS

Use the Eject Page option of the Print Menu frame any time the printer is turned on. It rolls the previous page up so that a new page is available for your next printed document.

Whenever you print a document, Framework III automatically moves the paper to the next page. Use this option to do the same thing.

TYPICAL OPERATION

This example shows you how to use the Eject Page option of the Print Menu frame.

Turn on your printer. You do not need to clear your desktop for this illustration. The shortcut key combinations, if applicable, are enclosed by braces.

1. {Press **Ctrl-P**}. Press **Ins** to move the cursor to the Main Menu line. Next, press the arrow (cursor) keys until the Print Menu frame is open on your desktop.
2. {Press **Ctrl-E**}. Using the arrow (cursor) keys, position the cursor on the Eject Page option and press **Enter**. The paper in the printer moves to the top of the next page.
3. {Press **Ctrl-P**, and then **Ctrl-E**}. Press **Ins** to move the cursor to the Main Menu line. The Print Menu frame is open on your desktop. With the cursor still positioned on the Eject Page option, press **Enter**. The paper in the printer again moves to the top of the next page.
4. {Press **Ctrl-D**}. Press **Ins** to move the cursor to the Main Menu line. Next, press the arrow (cursor) keys until the Disk Menu frame is open on your desktop.
5. {Press **Ctrl-Q**}. Using the arrow keys again, position the cursor on the QUIT Framework option and press **Enter**. Type **Y** when asked if you are sure you want to quit Framework III. This ends your Framework III session.
6. Turn to Module 14 to continue the learning sequence.

Module 30

EMPTY/WORD FRAME

DESCRIPTION

This type of frame is used for word processing activities. For example, you can write a letter, term paper, memo, or other similar document.

The first thing you do when you write a letter is get a clean sheet of paper. By selecting the Empty/Word Frame option of the Create Menu, you are doing the same thing. The Create Menu frame appears below.

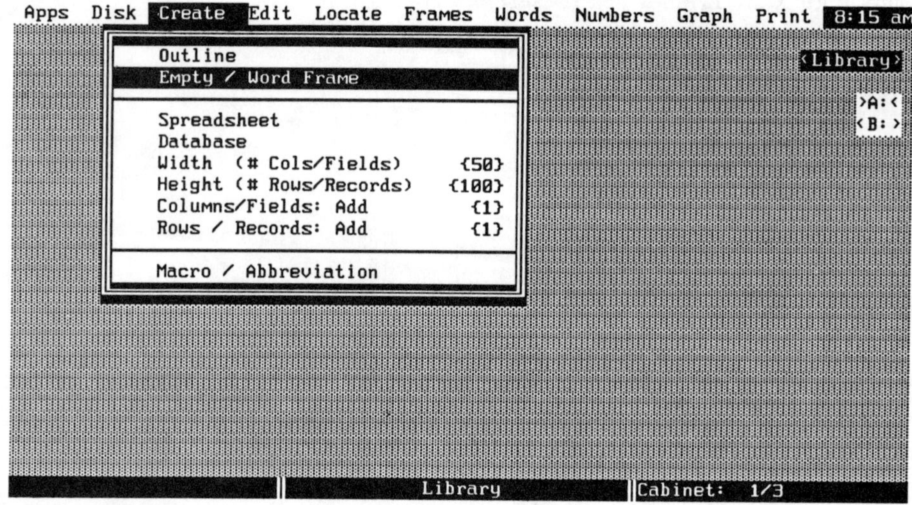

Create a frame for word processing or for containing other frames

By selecting the Empty/Word Frame option, your "sheet of paper" appears on your desktop as in the following display.

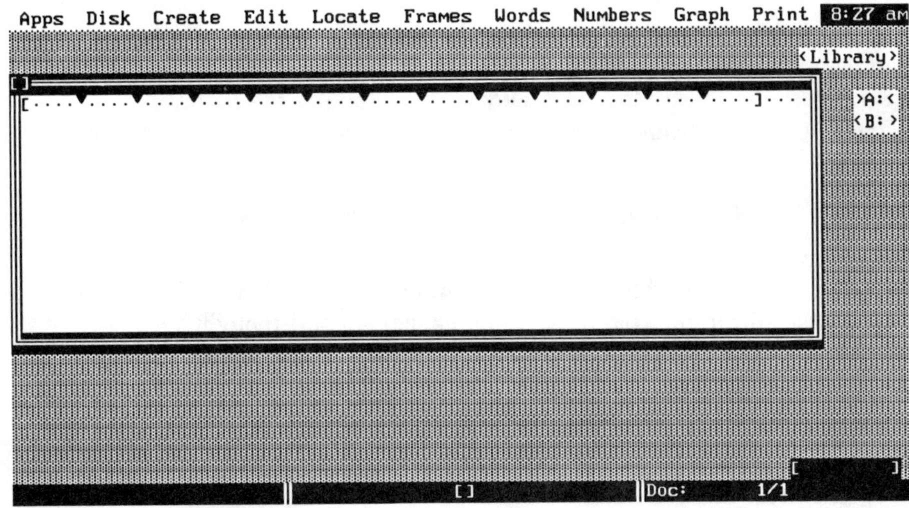

Create: Empty / Word Frame

The cursor is positioned on the top border of the word processing frame between the left and right brackets. This is where you assign a name to the document. The name which you type can be anything you choose.

Framework III uses the first eight characters of the name typed to create the name of the file which is saved on the disk. Only the first eight characters, or whatever you type if it is less than eight, are provided a suffix of .FW3 to develop a filename.

For example, if you type Birthday Party within the brackets, Framework III knows the document as BIRTHDAY.FW3. An underline replaces any blank space which exists within the first eight characters of the name.

Save your document with the Put Away or the Save and Continue options of the Disk Menu frame. Once the document is saved on the disk, it is later read from there to your desktop by using the Get File by Name { } option of the Disk Menu frame. All information which is saved on disk is available as though the document had never left your desktop.

As you type within the frame, you can set margins, tabs, typeface, etc. to make your document look the way you want it to look. Changes can be made quickly and easily by moving the cursor to where you want, and making the change.

Words, sentences, or even paragraphs can be moved from one area of the document to another area. This allows you to organize your thoughts even after you have typed them.

When you are ready, print the document on your printer using the Begin option of the Print Menu frame. This allows you to see the paragraph breakdown, column alignment, etc. as a whole document instead of being limited to what you see on your screen. When all changes are made, print the document again. Perform this edit and print activity as often as necessary.

Remember, however, that the document should be occasionally saved on your disk while you work. If your computer loses power, or some other type of problem occurs, only your latest saved version is available from your disk.

APPLICATIONS

Anytime you want to type something (for example, a memo or a letter), you must first open an empty word frame on your desktop. This is done by selecting the Empty/Word Frame option of the Create Menu. Once the frame is open, you can type inside the frame just like you would type on a typewriter.

There are several major advantages of using the Framework III word processor.

- Typing errors can be easily corrected.
- Whole words are moved to the next line automatically when you reach the right margin.
- You can use different typefaces to emphasize special thoughts.
- You can save the document as often as you want (complete or incomplete).
- You can print the document as often as you choose.

Once a document is created, review the Edit, Locate, Frames, Words, and Print Menu frames. These menu frames contain options for you to make changes, search for words and phrases, change the typeface, and print the document.

Feel free to experiment with the options as long as you save the document regularly. This prevents your work from being lost due to power failures as well as experiments which have gone bad.

TYPICAL OPERATION

In this illustration, an invitation to a birthday party is typed into a frame. It can then be printed by using the Print Menu option. The cursor is positioned on the drive B indicator and the desktop is clean. The shortcut key combinations, if applicable, are enclosed by braces in the following steps.

1. Type **FW** and press **Enter** to load Framework III. {Press **Ctrl-C**}. Press **Ins** to move the cursor to the Main Menu line. Press **Left Arrow** or **Right Arrow** until the Create Menu frame is open on your desktop.
2. {Press **Ctrl-E**}. Press **Down Arrow**, if necessary, to move the cursor to the Empty/Word Frame option of the Create Menu frame. Next, press **Enter** to select the option. An empty frame appears on your screen.
3. The cursor is positioned within the brackets at the top border of the frame. Type **BIRTHDAY** and press **Enter**. This is the name of the frame. When it is saved on the disk, it is named BIRTHDAY.FW3.
4. Press **Gray +**. Notice that the cursor is now positioned inside your open frame.
5. Type **P A R T Y !   P A R T Y !   P A R T Y !** and press **Enter**. Now, the cursor is positioned on the second line of your frame.

6. Type **Come help us celebrate Jerry Smith's birthday. We have a special surprise for him that will dazzle and amaze us all!** As you type, notice that you do not have to press Enter to move the cursor to the next line — Framework III does that automatically. Also, notice that a whole word moves to the next line when it is larger than the room on the line.

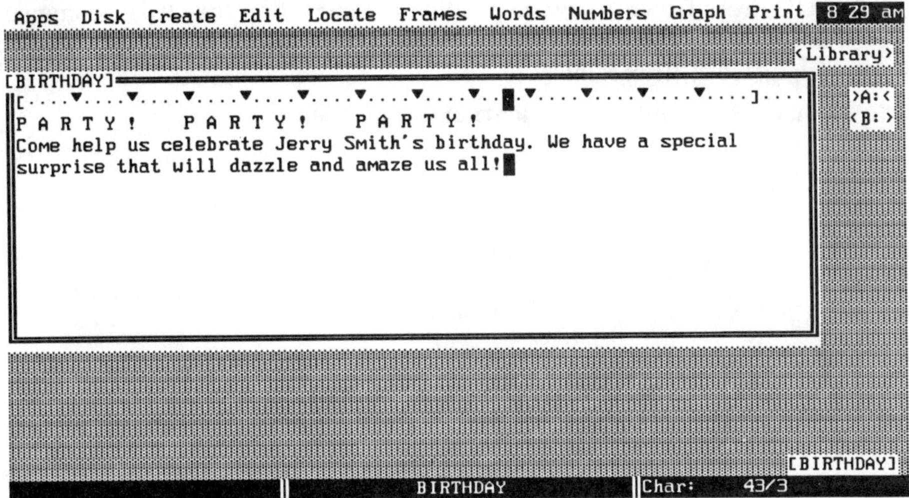

7. Press **Gray –** to move the cursor to the frame border. Next, press **Enter** to close the open frame. Notice that the cursor is positioned on the desktop tray in the lower right corner of the screen.

8. {Press **Ctrl-D**}. Press **Ins** to move the cursor to the Main Menu line. Next, press **Left Arrow** or **Right Arrow** until the following Disk Menu frame is open on your desktop.

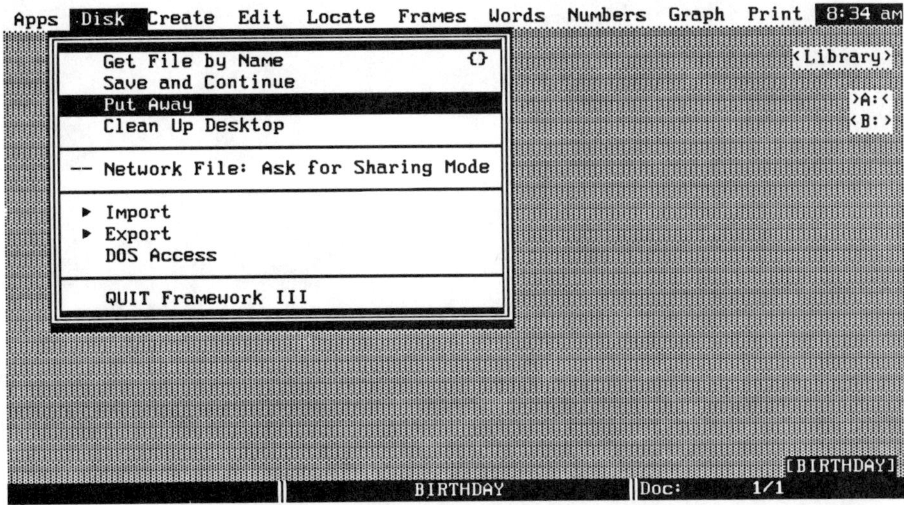

9. {Press **Ctrl-P**}. Press **Up Arrow** to position the cursor on the Put Away option and press **Enter**. This saves the invitation on the disk and cleans your desktop.
10. {Press **Ctrl-D**}. Press **Ins** to move the cursor to the Main Menu line. The Disk Menu frame is again open on your desktop.
11. {Press **Ctrl-Q**}. Press **Down Arrow** to position the cursor on the QUIT Framework option and press **Enter**. Type **Y** when asked if you are sure you want to quit Framework III. This ends your Framework III session.
12. Turn to Module 13 to continue the learning sequence.

Module 31

ENTRY FORMAT FOR DATA

DESCRIPTION

The Entry Format for Data option allows you to assign a data entry format (Character, Numeric, Date, Time, Logical, and Formula) for a field in a database, or cell in a spreadsheet. This allows you to assign a data type so you can use various data type specific functions.

For example, the @diffdate and @sumdate functions require database fields of date type. The Entry Format for Data Entry option is available from the Numbers menu as shown below.

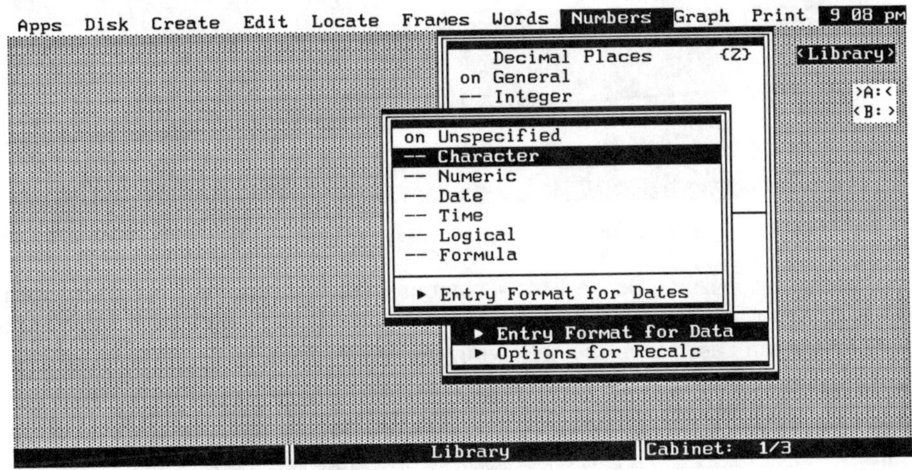

If you specify a data entry format, you do not have to press the Spacebar before entering character fields (even if they start with numbers). The default data type is "unspecified" if you do not specify a data entry format. This is unchanged from Framework II.

APPLICATIONS

The ability to specify entry formats for fields and cells speeds data entry. In addition, it allows you to specify alternate data types for calculations (date, time, Logical, etc.) that were unavailable in earlier versions of Framework III. This new feature also simplifies and streamlines formulas and FRED programs.

TYPICAL OPERATION

Use this illustration to learn how to use the Entry Format for Data option of the Numbers Menu frame. Close any open frames on your desktop and position the cursor on your data drive indicator (drive B in this example). The shortcut combinations, if applicable, are enclosed by braces.

1. {Press **Ctrl-D**}. Press **Ins** to move the cursor to the Main Menu line. Press **Left Arrow** or **Right Arrow**, if necessary, until the Disk Menu frame is open on your desktop. Your desktop should resemble the following display.

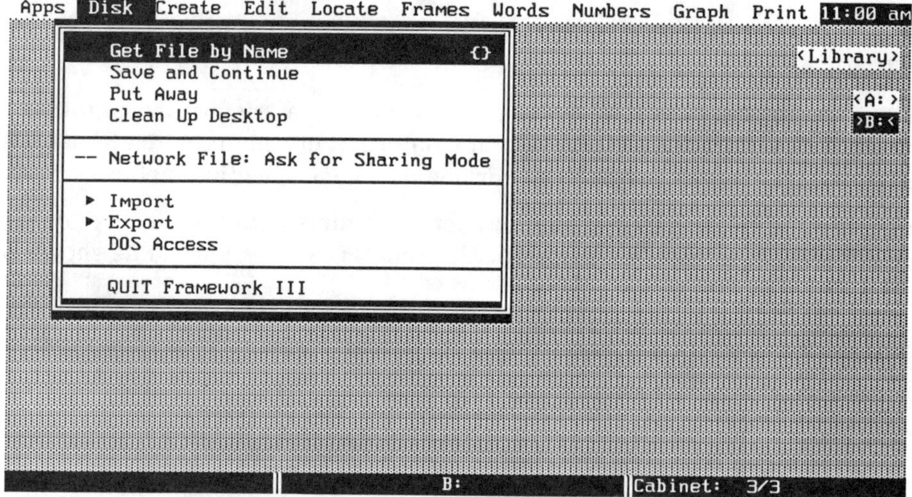

Bring specified file from disk and place beneath selected frame

2. {Press **Ctrl-G**}. By pressing **Down Arrow**, position the cursor on the Get File by Name option and press **Enter**. When prompted for the name of your file, type **PHONE_LI.FW3** and press **Enter**. Your screen resembles the following display.

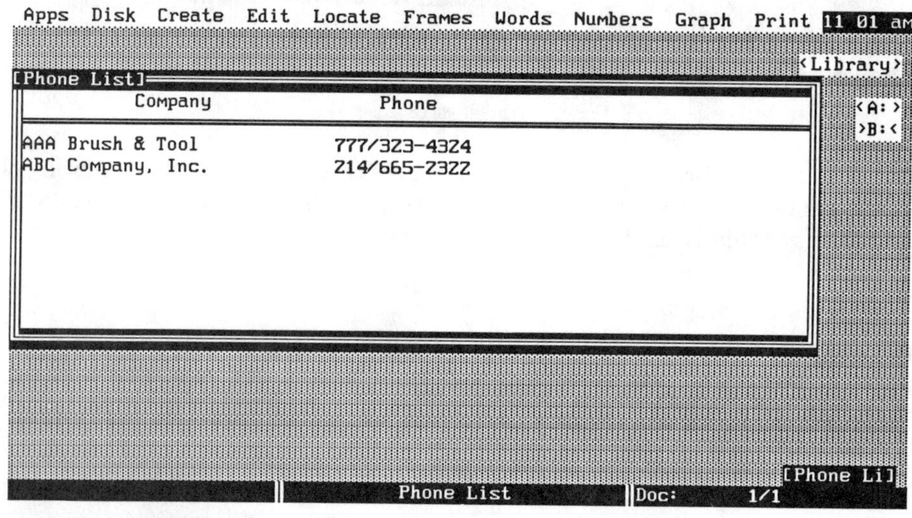

Disk: Get File by Name {PHONE LI}

3. Press **Gray +** to move into the frame. Press **Left Arrow** and **Right Arrow** to move your cursor to the third column. Make sure that your cursor is on the same line as the Company and Phone fields. Type **CONTDATE** and press **Enter**.
4. If you do not have enough room between the Phone number field and the CONTDATE field, position your cursor on the Phone Number field and press **F4** (Size).
5. Press **Right Arrow** until the field is the desired width and press **Enter**. Your screen resembles the following display.

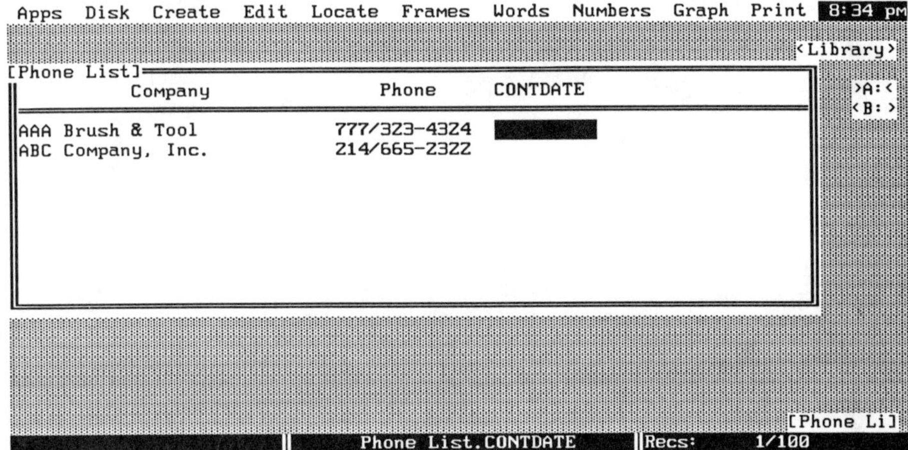

6. {Press **Ctrl-N** and then **Ctrl-E**}. Press **Ins** to move the cursor to the Main Menu line. Use your arrow keys to highlight the Entry Format for Data option and press **Enter**.
7. {Press **Ctrl-D**}. Use your arrow keys to highlight the Date option and press **Enter** to select the data entry format of date. Your screen should resemble the following display.

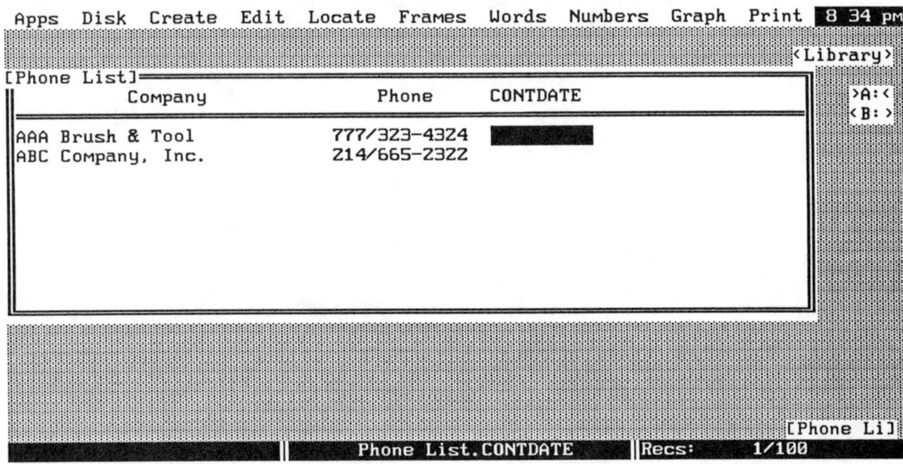

8. Use your arrow keys to move to the first CONTDATE field, type **03/23/89**, and press **Enter**. Notice that you did not have to press the Spacebar before entering the date field even though it began with a number and the prompt at the bottom of the screen indicates you are entering a date field.
9. Press **Gray –** to highlight the border of the PHONE_LI database. Press **Enter** to move the frame to your desktop. Press **Del** to delete the frame without saving your changes.
10. {Press **Ctrl-D** and then **Ctrl-Q**}. Press **Ins** and use your arrow keys to highlight the Disk menu and press **Enter**. Use your arrow keys to position the cursor on the QUIT Framework option and press **Enter**.
11. Turn to Module 62 to continue the learning sequence.

Module 32

EXPORT

DESCRIPTION

When using a software package, you use files which are formatted for that individual piece of software. However, that is not the case with Framework III. If you create a Framework III frame that you need in one of the popular software programs (dBASE, DisplayWrite IV (DCA), MultiMate, WordStar, etc.), use this submenu of options to convert the data in the frame to the new format.

The Export option is available through the Disk Menu frame. When selected, this option opens a submenu on your desktop. Several popular software packages are listed in the submenu as in the following display.

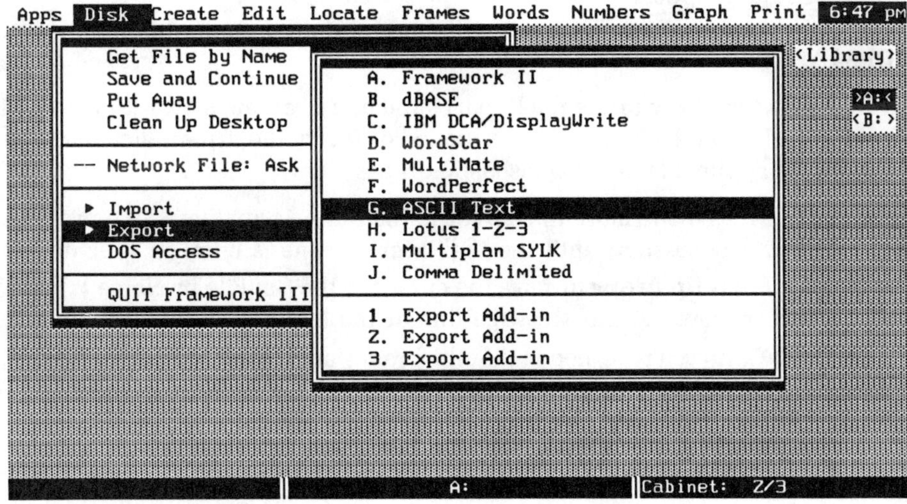

Write selection to disk as an ASCII text file

First, open the file you want to export on your desktop. If the file is for one of the packages in the list, position the cursor on that option and press Enter. Framework III opens and closes frames as it works. When complete, you see a message on the Message line that the file is saved on disk.

When exporting Framework III frames, the file is saved on the same disk as the Framework III file. It is given the same prefix when saved but the suffix identifies the type of file created. For example, a file with a prefix of TEST will have one of the following suffixes:

TEST.FW3	Framework III
TEST.WSD	WordStar
TEST.DBF	dBASE
TEST.TXT	ASCII
TEST.RFT	IBM DCA/DisplayWrite
TEST.DOC	MultiMate
TEST.WP	WordPerfect
TEST.WKS	Lotus 1-2-3
TEST.SYL	Multiplan

There are three Export Add-in options listed on the menu. If the Export option is not present for your file format, change one of the Add-in options to handle the export operation. Refer to the Add-in module in this book for more information.

APPLICATIONS

There is no sense in having to enter anything a second time when you need the same information for two software packages. If a file was created with Framework III, use one of the Export submenu options to make it available to one of the other popular software packages.

Framework III is preset for several popular packages. If yours is not on the list, add it by replacing one of the Export Add-in options.

TYPICAL OPERATION

This illustration shows you how to use the Export submenu to create a WordStar file. Make sure that your desktop is clear and the cursor is positioned on one of the drive indicators. The shortcut key combinations, if applicable, are enclosed by braces.

1. {Press **Ctrl-D**}. Press **Ins** to move the cursor to the Main Menu line. Next, press **Left Arrow** or **Right Arrow**, if necessary, until the Disk Menu frame is open on your desktop.
2. {Press **Ctrl-G**}. Press **Up Arrow** to move the cursor to the Get File by Name { } option. Press **Enter**. The cursor moves to the Message line at the bottom of your desktop.
3. Type **B:BIRTHDAY**. As you type, notice that the braces next to the Get File by Name { } option fill. When finished, press **Enter**. The disk is read and the frame you specified is opened on your desktop as follows.

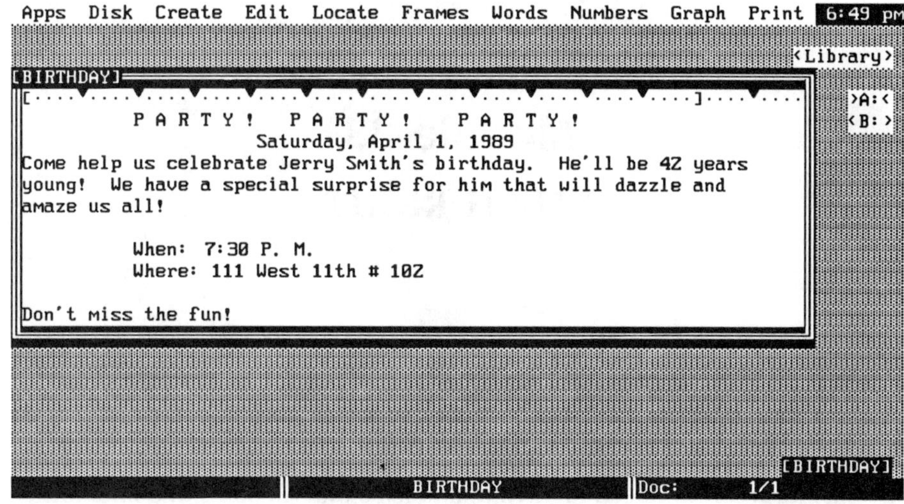

Disk: Get File by Name {birthday}

4. {Press **Ctrl-D**}. Reopen the Disk Menu frame.
5. {Press **Ctrl-E**}. Press **Down Arrow** to move the cursor to the Export option and then press **Enter**. Notice the submenu which opens on your desktop.
6. Press **Up Arrow** until the cursor is positioned on the WordStar { } option and press **Enter**. Framework III opens and closes several frames on your desktop. Each frame displayed includes a message on the Message line at the bottom of the screen. When finished, Framework III tells you that the export file was written. Since you no longer need the open file, press **Del** to remove the open Framework III file from your desktop.
7. {Press **Ctrl-D**}. Press **Ins** again to move the cursor to the Main Menu line. The Disk Menu frame is open on your desktop.
8. {Press **Ctrl-Q**}. Position the cursor on the QUIT Framework III option and press **Enter**. When asked if you really want to quit Framework III, type **Y**.
9. When the system prompt returns, type **TYPE B:BIRTHDAY.WSD** and press **Enter**. The new WordStar file is displayed on your screen. Notice that some dot commands are included at the top of the document.
10. You can now begin a WordStar session.
11. Turn to Module 83 to continue the learning sequence.

Module 33
FLUSH RIGHT

DESCRIPTION

Align Left, Justify, and Center are positioning options which are commonly used. To complete the spectrum of positioning text, the Flush Right option is available. Use it to align all text against the right margin of your open frame and cause the left side to be ragged.

This option is useful when you need to align numbers so that all decimal points form a straight line. First, set the right margin for the place where the numbers are to end. Then, type the first number, press Enter and type the next number. Continue this process until all numbers are typed.

The Flush Right option is available for word processing frames. Access it through the Words Menu frame.

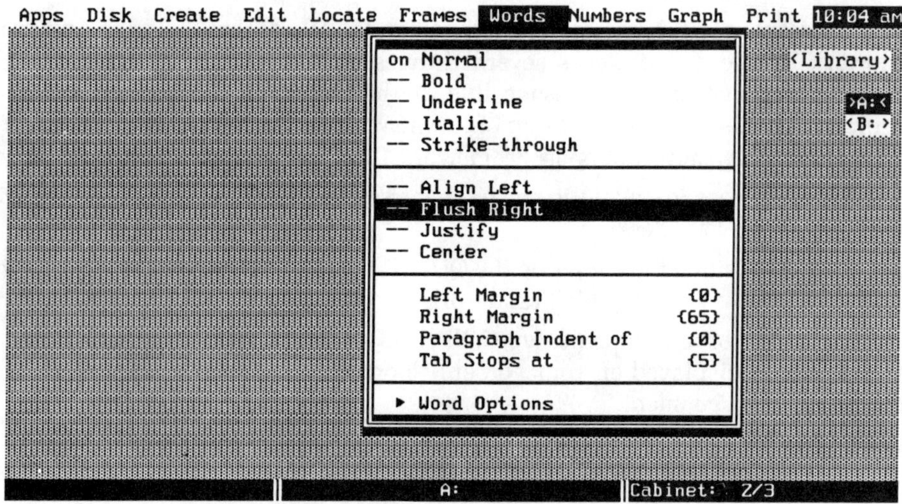

Align text of selected frames or paragraphs at the right margin

Framework III begins each new word processing frame with the Left and Right Margin options set so that Framework III knows when to move a word to the next line. Normally, the left side of your text forms a straight line at the left margin.

When turned on, the Flush Right option forces the right side to line up but not the left. As you type, this option immediately repositions the text against the right margin. Once turned on, it stays on until you select the Align Left, Justify, or Center option for your open frame.

As soon as one of the positioning options is selected, Framework III displays a message at the bottom of your screen. Press Enter to make the message disappear.

APPLICATIONS

This option is available for word processing frames only. Select this option when you want to align the text against the right margin.

Once the Flush Right option is selected, positioning is automatic. You must select one of the other positioning options in the Words Menu frame to turn it off.

TYPICAL OPERATION

This example shows you how to use the Flush Right option of the Words Menu frame. Close any open frames on your desktop and position the cursor on your data drive indicator (drive B in this example). The shortcut key combinations, if applicable, are enclosed by braces.

1. {Press **Ctrl-D**}. Press **Ins** to move the cursor to the Main Menu line. Next, press **Left Arrow** or **Right Arrow**, if necessary, until the Disk Menu frame is open on your desktop.
2. {Press **Ctrl-G**}. Press **Up Arrow** to move the cursor to the Get File by Name option and then press **Enter**. The cursor moves to the Message line at the bottom of your desktop.
3. Type **B:BIRTHDAY**. As you type, notice that the braces next to the Get File by Name option fill. When finished, press **Enter**. The disk is read and the frame you specified is opened on your desktop.
4. Press **Gray +** to move the cursor inside your open frame. Your cursor is positioned after the last change of the document. Press **Down Arrow** and **Left Arrow** until the cursor is positioned on the "C" in the word "Come."
5. Press **F6** (Extend) and notice the message at the bottom of your screen. This message tells you that by pressing the arrow (cursor) keys, you can enlarge the highlighted area. Press **Down Arrow** two times until all text is included in the highlighted area. Then press **Enter** to tell Framework III you have finished.

6. {Press **Ctrl-W**}. Press **Ins** to move the cursor to the Main Menu line. Next, press **Right Arrow** until the Words Menu frame is also open on your desktop. Notice that the Align Left option is currently turned on.

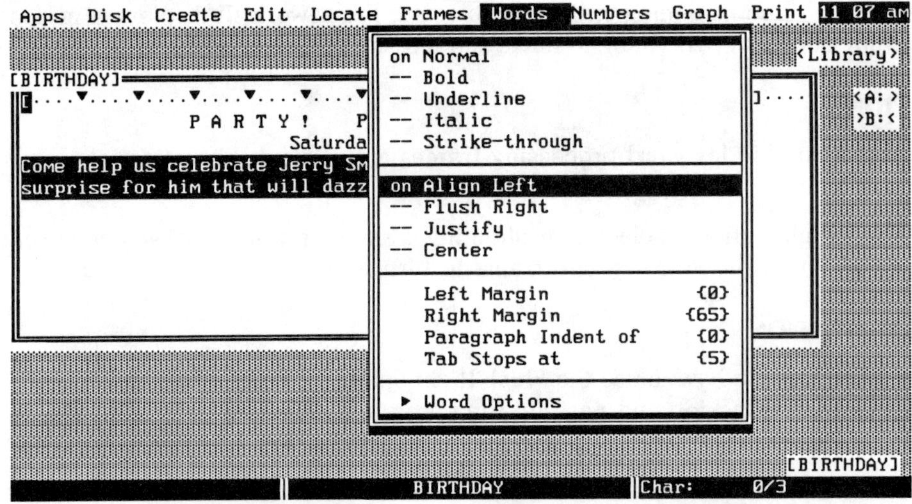

Align text of selected frames or paragraphs at the left margin

7. {Press **Ctrl-F**}. Press **Down Arrow** until the cursor is positioned on the Flush Right option. Press **Enter**. The Words Menu frame disappears from your desktop. Notice how the text forms a straight line against the right margin in the open frame.

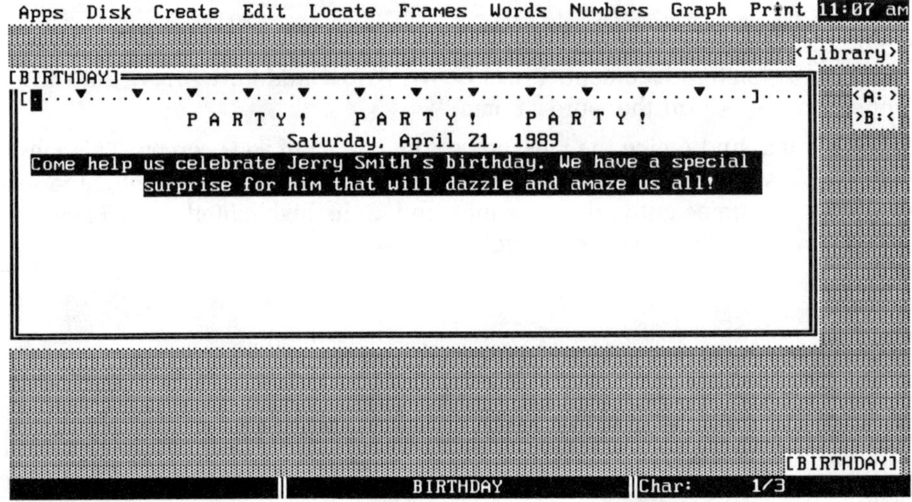

Words: Flush Right on

8. Press **Gray** – to move the cursor to the frame border.
9. {Press **Ctrl-D**}. Press **Ins** to move the cursor to the Main Menu line. Next, press **Left Arrow** until the Disk Menu frame is open on your desktop.
10. {Press **Ctrl-Q**}. Using the arrow keys again, position the cursor on the QUIT Framework option and press **Enter**. The file is closed and put into the tray. The computer beeps and asks if you want to save the new or modified document.
11. Type **Y** to save the file on the data disk and return to the DOS prompt.
12. Turn to Module 48 to continue the learning sequence.

Module 34
FOOTNOTES

DESCRIPTION

Use the Footnotes submenu to control the contents and numbering sequence of footnotes in frames and documents. These options are available through the Footnotes submenu of the Edit Menu as follows.

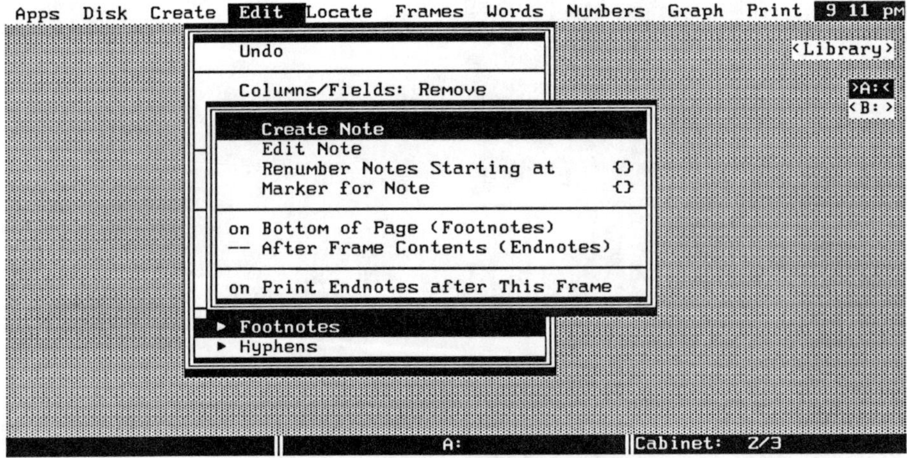

Select the Create Note option to enter new footnotes for a frame or document. Position the cursor in the document and enter the new footnote.

Use the Edit Note option to change an existing footnote. Position the cursor on the footnote and select the Edit Note option of the Footnotes submenu. To edit the note in full screen mode, press F9 (Zoom).

Framework III uses numbers as the default to identify a footnote. However, it allows you to select a special character to denote a footnote. Use the Marker for Note option to change the footnote identifier. For example, if you only have a few footnotes, you might want to use *, **, and *** to mark your footnotes.

Renumber the footnotes at any point in a document by selecting the Renumber Notes Starting at { } option. Then, enter a new number to start the numbering sequence.

Framework places footnotes at the bottom of the page if Bottom of Page (Footnotes) is turned on. The footnotes are placed at the end of the frame if the After Frame Contents (Endnotes) option is turned on.

Turn the Print Endnotes after This Frame option off to prevent the printing of footnotes after the current frame.

APPLICATIONS

Use the Footnotes submenu options to print footnotes at the bottom of each page or after each frame. Since several of the footnote options are available, it is easy to provide footnotes in your document.

TYPICAL OPERATION

This example shows you how to use the options of the Footnotes Menu. Turn on your printer. Make sure that your desktop is clean and the cursor is positioned on a drive indicator on the right side of your desktop. The shortcut key combinations, if applicable, are enclosed by braces.

1. {Press **Ctrl-D**}. Press **Ins** to move the cursor to the Main Menu line. Next, press **Left Arrow** or **Right Arrow**, if necessary, until the Disk Menu frame is open on your desktop.
2. {Press **Ctrl-G**}. Press **Up Arrow** to move the cursor to the Get File by Name option and then press **Enter**. The cursor moves to the Message line at the bottom of your desktop.
3. Type **B:BIRTHDAY**. As you type, notice that the braces next to the Get File by Name option fill. When finished, press **Enter** twice. The disk is read and the frame you specified is opened on your desktop as in the following display.

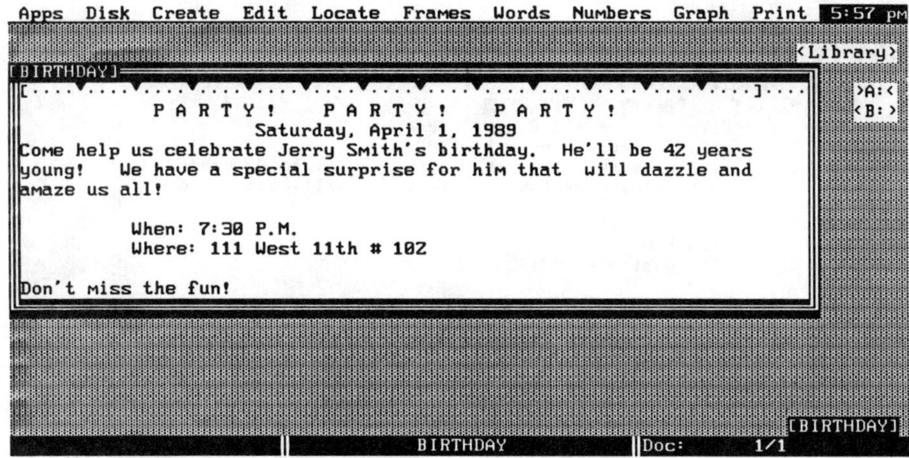

4. Position your cursor to the point just after Jerry Smith's name in the invitation.

5. {Press **Ctrl-E** and then **Ctrl-F**}. Press **Ins** to move the cursor to the Main Menu line. Next, press the arrow (cursor) keys until the Edit Menu frame is open on your desktop. Press **Down Arrow** until the cursor is positioned on Footnotes Options and press **Enter**.

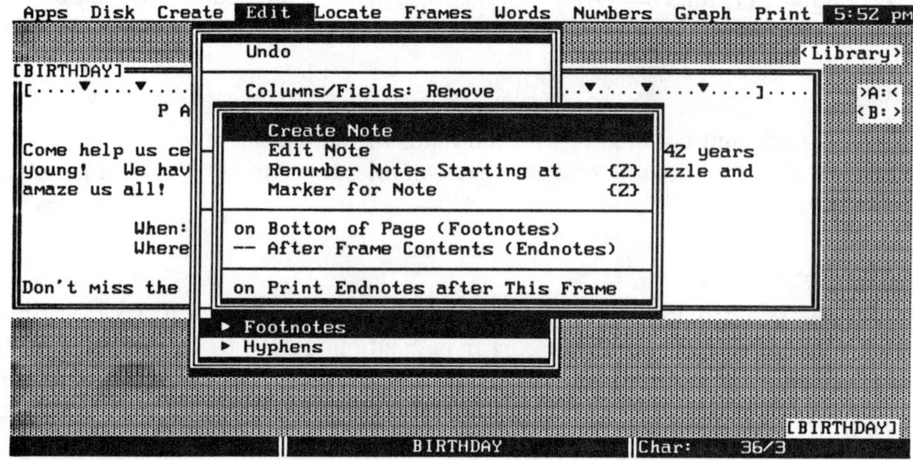

Create a new footnote or endnote with its marker at cursor location

6. {Press **Ctrl-C**}. If necessary, use your arrow keys to highlight the Create Note option and press **Enter**. Since this is your first footnote, the number 1 appears as the footnote number by default.
7. Type **International Marketing Manager** and press **Enter**.

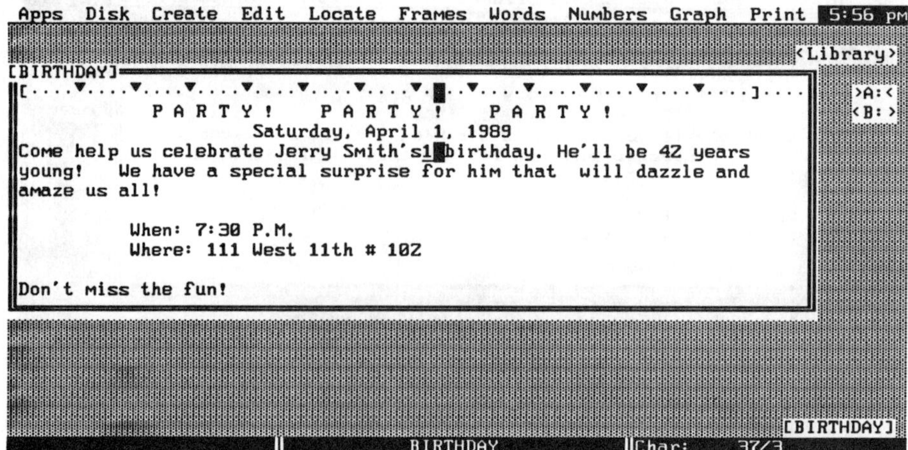

8. If necessary, position your cursor at the footnote again. {Press **Ctrl-E**, **Ctrl-F**, and then **Ctrl-E**}. Press **Ins** to move the cursor to the Main Menu line again. Use your arrow keys to move to the Edit Menu frame and open the Footnotes submenu. Press **Down Arrow** to highlight the Edit Note option and press **Enter**.
9. Change the note to **Texas Marketing Manager** and press **Enter**. Your screen should look like the following display.

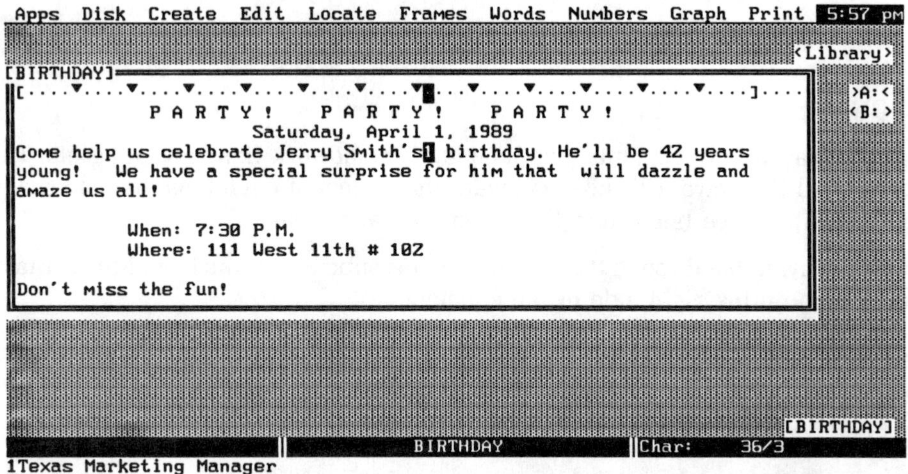

10. {Press **Ctrl-P** and then **Ctrl-B**}. Press **Ins** to move the cursor to the Main Menu line. Use your arrow keys to highlight the Print option. Position the cursor on the Begin option and press **Enter**. Your document prints on your printer. Notice that your footnote prints at the bottom of the page.
11. {Press **Ctrl-D and then Ctrl-Q**}. Open the Disk Menu. Using the arrow keys again, position the cursor on the QUIT Framework option and press **Enter**. Type **Q** to Quit without saving.
12. Turn to Module 37 to continue the learning sequence.

Module 35

FORMAT OPTIONS (FOOTERS)

DESCRIPTION

Customizing the way your documents print is one of Framework III's biggest assets. This set of options lets you tell Framework III how you want the bottom of each page to look. For example, print a centered title three lines from the bottom of each page.

These options are available through the Format Options submenu of the Print Menu frame. Notice the Footers section on the right side of the submenu.

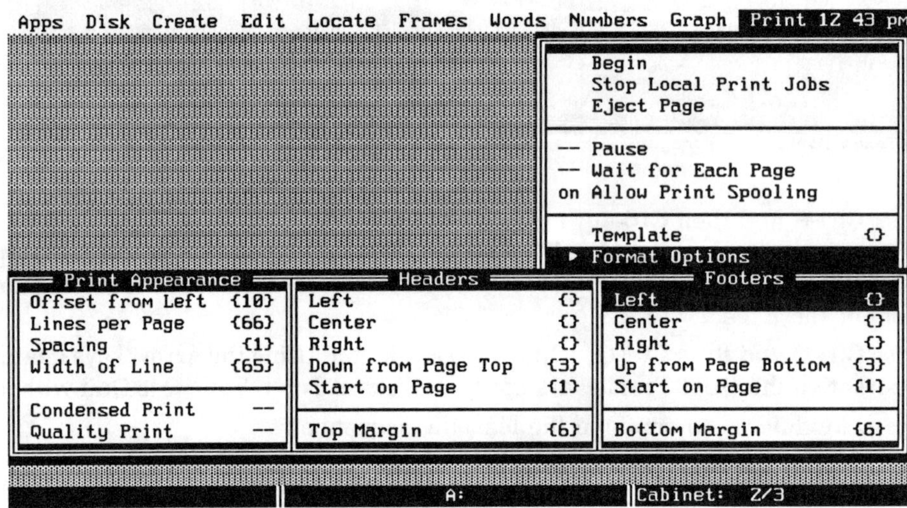

Specify the footer to be left aligned

When the submenu is opened, the cursor usually begins in the Print Appearance section of the submenu. Press Left Arrow or Right Arrow to move the cursor to the Footers section. Position the cursor on the option you want and press Enter. Then type or change the value within the braces to the value you want.

Left { } Position the cursor on this option and press Enter. The cursor moves to the bottom of your screen. Type the title you want to be printed on each page and press Enter. When printing the document, Framework III automatically includes this title on the bottom, left side of each page.

Center { } This option is selected the same way as the Left option. However, Framework III automatically includes this title centered on the bottom of each page.

Right { } This option is selected the same way as the Left option. However, Framework III automatically includes this title on the bottom, right side of each page.

Up from Page Bottom {3} Select this option when you want to move the footer up or down. Change the number of lines within the braces. Framework III is preset to print footers three lines above the bottom margin.

Start on Page {1} Change the page number within the braces to tell Framework III on which page to begin your footers. Framework III automatically begins on the first page and continues until the document is printed.

Bottom Margin {6} This option tells Framework III the number of lines at the bottom of the page you want left blank. Framework III is preset to allow a six-line bottom margin.

APPLICATIONS

Use these options when you want to print something at the bottom of each page of your document. Since these options are available, you don't have to type the footer on each page in the document.

Each option helps you position one or more footers exactly where you want them to print. Type the footer in the chosen set of braces and print a page of the document. Change any of these options until the footer prints properly.

TYPICAL OPERATION

This example shows you how to use the Footers options of the Format Options submenu. Turn on your printer. Make sure that your desktop is clean and the cursor is positioned on a drive indicator on the right side of your desktop. The shortcut key combinations, if applicable, are enclosed by braces.

1. {Press **Ctrl-D**}. Press **Ins** to move the cursor to the Main Menu line. Next, press **Left Arrow** or **Right Arrow**, if necessary, until the Disk Menu frame is open on your desktop.
2. {Press **Ctrl-G**}. Press **Up Arrow** to move the cursor to the Get File by Name option and then press **Enter**. The cursor moves to the Message line at the bottom of your desktop.
3. Type **B:BIRTHDAY**. As you type, notice that the braces next to the Get File by Name option fill. When finished, press **Enter** twice. The disk is read and the frame you specified is opened on your desktop.
4. {Press **Ctrl-P** and then **Ctrl-F**}. Press **Ins** to move the cursor to the Main Menu line. Next, press the arrow (cursor) keys until the Print Menu frame is open on your desktop. Press **Down Arrow** until the cursor is positioned on Format Options and press **Enter**.
5. If necessary, press **Right Arrow** to the Footers section.

6. Press **Down Arrow**, if necessary, until the cursor is positioned on the Left option of the Footers section and press **Enter**. The cursor moves to the bottom of the screen. Type * 15 times and press **Enter**. Then do the same for the Right option. Your desktop resembles the following display.

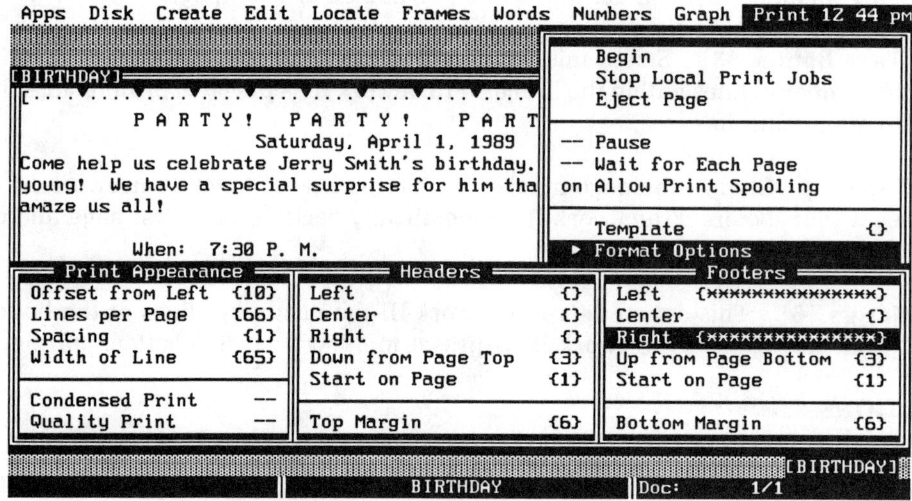

`Print: Format Options: Footers: Right {***************}`

7. Press **Esc** to get out of the submenu.
8. {Press **Ctrl-P**}. Press **Ins** to move the cursor to the Main Menu line again. The Print Menu frame is open on your desktop.
9. {Press **Ctrl-B**}. Using the arrow (cursor) keys, position the cursor on the Begin option and press **Enter**. The printout resembles the example on the following page.
10. Press **Del** to remove the document from your desktop.
11. {Press **Ctrl-D**}. Press **Ins** to move the cursor to the Main Menu line. Next, press the arrow (cursor) keys until the Disk Menu frame is open on your desktop.
12. {Press **Ctrl-Q**}. Using the arrow keys again, position the cursor on the QUIT Framework option and press **Enter**. Type **Y** when asked if you are sure you want to quit Framework III. This ends your Framework III session.
13. Turn to Module 63 to continue the learning sequence.

```
        P A R T Y !    P A R T Y !    P A R T Y !
                 Saturday, April 1, 1989
Come help us celebrate Jerry Smith's birthday.  He'll be 42 years
young!  We have a special surprise for him that will dazzle and
amaze us all!

            When: 7:30 P.M.
            Where: 111 West 11th # 102

Don't miss the fun!











 ***************                              ***************
```

Module 36

FORMAT OPTIONS (HEADERS)

DESCRIPTION

Customizing the way your documents print is one of Framework III's biggest assets. This set of options lets you tell Framework III how you want the top of each page to look. For example, print a centered title six lines from the top of each page.

These options are available through the Format Options submenu of the Print Menu frame. Notice the Headers section in the middle of the submenu.

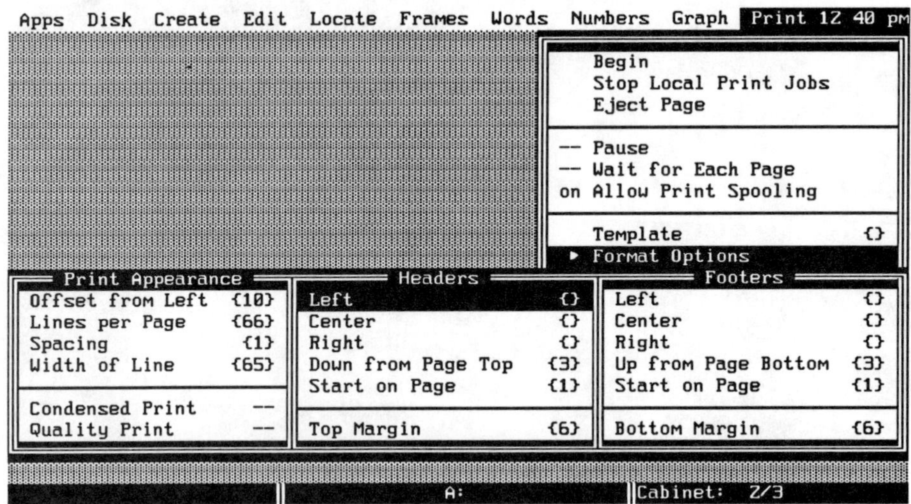

Specify the header to be left aligned

When the submenu is opened, the cursor usually begins in the Print Appearance section of the submenu. Press Right Arrow to move the cursor to the Headers section. Position the cursor on the option you want and press Enter. Then enter or change the value within the braces to the value you want.

Left { } Position the cursor on this option and press Enter. The cursor moves to the bottom of your screen. Type the title you want to be printed on each page and press Enter. When printing the document, Framework III automatically includes this text on the top left side of each page.

Center { } This option is selected the same way as the Left option. However, Framework III automatically includes this text centered at the top of each page.

Right { } This option is selected the same way as the Left option. However, Framework III automatically includes this text on the top-right side of each page.

Down From Page Top {3} Select this option when you want to move the header up or down. Change the number of lines within the braces. Framework III is preset to print headers three lines below the top margin.

Start on Page {1} Change the page number within the braces to tell Framework III on which page to begin your headers. Framework III automatically begins on the first page and continues until the document is printed.

Top Margin {6} This option tells Framework III the number of lines at the top of the page you want left blank. Framework III is preset to allow a six-line top margin.

APPLICATIONS

Use these options when you want to print something at the top of each page of your document. Since these options are available, you don't have to type the header information on each page in the document.

Each option helps you position text exactly where you want it to print. Type the text in the chosen set of braces and print a page of the document. Change any of these options until the header prints properly.

TYPICAL OPERATION

This example shows you how to use the Headers options of the Format Options submenu. Turn on your printer. Make sure that your desktop is clean and the cursor is positioned on a drive indicator on the right side of your desktop. The shortcut key combinations, if applicable, are enclosed by braces.

1. {Press **Ctrl-D**}. Press **Ins** to move the cursor to the Main Menu line. Next, press **Left Arrow** or **Right Arrow**, if necessary, until the Disk Menu frame is open on your desktop.
2. {Press **Ctrl-G**}. Press **Up Arrow** to move the cursor to the Get File by Name option and then press **Enter**. The cursor moves to the Message line at the bottom of your desktop.
3. Type **B:BIRTHDAY**. As you type, notice that the braces next to the Get File by Name option fill. When finished, press **Enter** twice. The disk is read and the frame you specified is opened on your desktop as follows.

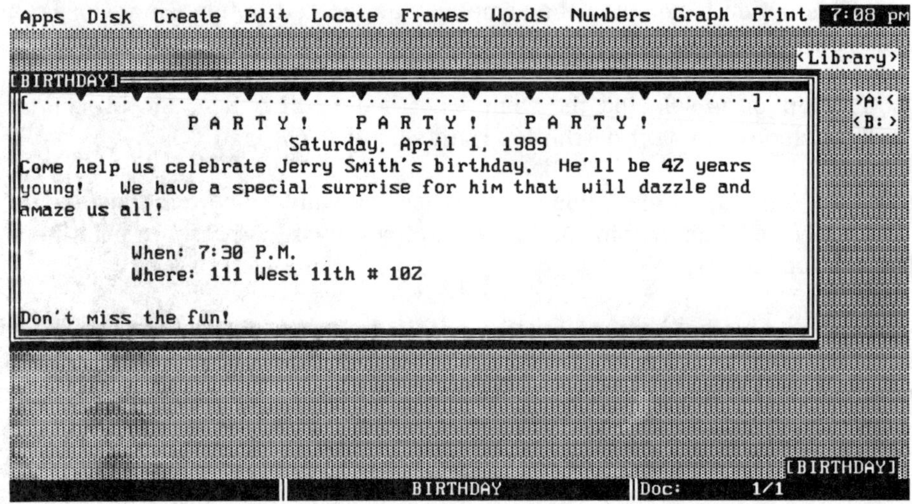

4. {Press **Ctrl-P** and then **Ctrl-F**}. Press **Ins** to move the cursor to the Main Menu line. Next, press the arrow (cursor) keys until the Print Menu frame is open on your desktop. Press **Down Arrow** until the cursor is positioned on Format Options and press **Enter**.
5. If necessary, press **Right Arrow** to move the cursor to the Headers section.
6. Press **Down Arrow**, if necessary, until the cursor is positioned on the Left option in the Headers section and press **Enter**. The cursor moves to the bottom of the screen. Type * 15 times and press **Enter**. Then do the same for the Right option. Now your desktop resembles the following display.

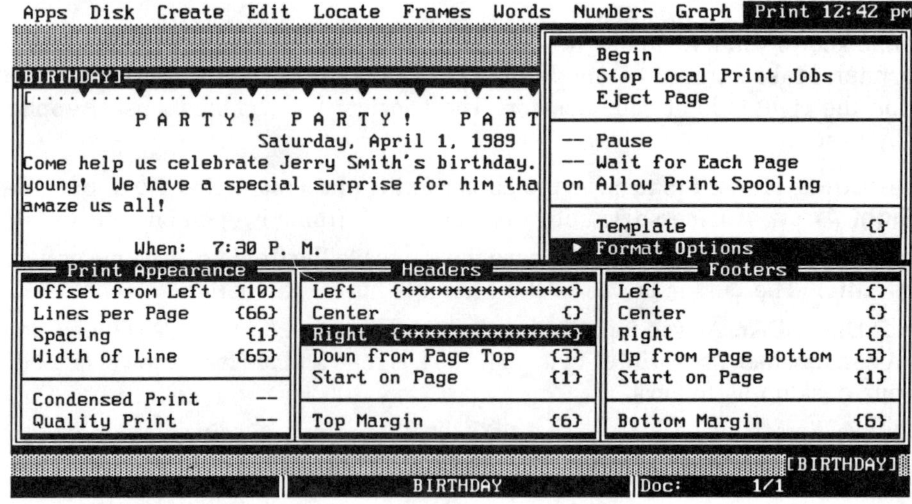

7. Press **Esc** to get out of the submenu.
8. {Press **Ctrl-P**}. Press **Ins** to move the cursor to the Main Menu line again. The Print Menu frame is open on your desktop.
9. {Press **Ctrl-B**}. Using the arrow (cursor) keys, position the cursor on the Begin option and press **Enter**. The printout resembles the following example.

```
***************                       ***************

       P A R T Y !   P A R T Y !   P A R T Y !
                Saturday, April 1, 1989
Come help us celebrate Jerry Smith's birthday.  He'll be 42 years
young!  We have a special surprise for him that will dazzle and
amaze us all!

           When: 7:30 P. M.
           Where: 111 West 11th # 102

Don't miss the fun!
```

10. Press **Del** to remove the document from your desktop.
11. {Press **Ctrl-D**}. Press **Ins** to move the cursor to the Main Menu line. Next, press the arrow (cursor) keys until the Disk Menu frame is open on your desktop.
12. {Press **Ctrl-Q**}. Using the arrow keys again, position the cursor on the QUIT Framework option and press **Enter**. Type **Y** when asked if you are sure you want to quit Framework III. This ends your Framework III session.
13. Turn to Module 35 to continue the learning sequence.

Module 37

FORMAT OPTIONS (PRINT APPEARANCE)

DESCRIPTION

This set of options lets you tell Framework III the general positioning of each page in your document. For example, specify the number of lines you want printed on each page. This is especially important if you're using paper that is only 8½ inches long.

These options are available through the Format Options submenu of the Print Menu frame. Notice the Print Appearance section on the left side of the submenu.

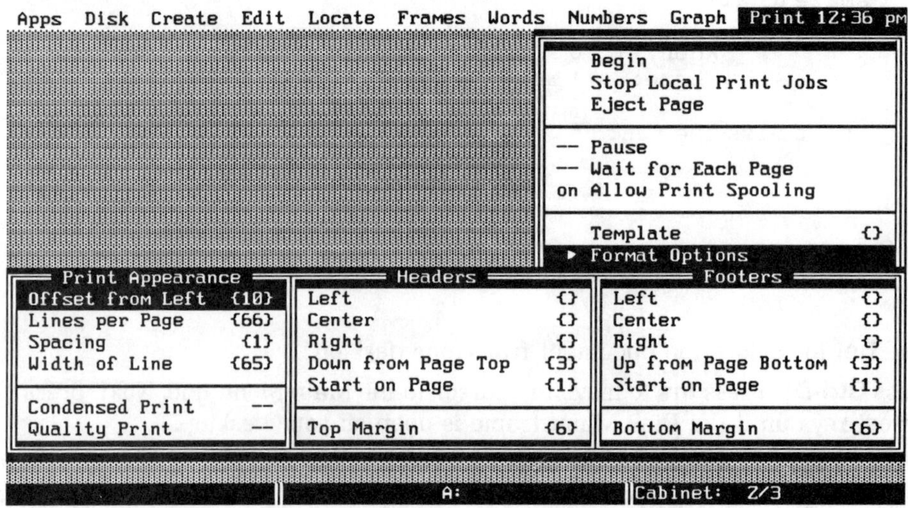

Specify the number of characters between left edge of page and left margin

When the submenu is opened, the cursor is usually located in the Print Appearance section of the submenu. If not, press Left Arrow to move the cursor to the Print Appearance section. Then position it on the option you want and press Enter. Type or change the value of the option and press Enter.

Offset From Left {10} Position the cursor on this option and press Enter. The cursor moves to the bottom of your screen. Type the number of blank spaces you want for the right margin and press Enter, otherwise, when printing the document, Framework III automatically positions each page of the document with a left margin of 10 spaces.

Lines Per Page {66} This option is changed like the Offset from Left option. Use it to tell Framework III how many lines the printer must move from one paper perforation to the next. Framework III is preset to allocate 66 lines per page.

Spacing {1} Select this option and type 2 if you wish Framework III to double-space each line of the document. Even though the document is single-spaced on the screen, changing this option lets you insert blank lines between each typed line.

Width of Line {65} Use this option to set the right margin of your printed page. The number within the braces is the maximum number of characters you want printed across each line. It is preset to print only 65 characters across.

Condensed Print Position the cursor on this option and press Enter. The word "on" or dashes (off) appear to the right of this option. If you have a dot matrix printer, turn this option on when you want to print the document in a very small print font. It is preset to dashes (off).

Quality Print This option is selected like the Condensed Print option. When turned on, your dot matrix printer uses the near letter quality font. It is preset to dashes (off).

APPLICATIONS

Change these options when you don't want to use Framework III's preset values. Each option helps you print your document the way you want.

Change any of these options until the document prints properly and save the frame on disk. The next time you print the document, all options remain as they were when you saved the frame.

TYPICAL OPERATION

This example shows you how to use the Print Appearance options of the Format Options submenu. Turn on your printer. Make sure that your desktop is clean and the cursor is positioned on a drive indicator on the right side of your desktop. The shortcut key combinations, if applicable, are enclosed by braces.

1. {Press **Ctrl-D**}. Press **Ins** to move the cursor to the Main Menu line. Next, press **Left Arrow** or **Right Arrow**, if necessary, until the Disk Menu frame is open on your desktop.
2. {Press **Ctrl-G**}. Press **Up Arrow** to move the cursor to the Get File by Name option and then press **Enter**. The cursor moves to the Message line at the bottom of your desktop.
3. Type **B:BIRTHDAY**. As you type, notice that the braces next to the Get File by Name option fill. When finished, press **Enter** twice. The disk is read and the frame you specified is opened on your desktop.
4. {Press **Ctrl-P** and then **Ctrl-F**}. Press **Ins** to move the cursor to the Main Menu line. Next, press the arrow (cursor) keys until the Print Menu frame is open on your desktop. Press **Down Arrow** until the cursor is positioned on Format Options and press **Enter**.
5. If necessary, press **Left Arrow** to move the cursor to the Print Appearance section.
6. Press **Down Arrow** until the cursor is positioned on the Lines per Page option in the Print Appearance section and press **Enter**. The cursor moves to the bottom of the screen. Type

33 and press **Enter**. Then move to the Condensed Print option and press **Enter** to turn it on. Now your desktop resembles the following display.

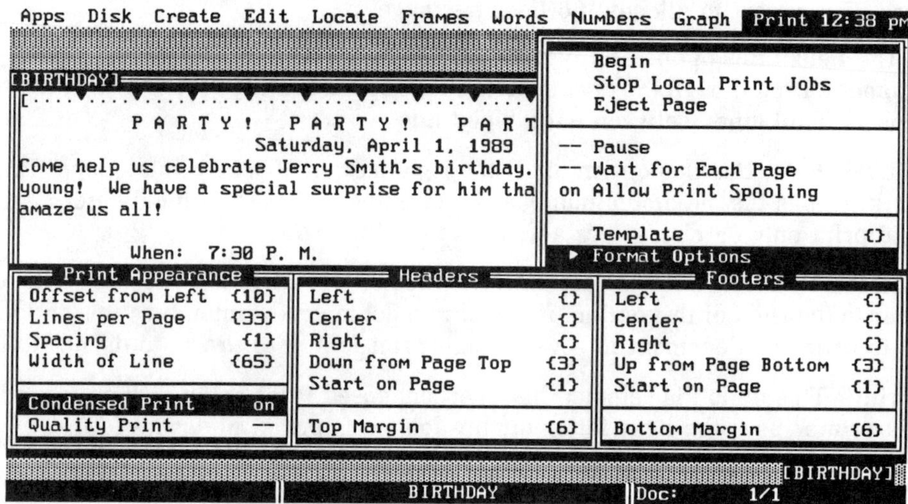

7. Press **Esc** to exit the submenu.
8. {Press **Ctrl-P**}. Press **Ins** to move the cursor to the Main Menu line again. The Print Menu frame is open on your desktop.
9. {Press **Ctrl-B**}. Using the arrow (cursor) keys, position the cursor on the Begin option and press **Enter**. The printout resembles the following example.

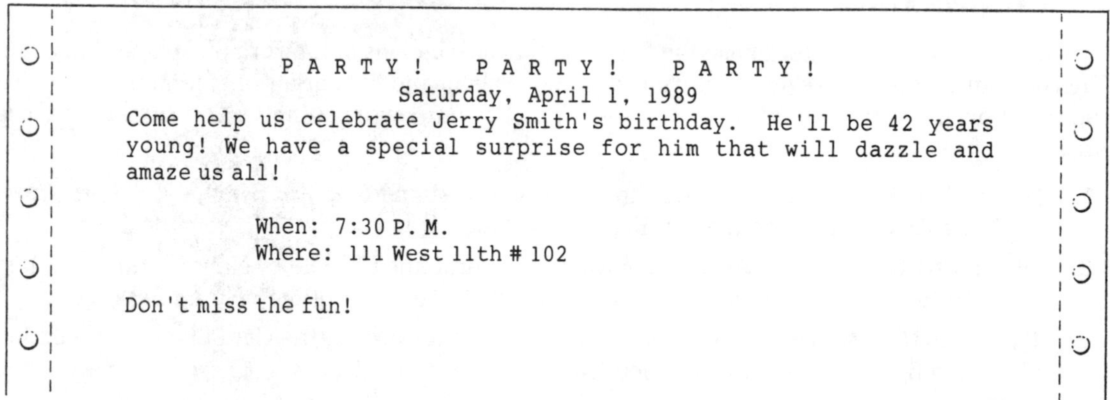

P A R T Y ! P A R T Y ! P A R T Y !
Saturday, April 1, 1989
Come help us celebrate Jerry Smith's birthday. He'll be 42 years young! We have a special surprise for him that will dazzle and amaze us all!

When: 7:30 P. M.
Where: 111 West 11th # 102

Don't miss the fun!

10. Press **Del** to remove the document from your desktop.
11. {Press **Ctrl-D**}. Press **Ins** to move the cursor to the Main Menu line. Next, press the arrow (cursor) keys until the Disk Menu frame is open on your desktop.
12. {Press **Ctrl-Q**}. Using the arrow keys again, position the cursor on the QUIT Framework option and press **Enter**. Type **Y** when asked if you are sure you want to quit Framework III. You have ended this Framework III session.
13. Turn to Module 36 to continue the learning sequence.

Module 38

FORMULAS INCLUDED

DESCRIPTION

When using the Search { } or Replace { } options, this option is used to find something within a spreadsheet or database frame. If the specified search value is used within the formula for a cell or field, Framework III presents the occurrence to you when this option is turned on.

Remember that the Contents Included option must also be turned on. Otherwise, Framework III ignores whatever is within a frame — that's where the formulas are kept.

The Formulas Included option is available through the Locate Menu frame.

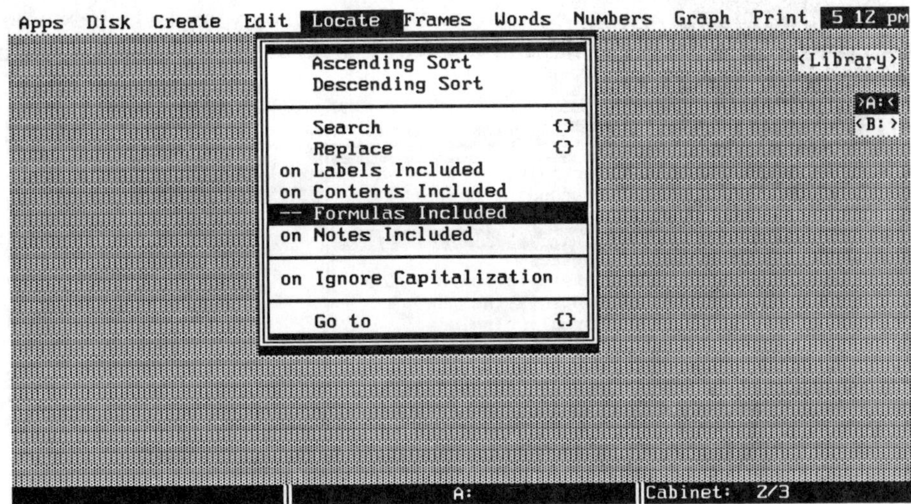

If ON, include formulas in Search/Replace

Selecting this option turns it on and off. This option is automatically turned off when you begin your Framework III session.

To turn it on or off, position the cursor on the Formulas Included option and press Enter. Then move the cursor to the Search { } or Replace { } option and press Enter. When Framework III looks through the document for the specified value, the formulas are included in the evaluation.

APPLICATIONS

The Formulas Included option is useful for spreadsheet or database frames. Select this option before doing a Search { } or Replace { } operation when you want to control what is evaluated by Framework III.

TYPICAL OPERATION

Use this illustration to learn how to use the Formulas Included option of the Locate Menu frame. Close any open frames on your desktop and position the cursor on your data drive indicator (drive B in this example). The shortcut key combinations, if applicable, are enclosed by braces.

1. {Press **Ctrl-D**}. Press **Ins** to move the cursor to the Main Menu line. Next, press **Left Arrow** or **Right Arrow**, if necessary, until the Disk Menu frame is open on your desktop.
2. {Press **Ctrl-G**}. Press **Up Arrow** to move the cursor to the Get File by Name option and then press **Enter**. The cursor moves to the Message line at the bottom of your desktop.
3. Type **B:CHECKBK**. As you type, notice that the braces next to the Get File by Name option fill. When finished, press **Enter**. The disk is read and the frame you specified is opened on your desktop.
4. {Press **Ctrl-L**}. Press **Ins** to move the cursor to the Main Menu line. Next, press **Left Arrow** or **Right Arrow** until the Locate Menu frame is also open on your desktop. Notice that the Formulas Included option is turned off. Press **Ctrl-F** to turn it on. Also, make sure the Ignore Capitalization is turned on.

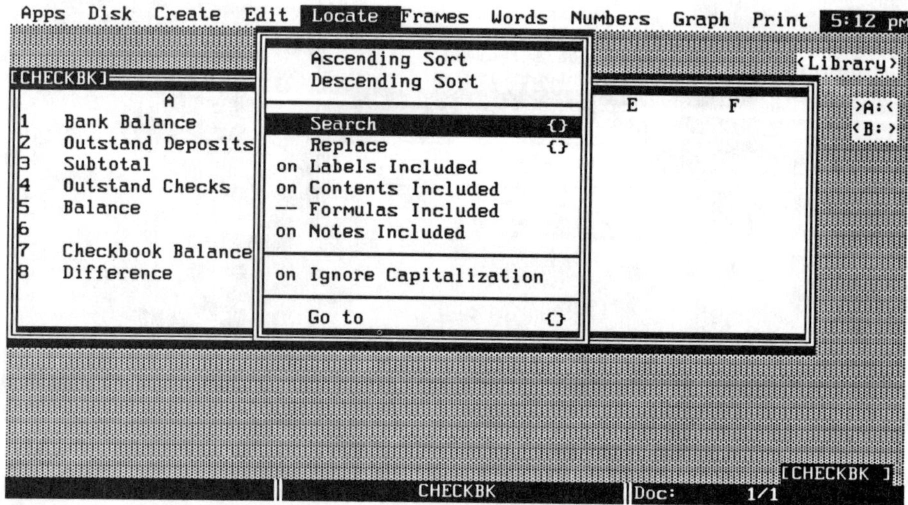

5. {Press **Ctrl-S**}. Press **Up Arrow** until the cursor is positioned on the Search { } option and press **Enter**. Type **B** and press **Enter**. The Locate Menu frame disappears from your desktop. Notice that the cursor is positioned on the frame border.

6. Press **Down Arrow** to see the cursor positioned within the frame on the word Bank. Continue pressing **Down Arrow** until the formulas are displayed on the Message line as a result of the Search { }. Press **Gray –** to return to the frame border.
7. {Press **Ctrl-L**}. Press **Ins** to move the cursor to the Main Menu line. The Locate Menu frame is again open on your desktop.
8. {Press **Ctrl-F**}. Press **Down Arrow** until the cursor is positioned on the Formulas Included option. Next, press **Enter** to turn it off.
9. {Press **Ctrl-S**}. Press **Up Arrow** until the cursor is positioned on the Search { } option and press **Enter.** Since B is already enclosed by the braces, press **Enter.** Notice that the cursor is positioned on the word "CHECKBK."
10. Press **Down Arrow** repeatedly to find all the occurrences of the Search { }. As you do so, notice that the formulas are not presented as part of the evaluation. When finished, Framework III reports that no other occurrence exists. When the Formulas Included option is turned off, Framework III ignores all formulas assigned to cells and fields.
11. Press **Gray –** to move the cursor to the frame border. Since the spreadsheet has not been changed, press **Del** to remove it from the desktop without saving it again on disk.
12. {Press **Ctrl-D**}. Press **Ins** to move the cursor to the Main Menu line. Next, press **Left Arrow** until the Disk Menu frame is open on your desktop.
13. {Press **Ctrl-Q**}. Using the arrow keys again, position the cursor on the QUIT Framework option and press **Enter.** Type **Y** when asked if you are sure you want to quit Framework III. You have ended this Framework III session.
14. Turn to Module 64 to continue the learning sequence.

Module 39

FRAME OPTIONS

DESCRIPTION

Desktop publishing software allows you to organize a document easily. Use the Frame Options submenu of the Frames Menu to provide desktop publishing capabilities for your Framework III documents. The submenu appears in the following display.

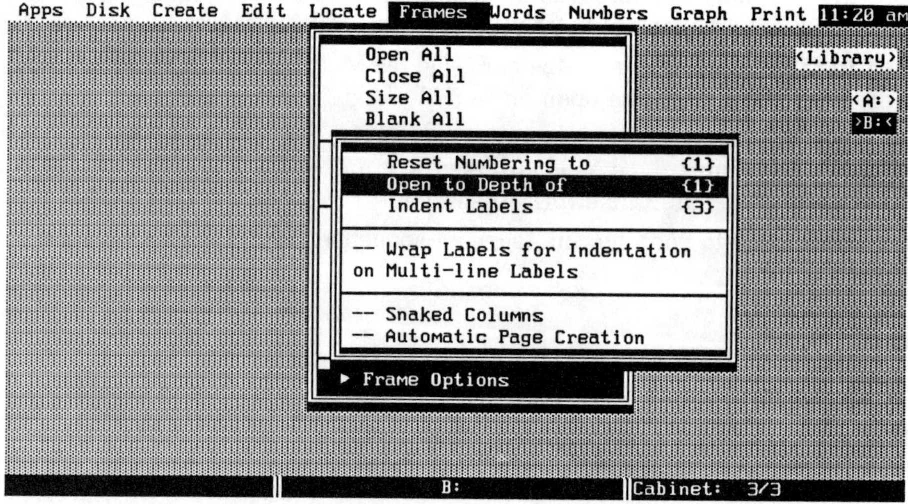

Set how many outline levels of current selection to display (close the rest)

Outline subframes are numbered automatically when you create them. Use the Reset Numbering to {1} option to change the current subframe number. Framework III renumbers all frames that follow the changed subframe automatically.

Control the number of outline frame levels that are opened automatically by changing the braced number in the Open to Depth of {1} option. When you set it to one, only major topic frames (e.g., 1 Body Building) are opened when you press F10 (View). Change it to two when you want to open two levels of frames (e.g., 1.1 Monday). All lower level frames are closed automatically.

Adjust the number of spaces for the left margin of an outline frame label by changing the braced number in the Indent Labels {3} option. For example, to indent all frame labels ten characters, move the cursor to the frame border of the outline, open the Frame Options submenu of the Frames Menu, select the Indent Labels option, and change the number to 10.

When you want to have the labels wrap to the next line automatically, select the Wrap Labels for Indentation option until it is turned on. Long labels are allowed for an outline; however, this option and the Multi-line Labels option let you change the way the label looks in Outline view.

Turn the Multi-line Labels option on when you want to see all lines of the outline labels. Otherwise, Framework III shows only the first line of the label while in Outline view. You must press F9 (Zoom) to see all label lines.

Select the Snaked Columns option when you want information to scroll from one outline subframe to the next. Position the cursor on the border of the major topic frame, open the Frames Menu, and select the Snaked Columns option until it is turned on. This sets all its subframes so when one fills up, the information adjusts to the next subframe. If you want only selected subframes to allow snaking, use the F6 (Extend) key to identify the subframes to be included in the snake activity.

Use the F3 (Drag) and F4 (Size) keys to adjust and arrange the subframes for a screen or printed page. The information that you type, move, or copy to the specified subframes shifts automatically. This technique lets you design a page of text that automatically adjusts itself around a graph or chart.

When using the Snaked Columns option, turn on the Automatic Page Creation option. When the page is filled, Framework III creates a duplicate page layout and continues the snaking activity on the new page.

APPLICATIONS

Use the options in the Frame Options submenu to design and change the page easily. For example, place a graph or chart on the page. Then size and organize text columns around the graph or chart so the printed document looks like a newspaper instead of a letter.

TYPICAL OPERATION

This example shows you how to use the Frame Option submenu of the Frames Menu frame. Make sure that your desktop is clean and the cursor is positioned on a drive indicator on the right side of your desktop. The shortcut key combinations, if applicable, are enclosed by braces.

1. {Press **Ctrl-C**}. Press **Ins** to move the cursor to the Main Menu line. Press **Left Arrow** or **Right Arrow** until the Create Menu frame is open on your desktop.
2. {Press **Ctrl-O**}. Press **Up Arrow** to move the cursor to the Outline option and then press **Enter**. An empty outline frame opens on your desktop.
3. Type **NEWSLETTER** and press **Enter** to name the new file.

4. Press **Gray +** to move inside the document frame and create the outline so it resembles the one in the following display. Press **Tab** to move to each item.

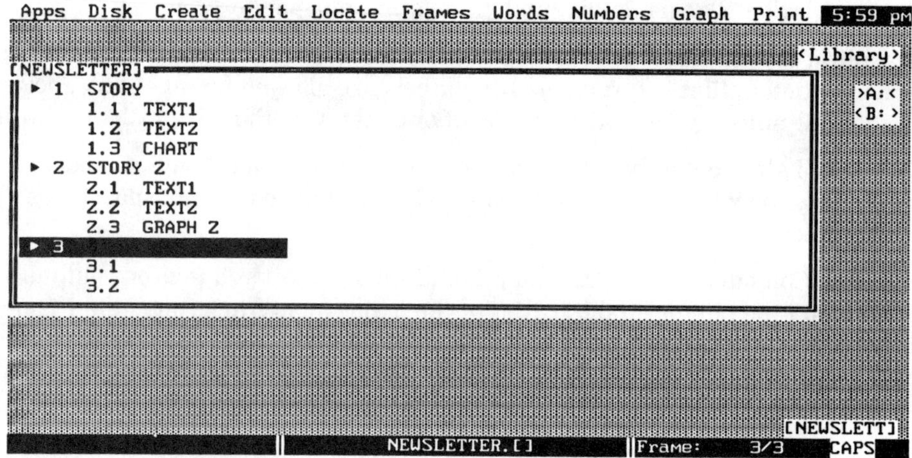

5. {Press **Ctrl-F** and **Ctrl-A**}. Press **Ins** to access the Main Menu line. Use the arrow keys to position the cursor on the Allow Free Dragging option. If it is turned off (dashes to the left of the option), press **Enter** to turn it on. The menu disappears from the desktop.
6. Position the cursor on the 1.1 subtopic and press **F6** (Extend). Press **Down Arrow** to extend the highlighted area to include 1.1 and 1.2. Press **Enter**.
7. {Press **Ctrl-F** and **Ctrl-F**}. Press **Ins** for the Main Menu. Open the Frames Menu. Then select Frame Options from the Frames submenu.
8. {Press **Ctrl-S**}. Position the cursor on the Snaked Columns option and press **Enter**. The message line reports that the snaked columns capability is turned on.
9. Move the cursor to the Story 1 line and press **F10** (View). Then press **F9** (Zoom) so all frames are available on the screen.
10. Press **F6** (Select) and highlight all three frames. Then press **Enter**. Press **F4** (Size) to help you resize the width of all three frames and press **Enter**. Press **Down Arrow** and then press **F3** (Drag) to move frame 1.3 to the top right and 1.2 to the lower right side of the screen. Continue sizing and dragging until the frame layout resembles the one in the following display. (Frame 1.1 is the long one on the left side, frame 1.3 is the top right, and 1.2 is the lower right.)

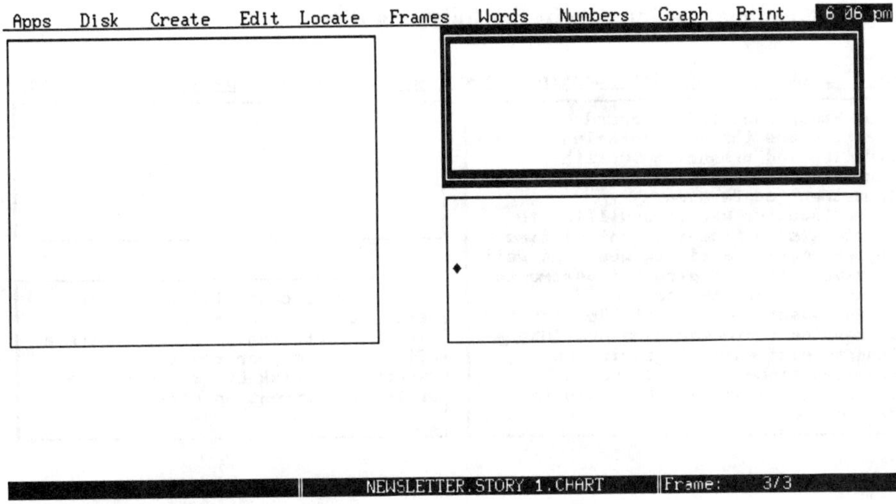

11. Move the cursor to the 1.1 frame border and press **Gray +**. Type the following information into the open frame. When frame 1.1 is filled, the cursor moves into frame 1.2 automatically.

Risk management and advanced planning are the key ingredients in creating and preserving wealth, according to strategists at a recent investment conference.

An investor who is unwilling to devote a significant amount of time to real estate activity would do well to steer clear of direct investments in homes or apartments.

An investor can limit the risk in a shopping center or warehouse where tenants must maintain their own premises since the landlord is typically responsible for only the external care.

One way of controlling risk in real estate is to invest in a limited partnership. However, these often produce poor results.

Reduce that risk by laying off part of the investment on others.

12. Compare your screen to the one in the following display.

```
Apps  Disk  Create  Edit  Locate  Frames  Words  Numbers  Graph  Print  6 30 pm

Risk management and advanced
planning are the key ingrediants in
creating and preserving wealth,
according to strategists at a recent
investment conference.
   An investor who is unwilling to
devote a significant amount of time
to real estate activity would do well
to steer clear of direct investments
in homes or apartments.
   An investor can limit the risk in
a shopping center or warehouse where
tenants must maintain their own
premises since the landlord is
typically responsible for only the
external care.

 One way of controlling risk in
real estate is to invest in a
limited partnership. However, these
often produce poor results.
Reduce that risk by laying off part
of the investment on others.

NEWSLETTER STORY 1.TEXT 2     Char:    26/6
```

13. Press **Gray –** three times to move the cursor to the Newsletter border. Then press **F10** (View) to return to the Outline View.
14. {Press **Ctrl-D** and **Ctrl-S**}. Press **Ins** to access the Main Menu line. Open the Disk Menu frame and select the Save and Continue option.
15. Press **Gray +**.
16. Use the arrow keys to move to the Story 2 topic line.
17. {Press **Ctrl-F** and **Ctrl-F**}. Select Frame Options from the Frames Menu. Turn on the Wrap Labels for Indentation and Multi-line Labels options.
18. Type the following in the label area and press **Enter**.

    This story is being done by Jerry Still. It is to cover
    the health benefits of various real estate classes.
19. Change the label by pressing **Spacebar** to allow editing. Change "Jerry" to "Terry" and press **Enter**.
20. Press **Spacebar** again. Then press **F9** (Zoom) to allow full-screen label editing. Change the label so it matches the following.

    This story is being done by Jerry Still. It is to cover
    the investment benefits of various real estate classes.
    This project is due by 9/1/89.

21. Press **Esc** to return to the Outline view.
22. Press **Gray –** to move the cursor to the Newsletter border.
23. {Press **Ctrl-D** and **Ctrl-P**}. Press **Ins**, open the Disk Menu, and select the Put Away option.
24. Press **Alt-F7** to play the Document macro. Answer the questions at the bottom of the screen by pressing **Enter** four times. A document opens on your desktop. This document has three columns across that allow snaking text. Change the size or position of any of the columns as done in the outline.
25. Press **Gray +** and type the text from a newspaper article to experiment with the form.
26. Press **Gray –** three times to return the cursor to the Document border. Press **Del** and answer Yes when asked if you really want to delete the frame.
27. {Press **Ctrl-D**}. Press **Ins** to move the cursor to the Main Menu line. Next, press **Left Arrow** until the Disk Menu frame is open on your desktop.
28. {Press **Ctrl-Q**}. Using the arrow keys again, position the cursor on the QUIT Framework III option and press **Enter**. Type **Y** when asked if you are sure you want to quit Framework III. This ends this Framework III session.
29. Turn to Module 60 to continue the learning sequence.

Module 40

GET FILE BY NAME { }

DESCRIPTION

Creating a frame full of work is usually a time-consuming activity. Using the Save and Continue option, you save it often on disk as you work so that you don't have to start from scratch again.

Later, when you want to use one of your saved frames, use the Get File by Name option to tell Framework III to get it for you. This option is available through the Disk Menu frame as in the following display.

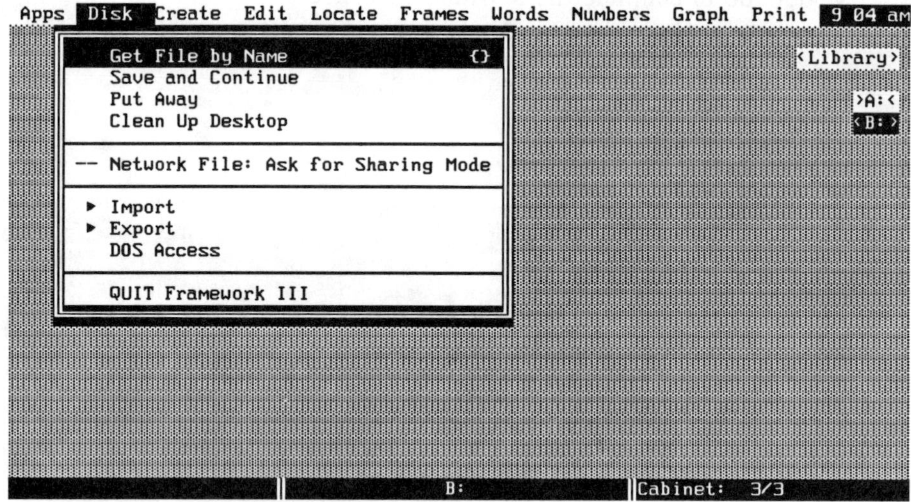

By selecting this option, Framework III lets you type the exact name of the frame (file). When you press Enter, the data disk is read and your frame is opened on your desktop.

If the file is not on the data disk, a new, empty frame is opened for you. To try again, press Del to delete the open frame, then select the Get File by Name option again. This time, however, type the drive you want Framework III to read, a colon, and then the frame name.

For example, if Framework III knows drive B is your data drive, that's the disk that is read. If you want the disk in drive A read instead, type A: before the name of the frame.

APPLICATIONS

You worked on a frame all day yesterday, got tired, and saved it on disk. Today you want to continue your work on that frame. It's on disk, so you need Framework III to get it for you.

There are two ways of reading a Framework III frame (file) which has been saved on disk. One is by using the Get File by Name option on the Disk Menu frame. The other is by opening a disk directory frame which contains filenames and selecting the one you want from the list.

Using the Get File by Name option is the easiest way — that is, if you remember what you named it. If not, tell Framework III to show you the names of all files on the data disk, and pick the one you want.

TYPICAL OPERATION

This exercise shows you how to tell Framework III to read a file from disk and open it on your desktop. Make sure that your desktop is clear and the cursor is positioned on one of the drive indicators. The shortcut key combinations, if applicable, are enclosed by braces.

1. {Press **Ctrl-D**}. Press **Ins** to move the cursor to the Main Menu line. Next, press **Left Arrow** or **Right Arrow**, if necessary, until the Disk Menu frame is open on your desktop.
2. {Press **Ctrl-G**}. Press **Up Arrow** to move the cursor to the Get File by Name option and then press **Enter**. The cursor moves to the Message line at the bottom of your desktop.
3. Type **B:BIRTHDAY.FW3**. As you type, notice that the braces next to the Get File by Name option fill. When finished, press **Enter**. The disk is read and the frame you specified is opened on your desktop as follows.

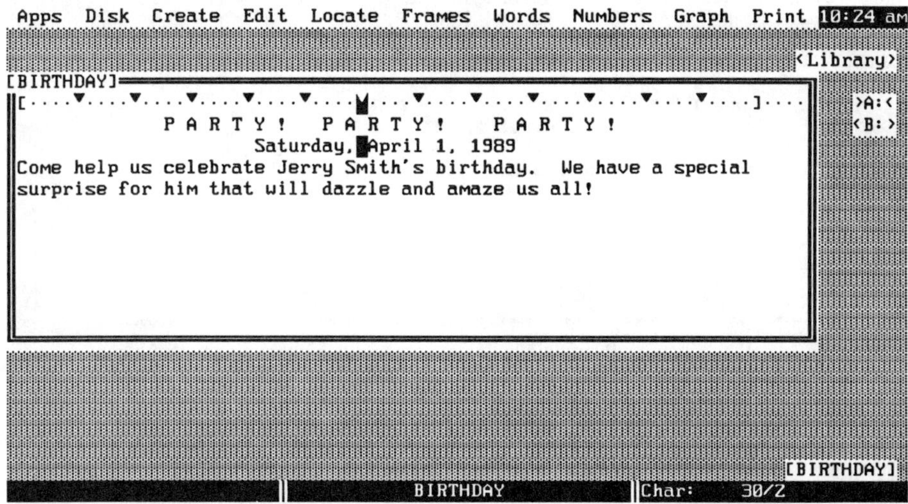

4. Press **Del** to delete the frame from your desktop. This does not affect the disk, it only cleared your desktop. Type "Y" in response to "Do you really want to delete frame(s)? (y/n).

5. Since the cursor is positioned on your data drive, press **Enter**. A frame opens on your desktop. Notice the following display.

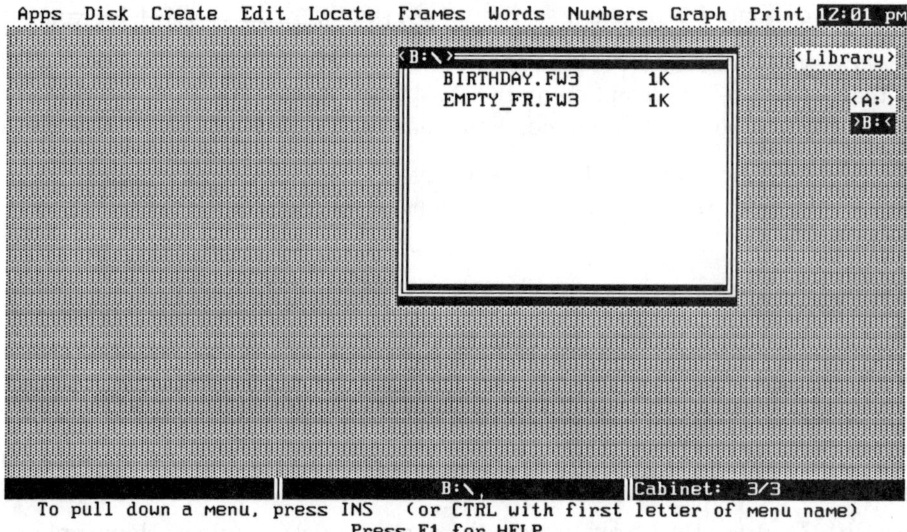

6. Since the cursor is positioned on the border of the open frame, press **Gray +**. Now you're inside the open frame. Since the cursor is already positioned on the filename BIRTHDAY.FW3, just press **Enter**. Another frame is opened on your desktop as in the following display.

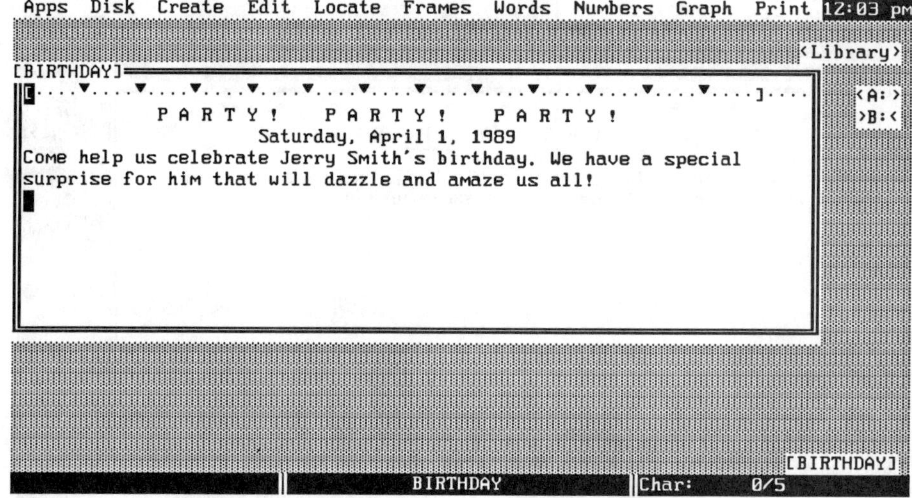

7. Press **Del** to delete the frame from your desktop. Again, this does not affect the disk, it only cleared the file from your desktop.
8. {Press **Ctrl-D**}. Press **Ins** to move the cursor to the Main Menu line. The Disk Menu frame is open on your desktop.
9. {Press **Ctrl-Q**}. Using the arrow keys again, position the cursor on the QUIT Framework option and press **Enter**. Type **Y** when asked if you are sure you want to quit Framework III. You have ended this Framework III session.
10. Turn to Module 5 to continue the learning sequence.

Module 41

GLOBAL OPTIONS

DESCRIPTION

Use the Setupfw program to select many of the Framework III options before beginning your session. Once the session is begun, use the Global Options Menu frame to adjust language, safety, and color.

If necessary, press the Ins key to access the menu at the top of your screen. Use the Left or Right Arrow to move the cursor on the Main Menu line from one menu option to another. Each time the cursor moves, the option's menu frame opens on the desktop.

Position the cursor on the Apps Menu option. Use the Up or Down Arrow to position the submenu cursor on the Global Options selection. The arrow next to the submenu option indicates another submenu frame of options. Press Enter to select the option and open the Global Options submenu as shown in the following display.

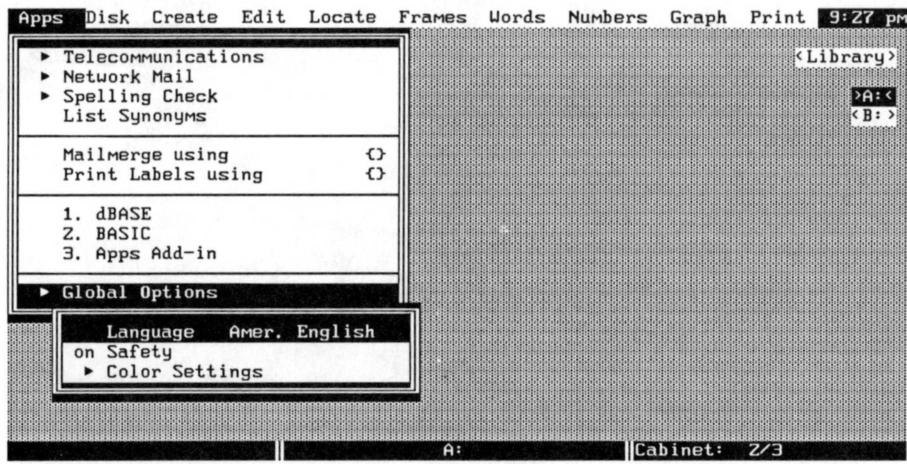

If you have purchased other language modules from Ashton-Tate, use the Language option to change to the appropriate language for proper spelling, synonyms, and hyphenation.

Select the Safety option to turn the safety feature on or off. When turned on, you are asked to verify the requested deletion activity. When turned off, the deletion occurs immediately. For example, a frame in the desktop tray is to be deleted. Position the cursor on the frame name and press the Delete key. If safety is turned on, you are asked if you really want to delete the frame. You must answer Yes to remove the frame from the desktop.

Use the Color Settings option to change the foreground and background colors for borders, frames, menus, clock, desktop, libraries, cabinets, status panel, message lines, ruler, negative values, and protected cells. Position the cursor on the foreground or background option for the item and press Enter to change the color. The message line describes the color settings as you press Enter.

APPLICATIONS

Use the Global Options submenu frame to modify your Framework III session. Change the language, set the safety feature, or customize the foreground and background color of each part on the desktop.

TYPICAL OPERATION

This example shows you how to use the Global Option submenu of the Apps Menu frame.

Make sure that your desktop is clean and the cursor is positioned on a drive indicator on the right side of your desktop. The shortcut key combinations, if applicable, are enclosed by braces.

1. {Press **Ctrl-A**}. Press **Ins** to access the Main Menu line. Use Left or Right Arrow to open the Apps Menu frame.
2. {Press **Ctrl-G**}. Press **Down Arrow** to move the cursor to the Global Options selection and press **Enter**.
3. {Press **Ctrl-C**}. Press **Down Arrow** to position the cursor on the Color Settings option and press **Enter**. The color selection frame on your screen resembles the following display.

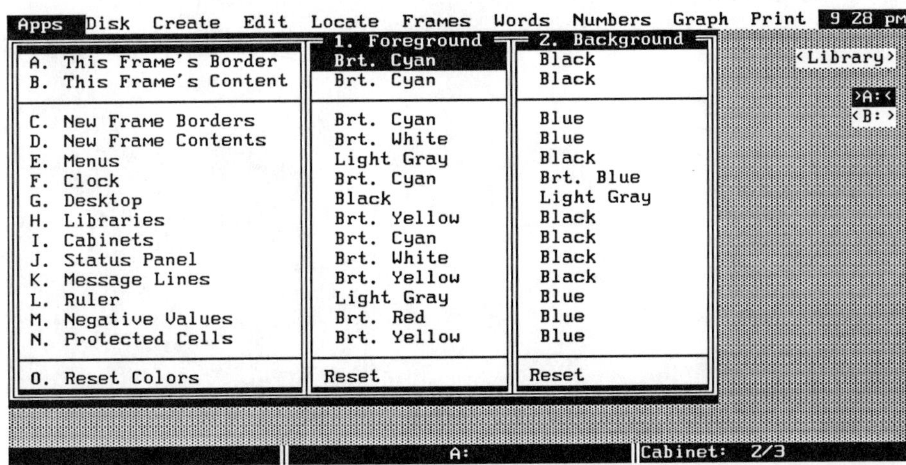

4. Use the arrow keys to position the cursor on the foreground column of the Menus line. Press **Enter** to see the color of the letters on the Main Menu line change. Notice the color information on the message line change each time you press **Enter**.
5. Press **Esc** to remove the color frame and return to the desktop.
6. Open the Global Options submenu frame and select the Safety option until it is turned on. Press **Esc** to return to the desktop.
7. {Press **Ctrl-D**}. Press **Ins** to move the cursor to the Main Menu line. Next, press **Right** or **Left Arrow** until the Disk Menu frame is open on your desktop.

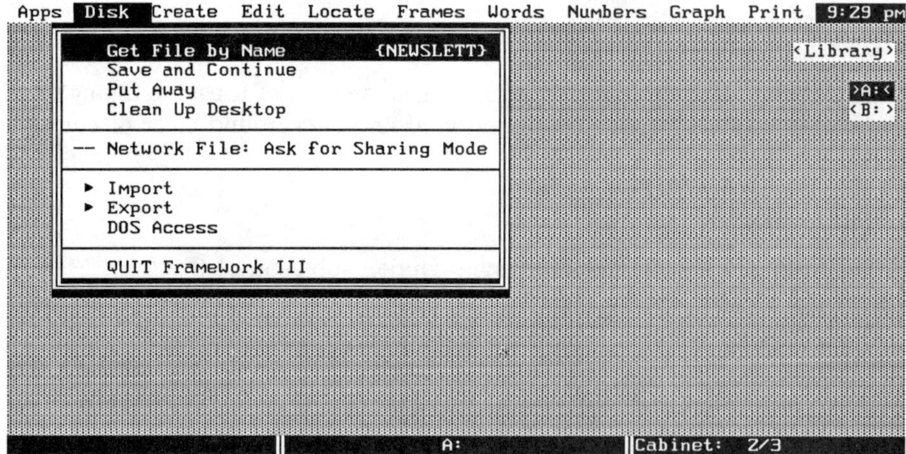

Bring specified file from disk and place beneath selected frame

8. {Press **Ctrl-Q**}. Using the arrow keys again, position the cursor on the QUIT Framework option and press **Enter**. Type **Y** when asked if you are sure you want to quit Framework III. This ends this Framework III session.
9. Turn to Module 30 to continue the learning sequence.

Module 42

GO TO { }

DESCRIPTION

The cursor (arrow) keys are used to move the cursor from one area to another on your desktop. The Go to { } option lets you tell Framework III exactly where to move the cursor.

For example, if you have a spreadsheet open and want to move the cursor from cell B1 to X10, just select the Go to { } option. Then type X10 and press Enter again. Framework III quickly moves the cursor to cell X10.

The Go to { } option is available through the Locate Menu frame.

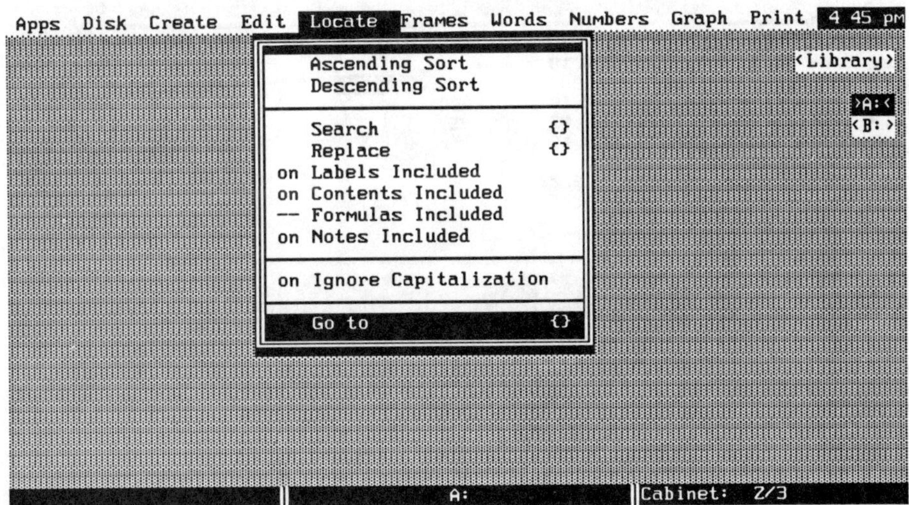

Go to the specified frame or cell

Use this option for outlines, spreadsheets, and databases. It helps you move quickly to a certain frame, cell, or field.

APPLICATIONS

This option is used for any type of frame except within a word processing frame. To use the Go to { } option, select it from the Locate Menu frame, type the frame, cell, or field identity, and then press Enter.

When used for outlines, specify the frame with which you need to work. Moving from one cell to another within a spreadsheet frame saves you time if you have far to go. The same is true of fields within a database.

TYPICAL OPERATION

Use this illustration to learn how to use the Go to { } option of the Locate Menu frame. Close any open frames on your desktop and position the cursor on your data drive indicator (drive B in this example). The shortcut key combinations, if applicable, are enclosed by braces.

1. {Press **Ctrl-D**}. Press **Ins** to move the cursor to the Main Menu line. Next, press **Left Arrow** or **Right Arrow**, if necessary, until the Disk Menu frame is open on your desktop.
2. {Press **Ctrl-G**}. Press **Up Arrow** to move the cursor to the Get File by Name option and then press **Enter**. The cursor moves to the Message line at the bottom of your desktop.
3. Type **B:CHECKBK**. As you type, notice that the braces next to the Get File by Name option fill. When finished, press **Enter**. The disk is read and the frame you specified is opened on your desktop as follows.

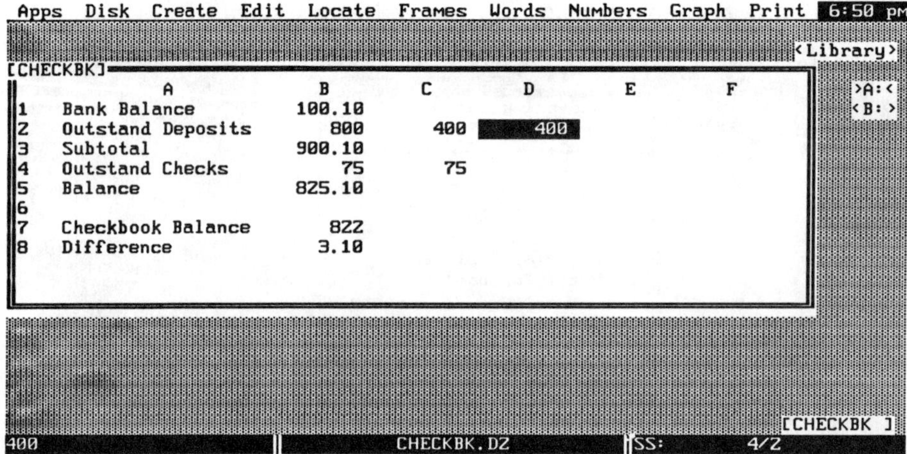

4. Press **Gray +** to move the cursor inside the open spreadsheet frame.
5. {Press **Ctrl-L**}. Press **Ins** to move the cursor to the Main Menu line. Next, press **Right Arrow** until the Locate Menu frame is also open on your desktop.

6. {Press **Ctrl-G**}. Press **Down Arrow** until the cursor is positioned on the Go to { } option and press **Enter**. Type **X4** and press **Enter**. The Locate Menu frame disappears from your desktop. Notice that the cursor is positioned on the cell you specified in the Go to { } option.

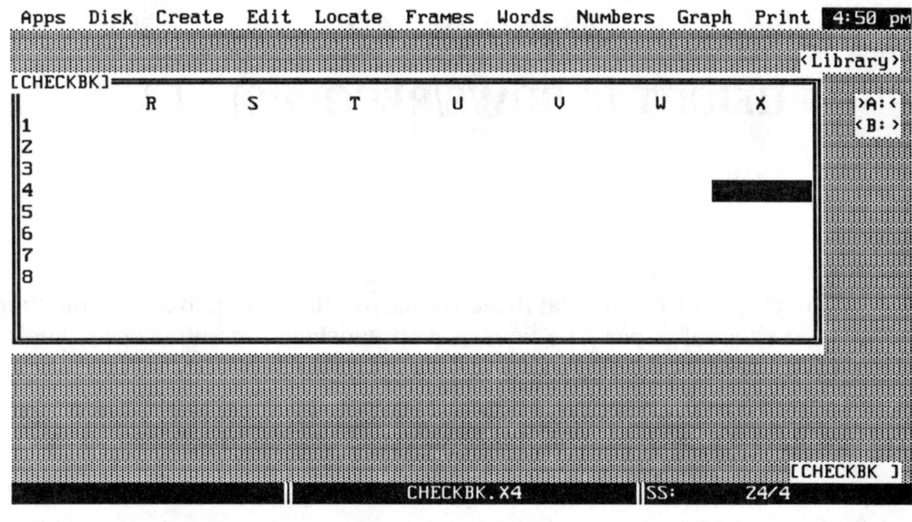

7. {Press **Ctrl-L**}. Press **Ins** to move the cursor to the Main Menu line. The Locate Menu frame is again open on your desktop.
8. {Press **Ctrl-G**}. Press **Down Arrow** until the cursor is positioned on the Go to { } option. Type **B2** and press **Enter**. The cursor is now positioned on cell B2.
9. Press **Gray –** to move the cursor to the frame border. Since the spreadsheet has not been changed, press **Del** to remove it from the desktop without saving it again on disk.
10. {Press **Ctrl-D**}. Press **Ins** to move the cursor to the Main Menu line. Next, press **Left Arrow** until the Disk Menu frame is open on your desktop.
11. {Press **Ctrl-Q**}. Using the arrow keys again, position the cursor on the QUIT Framework option and press **Enter**. Type **Y** when asked if you are sure you want to quit Framework III. You have ended this Framework III session.
12. Turn to Module 52 to continue the learning sequence.

Module 43

HEIGHT (# ROWS/RECORDS) { }

DESCRIPTION

Before creating a new spreadsheet or database frame, use this option to set the number of lines you want down your sheet of paper. The lines of a spreadsheet are called *rows*. Each line of a database is called a *record*.

If you use the {100} which is provided by Framework III, your file is created with 100 lines. By changing the number to 20, you can create a much shorter sheet of paper.

The Height option allows you to create a new spreadsheet or database which can hold more or fewer lines of information. Outlines and word processing frames are not affected by selecting or changing the number.

This option is available from the Create Menu frame which appears in the following display.

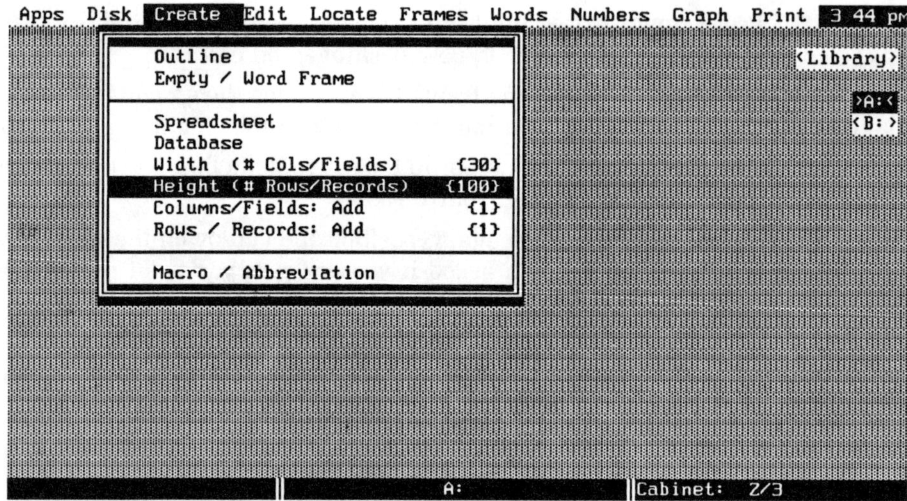

Set the number of rows/records for a new spreadsheet/database

Evaluate this option before creating a new spreadsheet or database since it determines the original size of your file. For example, you have 50 names of people and their phone numbers to store in a database. The 100 lines which Framework III automatically provides is too many for your information.

First, select the Height option and change the 100, which is the Framework III default (preset number), to 50. Next, review the Width (across) option just as you did the Height option. Then select the Spreadsheet or Database option to actually create your new file.

Remember that using this option does not affect the size of the frame on your desktop. The Height option only controls the number of lines a new file will have when you create it.

The frame size can be adjusted by the F4 (Size) key or the F9 (Zoom) key. By changing the size of the frame, you can see more of your file through the window. Each of the lines of your file is available to you when you scroll (move up and down) within your open frame.

If you create a new spreadsheet or database which is not big enough for your information, you can either create it again, or add new lines to the existing one. Your choice should be based on whether or not the current file is still empty.

To recreate it, first, delete the current one on your desktop by pressing the Del key. Next, select the Height option and change the number. Then create your new spreadsheet or database file. If you have already entered data into your file, the next choice is a better one.

To add new lines to your file, use the Rows/Records: Add option of the Create Menu frame. This option is covered in another module in this book.

APPLICATIONS

When you create a new spreadsheet or database, the size of the file is set at creation time. The Height option determines the number of lines (length or height) for your new file.

The number of lines (rows for a spreadsheet, records for a database) can be changed before selecting the Spreadsheet or Database option of the Create Menu frame. Framework III presets the number to 100 each time you begin a Framework III session. You can specify the number of lines you need by selecting the Height option, changing the 100 to the number you want, and then creating your new spreadsheet or database.

As you work with your new file, you may find that there are not enough lines for the information you need to keep. If this is the case, add new lines to the existing file. The new lines are added to the bottom of the file or inserted where needed by using the Rows/Records: Add option of the Create Menu frame.

The Height option is only for creating new spreadsheets and databases. It is available by opening the Create Menu frame.

TYPICAL OPERATION

This example creates a new spreadsheet which has five rows and 10 columns. Close any open frames on your desktop and position the cursor on one of the drive indicators. The shortcut key combinations, if applicable, are enclosed by braces.

1. {Press **Ctrl-C**}. Press **Ins** to move the cursor to the Main Menu line. Next, press **Left Arrow** or **Right Arrow**, if necessary, until the Create Menu frame is open on your desktop. Notice the Height and Width options.
2. Since the new spreadsheet is to have five rows, you need to change the number specified by the Height option. {Press **Ctrl-H**}. Move the cursor to the Height option by pressing the **Down Arrow** and press **Enter**. Notice that the cursor moves to the Message line.
3. Type **5** and press **Enter**. The 100 in the Create Menu frame has changed to 5 as in the following display.

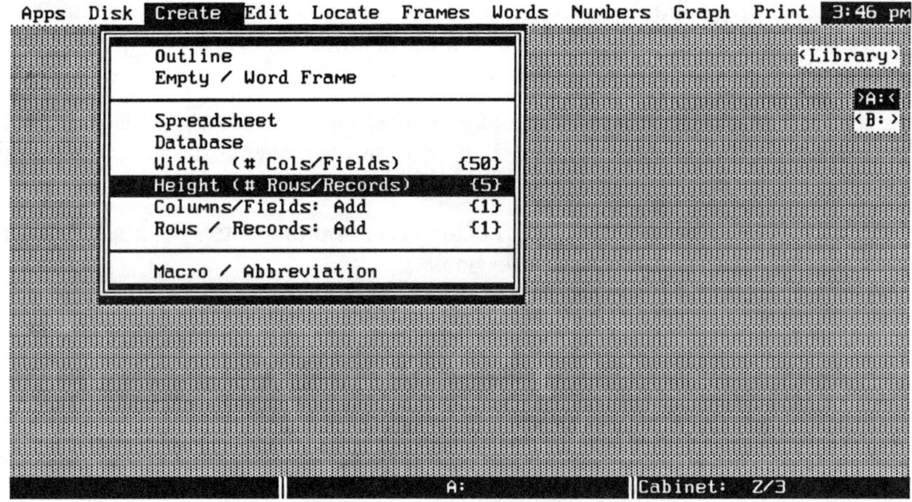

4. Since the new spreadsheet is to have 10 columns, change the number specified by the Width option. {Press **Ctrl-W**}. Move the cursor to the Width option by pressing the **Up Arrow** and press **Enter**. The cursor moves to the Message line.
5. Type **10** and press **Enter**. The 50 in the Create Menu frame has changed to 10.
6. {Press **Ctrl-S**}. Press **Up Arrow** to position the cursor on the Spreadsheet option. Press **Enter** to open the spreadsheet frame on your desktop. Notice that there are five lines or rows in your new spreadsheet. There are seven columns that you can see in your open frame although 10 columns are available.

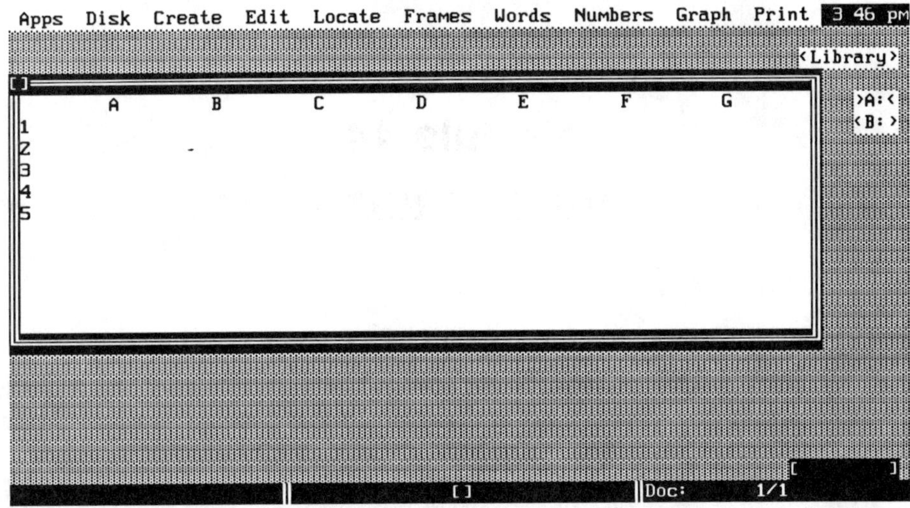

7. Since the cursor is still positioned on the border of the frame, press **Del** to delete the open frame from your desktop.
8. To create a new spreadsheet which has 10 rows, change the number specified by the Height option. {Press **Ctrl-C**}. Press **Ins** to move the cursor to the Main Menu line. The Create Menu frame appears on your desktop. {Press **Ctrl-H**}. Move the cursor to the Height option by pressing **Down Arrow**. Next, press **Enter**. The cursor moves to the Message line.
9. Type **10** and press **Enter**. The 5 in the Create Menu frame is now changed to 10.
10. Now it's time to create your new spreadsheet. {Press **Ctrl-S**}. Press **Up Arrow** to position the cursor on the Spreadsheet option. Next, press **Enter** to open the spreadsheet frame on your desktop. Notice that there are ten lines or rows in your open spreadsheet. There are seven columns that you can see in your open frame (ten columns are available).
11. If you want to save this spreadsheet on disk, refer to the Spreadsheet module. Otherwise, delete this frame from your desktop. Since the cursor is positioned on the border of the frame, press **Del** to delete the open frame from your desktop.
12. {Press **Ctrl-D**}. Press **Ins** to move the cursor to the Main Menu line. Using the arrow (cursor) keys, move the cursor to the Disk option.
13. {Press **Ctrl-Q**}. Press **Down Arrow** until you position the cursor on the QUIT Framework option and press **Enter**. Framework III asks if you are sure you want to end this session. Type **Y**. The system prompt reappears on your screen. This Framework III session is complete.
14. Turn to Module 88 to continue the learning sequence.

Module 44

HIDE BORDERS

DESCRIPTION

Hide Borders lets you remove or display frame borders. This is especially important when you want to print a document which contains subframes. Select this option through the Frames Menu frame.

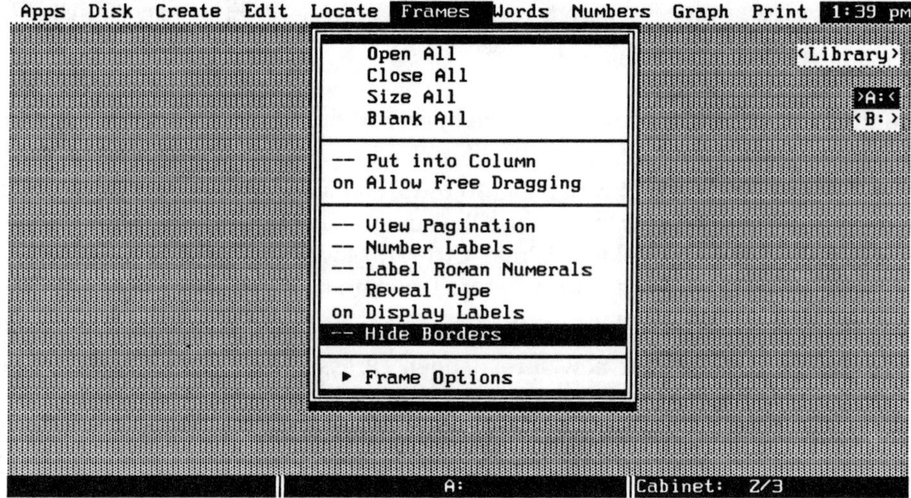

Hide the borders of the selected frames and all frames within them

The Hide Borders option is turned on and off when selected. If it is turned on, the border of the selected frame disappears from your desktop as in the following display.

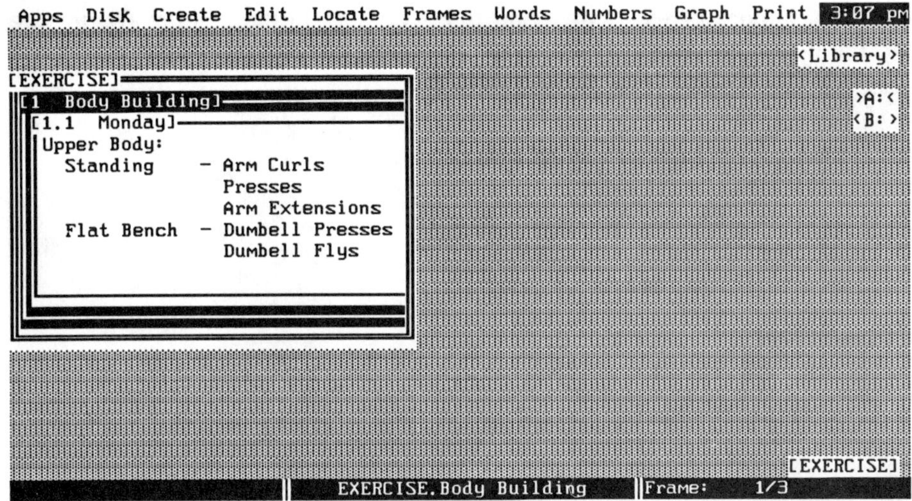

To help you keep track of which subframe is currently selected, Framework III provides a highlighted frame around it. Although it looks somewhat like a frame, it is not one.

When turned off, this option shows the borders on the screen so your desktop resembles the following display.

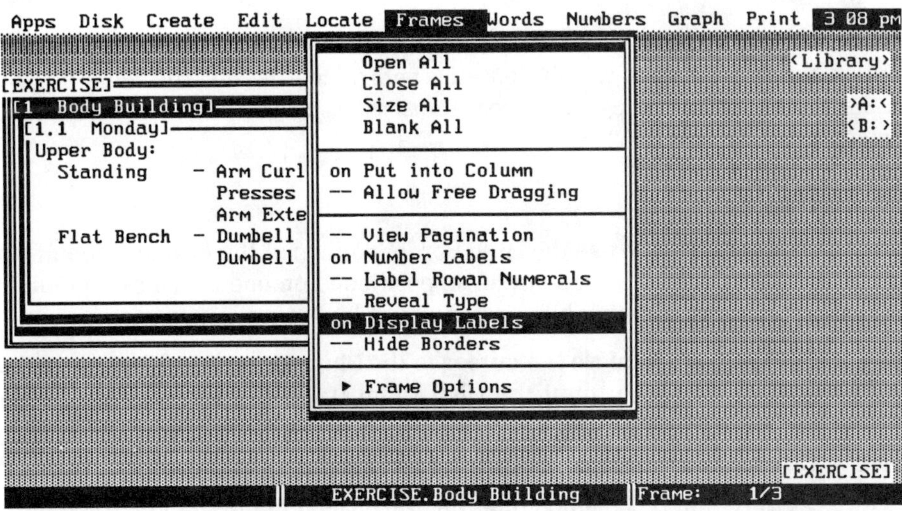

Display labels of frames within selection (in spreadsheet, display coordinates)

This is especially important when you send the document to the printer. By turning the Hide Borders on, the document prints as follows.

```
Upper Body:
  Standing   - Arm Curls
               Presses
               Arm Extensions
  Flat Bench - Dumbell Presses
               Dumbell Flys

Upper Body:
  Standing   - Arm Curls
               Presses
               Arm Extensions
  Flat Bench - Dumbell Presses
               Dumbell Flys
```

The printer skips an extra line for each side of an unhidden border. When the borders are suppressed, double spacing is avoided as shown.

APPLICATIONS

Use this option with any frame which contains subframes. It lets you show or hide frame borders on the screen. By removing them from the screen, they are ignored when you print the open document.

TYPICAL OPERATION

This illustration shows you how to use the Hide Borders option of the Frames Menu frame. Make sure that your desktop is clear and the cursor is positioned on one of the drive indicators. The shortcut key combinations, if applicable, are enclosed by braces.

1. {Press **Ctrl-D**}. Press **Ins** to move the cursor to the Main Menu line. Next, press **Left Arrow** or **Right Arrow**, if necessary, until the Disk Menu frame is open on your desktop.
2. {Press **Ctrl-G**}. Press **Up Arrow** to move the cursor to the Get File by Name { } option and then press **Enter**. The cursor moves to the Message line at the bottom of your desktop.
3. Type **EXERCISE**. As you type, notice that the braces next to the Get File by Name { } option fill. When finished, press **Enter**. The disk is read and the frame you specified is opened on your desktop. If it appears only in the desktop tray with the cursor, just press **Enter** to open it on your desktop.

4. Press **Gray +** to move the cursor to the inside of your open frame. Notice that the cursor is positioned on the first major topic of your outline.
5. Press **F10** (View). The contents of the subframe 1.1 is seen on your desktop.
6. {Press **Ctrl-P** and **Ctrl-B**}. Press **Ins** to move the cursor to the Main Menu line again. Next, press the arrow (cursor) keys until the Print Menu frame is open on your desktop. Turn on your printer and position the cursor on the Begin option and press **Enter**. The open frame prints as follows.

```
1.1 Monday

Upper Body:
  Standing    - Arm Curls
                Presses
                Arm Extensions
  Flat Bench  - Dumbell Presses
                Dumbell Flys

1.2 Tuesday

1.3 Wednesday

1.4 Thursday

Upper Body:
  Standing    - Arm Curls
                Presses
                Arm Extensions
  Flat Bench  - Dumbell Presses
                Dumbell Flys
```

7. {Press **Ctrl-F**}. Press **Ins** to move the cursor to the Main Menu line. Next, press **Left Arrow** until the Frames Menu frame is also open on your desktop. Notice that the Display Labels option is currently turned on.
8. {Press **Ctrl-H**}. Press **Up Arrow** or **Down Arrow** until the cursor is positioned on the Hide Borders option and press **Enter**. This causes the selected frame border and its subframe borders to disappear.
9. {Press **Ctrl-P** and **Ctrl-B**}. Open the Print Menu frame again and select the Begin option. This time the printed frame resembles the following.

```
Upper Body:
  Standing   - Arm Curls
               Presses
               Arm Extensions
  Flat Bench - Dumbell Presses
               Dumbell Flys

Upper Body:
  Standing   - Arm Curls
               Presses
               Arm Extensions
  Flat Bench - Dumbell Presses
               Dumbell Flys
```

10. Press **Gray –** to move the cursor to the frame border. Since the open frame has not been changed, press **Del** to remove the frame from your desktop without saving it on disk.
11. {Press **Ctrl-D**}. Press **Ins** to move the cursor to the Main Menu line. Next, press **Left Arrow** or **Right Arrow** until the Disk Menu frame is open on your desktop.
12. {Press **Ctrl-Q**}. Using the arrow (cursor) keys, position the cursor on the QUIT Framework option and press **Enter**. Type **Y** when Framework III asks if you're sure you want to quit Framework III. The system prompt appears on your screen. This ends this Framework III session.
13. Turn to Module 19 to continue the learning sequence.

Module 45

HYPHENS

DESCRIPTION

As you type, Framework III continues text on the next line automatically. There are times when hyphenation of a word is needed to make the document look better.

You have two choices. First, hyphenate words at the end of a line and adjust the rest of the paragraph. Or, second, let Framework III handle hyphenation when necessary.

Use the Insert Soft Hyphen option of the Hyphens submenu to identify possible hyphenation. Insert soft hyphens in long words to allow them to automatically hyphenate if editing forces the word to the next line of a document. The Hyphens submenu is available through the Edit Menu frame.

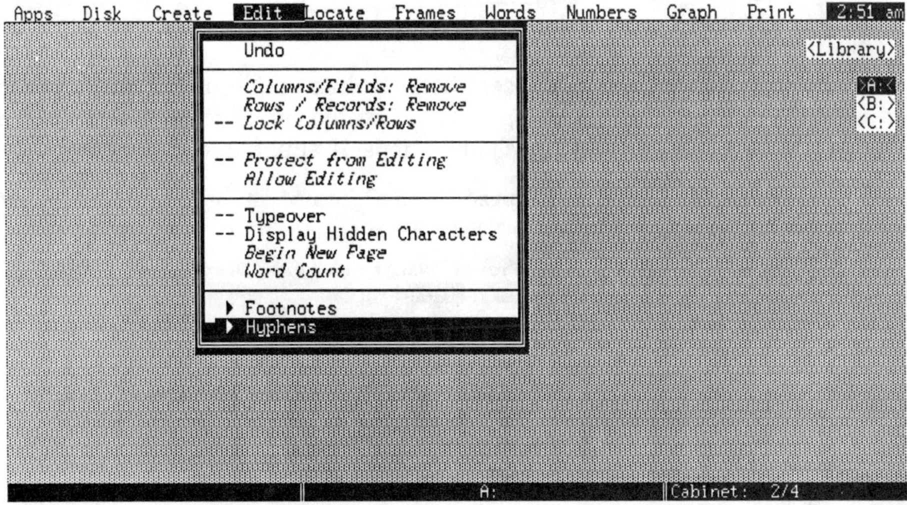

Choose options to hyphenate manually or automatically

The Hyphenate Selection option hyphenates the selected area or frame. However, the selected area does not maintain this hyphenation as editing occurs. Remember to hyphenate the selection again before you print or save the frame.

If you manually handle the word hyphenation, each line of the paragraph after the hyphenation must be adjusted. This is a time-consuming task which is compounded if you must change the paragraph again later.

Let Framework III do it. First, choose the word which might need to be broken to the next line. Position the cursor on the letter you want after the hyphen if the word must break. Open the Edit Menu frame, select Hyphens, and then select the Insert Soft Hyphen option.

The text does not look different to you, but Framework III has embedded a symbol. If the soft hyphenated word moves to the right margin when new text is inserted, Framework III hyphenates it automatically.

In short, you tell Framework III where a hyphen is allowed if necessary. If the word needs to be broken, Framework III does it. If the word fits on the line without hyphenation, Framework III does nothing to it.

APPLICATIONS

The Hyphens submenu is available for word frames. Use it when you want Framework III to handle word hypenation automatically.

Just identify words where hyphenation is acceptable by positioning the cursor on the letter you want after the hyphen. Then select an option from the Hyphens submenu.

Framework III embeds a symbol which is invisible to you unless you select the Display Hidden Characters option. Anytime Framework III encounters this hidden character within a word which crosses the right margin, the word breaks. Otherwise, the whole word moves to the next line.

TYPICAL OPERATION

This example shows you how to use the Insert Soft Hyphen option of the Edit/Hyphens Menu frame. Close any open frames on your desktop and position the cursor on your data drive indicator (drive B in this example). The shortcut key combinations, if applicable, are enclosed by braces.

1. {Press **Ctrl-D**}. Press **Ins** to move the cursor to the Main Menu line. Next, press **Left Arrow** or **Right Arrow**, if necessary, until the Disk Menu frame is open on your desktop.

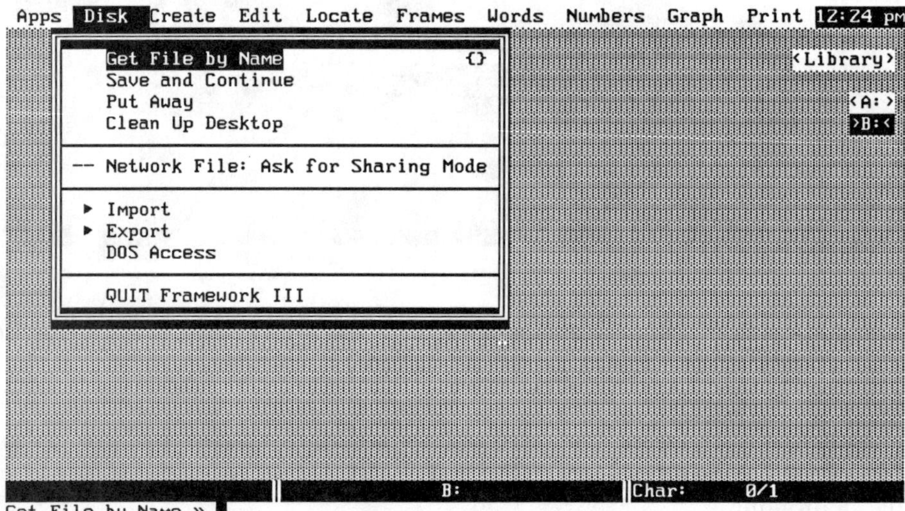

2. {Press **Ctrl-G**}. Press **Up Arrow** to move the cursor to the Get File by Name option and then press **Enter**. The cursor moves to the Message line at the bottom of your desktop.
3. Type **B:BIRTHDAY**. As you type, notice that the braces next to the Get File by Name option fill. When finished, press **Enter**. The disk is read and the frame you specified is opened on your desktop as follows.

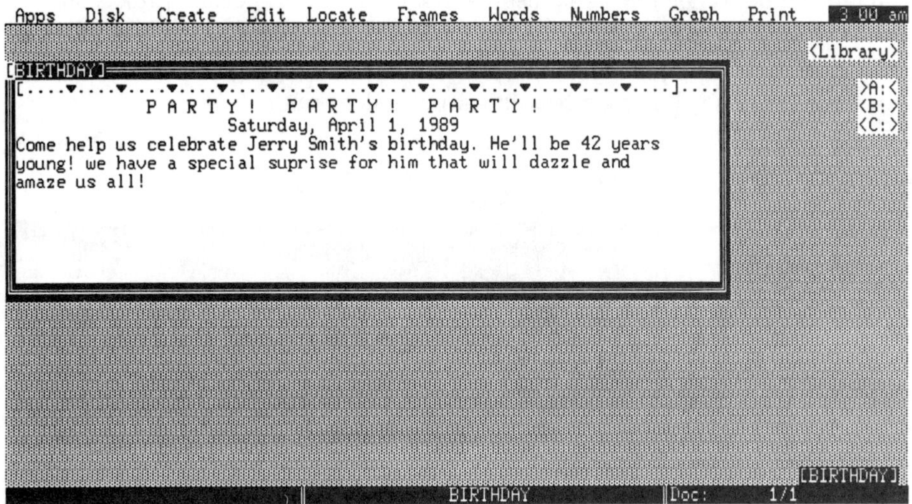

4. Press **Gray +** to move the cursor inside your open frame. Using the arrow (cursor) keys, position the cursor on the second "z" of "dazzle."
5. {Press **Ctrl-E**}. Press **Ins** to move the cursor to the Main Menu line. Next, press **Right Arrow** until the Edit Menu frame is also open on your desktop.

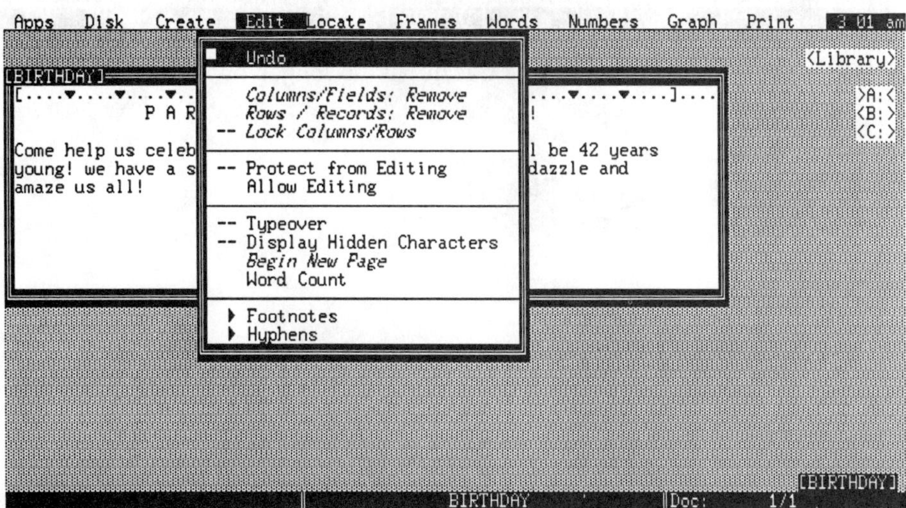

6. {Press **Ctrl-H**}. Press **Down Arrow** until the cursor is positioned on the Hyphens option and then press **Enter**. The Hyphens submenu appears.
7. {Press **Ctrl-I**}. Press **Down Arrow** until the cursor is positioned on the Insert Soft Hyphen option and then press **Enter**. The menu disappears but your text looks the same.
8. {Press **Ctrl-E** and **Ctrl-D**}. Reopen the Edit Menu frame and select the Display Hidden Characters option. When the menu disappears, the text has special symbols embedded within it. The wavy equals sign indicates a soft hyphen is available in the word "dazzle."
9. {Press **Ctrl-E** and **Ctrl-D**}. Reopen the Edit Menu frame and again select the Display Hidden Characters option so that your text looks normal again.
10. Press **Left Arrow** until the cursor is positioned on the exclamation point. Type **!** eight times. Framework III has hyphenated the word "dazzle."

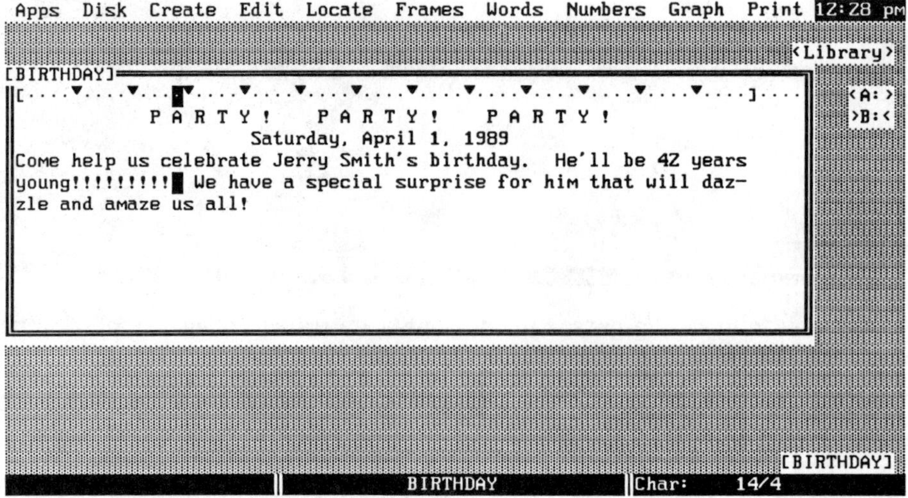

11. Press **Backspace** once and see that "dazzle" is no longer hyphenated.

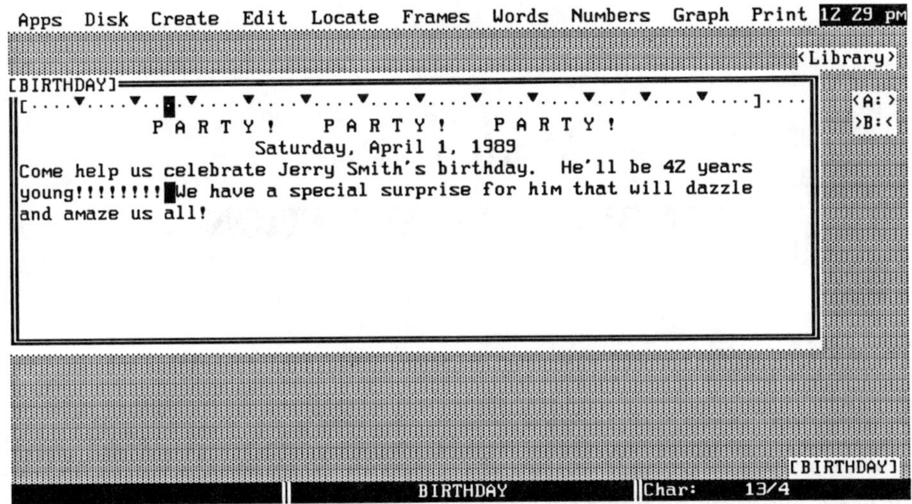

12. Since the frame is not changed (except in appearance), press **Gray –** to move the cursor to the frame border. Then press **Del** to remove it from your desktop. Type **Y** to delete the frame from your desktop.
13. Turn to Module 90 to continue the learning sequence.

Module 46
IGNORE CAPITALIZATION

DESCRIPTION

The words "Come" and "come" are not the same to the computer because the first begins with a capital letter while the second does not. When using the Search { } or Replace { } options of the Locate Menu frame, consider using this option too. By doing so, you tell Framework III that you want it to compare the letters regardless of case (uppercase versus lowercase).

This option is available for any type of frame. Access it through the Locate Menu frame.

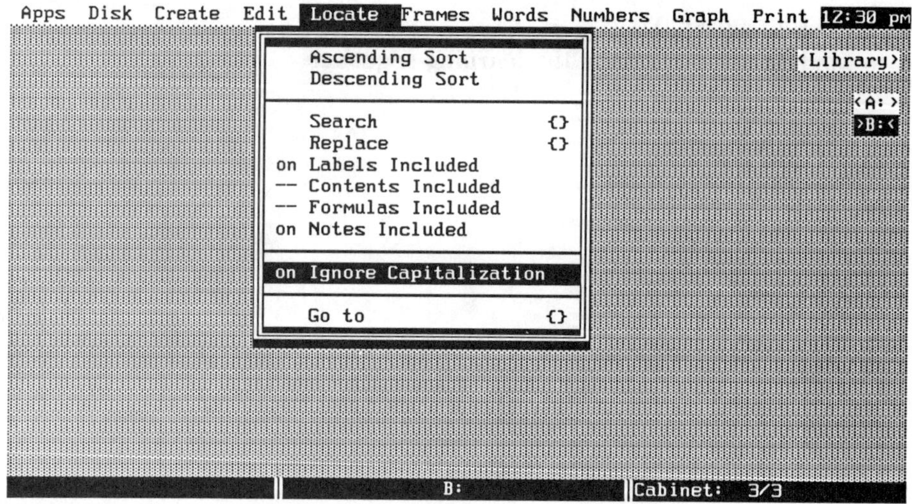

If ON, capitalization is NOT a factor in Sorting or Searching

This option is turned on or off when you position the cursor on it and press Enter. When on, "Come" and "come" are the same. When off, "Come" is not the same as "come."

Turn this option on or off before selecting the Search { } or Replace { } options of the Locate Menu frame. Framework III finds each occurrence of the word or phrase you type within the braces of these options. If Ignore Capitalization is turned off, the word must exactly match the contents of the braces. Otherwise, every occurrence is found and presented.

APPLICATIONS

The Ignore Capitalization option is available for any frame type. Use it with the Search { } or Replace { } options to find any combination of letters or numbers within an open frame.

When this option is turned on, Framework III ignores the case of the letters. Every occurrence of the text specified within the braces is found or replaced.

TYPICAL OPERATION

This example shows you how to use the Ignore Capitalization option of the Locate Menu frame. Close any open frames on your desktop and position the cursor on your data drive indicator (drive B in this example). The shortcut key combinations, if applicable, are enclosed by braces.

1. {Press **Ctrl-D**}. Press **Ins** to move the cursor to the Main Menu line. Next, press **Left Arrow** or **Right Arrow**, if necessary, until the Disk Menu frame is open on your desktop.
2. {Press **Ctrl-G**}. Press **Up Arrow** to move the cursor to the Get File by Name option and then press **Enter**. The cursor moves to the Message line at the bottom of your desktop.
3. Type **B:BIRTHDAY**. As you type, notice that the braces next to the Get File by Name option fill. When finished, press **Enter**. The disk is read and the frame you specified is opened on your desktop as follows.
4. Press **Gray +** to move the cursor inside the open frame.

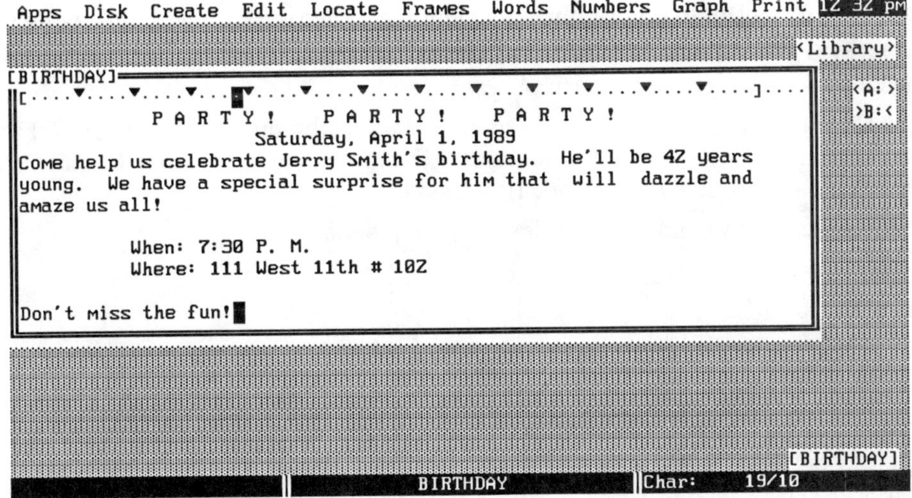

5. {Press **Ctrl-L**}. Press **Ins** to move the cursor to the Main Menu line. Next, press **Right Arrow** until the Locate Menu frame is also open on your desktop.
6. {Press **Ctrl-I**}. Press **Down Arrow** until the cursor is positioned on the Ignore Capitalization option and press **Enter**. It is now turned off as indicated by the dashes.

7. {Press **Ctrl-S**}. Press **Down Arrow** until the cursor is positioned on the Search { } option and press **Enter**. Type **Come** and press **Enter**. The Locate Menu frame disappears from your desktop. Notice that the cursor is positioned on the first occurrence of the word "Come." Press **Esc** to exit the Search { } operation.
8. {Press **Ctrl-L**}. Press **Ins** to move the cursor to the Main Menu line. The Locate Menu frame is again open on your desktop.
9. {Press **Ctrl-S**}. Press **Down Arrow** until the cursor is positioned on the Search { } option and press **Enter**. Type **COME** and press **Enter**. The Locate Menu frame disappears from your desktop. Notice that the cursor is positioned on the Message line. It says that the word was not found. Press **Esc** to exit the search.
10. {Press **Ctrl-L**}. Press **Ins** to move the cursor to the Main Menu line. The Locate Menu frame is again open on your desktop.
11. {Press **Ctrl-I**}. Press **Down Arrow** until the cursor is positioned on the Ignore Capitalization option and press **Enter**. It is now turned on as indicated by the word "on."
12. {Press **Ctrl-S**}. Press **Down Arrow** until the cursor is positioned on the Search { } option and press **Enter**. Type **COME** and press **Enter**. The Locate Menu frame disappears from your desktop. Notice that the cursor is positioned on the word "Come" within the open frame. This time Framework III found the word although the case was different. Press **Esc** to exit the search.
13. Press **Gray –** to move the cursor to the frame border. Since no changes were made to the open frame, press **Del** to remove the document from your desktop without saving it on disk.
14. {Press **Ctrl-D**}. Press **Ins** to move the cursor to the Main Menu line. Next, press **Left Arrow** until the Disk Menu frame is open on your desktop.
15. {Press **Ctrl-Q**}. Using the arrow keys again, position the cursor on the QUIT Framework option and press **Enter**. Type **Y** when asked if you are sure you want to quit Framework III. You have ended this Framework III session.
16. Turn to Module 80 to continue the learning sequence.

Module 47

IMPORT

DESCRIPTION

When using most software packages, you create files in a special format. To make one or more of those files available to another software package usually means you have to create it in the second package as well as the first.

However, that is not the case with Framework III. If you have created a document or file in another popular program (dBASE, DisplayWrite, MultiMate or WordStar, etc.) use the Import submenu to convert a file into a Framework III file.

The Import option is available through the Disk Menu frame. The supported packages are:

- Framework III
- dBASE
- IBM DisplayWrite
- WordStar
- MultiMate or MultiMate Advantage II
- WordPerfect
- ASCII Text
- Lotus 1-2-3
- Multiplan SYLK
- VisiCalc DIF

When selected, this option opens a submenu on your desktop.

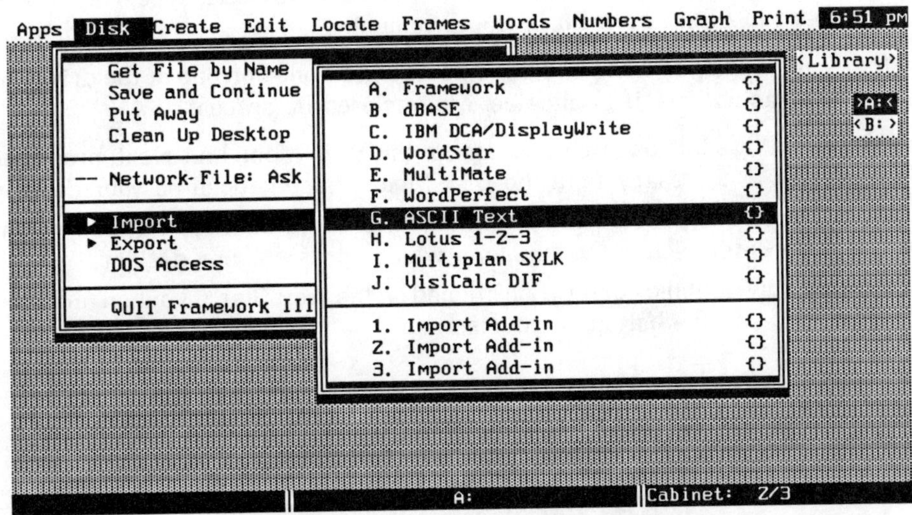

Read an ASCII text file into Framework III

If the file you want to import was created with one of the packages in the list, position the cursor on that option and press Enter. The cursor moves to the bottom of the screen. Type the name of the file you want to convert to a Framework III file and press Enter.

Framework III looks for the file. If found, it is checked for an expected format. If the format is correct for the selected option, Framework III checks the amount of available memory. If there is enough, the file is copied to a Framework file with the same name and .FW3 as the name's suffix.

Any error encountered during the checks that Framework III must make is reported to you. Usually you must make the decision to continue or quit. For example, if there isn't enough available computer memory, quit the import operation, make more memory available, and restart the import operation.

There are three Import Add-in options listed on the menu. If the program you used to create the file you want to import is not in the submenu, change one of these Add-in options to handle the import operation. Refer to the Add-in module in this book.

APPLICATIONS

It is not necessary to enter anything a second time when you need the same information for two software packages. If a file was created with another package, use one of the Import submenu options to make it available to Framework III.

Framework III is preset for several popular packages. If yours is not on the list, add it by replacing one of the Import Add-in options.

TYPICAL OPERATION

This illustration shows you how to use the Import submenu for a WordStar file.

1. Create and save a WordStar document called TEST on drive A. Type **This is a Wordstar file to be used in Framework III!** in the document.

Make sure that your desktop is clear and the cursor is positioned on one of the drive indicators. The shortcut key combinations, if applicable, are enclosed by braces.

2. {Press **Ctrl-D**}. Press **Ins** to move the cursor to the Main Menu line. Next, press **Left Arrow** or **Right Arrow**, if necessary, until the Disk Menu frame is open on your desktop.
3. {Press **Ctrl-I**}. Press **Up Arrow** and **Down Arrow** to move the cursor to the Import option and then press **Enter**. Notice the submenu which opens on your desktop.
4. Press **Down Arrow** until the cursor is positioned on the WordStar { } option and press **Enter**. The cursor moves to the bottom of your screen.

5. Type **TEST**. As you type, notice that the braces next to the option fill. When finished, press **Enter**. The disk is read and Framework III opens and closes several frames on your desktop. Each frame displayed includes a message on the Message line at the bottom of the screen. Framework III tells you there were no errors in the transfer. The new Framework III file is available in the open frame.

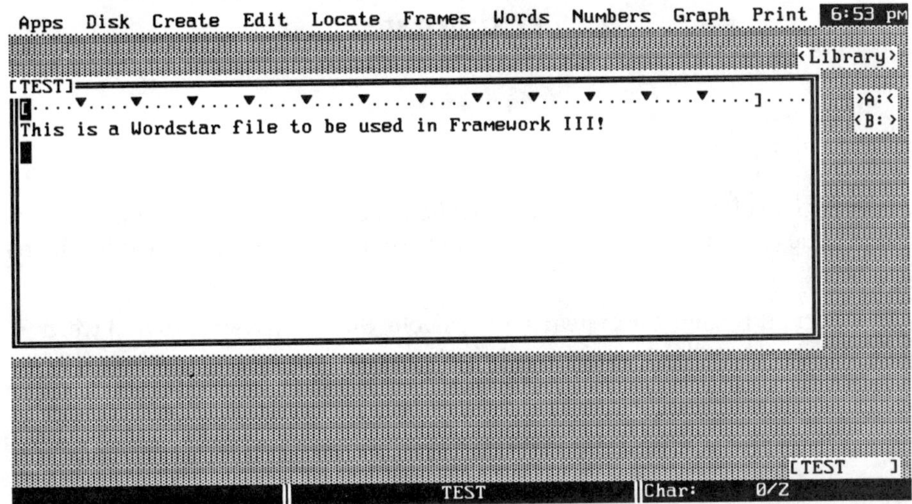

6. {Press **Ctrl-D**}. After all this work, you want to save the document on disk. Press **Ins** to move the cursor to the Main Menu line. The Disk Menu frame is also open on your desktop.
7. {Press **Ctrl-P**}. Using the **Up Arrow** key, position the cursor on the Put Away option and press **Enter**. This saves the new Framework III file on the disk and removes it from your desktop.
8. {Press **Ctrl-D**}. Press **Ins** again to move the cursor to the Main Menu line. The Disk Menu frame is open on your desktop.
9. {Press **Ctrl-Q**}. Position the cursor on the QUIT Framework option and press **Enter**. When asked if you really want to quit Framework III, type **Y**. This Framework III session is complete.
10. Turn to Module 32 to continue the learning sequence.

Module 48

JUSTIFY

DESCRIPTION

Books and newspapers often set text flush against both margins. This option eliminates the ragged look on the right side of your page. It inserts enough extra spaces within the text to cause a straight line appearance.

Doing this on a normal typewriter is nearly impossible. Smart typewriters and word processing software on computers handle centering, justification, spelling, and many other time-consuming activities easily.

This option is available for word processing frames. Access it through the Words Menu frame.

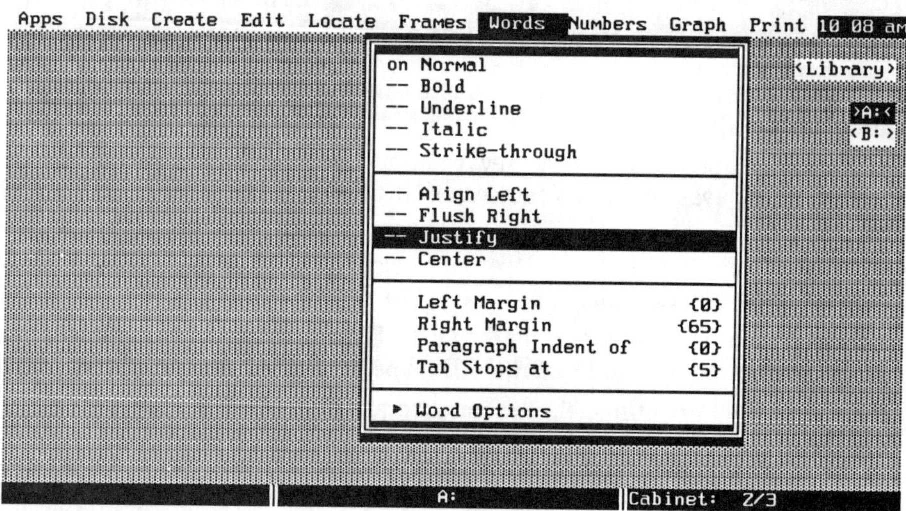

Framework III begins each new word processing frame with the Left and Right Margin options set so that Framework III knows when to move a word to the next line. The left side of your text forms a straight line at the left margin. The right side is left ragged.

When turned on, the Justify option forces the right side to line up too. As you type, this option immediately repositions the text within the left and right margins. Once turned on, it stays on until you select the Align Left, Flush Right, or Center option for your open frame.

As soon as one of the positioning options is selected, Framework III displays a message at the bottom of your screen. Framework III is telling you which option is currently turned on.

APPLICATIONS

This option is available for word processing frames only. Select this option when you want to align the text on both the left and right margins.

Once the Justify option is selected, positioning is automatic. You must select one of the other positioning options in the Words Menu frame to turn it off.

TYPICAL OPERATION

This example shows you how to use the Justify option of the Words Menu frame. Close any open frames on your desktop and position the cursor on your data drive indicator (drive B in this example). The shortcut key combinations, if applicable, are enclosed by braces.

1. {Press **Ctrl-D**}. Press **Ins** to move the cursor to the Main Menu line. Next, press **Left Arrow** or **Right Arrow**, if necessary, until the Disk Menu frame is open on your desktop.
2. {Press **Ctrl-G**}. Press **Up Arrow** to move the cursor to the Get File by Name option and then press **Enter**. The cursor moves to the Message line at the bottom of your desktop.
3. Type **B:BIRTHDAY**. As you type, notice that the braces next to the Get File by Name option fill. When finished, press **Enter**. The disk is read and the frame you specified is opened on your desktop. If the name only appears in the desktop tray with the cursor, press **Enter** to open it.

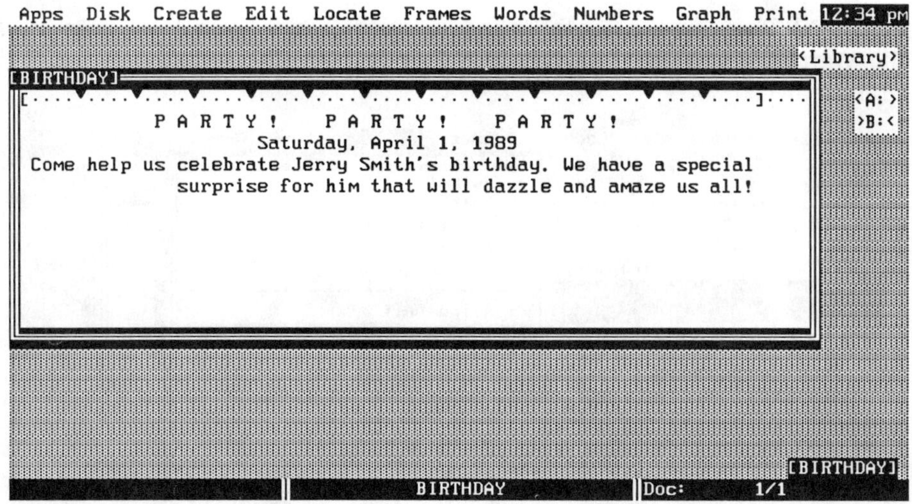

4. Press **Gray +** to move the cursor inside your open frame. Your cursor is positioned after the last change of the document. Press **Left Arrow** until the cursor is positioned on the "W" of "We have." Type **He'll be 42 years young!** and press **Spacebar** twice so that your document resembles the following display.

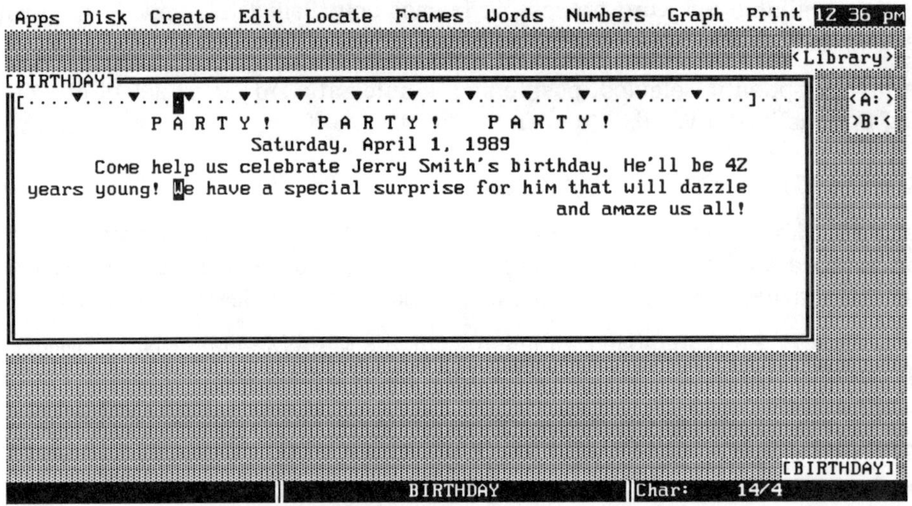

5. Use the arrow (cursor) keys to position the cursor on the "C" of the word "Come." Press **F6** (Extend) once and then press **Down Arrow** three times to highlight the whole paragraph. When done, press **Enter**.

6. {Press **Ctrl-W**}. Press **Ins** to move the cursor to the Main Menu line. Next, press **Right Arrow** until the Words Menu frame is also open on your desktop. Notice that the Flush Right option is currently turned on.

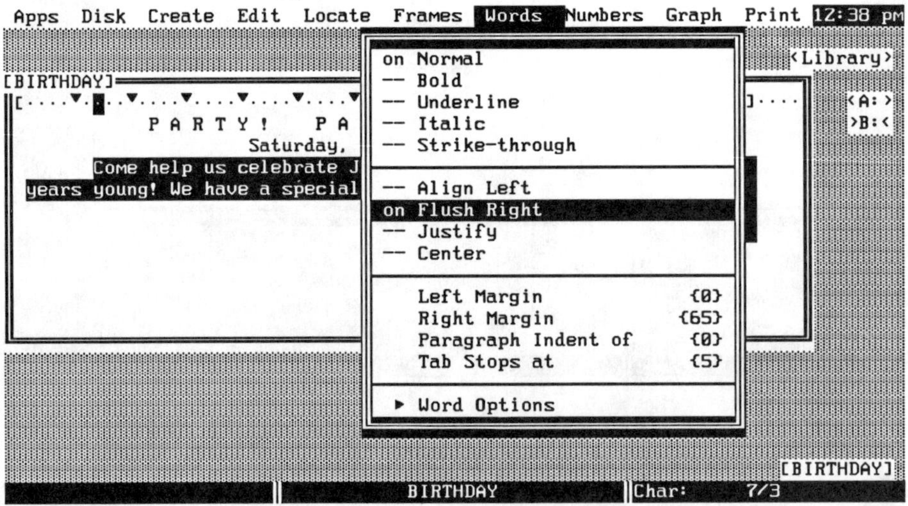

7. {Press **Ctrl-J**}. Press **Down Arrow** until the cursor is positioned on the Justify option. Press **Enter**. The Words Menu frame disappears from your desktop. Notice that the text forms a straight line on both sides of the open frame.
8. {Press **Ctrl-D**}. Press **Ins** to move the cursor to the Main Menu line. Next, press **Left Arrow** until the Disk Menu frame is also open on your desktop.
9. {Press **Ctrl-P**}. Using the arrow (cursor) keys, position the cursor on the Put Away option and then press **Enter**. The Message line displays the word "SAVING" and the disk drive lights. The frame name is not on your desktop.
10. Turn to Module 45 to continue the learning sequence.

Module 49

LABEL ROMAN NUMERALS

DESCRIPTION

When working with outlines, you often want the topics to have Roman numerals instead of Arabic. This option lets you change your outline's Arabic topic numbers (e.g., 1, 2, 3) to Roman topic numbers (e.g., I, II, III). At the same time, all subtopic numbers (e.g., 1.1, 1.2, 1.3) are changed to letters (e.g., A, B, C).

Select this option through the Frames Menu frame.

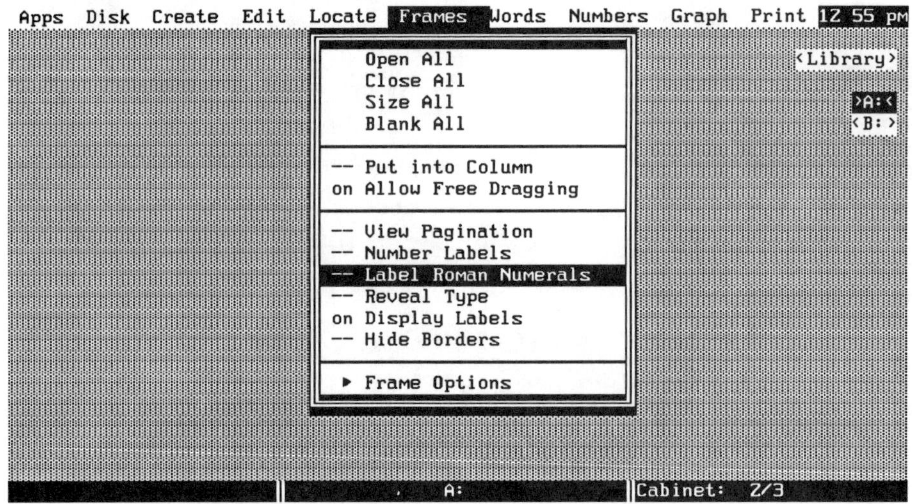

Use Roman Numerals to number the selected frames and all frames within them

The Label Roman Numerals option is turned on and off when selected. Framework III presets this option off so that Arabic numbers are used throughout the outline. Select this option at any time for an open outline frame.

APPLICATIONS

Use this option with any outline frame. It lets you change the topic and subtopic numbering system from Arabic to Roman style.

For example, topic number 1 is changed to I. Subtopic 1.1 is changed to A. The whole outline is affected unless you specify one topic or press F6 (Extend) to specify which part of the outline you want changed.

TYPICAL OPERATION

This illustration shows you how to use the Label Roman Numerals option of the Frames Menu frame. Make sure that your desktop is clear and the cursor is positioned on one of the drive indicators. The shortcut key combinations, if applicable, are enclosed by braces.

1. {Press **Ctrl-D**}. Press **Ins** to move the cursor to the Main Menu line. Next, press **Left Arrow** or **Right Arrow**, if necessary, until the Disk Menu frame is open on your desktop.
2. {Press **Ctrl-G**}. Press **Up Arrow** to move the cursor to the Get File by Name option and then press **Enter**. The cursor moves to the Message line at the bottom of your desktop.
3. Type **EXERCISE**. As you type, notice that the braces next to the Get File by Name option fill. When finished, press **Enter**. The disk is read and the frame you specified is opened on your desktop. If it appears only in the desktop tray with the cursor, just press **Enter** to open it on your desktop.
4. {Press **Ctrl-F**}. Press **Ins** to move the cursor to the Main Menu line. Next, press **Right Arrow** until the Frames Menu frame is also open on your desktop.

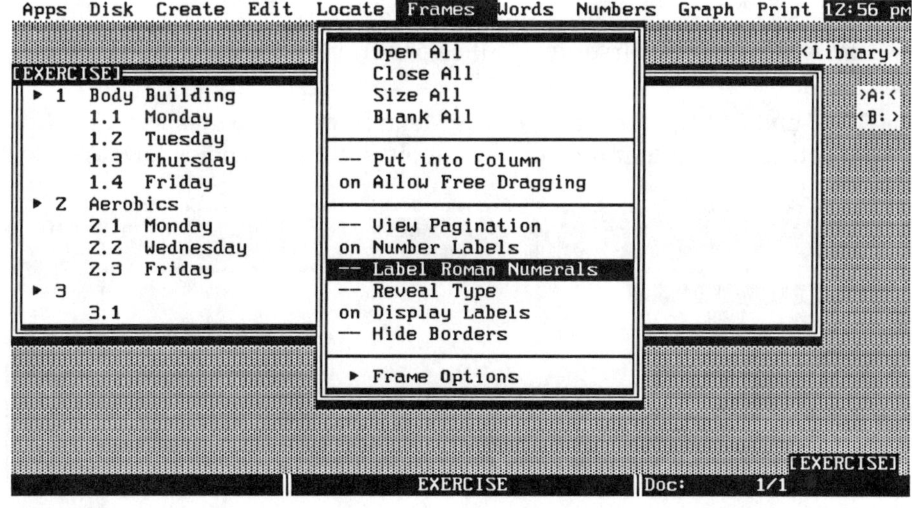

5. {Press **Ctrl-L**}. Press **Up Arrow** until the cursor is positioned on the Label Roman Numerals option and press **Enter**. The menu frame disappears and your outline is changed to resemble the following display.

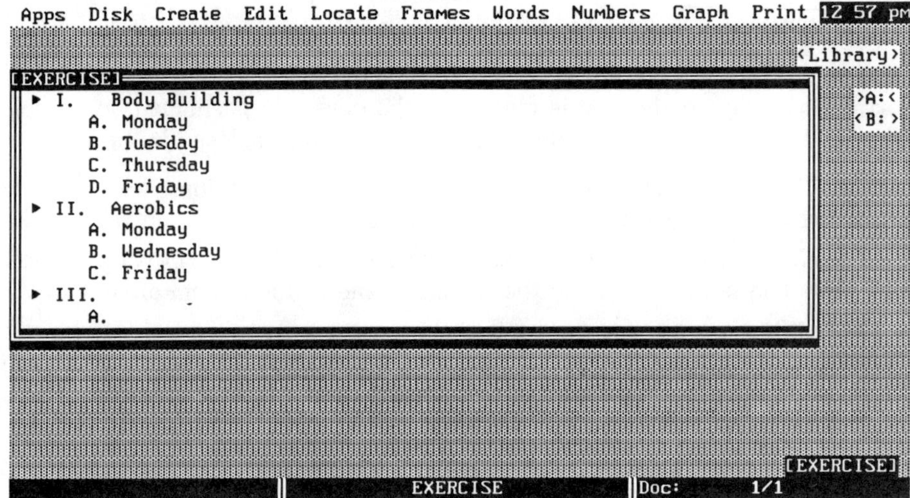

6. Press **Gray +** to move the cursor inside the open frame. Position it on the first topic of the outline.

7. {Press **Ctrl-F** and **Ctrl-L**}. Open the Frames Menu frame again and select the Label Roman Numerals option. Notice that only the first topic and its subtopics have Arabic numbers.

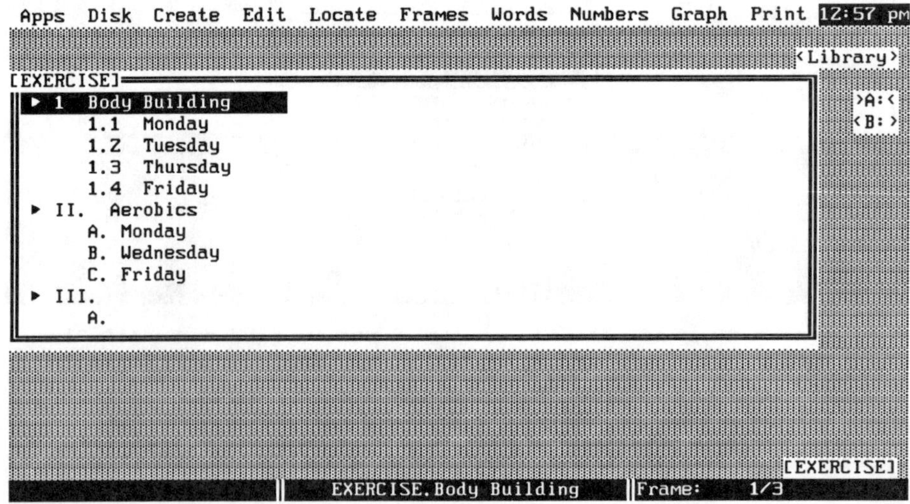

8. Press **Gray –** to move the cursor to the EXERCISE frame border.
9. The outline on your desktop has been changed but there is no reason to save this change on disk. Press **Del** to remove the frame from your desktop without saving it.
10. {Press **Ctrl-D**}. Press **Ins** to move the cursor to the Main Menu line. Next, press **Left Arrow** until the Disk Menu frame is open on your desktop.
11. {Press **Ctrl-Q**}. Using the arrow (cursor) keys, position the cursor on the QUIT Framework option and press **Enter**. Type **Y** when Framework III asks if you're sure you want to quit Framework III. The system prompt appears on your screen. This ends this Framework III session.
12. Turn to Module 59 to continue the learning sequence.

Module 50
LABELS INCLUDED

DESCRIPTION

When using the Search { } or Replace { } options inside a frame, only the contents of the frame are reviewed unless this option is turned on. Turn Labels Included on to include the frame labels during the search or replace activity.

The Labels Included option is available through the Locate Menu frame.

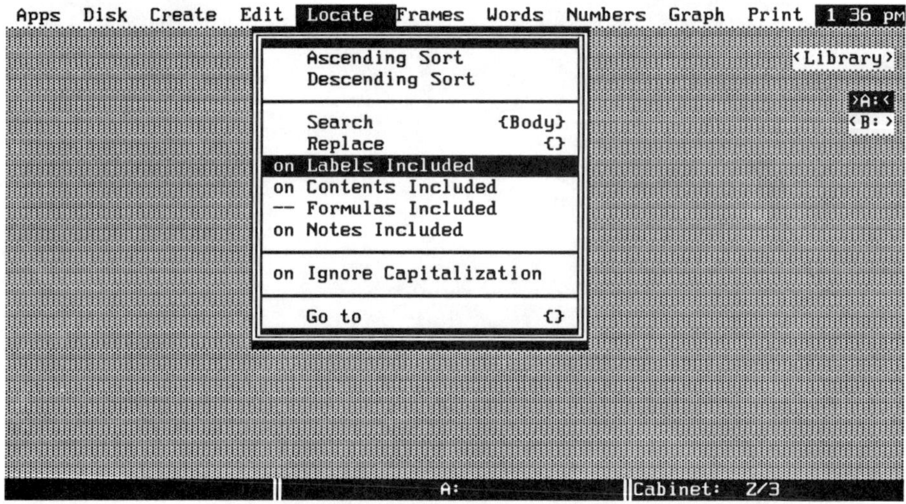

If ON, include frame labels in Search/Replace

Selecting this option turns it on and off. Labels Included is automatically turned on when you begin your Framework III session.

If it is turned off, position the cursor on the Labels Included option and press Enter. Then move the cursor to the Search { } or Replace { } option and press Enter. When Framework III looks through the frame for the specified text, the labels are included in the review.

APPLICATIONS

The Labels Included option is most useful when outline frames are involved. Select this option before doing a search or replace operation when you want the frame labels to be reviewed.

TYPICAL OPERATION

Use this illustration to learn how to use the Labels Included option of the Locate Menu frame. Close any open frames on your desktop and position the cursor on your data drive indicator (drive B in this example). The shortcut key combinations, if applicable, are enclosed by braces.

1. {Press **Ctrl-D**}. Press **Ins** to move the cursor to the Main Menu line. Next, press **Left Arrow** or **Right Arrow**, if necessary, until the Disk Menu frame is open on your desktop.
2. {Press **Ctrl-G**}. Press **Up Arrow** to move the cursor to the Get File by Name option and then press **Enter**. The cursor moves to the Message line at the bottom of your desktop.
3. Type **B:EXERCISE**. As you type, notice that the braces next to the Get File by Name option fill. When finished, press **Enter** twice. The disk is read and the frame you specified is opened on your desktop as follows:

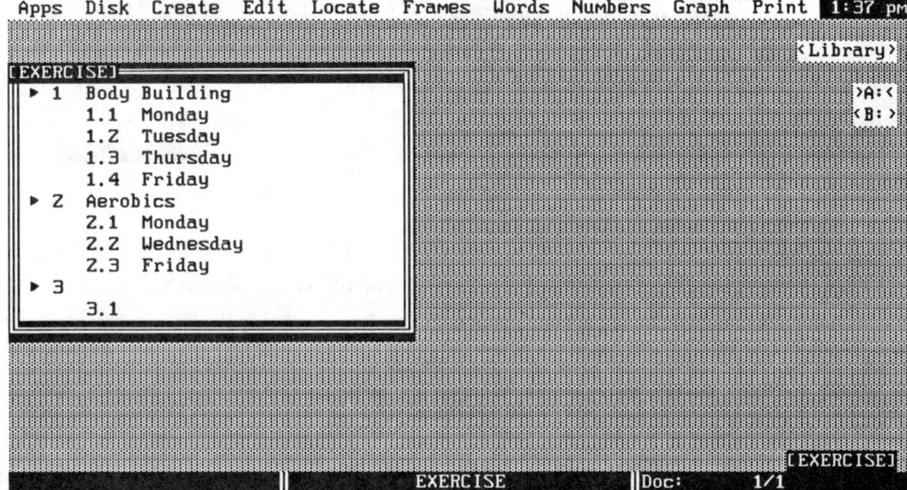

4. {Press **Ctrl-L**}. Press **Ins** to move the cursor to the Main Menu line. Next, press **Right Arrow** until the Locate Menu frame is also open on your desktop. Notice that the Labels Included option is turned on. (If not, press **Ctrl-L** to turn it on. Also turn on Contents Included if it is not currently on.)
5. {Press **Ctrl-S**}. Press **Up Arrow** until the cursor is positioned on the Search { } option and press **Enter**. Type **Body** and press **Enter**. The Locate Menu frame disappears from your desktop. Notice that the cursor is positioned on the Body Building topic.

6. Press **Down Arrow** to see the cursor positioned within the subframe on the word you specified in the Search { } option. Your frame resembles the following display.

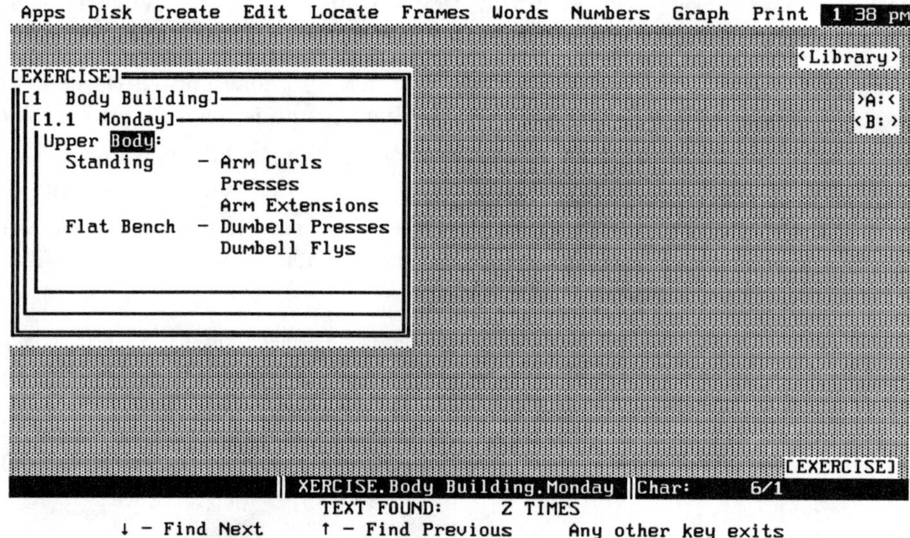

7. Press **Esc** to discontinue the Search activity. Press **F10** to return to the outline view. Then press **Gray –** twice until the cursor is positioned on the EXERCISE frame border.
8. {Press **Ctrl-L**}. Press **Ins** to move the cursor to the Main Menu line. The Locate Menu frame is again open on your desktop.
9. {Press **Ctrl-L**}. Press **Down Arrow** until the cursor is positioned on the Labels Included option. Next, press **Enter** to turn it off.
10. {Press **Ctrl-S**}. Press **Up Arrow** until the cursor is positioned on the Search { } option and press **Enter**. Since the word "Body" is already enclosed by the braces, just press **Enter**. Notice that the cursor is positioned within the Monday frame. The "Body" on the Body Building frame border was ignored. When the Labels Included option is turned off, Framework III ignores all frame labels.
11. Press **F10** to return to the outline view.
12. Press **Gray –** twice to move the cursor to the EXERCISE frame border. Since the outline has not been changed, press **Del** to remove it from the desktop without saving it again on disk.
13. {Press **Ctrl-D**}. Press **Ins** to move the cursor to the Main Menu line. Next, press **Left Arrow** until the Disk Menu frame is open on your desktop.
14. {Press **Ctrl-Q**}. Using the arrow keys again, position the cursor on the QUIT Framework option and press **Enter**. Type **Y** when asked if you are sure you want to quit Framework III. You have ended this Framework III session.
15. Turn to Module 58 to continue the learning sequence.

Module 51

LEFT MARGIN { }

DESCRIPTION

When you type a word processing document, Framework III begins each new line next to the left border of the frame. To temporarily change this default (preset) condition, use the Left Margin option of the Words Menu frame.

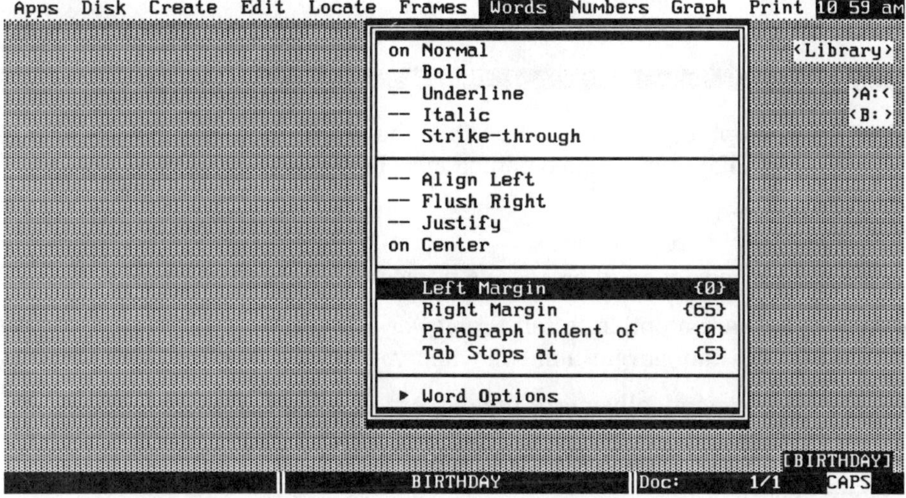

Notice that the Left Margin option is currently set to 0. This means that each line of the text you type begins at the left border of the frame. Change this number anytime during a word processing activity.

For example, the following party invitation has the left margin of 0 spaces set for the description of the party. "When:" and "Where:" are indented by 10 spaces.

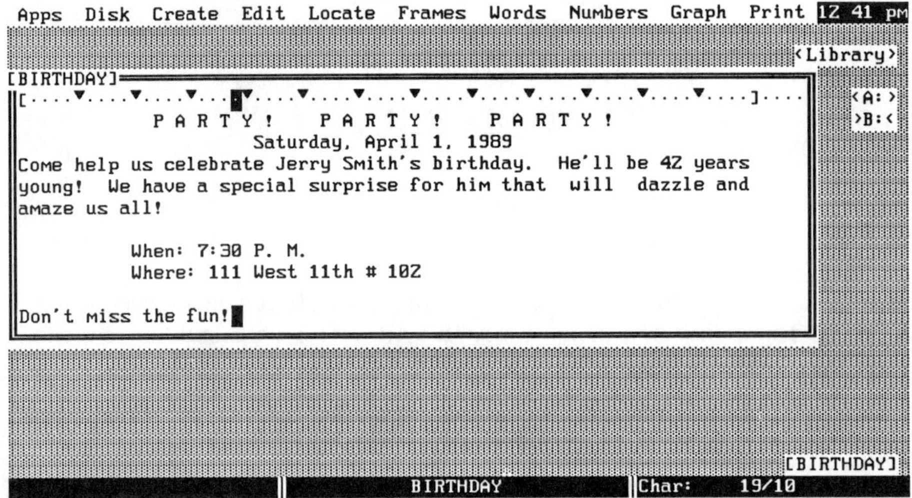

First, the Left Margin option begins as {0}. When the description is complete, change the Left Margin option to {10} before typing the indented text. Then change it back to 0 before continuing.

APPLICATIONS

This option is available only for word processing frames — not spreadsheets, databases, or graphs.

Use it and the Right Margin option to tell Framework III where to begin and end each line of your document. Change the margin number when you need to set new limits for the cursor.

Since Framework III automatically moves the cursor to the left margin of the next line when the current one is filled, you don't have to remember to do so. Just type!

TYPICAL OPERATION

This illustration shows you how to change the left margin for a birthday party invitation. Close any open frames on your desktop and position the cursor on your data drive indicator (drive B in this example). The shortcut key combinations, if applicable, are enclosed by braces.

1. With the cursor positioned on the data drive indicator, press **Enter**.
2. Since the cursor is positioned on the border of the open frame, press **Gray +**. Now you're inside the open frame. With the cursor positioned on the filename BIRTHDAY.FW3, press **Enter**. If necessary, press **Enter** again to move the frame from the tray to the desktop.
3. Press **Gray +** to move the cursor from the frame border to the text inside the frame.
4. The cursor is positioned on the last change made to the document. Press **Down Arrow** to move the cursor to the end of the text. Then press **Enter** twice. Notice that the cursor is positioned on the left border of the frame.

5. {Press **Ctrl-W**}. Press **Ins** to move the cursor to the Main Menu line. Next, press **Left Arrow** or **Right Arrow** until the Words Menu frame is also open on your desktop. Notice that the Left Margin option is set to 0.
6. {Press **Ctrl-L**}. Press **Down Arrow** until the cursor is positioned on the Left Margin option and then press **Enter**. The cursor moves to the Message line at the bottom of your screen. Type **10** and press **Enter**. The Words Menu frame disappears. However, the cursor is positioned at your new left margin.
7. Type **When: 7:30 P. M.** and press **Enter**. Notice that your cursor moves to the new margin on the next line.
8. Type **Where: 111 West 11th # 102**. Press **Enter** twice.
9. {Press **Ctrl-W**}. Press **Ins** to move the cursor to the Main Menu line. The Words Menu frame is open on your desktop. Notice that the Left Margin option is set to 10.
10. {Press **Ctrl-L**}. With the cursor positioned on the Left Margin option, press **Enter**. The cursor moves to the Message line at the bottom of your screen. Type **0** and press **Enter**. The Words Menu frame disappears. However, the cursor is positioned at your new left margin.
11. Type **Don't miss the fun!** Make sure your desktop resembles the following display.

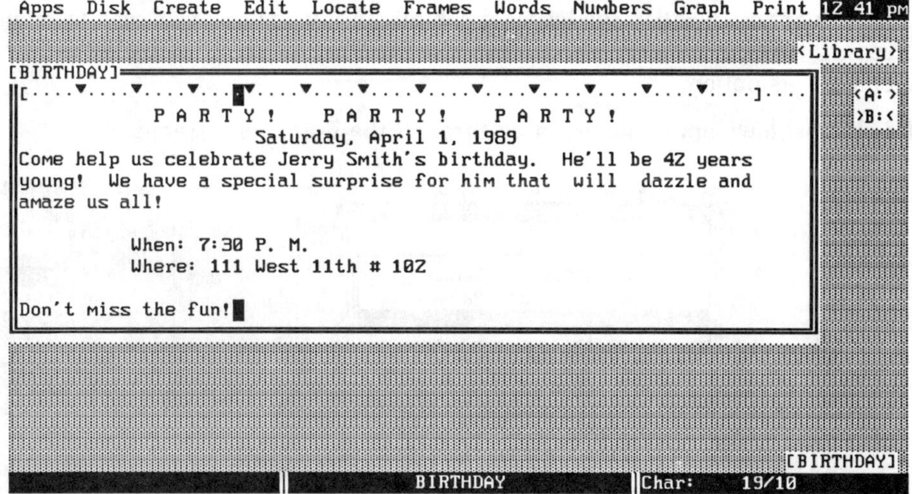

12. Press **Gray –** to move the cursor to the frame border and then press **Enter**. The frame closes and is put in your desktop tray.
13. {Press **Ctrl-D**}. Press **Ins** to move the cursor to the Main Menu line. Next, press the arrow (cursor) keys until the Disk Menu frame is again open on your desktop.
14. {Press **Ctrl-Q**}. Position the cursor on the QUIT Framework option and press **Enter**. Type **Y** when asked if you want to save the new or modified frames. You are returned to the DOS prompt.
15. Turn to Module 74 to continue the learning sequence.

Module 52

LOCK COLUMNS/ROWS

DESCRIPTION

When you move the cursor across a large spreadsheet, the upper columns and leftmost rows disappear from view. Since these columns or rows are usually where labels are kept, it's hard to know what is actually stored in each cell.

You can use the column letters (A, B, C) and the row numbers (1, 2, 3), however, the labels are more helpful.

The Lock Columns/Rows option can be used to lock any number of rows and columns on the screen. Before using this option, position the leftmost column and upper row you wish to remain on the screen. If you want to lock column A and row 1, use the Grey – key to highlight the frame border before selecting this option.

The Lock Columns/Rows option is available through the Edit Menu frame.

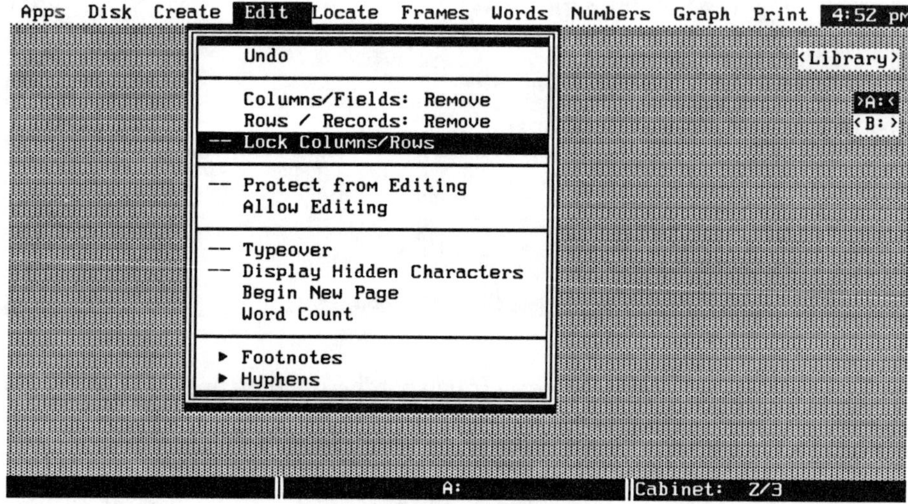

Lock columns left of and rows above the selection in spreadsheet or database

This option is turned on or off when it is selected. When your session begins, it is turned off. By moving the cursor from cell B4 to X4, the labels disappear from view as shown in the following display.

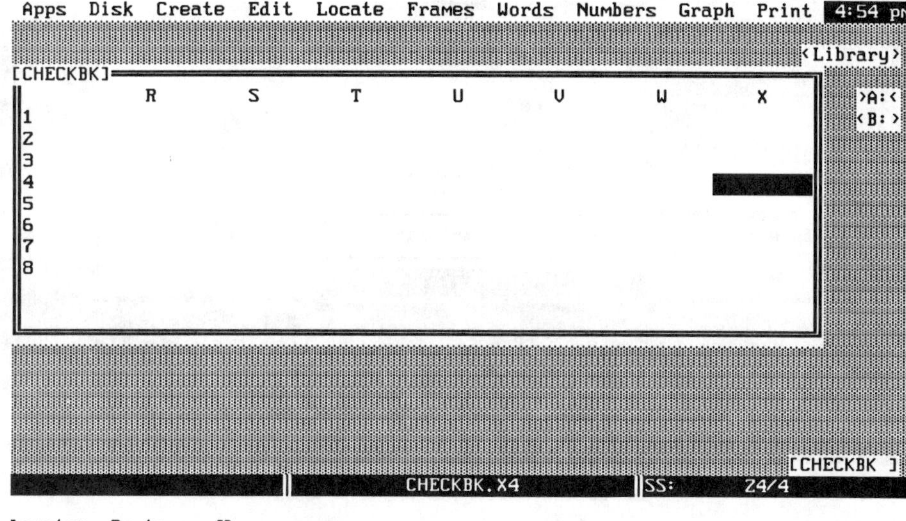

By selecting the Lock Columns/Rows option, the locked columns and rows remains in view when you move the cursor around the spreadsheet.

APPLICATIONS

This option is used to prevent information labels from scrolling off your screen when navigating in database and spreadsheet frames.

TYPICAL OPERATION

Use this illustration to learn how to use the Lock Columns/Rows option of the Edit Menu frame. Close any open frames on your desktop and position the cursor on your data drive indicator (drive B in this example). The shortcut key combinations, if applicable, are enclosed by braces.

1. {Press **Ctrl-D**}. Press **Ins** to move the cursor to the Main Menu line. Next, press **Left Arrow** or **Right Arrow**, if necessary, until the Disk Menu frame is open on your desktop.
2. {Press **Ctrl-G**}. Press **Up Arrow** to move the cursor to the Get File by Name option and then press **Enter**. The cursor moves to the Message line at the bottom of your desktop.
3. Type **B:CHECKBK**. As you type, notice that the braces next to the Get File by Name option fill. When finished, press **Enter**. The disk is read and the frame you specified is opened on your desktop.
4. Press **Gray +** to move the cursor inside the open spreadsheet frame.

5. {Press **Ctrl-L**}. Press **Ins** to move the cursor to the Main Menu line. Next, press **Right Arrow** until the Locate Menu frame is also open on your desktop.

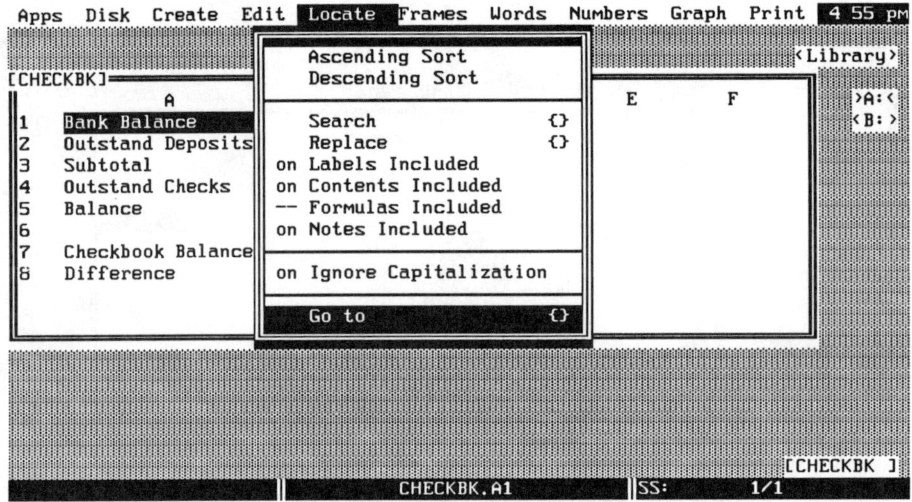

6. {Press **Ctrl-G**}. Press **Down Arrow** until the cursor is positioned on the Go to { } option and press **Enter**. Type **X4** and press **Enter**. The Locate Menu frame disappears from your desktop. Notice that the cursor is positioned on the cell you specified in the Go to { } option.

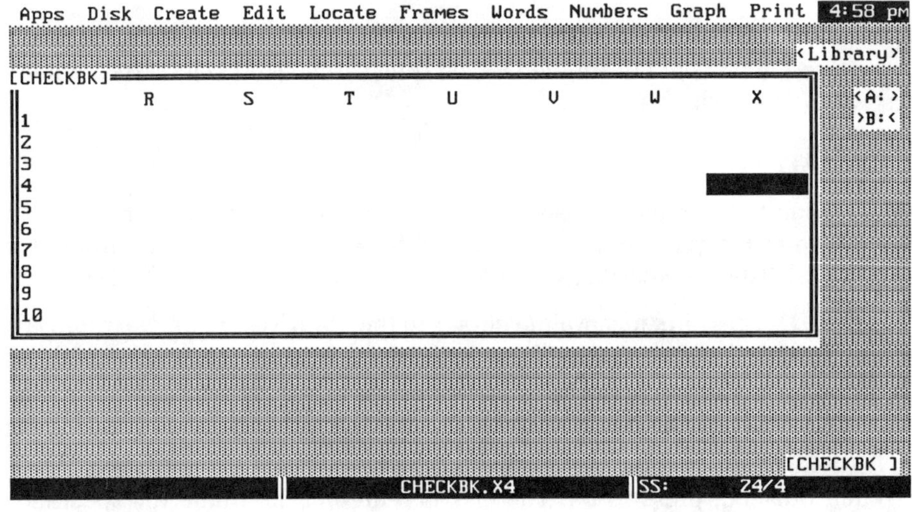

7. Press **Ctrl-Home** to return to column A, row 1.
8. Press **Gray –** to highlight the frame border.
9. Press **Ctrl-E** and **Ctrl-L** to access the Edit Menu frame and turn the Lock Columns/Rows option on.
10. Press **Gray +** to enter the frame. Press **Ctrl-L** to access the Locate Menu frame.
11. {Press **Ctrl-G**}. With the cursor positioned on the Go to { } option, type **X4** and press **Enter**. The cursor is now positioned on cell X4 and the labels in column A are still visible within the frame.

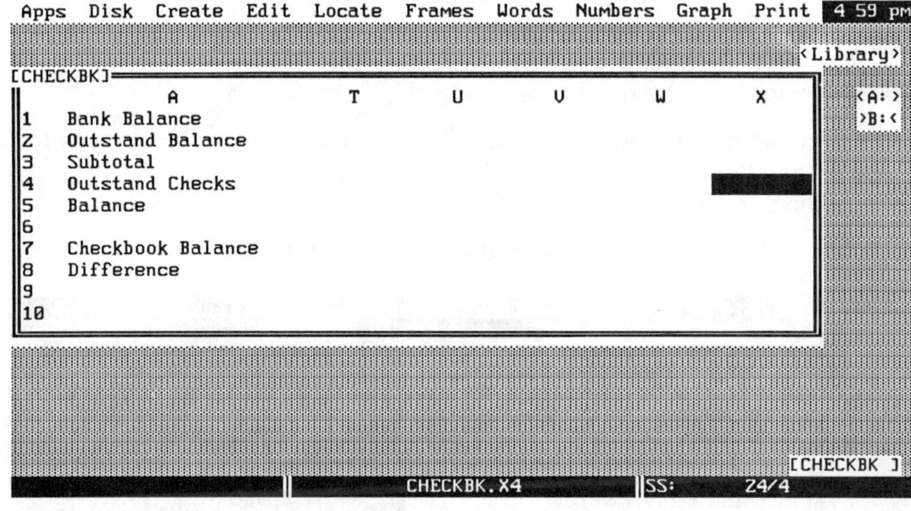

12. Press **Gray –** to move the cursor to the frame border. Since the spreadsheet has not been changed, press **Del** to remove it from the desktop without saving it again on disk.
13. {Press **Ctrl-Q**}. Using the arrow keys again, position the cursor on the QUIT Framework option and press **Enter**. Type **Y** when asked if you are sure you want to quit Framework III. You have ended this Framework III session.
14. Turn to Module 91 to continue the learning sequence.

Module 53

MACRO/ABBREVIATION

DESCRIPTION

Everyone loves shortcuts — the quicker, the better!

This option lets you set up your own shortcuts. For example, set up abbreviations for states so you don't have to type the full name in your documents. Set up macros so a shortcut key press opens your checkbook reconciliation spreadsheet.

The Macro/Abbreviation option is available through the Create Menu frame.

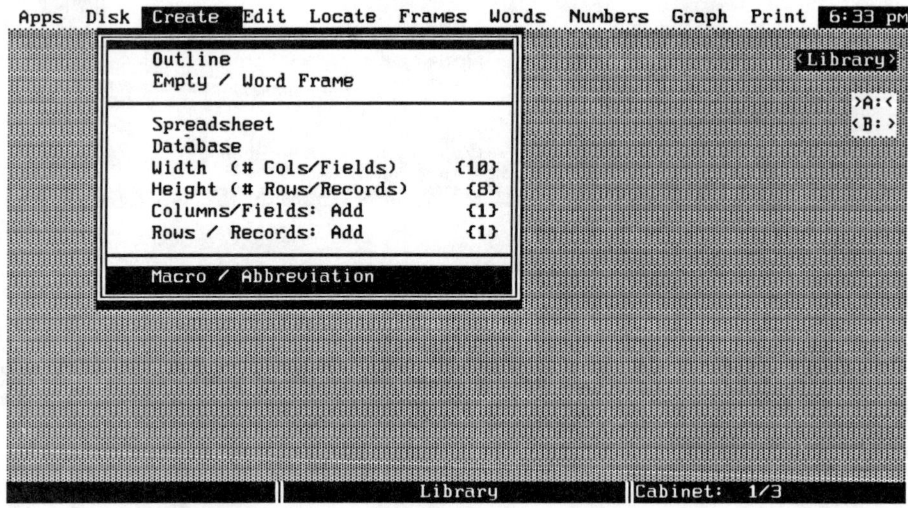

Begin recording a macro or abbreviation to be saved in the Library

When this option is selected, Framework III expects you to type the abbreviation or macro you need available in the Library Cabinet. To see what's currently in the Library Cabinet, press Up Arrow to position the cursor on the <Library> word of your desktop. When you press Enter, the Library frame opens.

```
Apps  Disk  Create  Edit  Locate  Frames  Words  Numbers  Graph  Print  6:35 pm
▸ Macros
   - {ALT-F1} : Out of indent
   - {ALT-F2} : New first frame on current level
   - {ALT-F3} : Type Current Date
   - {ALT-F4} : Show print width of ss or db
   - {ALT-F5} : Available Memory
   ▸ 1   {ALT-F6} : Memos and Letters
        1.1  Memorandum
        1.2  Company Letter
        1.3  Exit
   ▸ {ALT-F7} : Snaked columns template
      - Main
      - Get Number
   - {ALT-F8} : Sum column (start with selection below numbers)
   - {ALT-F9} :-Strip hard CR's
   - {ALT-F10}: Calculator
▸ Abbreviations
   - CA:  California
   - Fed: Federal Government
▸ Printing Templates
   - Memo
                          Library.Macros          Frame:     1/5
   To pull down a menu, press INS   (or CTRL with first letter of menu name)
                               Press F1 for HELP
```

The arrows to the left of the topics indicate that they contain subframes. The dash identifies the topic as a subframe.

A macro is a frame which is created and saved in the Library Cabinet. Framework III is preset with several macros as seen by entering the Library frame, selecting the Macro topic, and pressing F9 (Zoom).

When you press Alt-F3 while in an open word processing frame, the current date is immediately written where you positioned the cursor. Press Alt-F6 to automatically create the intro section of a memo or letter. Press Alt-F5 to determine the amount of available memory. You might also create your own macro to open and enter your checkbook reconciliation spreadsheet.

After adding your own abbreviations to the Library, typing an abbreviation in your document causes Framework III to expand it. (You must turn Expand Abbreviations in the Word options submenu of the Words Menu on.) The abbreviation is immediately replaced by the full word or phrase you specified in the abbreviation macro. Framework III is preset with abbreviations for California and Federal Government.

The whole idea of using macros is to save yourself time and keystrokes by identifying procedures that you do often and saving them in the Library Cabinet. Framework III makes all Library functions available at any time during your Framework III session.

APPLICATIONS

Use this option when you want to add a macro or abbreviation to the Library Cabinet. Each new function you save in the Library is always available since Framework III puts it in memory when the session begins.

Choose anything you do often and set up a macro for that operation. Add words or phrases that you are tired of typing to the Abbreviations list in the Library Cabinet. Just remember that the Library Cabinet is read into memory when your session begins. Make sure you have enough available memory for your additions.

TYPICAL OPERATION

This example shows you how to add abbreviations and macros to your library. There are several methods available for adding to the Library Cabinet. Use the one with which you feel most comfortable when adding a macro or an abbreviation.

Make sure that your desktop is clean and the cursor is positioned on the Library indicator on the right side of your desktop. The shortcut key combinations, if applicable, are enclosed by braces.

1. With the cursor positioned on the Library indicator, press **Enter**. The Library frame is opened on your desktop.

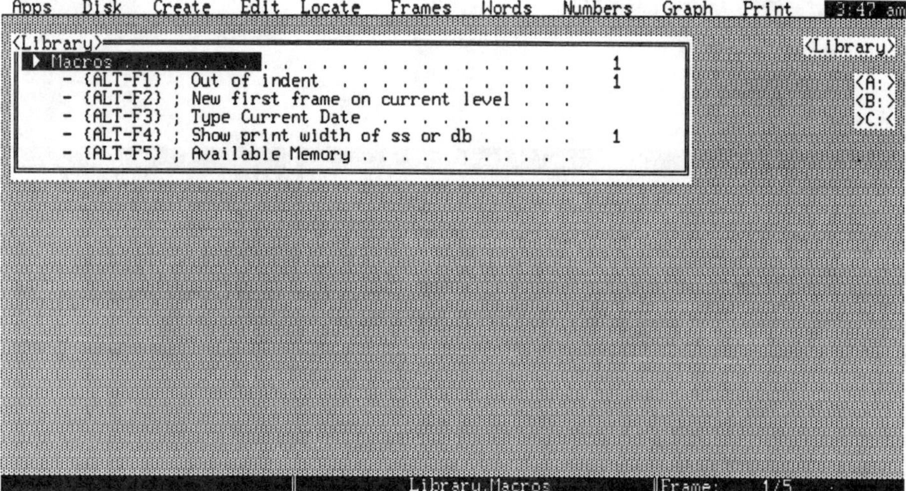

2. Press **F9** (Zoom) so that the frame fills your desktop as in the following display. If the macros' subtopics are not listed, just position the cursor on the Macros topic and press **Enter**.

```
Apps  Disk  Create  Edit  Locate  Frames  Words  Numbers  Graph  Print   3:49 am
▶ Macros . . . . . . . . . . . . . . . . . . . . . . . . 1
   - {ALT-F1} ; Out of indent . . . . . . . . . . . . . 1
   - {ALT-F2} ; New first frame on current level . . .
   - {ALT-F3} ; Type Current Date . . . . . . . . . . .
   - {ALT-F4} ; Show print width of ss or db . . . . . 1
   - {ALT-F5} ; Available Memory . . . . . . . . . . .
   ▶ 1   {ALT-F6} ; Memos and Letters . . . . . . . . . 1
        1.1  Memorandum . . . . . . . . . . . . . . .
        1.2  Company Letter . . . . . . . . . . . . .
        1.3  Exit . . . . . . . . . . . . . . . . . .
   ▶ {ALT-F7} ; Snaked columns template . . . . . . .
      - Main . . . . . . . . . . . . . . . . . . . .
      - Get Number . . . . . . . . . . . . . . . . .
   - {ALT-F8} ; Sum column (start with selection belo
   - {ALT-F9} ; Strip hard CR's . . . . . . . . . . .
   - {ALT-F10}; Calculator . . . . . . . . . . . . . .
▶ Abbreviations . . . . . . . . . . . . . . . . . . . . 1
   - CA;  California . . . . . . . . . . . . . . . . . 1
   - Fed; Federal Government . . . . . . . . . . . . .
▶ Printing Templates . . . . . . . . . . . . . . . . . . 1
   - Memo . . . . . . . . . . . . . . . . . . . . . . . 1
   ▶ Business Letter . . . . . . . . . . . . . . . . .
      - Pica . . . . . . . . . . . . . . . . . . . . .
      - Elite . . . . . . . . . . . . . . . . . . . . .
   - Pica Type  ; IBM codes supplied. Replace with co
                              Library.Macros              Frame:    1/5
      To pull down a menu, press INS  (or CTRL with first letter of menu name)
                              Press F1 for HELP
```

3. Press **Down Arrow** until the cursor is on Abbreviations. If the Abbreviations section is closed, press **Enter**. Press **Down Arrow** until the cursor is positioned on the California abbreviation.
4. {Press **Ctrl-C** and **Ctrl-E**}. Open the Create Menu frame and select the Empty/Word Frame option. A blank line is opened after the California abbreviation. Type **TX ; Texas** and press **Enter**. Your screen should resemble the following display.

```
Apps  Disk  Create  Edit  Locate  Frames  Words  Numbers  Graph  Print  9:50 pm
▶ Macros
   - {ALT-F1} : Out of indent
   - {ALT-F2} : New first frame on current level
   - {ALT-F3} : Type Current Date
   - {ALT-F4} : Show print width of ss or db
   - {ALT-F5} : Available Memory
   ▶ 1   {ALT-F6} : Memos and Letters
         1.1  Memorandum
         1.2  Company Letter
         1.3  Exit
   ▶ {ALT-F7} : Snaked columns template
      - Main
      - Get Number
   - {ALT-F8} : Sum column (start with selection below numbers)
   - {ALT-F9} : Strip hard CR's
   - {ALT-F10}: Calculator
▶ Abbreviations
   - CA:  California
   - TX:  Texas
   - Fed: Federal Government
▶ Printing Templates
                    || Library.Abbreviations.TX   ||Frame:    2/3
   To pull down a menu, press INS  (or CTRL with first letter of menu name)
                              Press F1 for HELP
```

5. Press **F10** (View) to open the new subframe. Press **Gray +** to move the cursor inside the open frame. Type **Texas**. Then press **Gray –** to move to the frame border and press **F10** (View) again.
6. Press **F9** (Zoom) to return to the frame view. Then press **Gray –** twice until the cursor is positioned on the Library frame border and press **Enter** to close the frame.
7. Press **Ctrl-Enter** to save the new abbreviation to the Library.
8. {Press **Ctrl-W** and then **Ctrl-W** and then **Ctrl-E**}. Open the Word Menu frame and select the Word Options menu. Select Expand abbreviations and press **Enter**.
9. {Press **Ctrl-C** and then **Ctrl-E**}. Open the Create Menu frame and select the Empty/Word Frame option.
10. Press **Gray +** to move the cursor inside the open frame. Type **TX** and press **Spacebar**. Notice that the abbreviation is replaced by the full word "Texas."
11. Press **Gray –** to move the cursor to the frame border. Press **Del** to remove the frame from your desktop without saving it on disk.
12. {Press **Ctrl-C** and then **Ctrl-M**}. Open the Create Menu frame again and select the Macro/Abbreviation option.
13. Press **Alt-R** for the frame name. Any key you press now is entered inside the open subframe. The description must be added after completing the macro — not now!
14. Press **Ctrl-D** and then **Ctrl-G**. Type **CHECKBK** and press **Enter**. The spreadsheet opens on your desktop.

15. Press **Gray +** to move the cursor inside the open spreadsheet frame.
16. Press **Ctrl-L** and then **Ctrl-G** to open the Locate Menu frame and select the Go to { } option. Type **B1** and press **Enter** to move the cursor to cell B1.
17. Press **Ctrl-Break** to stop filling the macro frame.
18. Press **Gray –** to move the cursor to the CHECKBK frame border and press **Del**. The frame is removed from the desktop.
19. Open the Library frame and press **Gray +** to move the cursor inside the open frame. Press **Up Arrow** to position the cursor on the Alt-R option. Type {**Alt-R**} **; Reconcile Checkbook** and press **Enter**.
20. Press **F9** (Zoom) to open the subframe. The frame contains every keystroke you performed during the Macro/Abbreviation operation. If your screen does not resemble the following display, exit the {Alt-R} subframe. Position the cursor on {Alt-R} subtopic and press **Del**. Then try it again.

```
Apps  Disk  Create  Edit  Locate  Frames  Words  Numbers  Graph  Print  6 06 pm
{CTRL-D}{CTRL-G}CHECKBK{RETURN}{IN}{CTRL-L}{CTRL-G}B1{RETURN}
```

```
Library.Macros.[{ALT-R}]  Char:    60/1
```

21. When the macro is correct, get out of the Library Cabinet frame. Press **Ctrl-Enter** to save the new macro.
22. Press **Alt-R** and watch Framework III open your spreadsheet and position the cursor. Then remove the open frame from your desktop.
23. {Press **Ctrl-D** and **Ctrl-Q**}. Open the Disk Menu frame and select the QUIT Framework option. When asked, type **Y** to end this Framework III session.
24. Turn to Module 25 to continue the learning sequence.

Module 54

MAILMERGE USING { }

DESCRIPTION

Everyone likes to get an original copy of a letter! This option lets you print as many custom letters as you have names in a database. All you need is a database of names and addresses and a layout frame.

The layout frame is just a word processing frame. You mark where you want the fields from the database printed. Then select the Mailmerge using { } option of the Apps Menu frame and provide a database frame name within the braces.

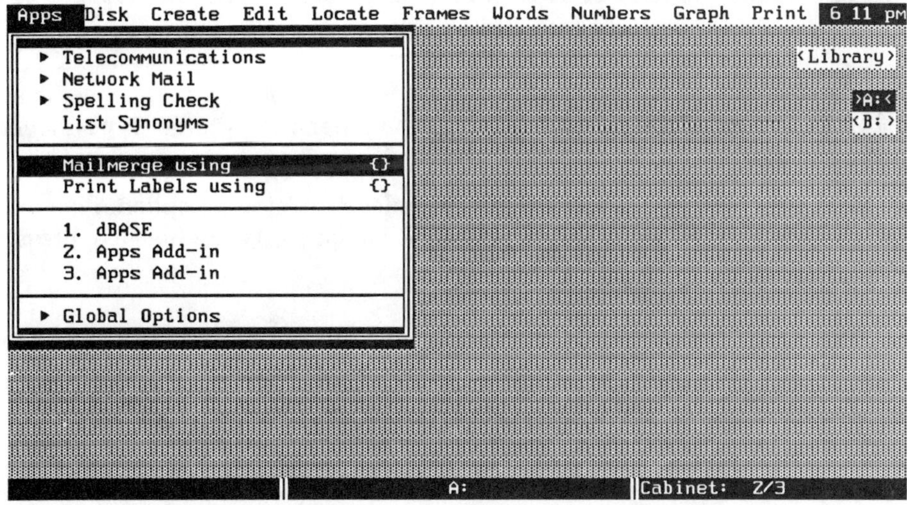

First, read your database from disk to your desktop. Next, open and enter a word processing frame. Type the fieldnames from the database within the open frame and enclose them with angle brackets as in the following example.

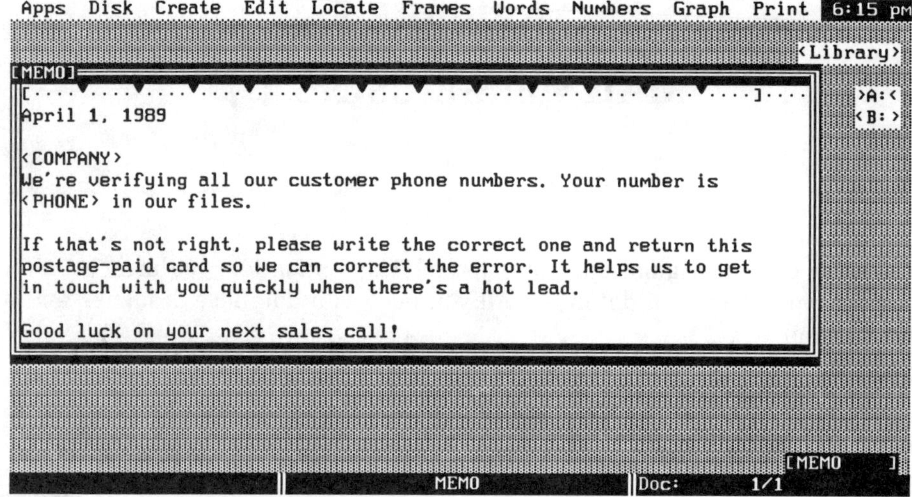

Make sure your printer is turned on. Open the Print Menu frame and change the Lines per Page option as well as any other format options. Print the letter until you get it positioned the way you need it.

Next, open the Apps Menu frame and select the Mailmerge Using { } option. Type the database frame name so that it appears within the braces of the option. When finished, press Enter and watch your letters print.

APPLICATIONS

Use this option when you need to send the same letter to many people. Make the letter as fancy or plain as you want.

For example, print the phone number in boldface type so that it is easy to find within the text. To do this, just highlight the field <PHONE> with the F6 (Extend) key. Then open the Words Menu frame and select the Bold option.

TYPICAL OPERATION

In this illustration, a letter model is typed into a frame. It is then used to print phone cards for a card file. Make sure that your desktop is clean and the cursor is positioned on the drive B indicator. The shortcut key combinations, if applicable, are enclosed by braces.

1. {Press **Ctrl-D**}. Press **Ins** to move the cursor to the Main Menu line. Next, press **Left Arrow** or **Right Arrow**, if necessary, until the Disk Menu frame is open on your desktop.
2. {Press **Ctrl-G**}. Press **Up Arrow** to move the cursor to the Get File by Name { } option and then press **Enter**. The cursor moves to the Message line at the bottom of your desktop.

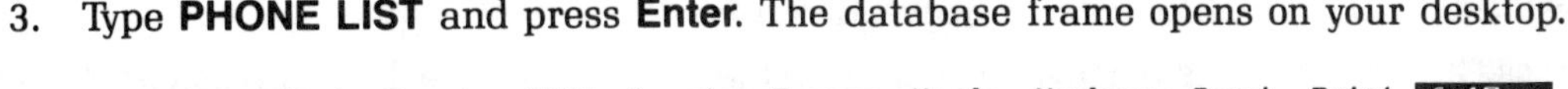

3. Type **PHONE LIST** and press **Enter**. The database frame opens on your desktop.

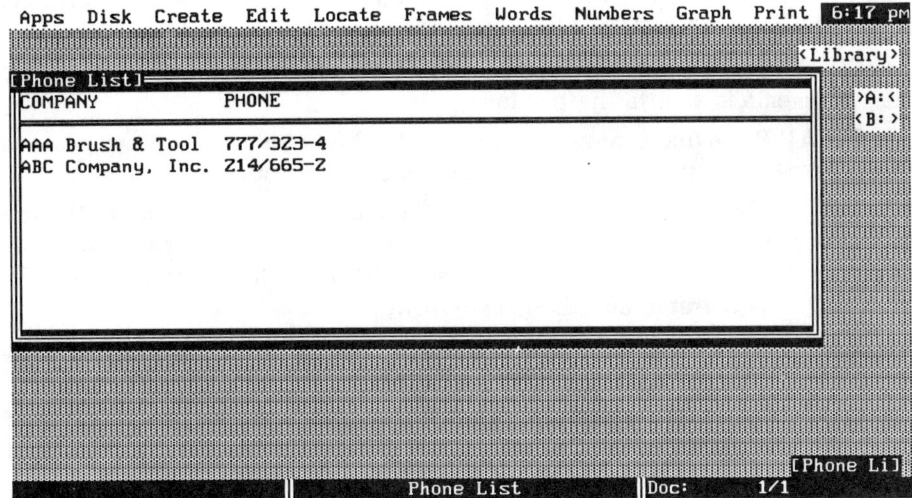

4. {Press **Ctrl-C**}. Press **Ins** to move the cursor to the Main Menu line. Next, press **Right Arrow** until the Create Menu frame is open on your desktop.
5. {Press **Ctrl-E**}. Press **Down Arrow**, if necessary, to move the cursor to the Empty/Word Frame option of the Create Menu frame. Next, press **Enter** to select the option. An empty frame appears on your screen.
6. The cursor is positioned within the brackets at the top border of the frame. Type **MEMO** and press **Enter**. This is the name of the frame. When it is saved on the disk, it is named MEMO.FW3.
7. Press **Gray +**. Notice that the cursor is now positioned inside your open frame.
8. Type the memo you see in the following display.

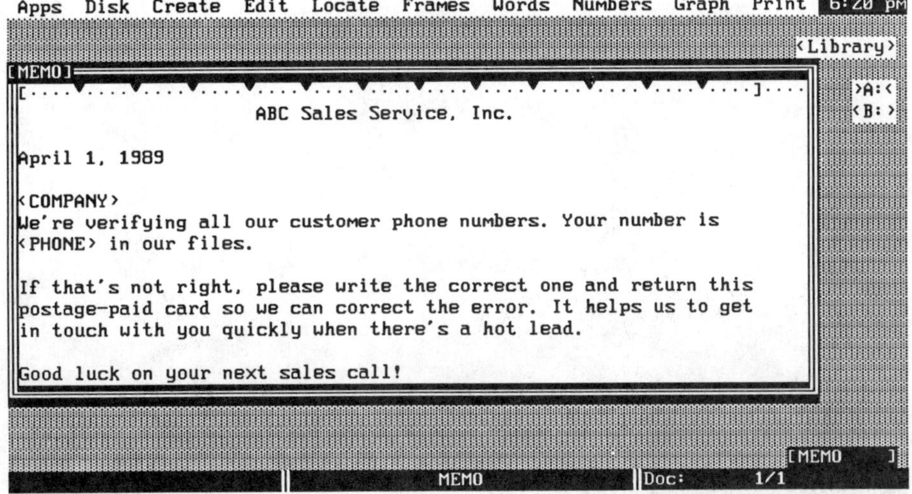

9. Press **Gray –** to move the cursor to the frame border.
10. {Press **Ctrl-P**}. Press **Ins** to move the cursor to the Main Menu line. Next, press **Left Arrow** or **Right Arrow** until the Print Menu frame is open on your desktop.
11. {Press **Ctrl-B**}. Press **Up Arrow** to move the cursor to the Begin option of the Print Menu frame. The memo is sent to the printer.
12. {Press **Ctrl-A**}. Press **Ins** to move the cursor to the Main Menu line. Next, press **Left Arrow** or **Right Arrow** until the Apps Menu frame is open on your desktop.
13. {Press **Ctrl-M**}. Press **Down Arrow** to move the cursor to the Mailmerge Using { } option of the Apps Menu frame and press **Enter**. Type **PHONE_LIST**, turn on your printer, and press **Enter**. Your letters begin printing. (Press **Ctrl-Break** to stop the printer.) Press **Enter** to close the MEMO frame into the desktop tray.
14. {Press **Ctrl-D**}. Press **Ins** to move the cursor to the Main Menu line. Next, press **Right Arrow** until the Disk Menu frame is open on your desktop.
15. {Press **Ctrl-P**}. Press **Down Arrow** to move the cursor to the Put Away option of the Disk Menu frame and press **Enter**. Now, your letter model is saved on disk. Press **Del** to delete the PHONE_LIST frame.
16. {Press **Ctrl-D**}. Press **Ins** to move the cursor to the Main Menu line. The Disk Menu frame is again open on your desktop.
17. {Press **Ctrl-Q**}. Position the cursor on the QUIT Framework option and press **Enter**. Type **Y** when asked if you are sure you want to quit Framework III. You have ended this Framework III session.
18. Turn to Module 67 to continue the learning sequence.

Module 55

NETWORK FILE

DESCRIPTION

Framework III has special locking features that allow users to share files on Local Area Networks (LAN). These locks prevent other users from loading the same frame you are updating.

If Framework III did not have locks, another user could load the same file, make changes, and save the document to disk thereby wiping out any changes you made. Framework III has three kinds of file access to prevent this from happening.

EXCLUSIVE — When you load a file with exclusive access, all other users are locked out of the file.

LOAD — Gives you the right to load the file, however, you cannot save the frame.

SAVE — (The default lock type) When you load a file with SAVE access, you can both load and save the file. However, other users are allowed to load the file but are prevented from saving the file. If you load a frame that another user has locked with a SAVE lock, you can still save your work. Just save the frame with another name or place it in another subdirectory.

If you are the user that has locked a frame, remember to select the Put Away option from the Disk Menu when you are finished so it is available to other users.

When you attempt to open a frame, the default access method is SAVE. If you want to use a different access method, press Alt-Enter when opening a file. If you are using Framework III on a LAN, a menu opens with the available file access options. If you are not working on a LAN, it is ignored.

Cause Framework III to automatically ask you for a sharing mode by turning the Network File: Ask for Sharing Mode option on as shown in the following display.

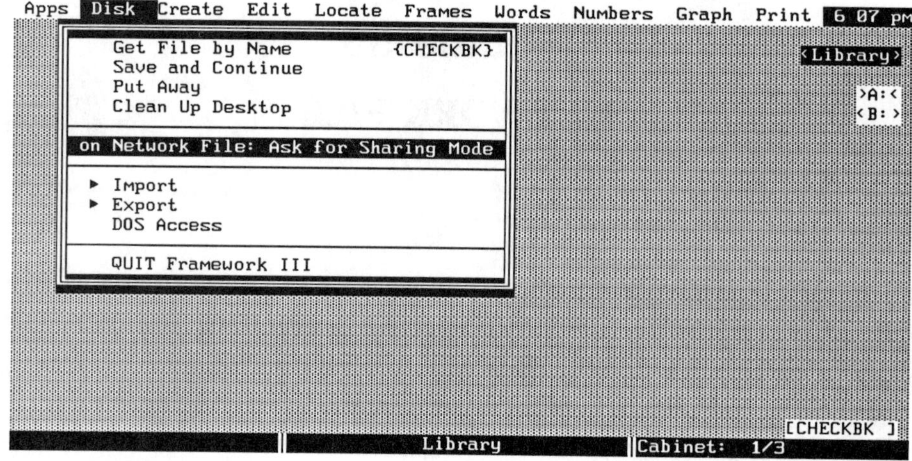

If ON, menu of lock types appears when you load a file from network

APPLICATIONS

File sharing allows groups to update common documents. For example, file sharing allows each department (Accounting, Information Systems, Manufacturing, etc.) to view and update a budget. Another use might be a shared "diary" or passdown log.

TYPICAL OPERATION

Network file sharing applies to the Framework III LAN package so no Typical Operation section is provided. Please turn to Module 56 to continue the learning sequence.

Module 56

NETWORK MAIL

DESCRIPTION

The Framework III Network Mail option allows you to exchange files, messages, and documents with other Local Area Network (LAN) and EMAIL users. Before you can use Framework mail, you must install the optional MHS (Message Handling Service) software package or a compatible package that shares the MHS file format. MHS acts as the post office in routing messages and files to the proper recipient.

You can send messages to other users on your LAN, other remote LANs, and even mainframes (requires an optional gateway software package).

Framework uses your mail-ID as an address to know where to send mail. After you install mail, you will be prompted for your user name and password each time you start Framework III. You can automatically tell Framework III your name and password by setting the following environmental variables.

NOTE

Any user that can read your AUTOEXEC.BAT or Framework start-up batch file will have access to your password.

```
SET USR = username
SET PWD = password
```

Framework mail is available from the Application Menu as illustrated below.

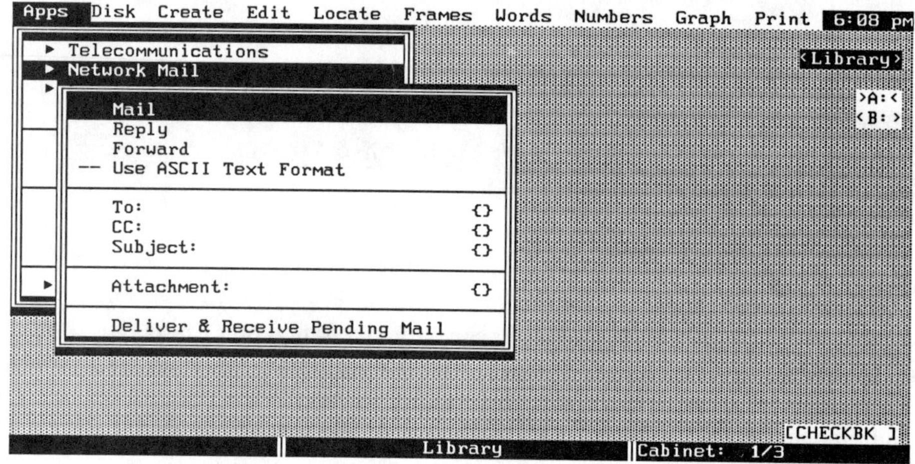

Send selected frame as mail to recipients listed in To: and CC:

If you have Framework mail installed, you have a Mailbox frame under the Library frame on the desktop. To view your mail, simply open the mailbox the same way you would open your default drive or the Library.

When you have the mailbox open, all new unread mail appears at the top of the list. Mail messages come in several types:

- >	(Arrow) Unread mail.
(=)	(Trashcan symbol) Mail that has been read but not saved is moved to the Trashcan directory. When the mail session ends, all read but unsaved files are moved to the Trashcan directory. These files are automatically saved for seven days unless they are later saved.
Blank	Mail you have read and saved.
Nonmail	Files you moved to the mailbox for mailing.
Directories	Mail directories like the Trashcan directory.

When you receive mail, Framework beeps, places a message in the message area, and displays Mail on the right side of the message area. By default, Framework checks for new mail every five minutes. Use the customization program (SETUPFW) to change the time interval.

To read a mail message, select the message by moving the highlighted bar to it and press Enter. Save the mail message by pressing Ctrl-Enter.

To send mail, create or load a document, select the Mail menu, fill in the name of the person to receive the mail, and select send to mail the document.

APPLICATIONS

Network Mail is a great way to improve communications for your entire work group. Supervisors can assign tasks, respond to queries from workers and broadcast news without the problem of getting the entire work group together for a meeting.

Electronic filing of correspondence also reduces the amount of paper floating around the office and improves productivity by allowing any EMAIL user to refer to old messages and notes.

TYPICAL OPERATION

Network Mail requires the optional MHS software package or another optional mail package. As a result of this, no Typical Operation section is specified. Congratulations!, this concludes the learning sequence.

Module 57

NORMAL, BOLD, UNDERLINE, ITALIC, STRIKE-THROUGH

DESCRIPTION

When you want to draw attention to a word or thought, use a different style. Framework III provides five choices — normal, bold, underline, italic, and strike-through. These options are available in the Words Menu frame as follows.

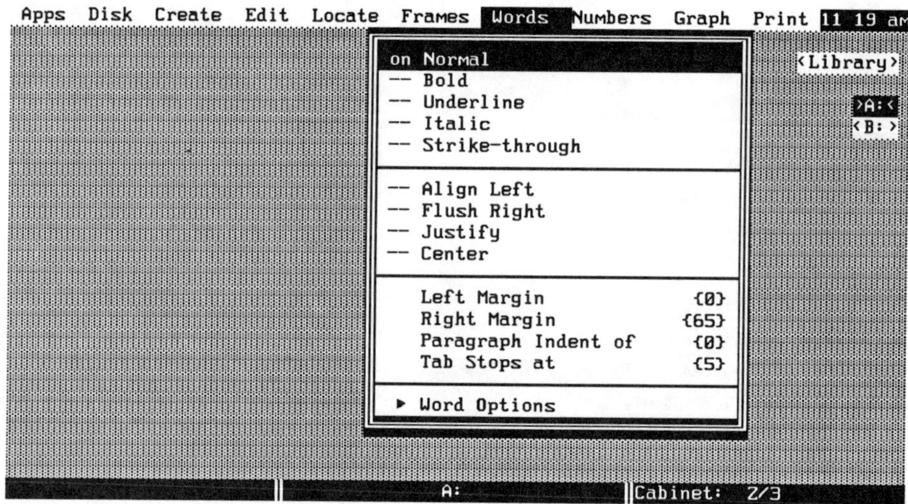

Turn OFF all text styles on current selection

Framework III defaults (presets) to the Normal option. The word "on" appears to the left of the selected option. As you type, letters in the selected style appear on the screen. When the document is printed on a dot matrix printer, the different style of text appears on the printed page.

While typing a new line, the selected style remains set. Each keystroke produces a letter in that style.

To change the style of a word or phrase, the F6 (Extend) activity must be used. First, highlight the word or phrase. Then open the Words Menu frame and select a different style. When the Words Menu frame disappears from your desktop, the highlighted area is changed to the selected style.

APPLICATIONS

Use this option anytime. It is available for any frame type (word processing, spreadsheet, database, graph, and yes even frame borders).

Some computers are not able to display (on the screen) the type style you select. However, when you print the document on a dot matrix or laser printer, the style change appears as you specified.

TYPICAL OPERATION

This illustration shows you how to use different type styles in the birthday party invitation created in the Empty/Word Frame module. Clear your desktop of any open frames and position the cursor on your data disk indicator (drive B in the illustration). The shortcut key combinations, if applicable, are enclosed by braces.

1. With the cursor positioned on the data drive indicator, press **Enter**.
2. Since the cursor is positioned on the border of the open frame, press **Gray +**. Now you're inside the open frame. With the cursor positioned on the filename BIRTHDAY.FW3 press **Enter**. Press **Enter** again. Another frame is opened on your desktop as in the following display.

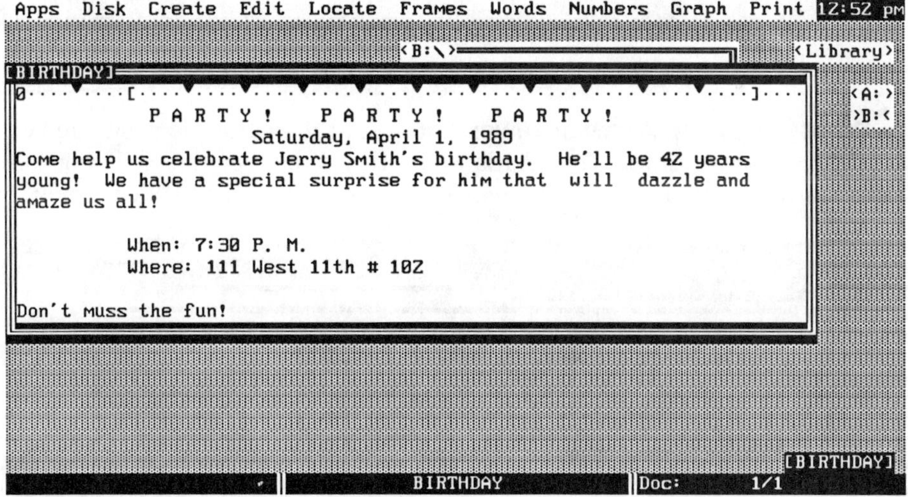

3. Press **Gray +** to move the cursor from the frame border to the text inside the frame.
4. Position the cursor on the first letter of the first line. You need to expand the cursor to include all words on the first line. To do this, press **F6** (Extend) to tell Framework III you want to extend or stretch the cursor. The message at the bottom tells you to start stretching.
5. Press **Right Arrow** until all letters on the line have been included in the highlighted area. Press **Enter** to stop the stretching. You have now specified what is to be affected by your typeface choice.

6. {Press **Ctrl-W**}. Press **Ins** to move the cursor to the Main Menu line. Next, press **Left Arrow** or **Right Arrow** until the Words Menu frame is also open on your desktop. Notice that the Normal option is "on" as in the following display.

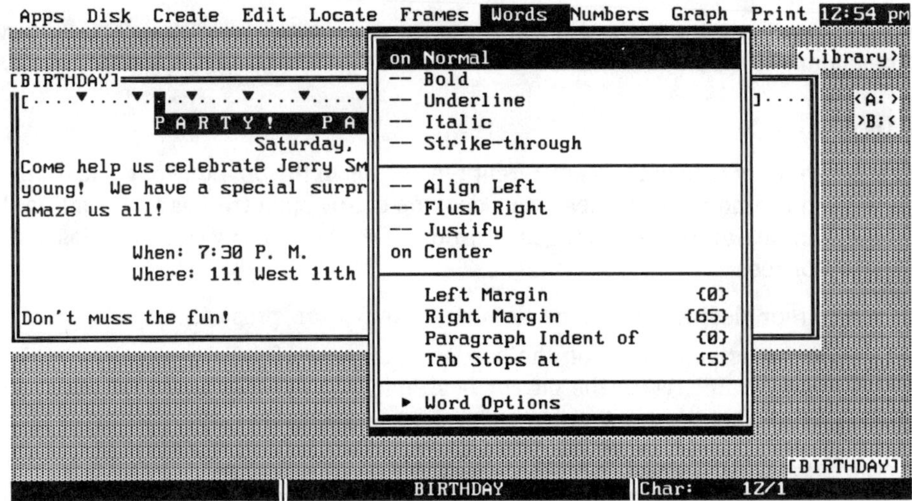

Turn OFF all text styles on current selection

7. {Press **Ctrl-B**}. Press **Up Arrow** or **Down Arrow** until the cursor is positioned on the Bold option and then press **Enter**. The Words Menu frame disappears. However, all letters in the area you highlighted are now in heavier type style (bold) as shown below.

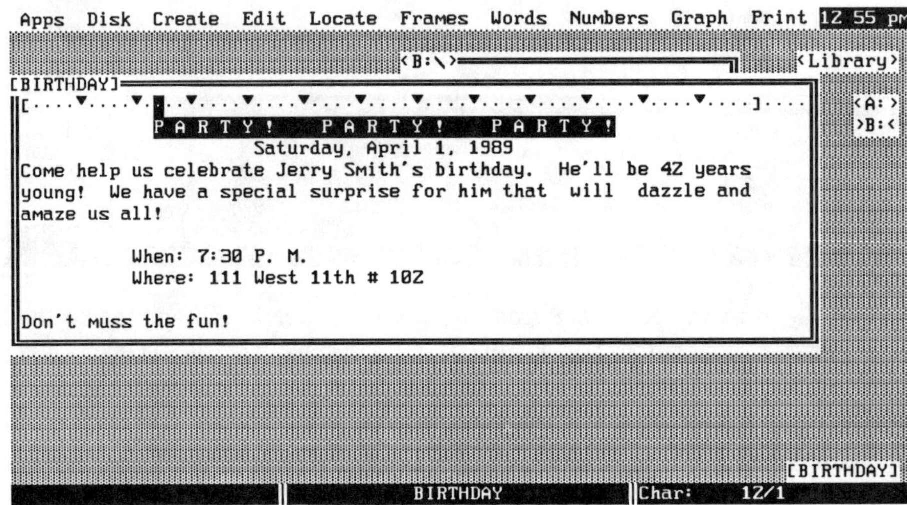

Words: Bold on

8. {Press **Ctrl-W** and then **Ctrl-U**}. Since the area is still highlighted, open the Words Menu again, but select the Underline option this time. Now, your invitation resembles the following display.

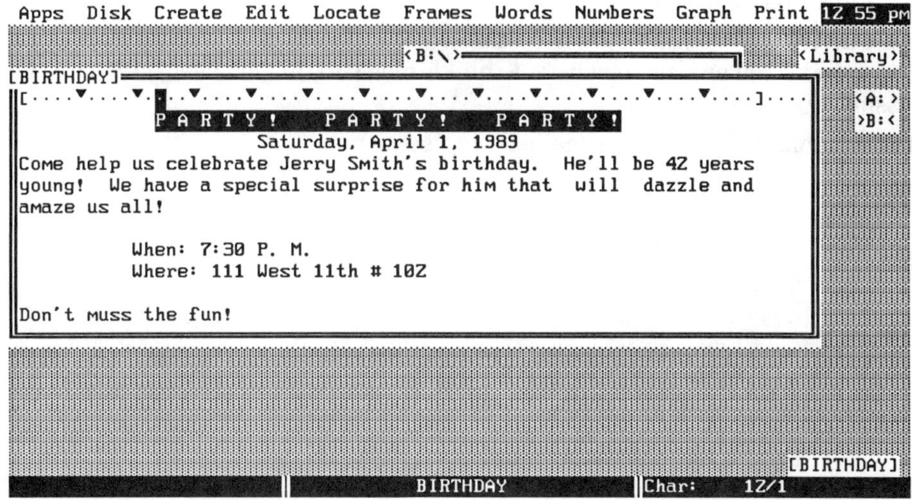

Words: Underline on

9. {Press **Ctrl-W** and then **Ctrl-N**}. Now change it back to normal type style without an underline.
10. Press **Gray –** to move the cursor to the border. Then press **Enter** to move the frame to the desktop tray.
11. {Press **Ctrl-D**}. Press **Ins** to move the cursor to the Main Menu line. Press **Left Arrow** until the following Disk Menu frame is open on your desktop.

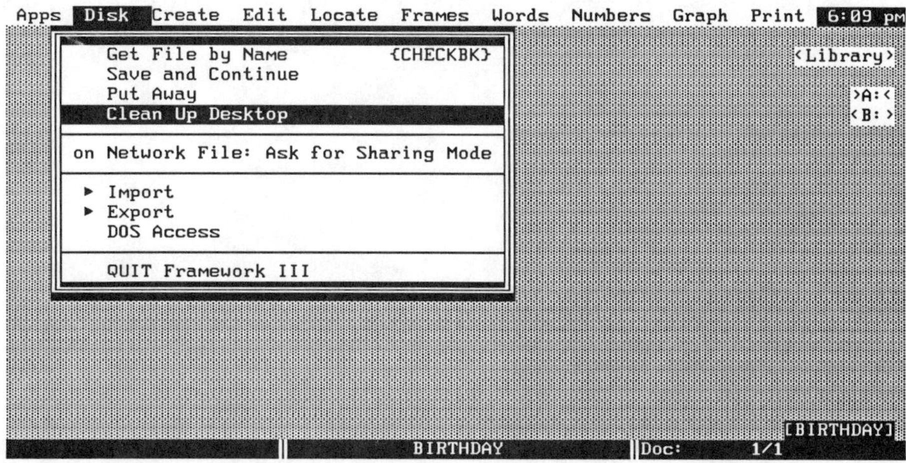

Close and stack all documents and cabinets

12. {Press **Ctrl-P**}. Position the cursor on the Put Away option and press **Enter**. This saves the invitation on the disk and cleans your desktop. Press **Enter** again to close the directory frame.
13. {Press **Ctrl-D**}. Press **Ins** to move the cursor to the Main Menu line. The Disk Menu frame is again open on your desktop.
14. {Press **Ctrl-Q**}. Position the cursor on the QUIT Framework option and press **Enter**. Type **Y** when asked if you are sure you want to quit Framework III. You have ended this Framework III session.
15. Turn to Module 26 to continue the learning sequence.

Module 58

NOTES INCLUDED

DESCRIPTION

When using the Search { } or Replace { } options, only the contents of a frame are reviewed unless Labels Included or Notes Included are turned on. Notes Included causes Framework III to review the footnotes during the search or replace activity. The Notes Included option is available through the Locate Menu frame.

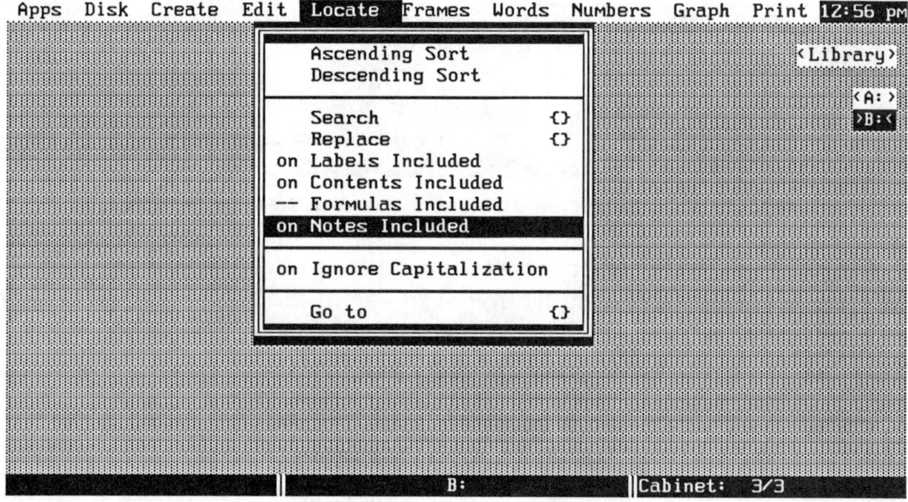

If ON, include footnotes and endnotes in Search/Replace

Selecting Notes Included turns it on and off. This option is automatically turned on when you begin your Framework III session.

If it is turned off (dashes next to the option), position the cursor on the Notes Included option and press Enter. Then move the cursor to the Search { } or Replace { } option and press Enter. When Framework III looks through the document for the specified text, the footnotes are included in the review.

APPLICATIONS

The Notes Included option is most useful when searching long documents with several footnotes. Select this option before doing a search or replace operation when the footnotes are to be reviewed like the main text.

TYPICAL OPERATION

Use this illustration to learn how to use the Notes Included option of the Locate Menu frame. Close any open frames on your desktop and position the cursor on your data drive indicator (drive B in this example). The shortcut key combinations, if applicable, are enclosed by braces.

1. {Press **Ctrl-D**}. Press **Ins** to move the cursor to the Main Menu line. Press **Left Arrow** or **Right Arrow**, if necessary, until the Disk Menu frame is open on your desktop.

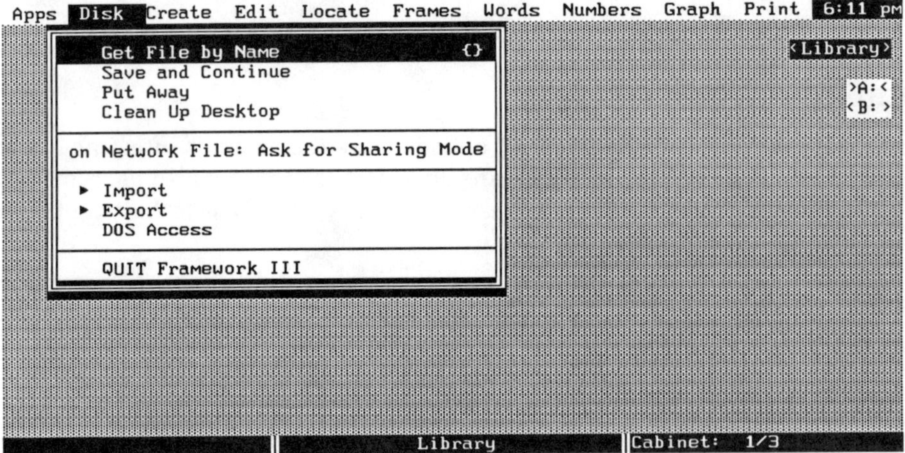

Bring specified file from disk and place beneath selected frame

2. {Press **Ctrl-G**}. Press **Up Arrow** to move the cursor to the Get File by Name option and then press **Enter**. The cursor moves to the Message line at the bottom of your desktop.
3. Type **B:BIRTHDAY**. As you type, notice that the braces next to the Get File by Name option fill. When finished, press **Enter** twice. The disk is read and the frame you specified is opened on your desktop as follows.

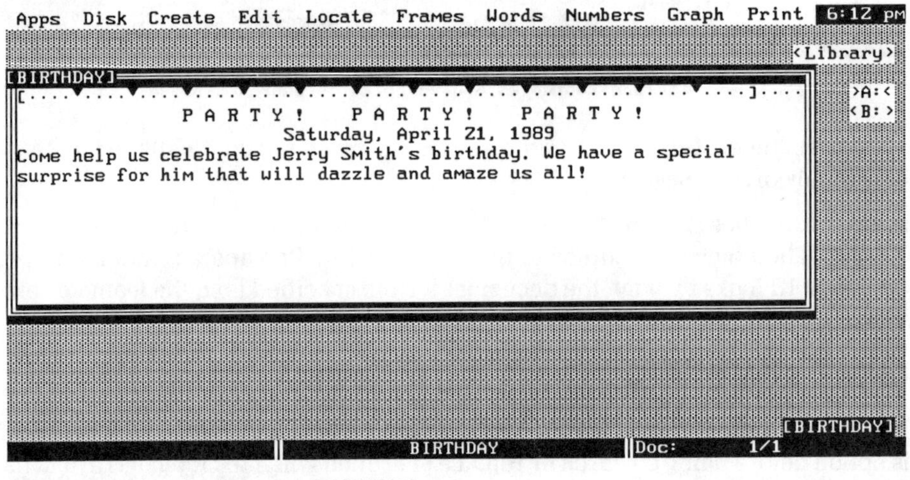

4. Press **Grey +** and position your cursor to the point just after Jerry Smith's name in the invitation.
5. {Press **Ctrl-E** and then **Ctrl-F**}. Press **Ins** to move the cursor to the Main Menu line. Press the arrow (cursor) keys until the Edit Menu frame is open on your desktop. Press **Down Arrow** until the cursor is positioned on Footnotes Options and press **Enter**.

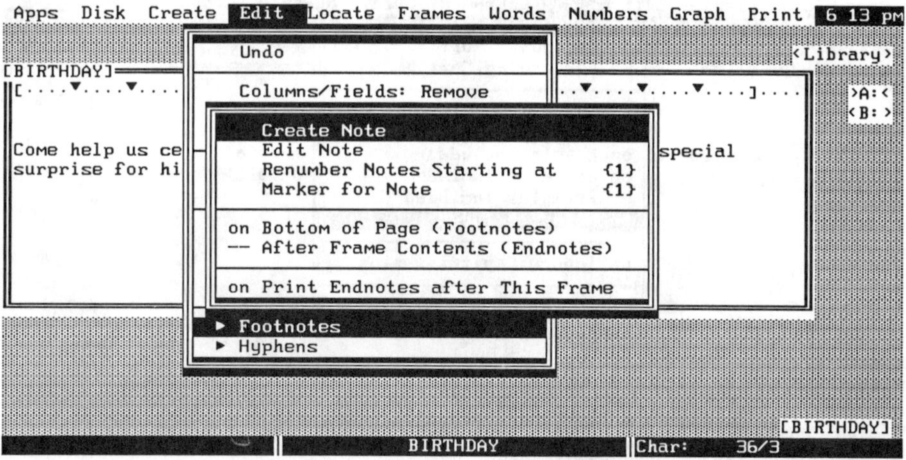

6. {Press **Ctrl-C**}. If necessary, use your arrow keys to highlight the Create Note option and press **Enter**. Since you are creating a footnote, the number 1 appears as the footnote number by default.
7. Type **Jerry is our marketing manager.** and press **Enter**.

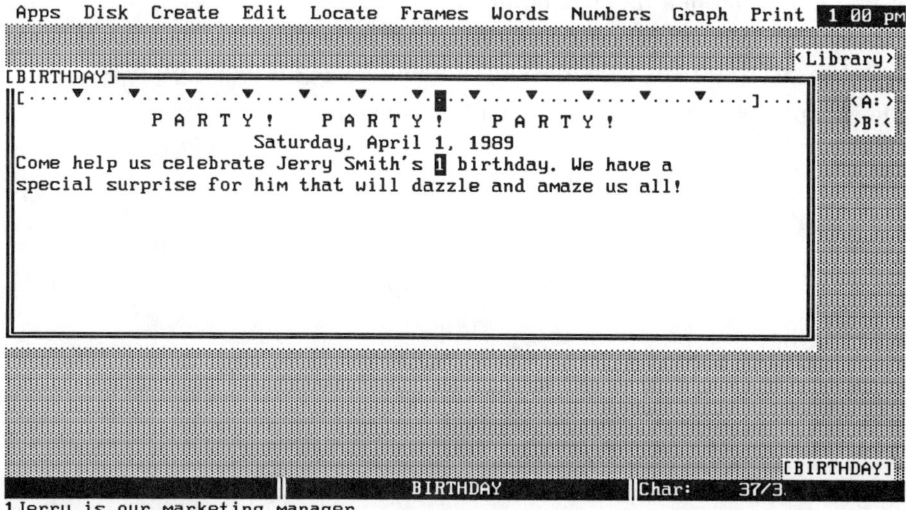

8. Press **Esc** to remove the submenu and return to the document.
9. {Press **Ctrl-L**}. Press **Ins** to move the cursor to the Main Menu line. Press **Right Arrow** until the Locate Menu frame is also open on your desktop. Notice that the Notes Included option is turned on. (If not, press **Ctrl-N** to turn it on. Also turn on Contents Included if it is not currently on.)

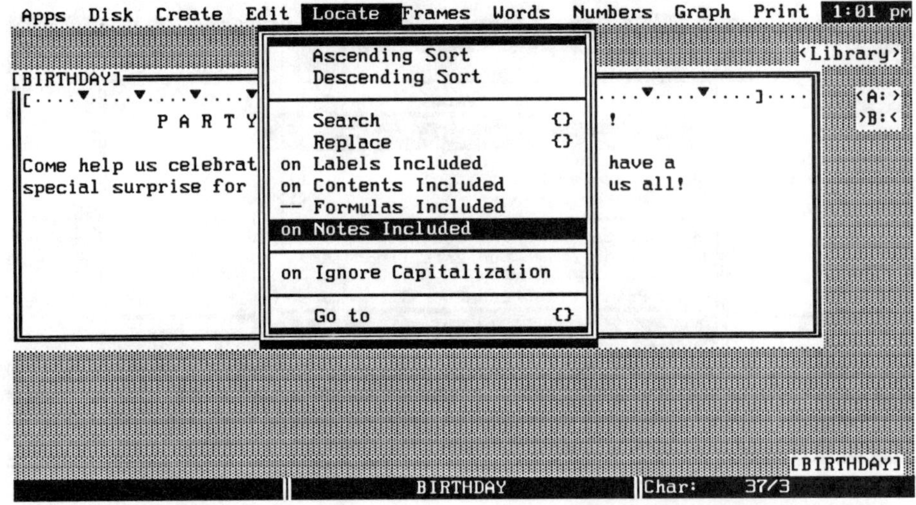

10. {Press **Ctrl-S**}. Press **Up Arrow** until the cursor is positioned on the Search { } option and press **Enter**. Type **Marketing** and press **Enter**. The Locate Menu frame disappears from your desktop. Notice that the cursor is positioned on the word Marketing in the footnote.
11. Press **Esc** to discontinue the Search activity.
12. Press **Gray –** twice to highlight the BIRTHDAY frame. Since the file has not been changed, press **Del** to remove it from the desktop without saving it again on disk.
13. Turn to Module 44 to continue the learning sequence.

Module 59

NUMBER LABELS

DESCRIPTION

When printing outlines, you often don't want to print the numbers with the topic and subtopic headings. To remove the numbering system, just select the Number Labels option. This option is available through the Frames Menu frame.

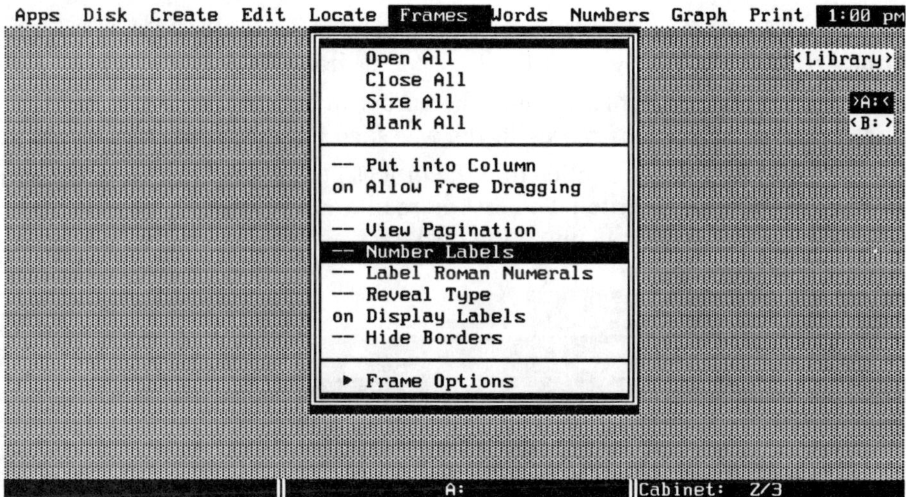

The Number Labels option is turned on and off when selected. Framework III presets this option on so that each new outline is created with the numbers displayed throughout the outline. When turned off, your outline resembles the following display.

Select this option at any time for an open outline frame. Position the cursor on the frame and select this option. The numbers are removed from all topic and subtopic headings.

By positioning the cursor on a topic and selecting this option, you limit the effect of this option. Only the numbers for the subtopics related to the selected topic are removed or displayed.

APPLICATIONS

Use this option with any outline frame. It lets you remove or display the topic and subtopic numbering system. This is useful when you are printing the topic outline but don't want the numbering system on the printed document.

TYPICAL OPERATION

This illustration shows you how to use the Number Labels option of the Frames Menu frame. Make sure that your desktop is clear and the cursor is positioned on one of the drive indicators. The shortcut key combinations, if applicable, are enclosed by braces.

1. {Press **Ctrl-D**}. Press **Ins** to move the cursor to the Main Menu line. Next, press **Left Arrow** or **Right Arrow**, if necessary, until the Disk Menu frame is open on your desktop.
2. {Press **Ctrl-G**}. Press **Up Arrow** to move the cursor to the Get File by Name { } option and then press **Enter**. The cursor moves to the Message line at the bottom of your desktop.
3. Type **EXERCISE**. As you type, notice that the braces next to the Get File by Name { } option fill. When finished, press **Enter**. The disk is read and the frame you specified is opened on your desktop. If it appears only in the desktop tray with the cursor, just press **Enter** to open it on your desktop.

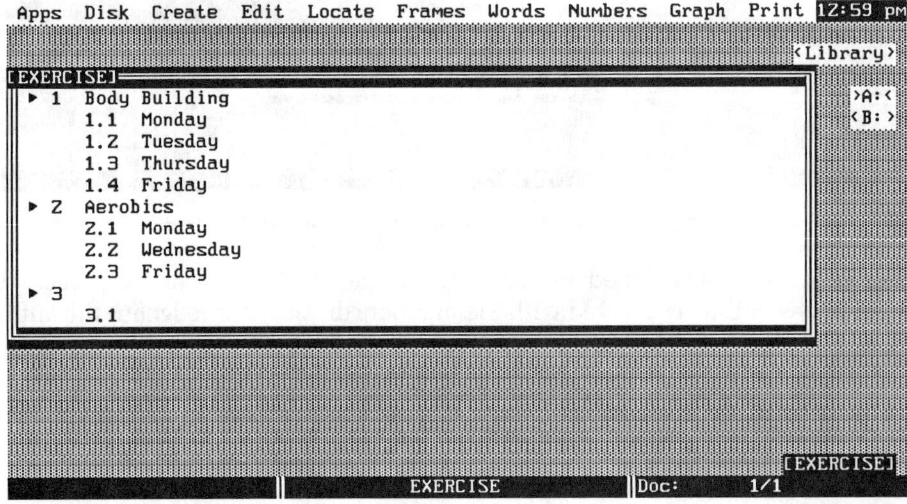

4. {Press **Ctrl-F**}. Press **Ins** to move the cursor to the Main Menu line. Next, press **Right Arrow** until the Frames Menu frame is also open on your desktop.

5. {Press **Ctrl-N**}. Press **Up Arrow** until the cursor is positioned on the Number Labels option and press **Enter**. The menu frame disappears and your outline is changed to resemble the following display.

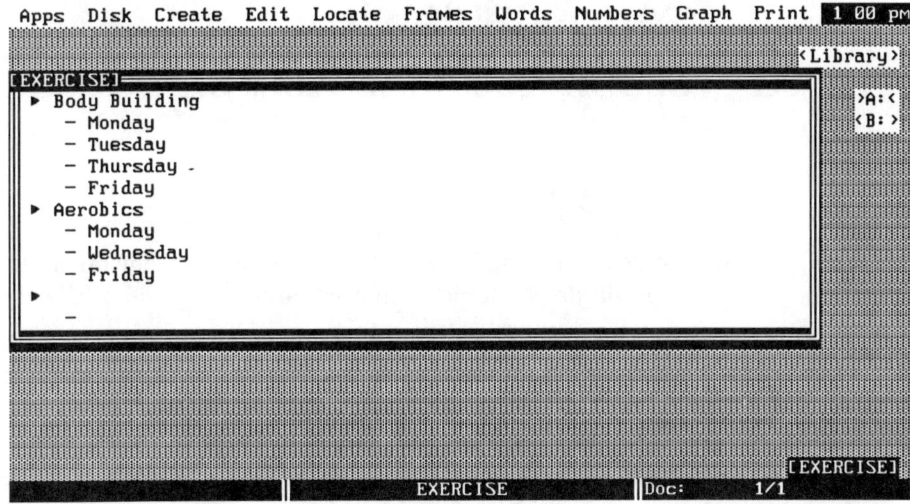

Frames: Number Labels off

6. Press **Gray +** to move the cursor inside the open frame. Position it on the first topic of the outline.
7. {Press **Ctrl-F** and **Ctrl-N**}. Open the Frame Menu frame again and select the Number Labels option. Notice that only the first topic and its subtopics have numbers displayed.
8. The outline on your desktop has been changed but there is no reason to save this change on disk. Press **Gray –** and then **Del** to remove the frame from your desktop without saving it.
9. {Press **Ctrl-D**}. Press **Ins** to move the cursor to the Main Menu line. Next, press **Left Arrow** until the Disk Menu frame is open on your desktop.
10. {Press **Ctrl-Q**}. Using the arrow (cursor) keys, position the cursor on the QUIT Framework option and press **Enter**. Type **Y** when Framework III asks if you're sure you want to quit Framework III. The system prompt appears on your screen. This ends this Framework III session.
11. Turn to Module 73 to continue the learning sequence.

Module 60

OPEN ALL, CLOSE ALL, SIZE ALL, BLANK ALL

DESCRIPTION

There are many times when you want to affect several or all frames in your open outline. Just position the cursor on the frame border or topic of interest and select one of these options.

For example, you want to change the size of all frames in the outline. Instead of using the F6 (Extend) key to expand the size of the cursor, just position the cursor on the outer frame border or topic and select the Size All option.

Each of these options are available through the Frames Menu frame.

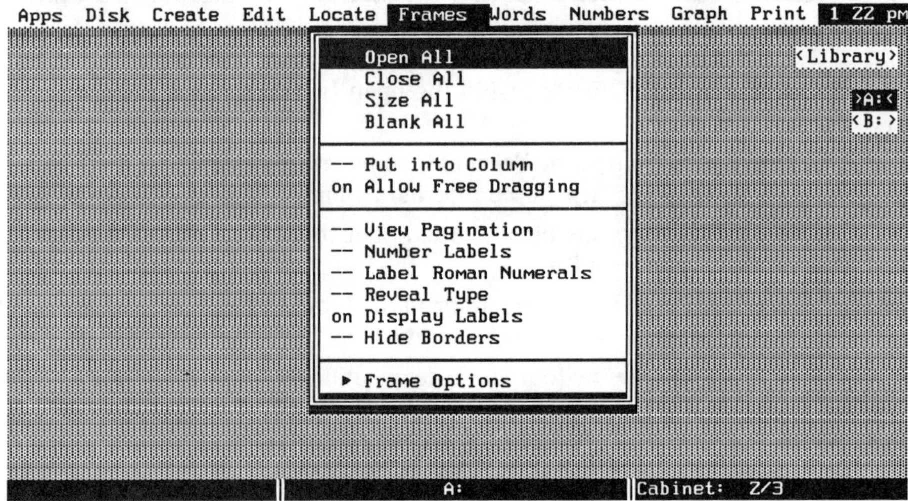

Open the selected frames and all frames within them

Open All This option makes all subframes within the selected frame or topic available to you. For example, if you collapsed an outline with the Close All option, select this option to reopen the outline frames.

It is also used for databases. When using a FRED command to filter the database, Framework III restricts the records seen within the open frame. Selecting the Open All option releases the filter so that all records are again seen.

Close All Use this option when your outline gets too large for your open window. When you position the cursor on the outermost frame and select the Close All option, only the major topics of your outline are displayed as in the following desktop.

Next, move the cursor to the topic with which you want to work and select the Open All option. This opens only the frames for the selected topic. Select the topic heading again and use the Close All option.

Size All This option lets you use the F4 (Size) key without first extending the size of the cursor by pressing F6 (Extend). Just position the cursor on the topic or subtopic which you need to affect. Then select the Size All option from the Frames Menu frame. Now, when the F4 (Size) key is pressed, all subframes within the selected topic change with each press of the arrow (cursor) keys.

Blank All Use this option to erase the contents of all selected frames. Just position the cursor on the topic or subtopic which you want emptied. Open the Frames Menu frame and select the Blank All option. Each subtopic frame is then empty.

APPLICATIONS

Use these options with any frame which contains subframes. You affect the status of each subframe within the topic selected by your cursor when the Open All, Close All, Size All, or Blank All option is selected.

TYPICAL OPERATION

This illustration shows you how to affect several frames within your open outline frame by selecting any of these options. Make sure that your desktop is clear and the cursor is positioned on one of the drive indicators. The shortcut key combinations, if applicable, are enclosed by braces.

1. {Press **Ctrl-D**}. Press **Ins** to move the cursor to the Main Menu line. Next, press **Left Arrow** or **Right Arrow**, if necessary, until the Disk Menu frame is open on your desktop.
2. {Press **Ctrl-G**}. Press **Up Arrow** to move the cursor to the Get File by Name { } option and then press **Enter**. The cursor moves to the Message line at the bottom of your desktop.

3. Type **EXERCISE**. As you type, notice that the braces next to the Get File by Name { } option fill. When finished, press **Enter**. The disk is read and the frame you specified is opened on your desktop. If it appears only in the desktop tray with the cursor, just press **Enter** to open it on your desktop.

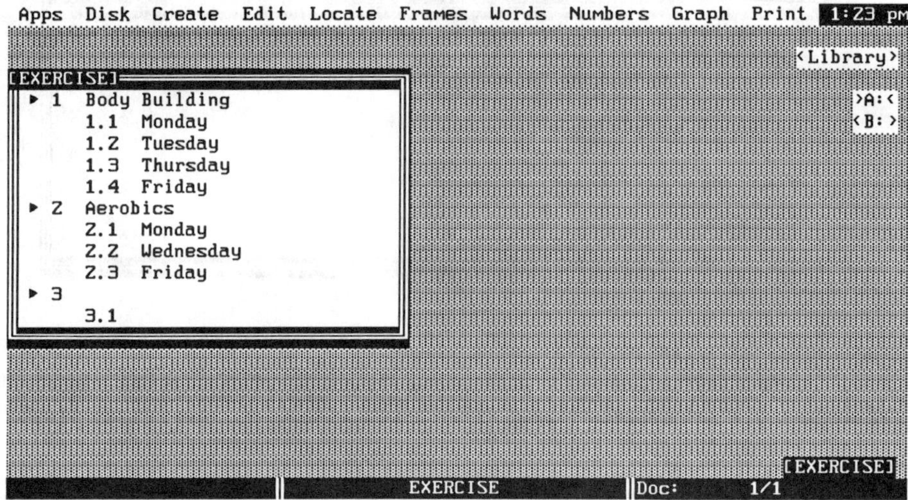

4. {Press **Ctrl-F**}. Press **Ins** to move the cursor to the Main Menu line. Next, press **Right Arrow** until the Frames Menu frame is also open on your desktop.
5. {Press **Ctrl-C**}. Press **Up Arrow** until the cursor is positioned on the Close All option and press **Enter**. This tells Framework III that you want to collapse the outline to just the major topics. Your desktop now resembles the following display.

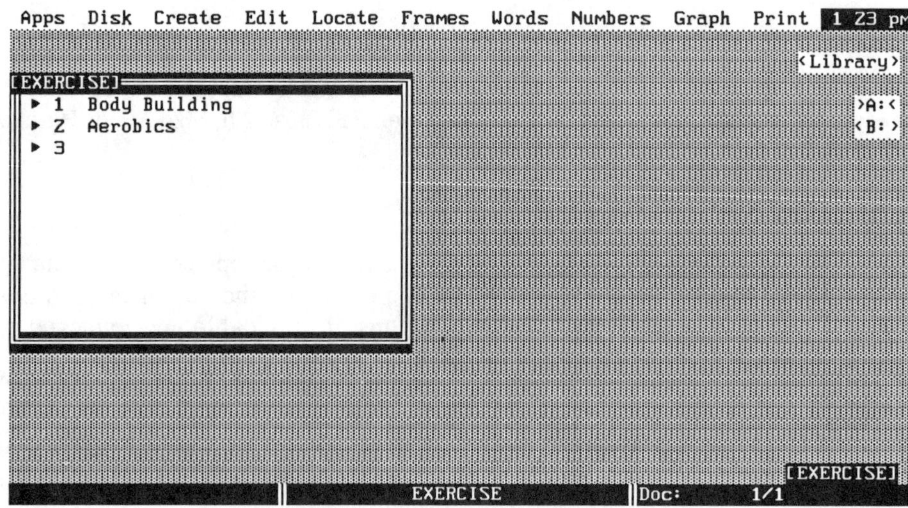

Frames: Close All

6. Press **Gray +** to move the cursor inside the open outline frame. Using the arrow keys, position the cursor on the first topic.
7. {Press **Ctrl-F**}. Press **Ins** to move the cursor to the Main Menu line. The Frames Menu frame is again open on your desktop.
8. {Press **Ctrl-O**}. Press **Up Arrow** until the cursor is positioned on the Open All option and press **Enter**. This tells Framework III that you want to expand the outline.
9. Press **F9** (Zoom). Notice the size of the frame borders. Then press **Up Arrow** until the cursor is positioned on the Monday topic heading.

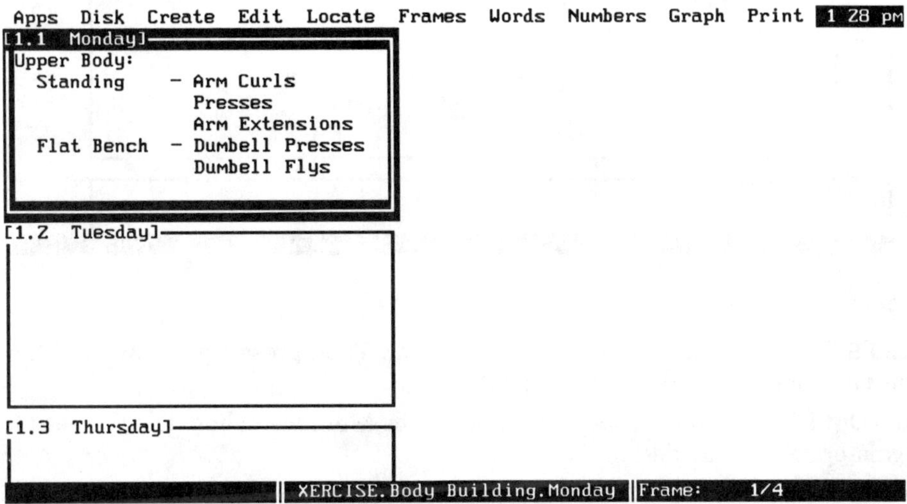

10. Press **F9** (Zoom) to return to Outline view. Then press **Up Arrow** move the cursor to the Body Building topic.
11. {Press **Ctrl-F**}. Press **Ins** to move the cursor to the Main Menu line. The Frames Menu frame is again open on your desktop.
12. {Press **Ctrl-S**}. Select the Size All option. This has the same effect as pressing **F6** (Extend) and **F4** (Size) to change the size of the frame borders.

13. Press **F9** (Zoom) to see the following display.

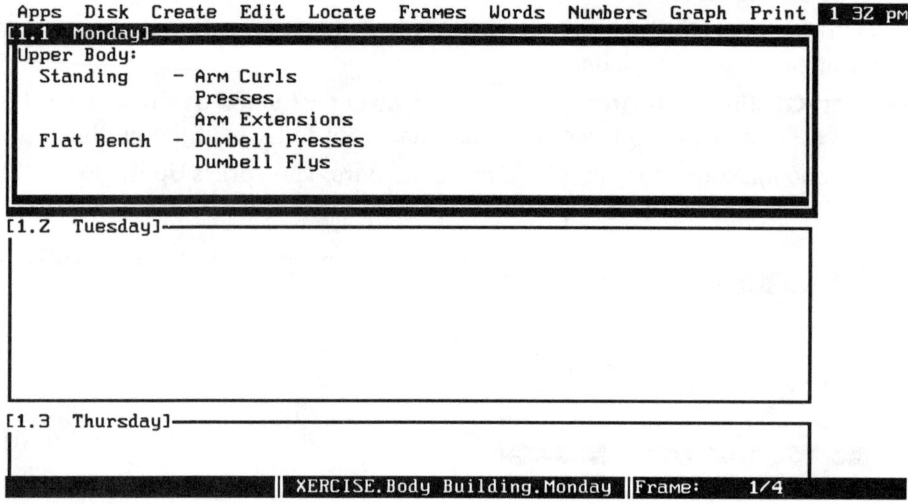

Notice the size of the frame borders.

14. Press **F9** (Zoom) again to return to Outline view. Then press **Up Arrow** until the cursor is again positioned on Body Building topic.
15. {Press **Ctrl-F**}. Press **Ins** to move the cursor to the Main Menu line. The Frames Menu frame is again open on your desktop.
16. {Press **Ctrl-B**}. Select the Blank All option. The computer beeps and a message appears on the Message line. It's telling you that this option is "undoable." Type **Y** to continue. When the message disappears, press **F9** (Zoom) and notice that each subframe is now empty.
17. Press **F9** (Zoom) again to return to the Outline view. Press **Gray –** twice to move the cursor to the EXERCISE frame border.
18. Don't save the outline since it is now empty. Just press **Del** to remove it from the desktop without saving it on disk.
19. {Press **Ctrl-D**}. Press **Ins** to move the cursor to the Main Menu line. Next, press **Left Arrow** until the Disk Menu frame is open on your desktop.
20. {Press **Ctrl-Q**}. Using the arrow (cursor) keys, position the cursor on the QUIT Framework option and press **Enter**. Type **Y** when Framework III asks if you're sure you want to quit Framework III. The system prompt appears on your screen. This ends this Framework III session.
21. Turn to Module 18 to continue the learning sequence.

Module 61

OPTIONS (FOR GRAPH)

DESCRIPTION

When you use Framework III to draw a graph, you paint a picture of numeric information. There are times when you need to change the look of your graph.

For example, you need to title each side of the graph or set the scale of the graph marks. This is where the Options submenu is handy. It is available through the Graph Menu frame.

The pointer next to the Options selection identifies it as a submenu. In other words, by selecting Options from the Graph Menu frame, you open a submenu from which you may choose. The submenu is open on the following desktop.

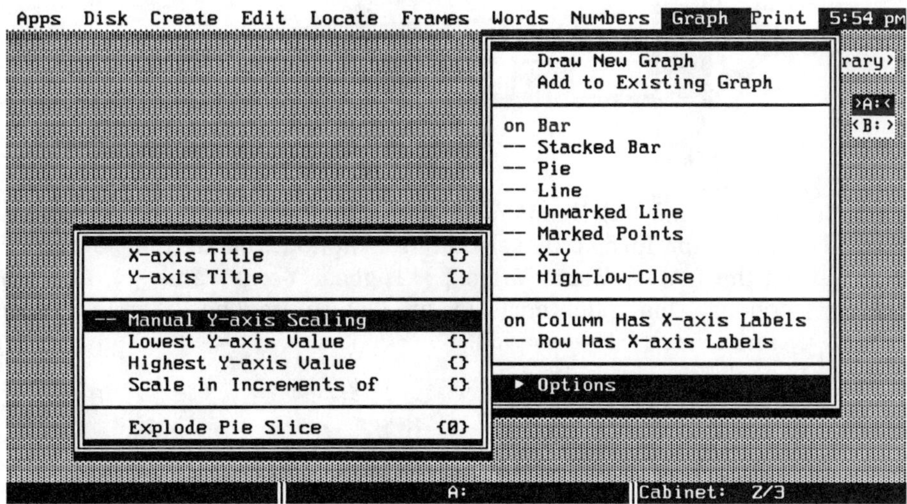

If ON, use the three options below to set scale for next graph drawn

The options with braces are used to provide more information to Framework III. When the option is selected, the cursor moves to the bottom of your desktop so that you can type the additional information. The Manual Y-axis Scaling is turned on and off when it is selected.

Each of the customizing options are as follows. Use one or any combination of these options before drawing your graphs.

X-axis Title To label the horizontal axis, select this option. The label you type for the X-axis Title is displayed below the X-axis numbers. The following example has "Sales Months" as the X-axis Title.

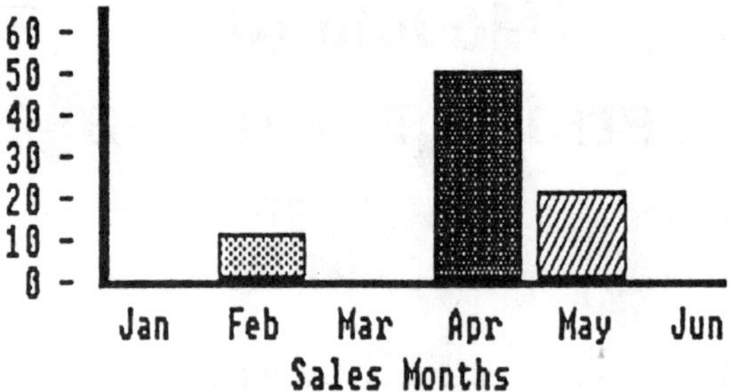

Y-axis Title This option is similar to the X-axis Title. It, however, assigns a title to the vertical line. The Y-axis title is "Millions."

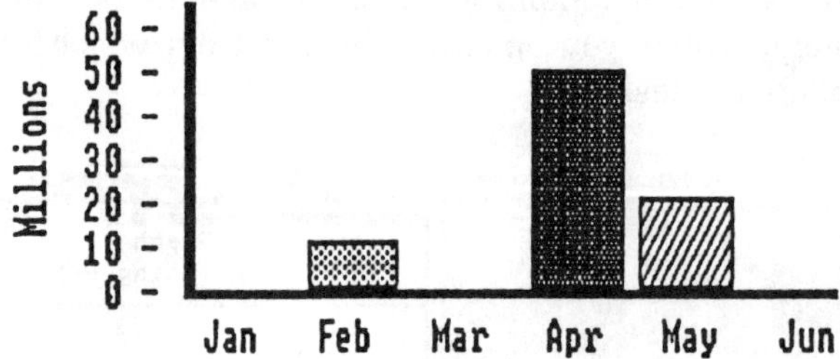

Manual Y-axis Scaling Framework III automatically sets the scaling of each axis when you draw a graph (excluding pie graph forms). By selecting this option, you set the Y-axis scale. This is done by also setting the Lowest Y-axis Value { }, Highest Y-axis Value { }, and the Scale in Increments of { } options. This option must be "on" before drawing the graph; otherwise, the graph is scaled by Framework III — not you.

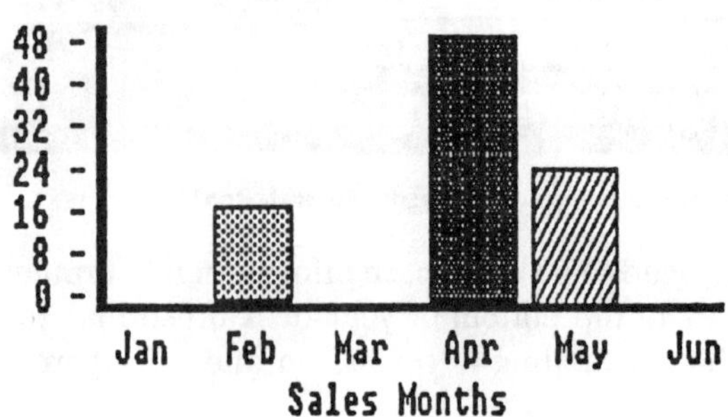

Lowest Y-axis Value { } When you select this option, type the lowest value you want for the Y-axis of your graph. The number you type appears at the bottom of the Y-axis. Remember that the Manual Y-axis Scaling option must be turned on before drawing the graph.

Highest Y-axis Value { } When you select this option, type the largest value you want for the Y-axis of your graph. The number you type appears at the top of the Y-axis. Remember that the Manual Y-axis Scaling option must be turned on before drawing the graph.

Scale in Increments of { } Select this option to type the amount you want added to the Lowest Y-axis Value for the next position on the Y-axis scale. This number is added to each position until the Highest Y-axis Value is reached. Remember that the Manual Y-axis Scaling option must be turned on before drawing the graph.

Explode Pie Slices {0} You can specify one, several, or all slices of the pie to move away from the circle. This draws attention to that segment of the graph. When this option is selected, Framework III asks how many slices you want to explode. By typing –1, you tell Framework III that all slices are to be separate. Typing 0 allows no explosion. When you type 1, Framework III separates the slice which identifies the first number selected from the spreadsheet or database.

After you have selected all the Graph Menu options you want, move the cursor to the Draw New Graph option and press Enter. Your picture is on its way.

APPLICATIONS

Use the Options submenu when you want Framework III to do more than just draw a graph. Provide titles or set the scale before letting Framework III draw your graph. These options let you enhance the picture to meet your needs.

TYPICAL OPERATION

This illustration shows you how to use some of the Options submenu selections to change the looks of your graph. Make sure that your desktop is clear and the cursor is positioned on one of the drive indicators. The shortcut key combinations, if applicable, are enclosed by braces.

1. {Press **Ctrl-D**}. Press **Ins** to move the cursor to the Main Menu line. Next, press the arrow (cursor) keys until the Disk Menu frame is open on your desktop.
2. {Press **Ctrl-G**}. Press **Up Arrow** until the cursor is positioned on the Get File by Name option and press **Enter**. The cursor then moves to the Message line at the bottom of your desktop. Type **SALES** and press **Enter**. The spreadsheet opens on your desktop.
3. Press **Gray +** to move the cursor inside the open frame.
4. Press **Esc** to change the cursor size. Press **Up Arrow** until the cursor is positioned on cell B2. Press **F6** (Extend). Press **Right Arrow** twice until cells B2, C2, and D2 are highlighted. When finished, press **Enter**.
5. {Press **Ctrl-G** and then **Ctrl-O**}. Press **Ins** to move the cursor to the Main Menu line. Press **Right Arrow** until the Graph Menu is also open on your desktop. Press **Down Arrow** until the cursor is positioned on the Options option and press **Enter**. The submenu also opens on your desktop.

6. Select each of the submenu options until your desktop resembles the following display.

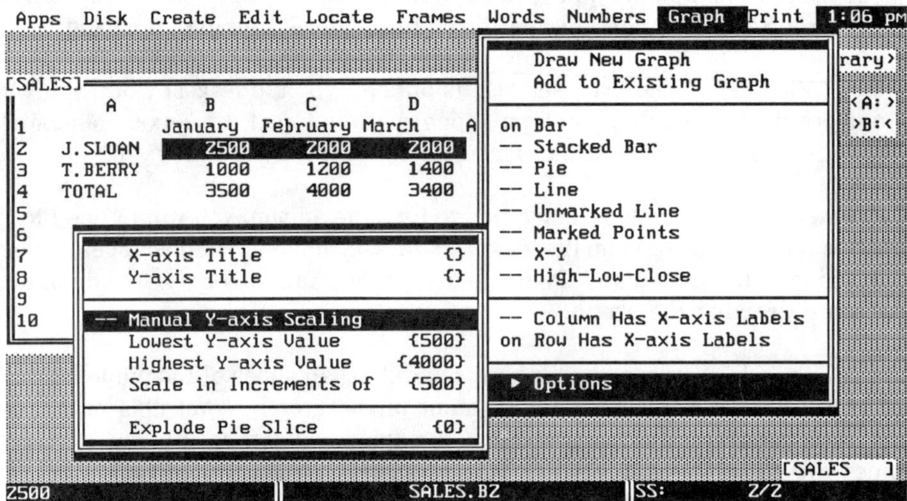

7. Press **Esc** to close the open menus.
8. {Press **Ctrl-G**}. Press **Ins** to move the cursor to the Main Menu line. The Graph Menu frame is again open on your desktop.
9. {Press **Ctrl-L** and then **Ctrl-D**}. Select the Line option so it is turned on. Then select the Draw New Graph option. Framework III asks if you want to draw it in the open frame or a new one. Just press **Enter** to use a new frame. The graph resembles the following display.

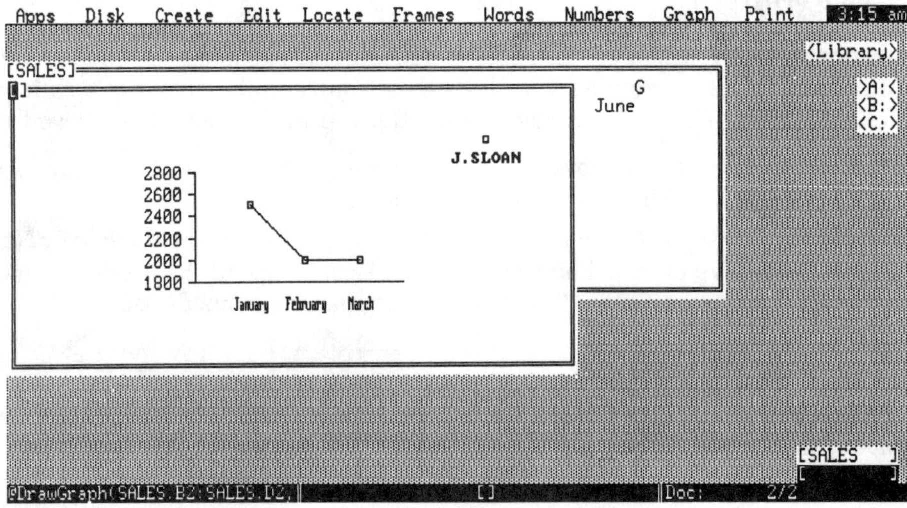

10. Press **Del** twice to remove both open frames from your desktop.
11. {Press **Ctrl-D**}. Press **Ins** to move the cursor to the Main Menu line. Press **Left Arrow** until the Disk Menu frame is open.
12. {Press **Ctrl-Q**}. Select the QUIT Framework option. When asked if you are sure you want to quit, type **Y**. This is the end of your Framework III session.
13. Turn to Module 4 to continue the learning sequence.

Module 62

OPTIONS FOR RECALC

DESCRIPTION

This option opens a submenu to be used for spreadsheets or databases which contain calculated cells or fields. Framework III is preset to automatically rework every formula you specify within a spreadsheet or database.

If there are many calculations, you have to wait until they are completed before you continue. By selecting options from the Options for Recalc submenu, you gain control over the recalculations. This submenu is available through the Numbers Menu frame.

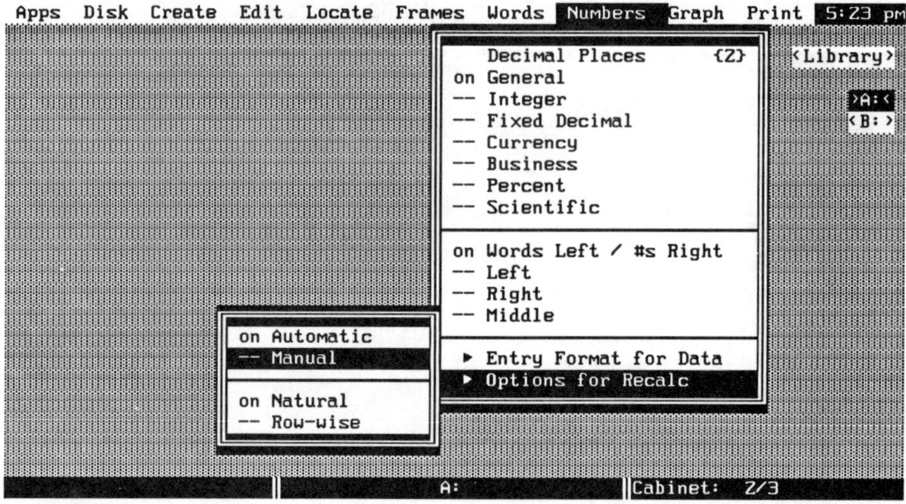

If ON, spreadsheet/database formulas recalculate only when you press F5 RECALC

The options within the submenu are turned on when selected. Selecting the Manual option turns that option on and the Automatic option off. When the Automatic option is selected again, the Manual option is turned off. The same is true of the Natural and Row-wise options. When the Row-wise option is selected, the Natural option is turned off.

If the Manual option is turned on, all calculations are reworked only when you press the F5 (Recalc) key. This lets you change the numbers within the spreadsheet without having to wait for the calculated fields to be changed. When you want Framework III recalculations, just press F5 (Recalc).

The Natural and Row-wise options let you tell Framework III the order in which you want recalculation to occur. By selecting the Natural option, you want each cell reviewed before recalculation occurs. For example, if the cell A6 uses B10 and D8, Framework III reviews and reworks the used cells first. This way, each calculation is performed in order of importance. This direction is best for most spreadsheets.

When the Row-wise option is turned on, Framework III works its way across the spreadsheet or database. Each calculation is reworked line by line. All cells from left to right in row or record 1 are done first. Next, Framework III reworks those in row 2. This direction is best for databases.

APPLICATIONS

Use this submenu of options when you are working with a spreadsheet or database which does several calculations. The frequency and direction of recalculation is your choice.

For example, suppose you need to change the numbers in 12 cells of a spreadsheet. If those 12 cells affect 10 cells which are calculated, you should consider selecting the Manual option.

By turning the Manual option on, you are able to first change all the cells in the spreadsheet. When finished, press F5 (Recalc) so that the 10 formulas are reworked.

The direction of recalculation is especially important. For example, cells A6, B10, and C10 are all calculated cells. Cell A6 equals cell B10 plus cell C10. You want cells B10 and C10 reworked before cell A6, so the Natural option must be turned on.

If the Row-wise option is selected instead, cell A6 is calculated with the numbers currently in cells B10 and C10. When the Row-wise option is turned on, cell B10 is changed and then cell C10. When you look at the spreadsheet and do the calculations yourself, you find that cell A6 is wrong.

Use the Manual option when you have a spreadsheet or database that needs many changes or calculations. Use the Row-wise option on spreadsheets or databases which need to calculate across each row before going on to the next one.

Remember, when the Automatic option is turned on, the Manual option is turned off. When the Natural option is turned on, the Row-wise option is turned off.

TYPICAL OPERATION

This illustration shows you the differences in a spreadsheet when using the Options for Recalc submenu. Make sure that your desktop is clear and the cursor is positioned on one of the drive indicators. The shortcut key combinations, if applicable, are enclosed by braces.

1. {Press **Ctrl-D**}. Press **Ins** to move the cursor to the Main Menu line. Next, press **Left Arrow** or **Right Arrow**, if necessary, until the Disk Menu frame is open on your desktop.
2. {Press **Ctrl-G**}. Press **Up Arrow** to move the cursor to the Get File by Name { } option and then press **Enter**. The cursor moves to the Message line at the bottom of your desktop.

3. Type **CHECKBK**. As you type, notice that the braces next to the Get File by Name { } option fill. When finished, press **Enter**. The disk is read and the frame you specified is opened on your desktop. If it appears only in the desktop tray with the cursor, just press **Enter** to open it on your desktop.
4. Press **Gray +** to move the cursor inside the spreadsheet.
5. Press **Up Arrow** and **Right Arrow** until the cursor is positioned on cell E1. Type **Difference** and press **Enter**.
6. Press **Right Arrow** to cell F1. Type **+B5−B7** and press **Enter**. This cell is the same as cell B8 but is located before the cells it uses for its calculation. Since the Automatic and Natural options of the Options for Recalc submenu are turned on, the cell is immediately filled with "3.10."

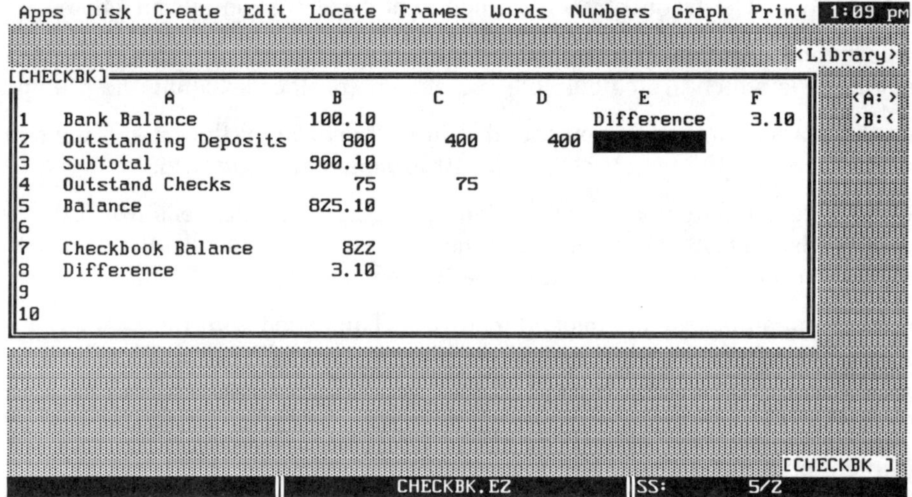

7. {Press **Ctrl-N**}. Press **Ins** to move the cursor to the Main Menu line. Press **Right Arrow** until the Numbers Menu frame is open.
8. {Press **Ctrl-O**}. Use the arrow (cursor) keys to position the cursor on the Options for Recalc option and press **Enter**. The submenu frame is also opened on your desktop.

9. {Press **Ctrl-R**}. Position the cursor on the Row-wise option and press **Enter**. Move the cursor to cell C4, type **78.10**, and press **Enter**. Cells B4, B5, and B8 change as a result of the Outstanding Checks; however, cell F1 is still 3.10, because the Row-wise option is turned on. When cell F1 is calculated, B5 is 825.10 and cell B7 is 822.

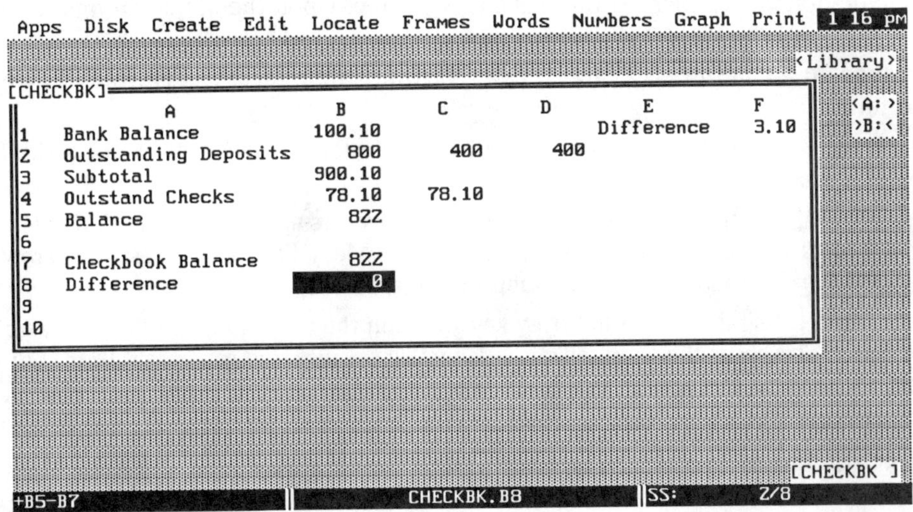

10. Press **F5** (Recalc) to force cell E1 to refigure the formula with the new numbers. Now, cell F1 contains 0.
11. {Press **Ctrl-N**, then **Ctrl-O** and **Ctrl-M**}. Again, open the Numbers Menu frame. Select the Options for Recalc option and turn on the Manual option. Now, type **75** and press **Enter** in cell C4. Notice that none of the formula cells are reworked.

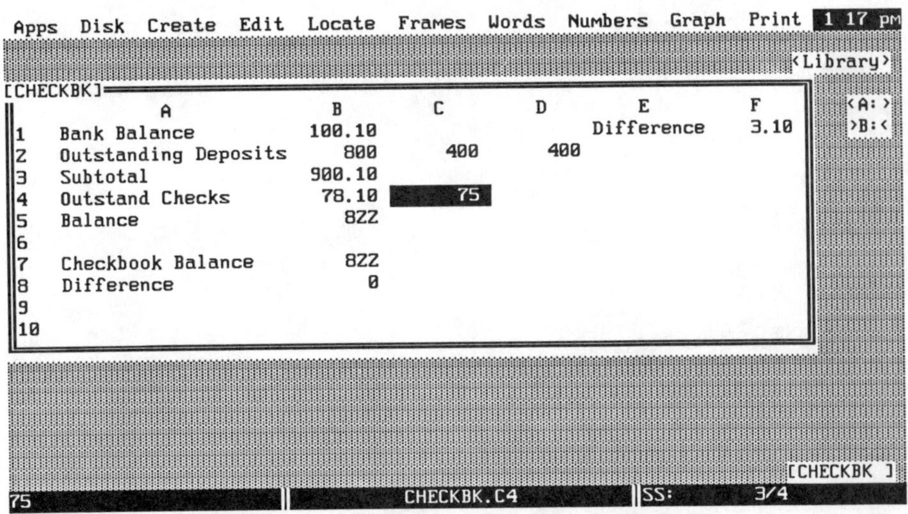

12. Press **F5** (Recalc) to refigure all calculated cells. Notice that cell F1 still contains 0 since the Row-wise option is still turned on. This shows you how the Row-wise option should be used only in certain conditions.
13. {Press **Ctrl-N**, then **Ctrl-O** and **Ctrl-A**}. Open the Numbers Menu frame. Select the Options for Recalc option and turn on the Automatic option. Open the submenu again and select the Natural option.
14. Now, type **78.10** and press **Enter** in cell C4. Notice that cell F1 is reworked — cell B8 is not right.
15. Press **Gray –** to move the cursor to the frame border. Press **Enter** to close the frame to the desktop tray.
16. {Press **Ctrl-D**}. After all this work, you want to save the spreadsheet so that it is available next month. Press **Ins** to move the cursor to the Main Menu line. Next, press the arrow (cursor) keys until the Disk Menu frame is open on your desktop.
17. {Press **Ctrl-P**}. Using the **Down Arrow** key, position the cursor on the Put Away option and press **Enter**. This saves the changed spreadsheet on the disk and removes it from your desktop.
18. {Press **Ctrl-D**}. Press **Ins** again to move the cursor to the Main Menu line. The Disk Menu frame is open on your desktop.
19. {Press **Ctrl-Q**}. Position the cursor on the QUIT Framework option and press **Enter**. When asked if you really want to quit Framework III, type **Y**. This Framework III session is complete.
20. Turn to Module 28 to continue the learning sequence.

Module 63

OUTLINE

DESCRIPTION

The outline capability of Framework III is a perfect tool for writing documents like term papers, business proposals, or books. You can include text, graphs, spreadsheets, etc. in your outline.

The Outline option is available through the Create Menu.

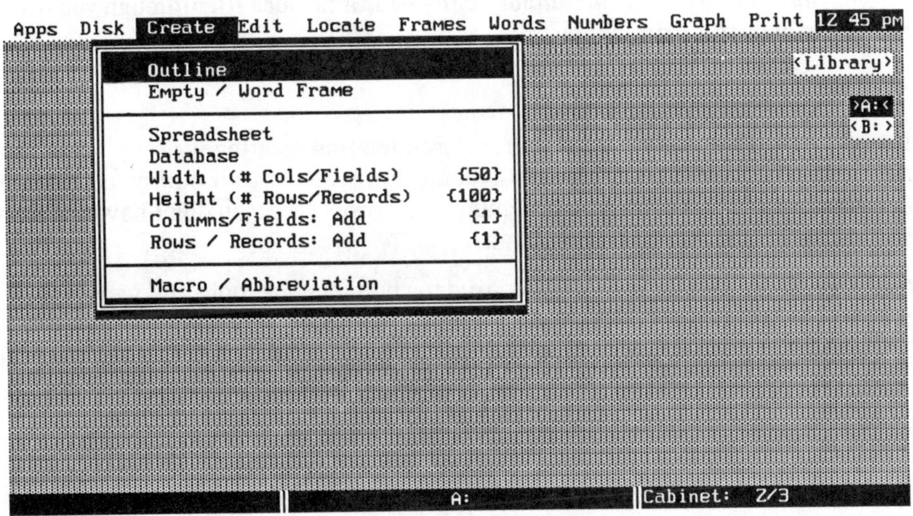

Create an outline of nested frames

By selecting the Outline option, an empty outline frame is opened on your desktop. It resembles the following frame.

Begin by building an outline of topics and subtopics. This outline can be changed at any time so don't feel that you have to have everything finalized before using Framework III.

Topics and subtopics can be added to or deleted from your outline frame. For example, if you need five subtopics under topic number 1, insert two more. If you don't need topic number 3 at all, delete it.

Each subtopic of the outline is written in a frame of its own. Use the Framework III options which apply to the current frame type.

The frames are usually word frames (text) but include other types of frames when you need them. For example, include graphs as part of the document.

Rearrange the outline as often as you want — when you want. As you move topics on the outline frame, each frame within the topic is also moved. It's just like rearranging sheets of paper into another order.

When you are ready to print, send each frame separately or the whole document to the printer. Page numbering, margins, etc. are set automatically by Framework III, although you are in control of each option through the Print Menu.

APPLICATIONS

The Outline option of Framework III is a great organization tool for writing. Create an outline of topics and subtopics much like a Table of Contents. Each line of your outline consists of a frame which is accessed quickly. Unlike using a regular word processor, you don't have to wade through many pages of text to find a specific subject.

Also, there are times when you are more prepared to complete one topic and wait to do the others. Piece by piece, your document begins to take shape. The order may change again (at least once more) to accommodate a smoother flow as you expand a topic, delete another, and move paragraphs. Framework III helps you do the required rearrangement easily.

TYPICAL OPERATION

This illustration shows you how to use the outline capabilities of Framework III. Make sure that your desktop is clear and the cursor is positioned on one of the drive indicators. The shortcut key combinations, if applicable, are enclosed by braces.

1. {Press **Ctrl-C**}. Press **Ins** to move the cursor to the Main Menu line. Next, press **Left Arrow** or **Right Arrow**, if necessary, until the Create Menu frame is open on your desktop.
2. {Press **Ctrl-O**}. Press **Up Arrow** to move the cursor to the Outline option and then press **Enter**. The following outline model appears.

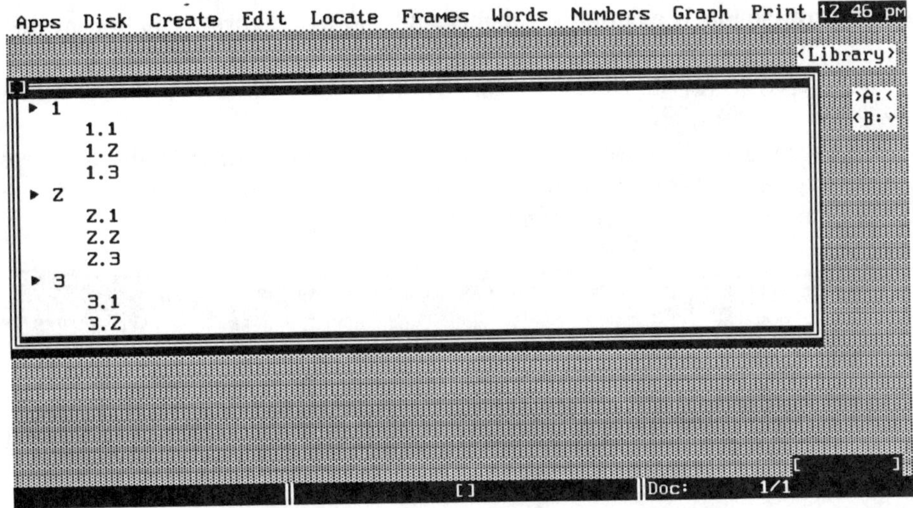

3. The cursor is positioned within the brackets on the top border of the frame. Type **EXERCISE** within the brackets and press **Enter**. This is the name of the outline file which is to be saved on disk. When it is saved, it is named EXERCISE.FW3. As you type each letter, notice that the same letters are being typed into your tray and on the left side of the Message line.
4. Press **Gray +** to move the cursor to the inside of your open frame. Notice that the cursor is positioned on the first topic of your outline. Type **Body Building** and press **Enter**.
5. Press **Down Arrow** until the cursor is positioned on subtopic 1.3. {Press **Ctrl-C** and **Ctrl-E**}. Press **Ins** to move the cursor to the Main Menu line. Reopen the Create Menu frame and select the Empty/Word Frame option. Notice that subtopic 1.4 is added to your outline.
6. Press **Down Arrow** to move the cursor to topic 2, type **Aerobics** and press **Enter**.
7. Press **Down Arrow** to position the cursor on topic 3 and press **Del**. This removes the third topic and its subtopics from your outline.
8. Press **Up Arrow** to move the cursor to subtopic 1.1, type **Monday** and press **Enter**. Continue this process so that your outline resembles the following display.

```
[EXERCISE]
▸ 1  Body Building
     1.1  Monday
     1.2  Tuesday
     1.3  Thursday
     1.4  Friday
▸ 2  Aerobics
     2.1  Monday
     2.2  Wednesday
     2.3  Friday
```

9. Press **Up Arrow** so that the cursor highlights subtopic 1.1 and press **F10** to view the subtopic frame. Notice that there are actually two frames open on your desktop. The outside one is the topic frame (upper level) and the inside one is the subtopic frame (lower level or subframe).
10. Press **Gray +** to move the cursor inside the subframe. Type **Upper Body:** and press **Enter**. Remember to press **Enter** to move to the next line, press **Backspace** or **Del** to delete a letter. Complete your frame so that it resembles the following display.

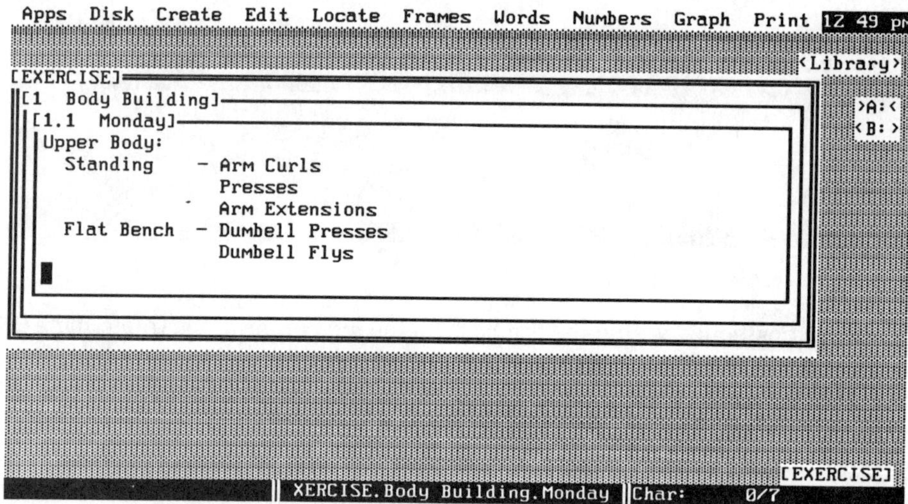

11. Press **Gray –** to move the cursor to the frame border. Press **F10** to return to the Outline view.
12. {Press **Ctrl-D**}. Press **Ins** to move the cursor to the Main Menu line. Next, press **Left Arrow** until the Disk Menu frame is open on your desktop.
13. {Press **Ctrl-P**}. Press **Down Arrow** or **Up Arrow** to the Put Away option and press **Enter**. This option clears your desktop and saves the file called EXERCISE.FW3 on the data disk.
14. {Press **Ctrl-D**}. Press **Ins** to move the cursor to the Main Menu line. The Disk Menu frame is again open on your desktop.
15. {Press **Ctrl-Q**}. Using the arrow (cursor) keys, position the cursor on the QUIT Framework option and press **Enter**. Type **Y** when Framework III asks if you're sure you want to quit Framework III. The system prompt appears on your screen. This ends this Framework III session.
16. Turn to Module 27 to continue the learning sequence.

Module 64

OUTPUT OPTIONS

DESCRIPTION

This selection presents a submenu of options from which you choose what part of your open frame you print. For example, there are times when you need to print only one or two pages of a document or you want Framework III to print three copies instead of just one.

To open the submenu, use the Output Options selection of the Print Menu frame. The pointer on the left of the option indicates that selecting it causes a submenu of options to open on your desktop. The Print Menu frame and the submenu for Output Options appears in the following display.

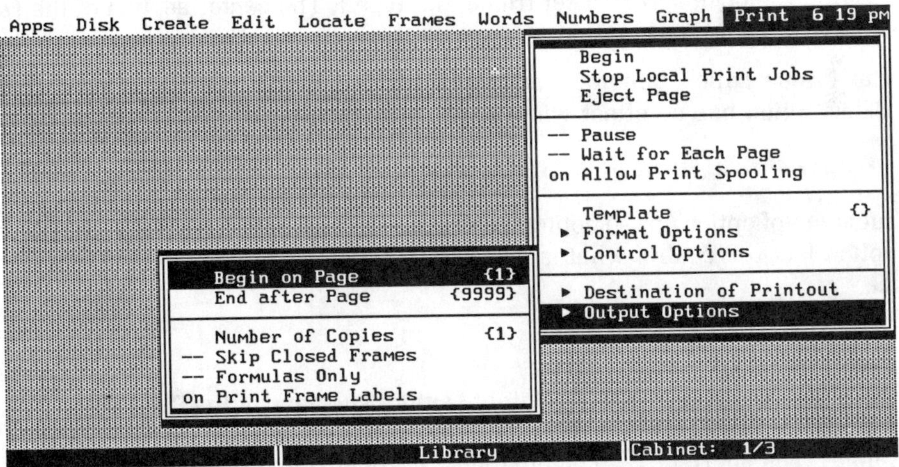

When you select one of the options in the submenu, don't expect anything to happen until you later select the Begin option of the Print Menu frame. The submenu options are used to tell Framework III what you want done when you select the Begin option.

Select the Begin on Page { } option to tell Framework III which page of the document you want first. Position the cursor on the option, press Enter, type the page number of the part of the document you want to print and press Enter. The same process is used to set the End after Page { } option.

For example, to print only page number five of your document, select the Begin on Page { } option, type 5, and press Enter. Next, do the same process with the End after Page { } option. This tells Framework III that you want to skip to page five, print that one page, and then skip the rest of the document.

If the End after Page { } option is not changed from 9999, Framework III prints from page five until the rest of the document is printed. If you need pages five and eight, change both options to 5 and print that page. When it printed, change both options to 8 and print that page.

The Number of Copies { } option lets you tell Framework III how many copies you want to print. Unless you change the number within the braces, only one copy is printed when the Begin option is selected.

The other three options of the submenu are turned on and off when selected. Just position the cursor on the option and press Enter. The dashes (off) change to the word "on."

Use the Skip Closed Frames option when printing an outline. When on, this option prints only the frames which are open on your desktop instead of the whole document.

The Formulas Only option lets you print all the formulas used within the open spreadsheet or database frame. Spreadsheet formulas are printed with the cell identifiers (e.g. CHECKBK.G3) or with English-like names (e.g. CHECKBK.[0].[Balance]). To choose the type of cell names, position the cursor within the open spreadsheet frame and type !. The center section of the status line tells you which form you've requested.

Use the Print Frame Labels option to include or exclude the frame labels when printing the document. This option has no effect when printing outlines.

APPLICATIONS

Open the submenu of options by selecting the Output Options option from the Print Menu. Each submenu option lets you control what is printed when you select the Begin option of the Print Menu frame.

TYPICAL OPERATION

This example shows you how to use the Output Options submenu of the Print Menu frame. Close any open frames on your desktop and position the cursor on your data drive indicator (drive B in this example). The shortcut key combinations, if applicable, are enclosed by braces.

1. {Press **Ctrl-D**}. Press **Ins** to move the cursor to the Main Menu line. Next, press **Left Arrow** or **Right Arrow**, if necessary, until the Disk Menu frame is open on your desktop.
2. {Press **Ctrl-G**}. Press **Up Arrow** to move the cursor to the Get File by Name { } option and press **Enter**. The cursor moves to the Message line at the bottom of your desktop.

3. Type **B:CHECKBK**. As you type, notice that the braces next to the Get File by Name { } option fill. When finished, press **Enter**. The disk is read and the frame you specified is opened on your desktop.
4. {Press **Ctrl-P** and **Ctrl-O**}. Press **Ins** to move the cursor to the Main Menu line. Open the Print Menu frame, select Output Options to open the submenu.

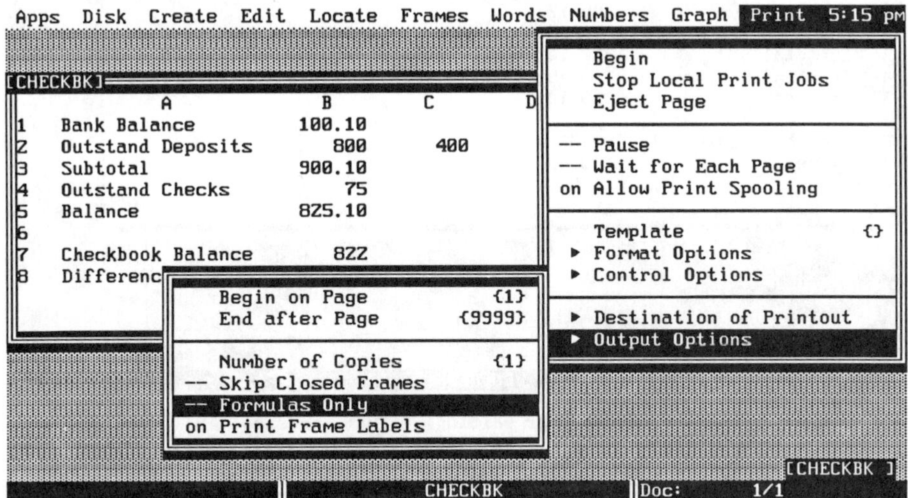

If ON, print only the formulas

5. Using the arrow (cursor) keys, position the cursor on the Formulas Only option and press **Enter**. The word "on" appears to the left of the option. Press **Esc** to close the submenu.
6. Reopen the Print Menu frame and select the Begin option. Before you press **Enter**, make sure that the printer is on. A sample of the printout follows.

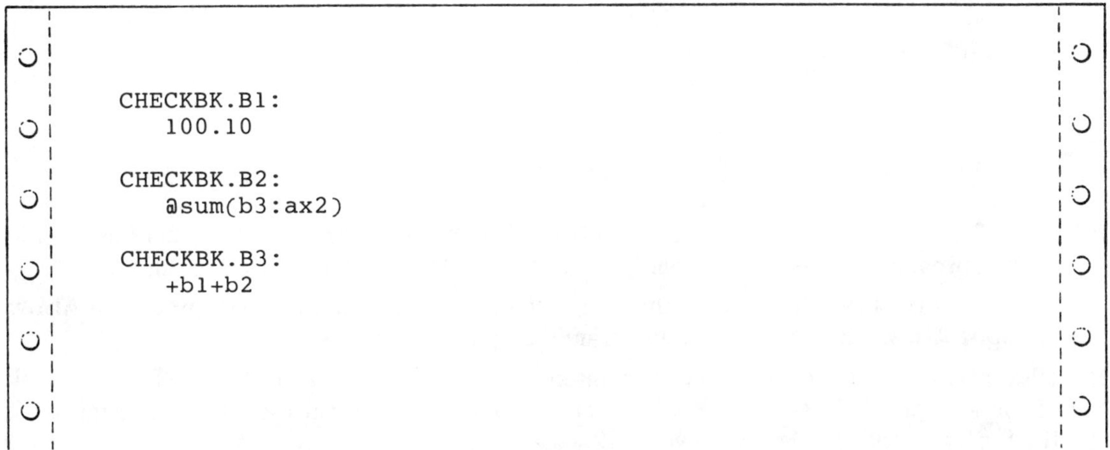

```
CHECKBK.B1:
   100.10

CHECKBK.B2:
   @sum(b3:ax2)

CHECKBK.B3:
   +b1+b2
```

7. Press **Gray +** to move the cursor inside your open frame. Type **!** and notice the center of the status line.

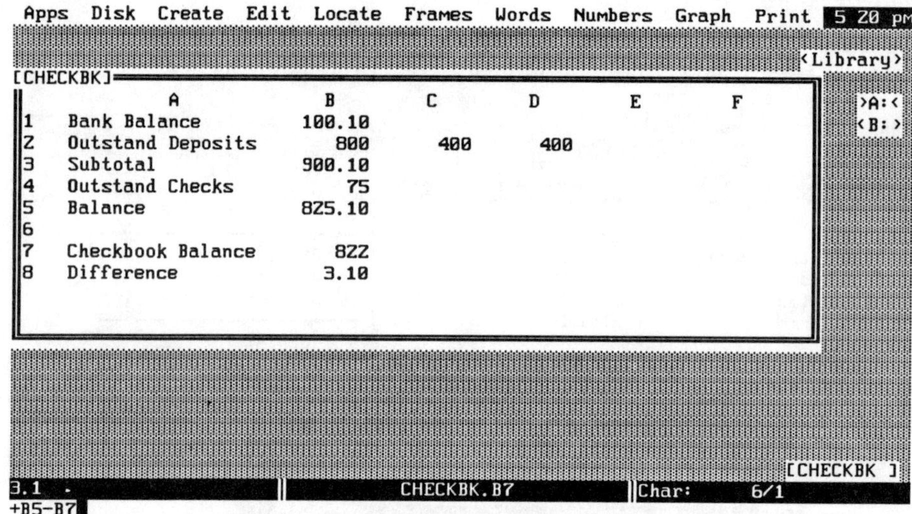

8. Reopen the Print Menu frame and select the Begin option. Before you press **Enter**, make sure that the printer is on. A sample of the printout follows.

```
CHECKBK.[100.10].Bank Balance:
   100.10

CHECKBK.[800].Outstand Deposits:
   @sum(b3:ax2)

CHECKBK.[900.10].[ Subtotal]:
   +b1+b2
```

9. Press **Gray –** to move the cursor to the frame border. Since changes have not been made to the spreadsheet, remove it from your desktop without saving it by pressing **Del**.
10. {Press **Ctrl-D**}. Press **Ins** to move the cursor to the Main Menu line. Next, press **Left Arrow** or **Right Arrow** until the Disk Menu frame is open on your desktop.
11. {Press **Ctrl-Q**}. Using the arrow keys again, position the cursor on the QUIT Framework option and press **Enter**. Type **Y** when asked if you are sure you want to quit Framework III. You have ended this Framework III session.
12. Turn to Module 31 to continue the learning sequence.

Module 65

PARAGRAPH INDENT OF { }

DESCRIPTION

When you type a word processing document, Framework III begins each new line next to the left border of the frame. This option is used to tell Framework III the number of spaces to indent the first line of every paragraph you type. It is preset to 0.

The Paragraph Indent option is available in the Words Menu frame.

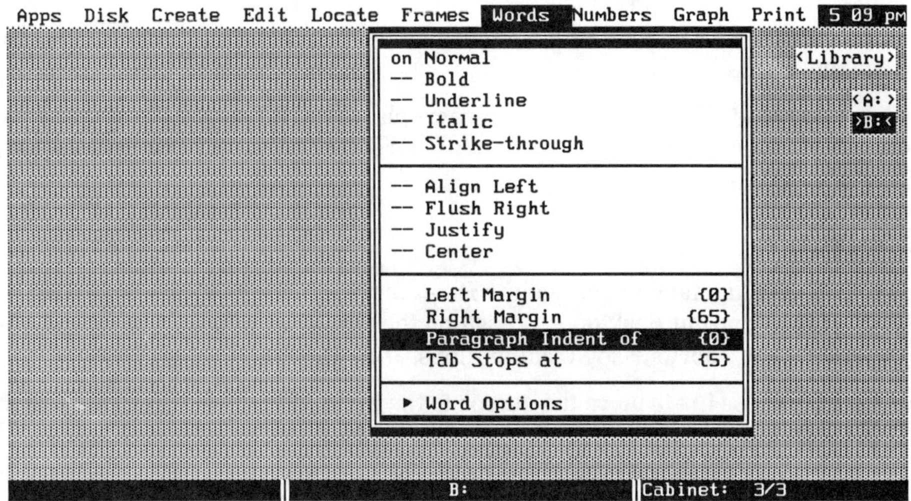

Set the indentation of paragraph's first line, relative to left margin

Notice that the Paragraph Indent is currently set to 0. This means that each line of text that you type begins at the left border of the frame. Change this number any time during a word processing activity.

For example, the following article has been typed with the Paragraph Indent option set to 0.

```
Apps Disk Create Edit Locate Frames Words Numbers Graph Print 5:14 pm
[....▼....▼....▼....▼....▼....▼....▼....▼....▼....▼....▼....]....▼.......
The name Texas is derived from Tejas, the name which the
Spaniards gave to the Hasinia Indians who lived in the eastern
portion of the state.
Texas known as the Lone Star State because the flag, which also
served the Republic of Texas, carries a single star, entered the
Union on Dec. 29, 1845, as the twenty-eighth state.
```

By changing the indent option to 5, you indent the first line of each paragraph. Now, the article looks like the following display.

```
Apps  Disk  Create  Edit  Locate  Frames  Words  Numbers  Graph  Print  5 16 pm
[----#....▼....▼....▼....▼....▼....▼....▼....▼....▼....▼....▼....]....▼....▼....
     The name Texas is derived from Tejas, the name which the
Spaniards gave to the Hasinia Indians who lived in the eastern
portion of the state.
     Texas known as the Lone Star State because the flag, which
also served the Republic of Texas, carries a single star, entered
the Union on Dec. 29, 1845, as the twenty-eighth state.
```

If the document already exists without paragraph indention, Framework III knows the Paragraph Indent option is set to 0. You must first position the cursor on the paragraph you want to indent. Then, open the Words Menu frame to select and set the Paragraph Indent option.

APPLICATIONS

This option is available only for word processing frames — not spreadsheets, databases, or graphs.

Use it to tell Framework III the number of spaces to indent each paragraph. Change the option's number when you want.

Pressing Enter on the last line of a paragraph tells Framework III that you have ended it and are starting a new one. It is not necessary to skip a blank line as long as you have pressed Enter.

TYPICAL OPERATION

This illustration shows you how to change the Paragraph Indent option when writing an article. Close any open frames on your desktop and position the cursor on your data drive indicator (drive B in this example). The shortcut key combinations, if applicable, are enclosed by braces.

1. {Press **Ctrl-C**}. Press **Ins** to move the cursor to the Main Menu line. Next, press **Right Arrow** until the Create Menu frame is open on your desktop.
2. {Press **Ctrl-E**}. Press **Down Arrow**, if necessary, to move the cursor to the Empty/Word Frame option of the Create Menu frame. Next, press **Enter** to select the option. An empty frame appears on your screen.
3. The cursor is positioned within the brackets at the top border of the frame. Type **TEXAS** and press **Enter**. This is the name of the frame. When it is saved on the disk, it is named TEXAS.FW3.
4. Press **Gray +** to move the cursor inside your open frame.
5. Type **The name Texas is derived from Tejas, the name which the Spaniards gave to the Hasinai Indians who lived in the eastern portion of the state.** As you type, notice that you do not have to press Enter to move the cursor to the next line — Framework III does that automatically. When it's typed, press **Enter** and see the following display.

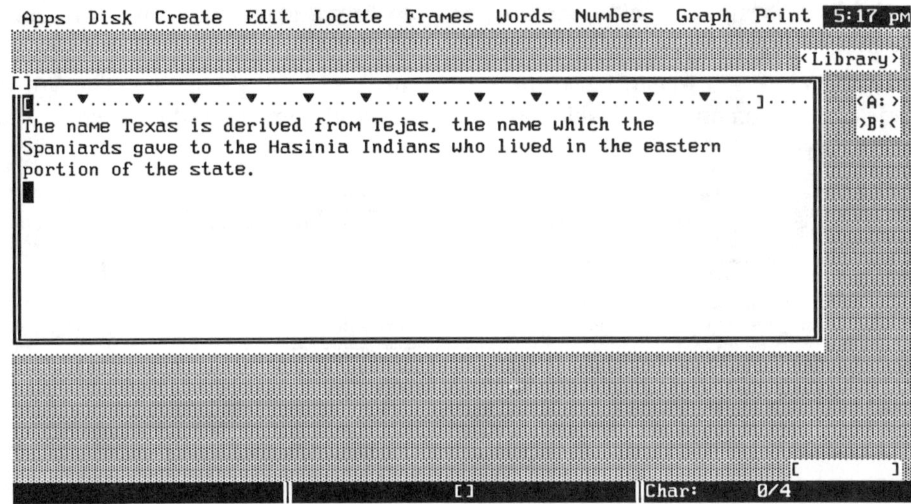

6. {Press **Ctrl-W**}. Press **Ins** to move the cursor to the Main Menu line. Next, press **Right Arrow** until the Words Menu frame is also open on your desktop. Notice that the Paragraph Indent is set to 0 as in the following display.

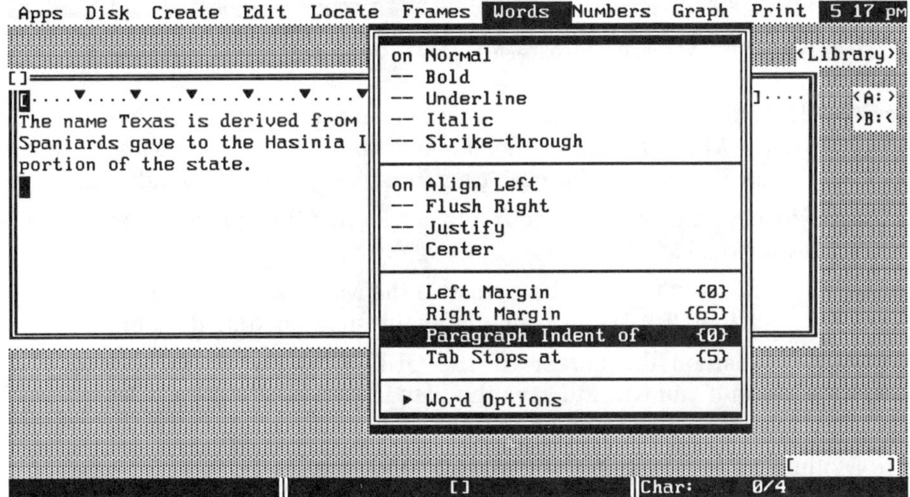

Set the indentation of paragraph's first line, relative to left margin

7. {Press **Ctrl-P**}. Press **Down Arrow** until the cursor is positioned on the Paragraph Indent option and then press **Enter**. The cursor moves to the Message line at the bottom of your screen. Type **5** and press **Enter**. The Words Menu frame disappears. Notice that the cursor is positioned five spaces from the left border. This is your paragraph indention.
8. Type **Texas, known as the Lone Star State because the flag, which also served the Republic of Texas, carries a single star, entered the Union on Dec. 29, 1845, as the twenty-eighth state.**

9. Since the first paragraph isn't indented, press **Up Arrow** to move the cursor to the first line of the first paragraph.
10. {Press **Ctrl-W**}. Press **Ins** to move the cursor to the Main Menu line. The Words Menu frame is again open on your desktop. Notice that the Paragraph Indent is set to 0 as in the following display.

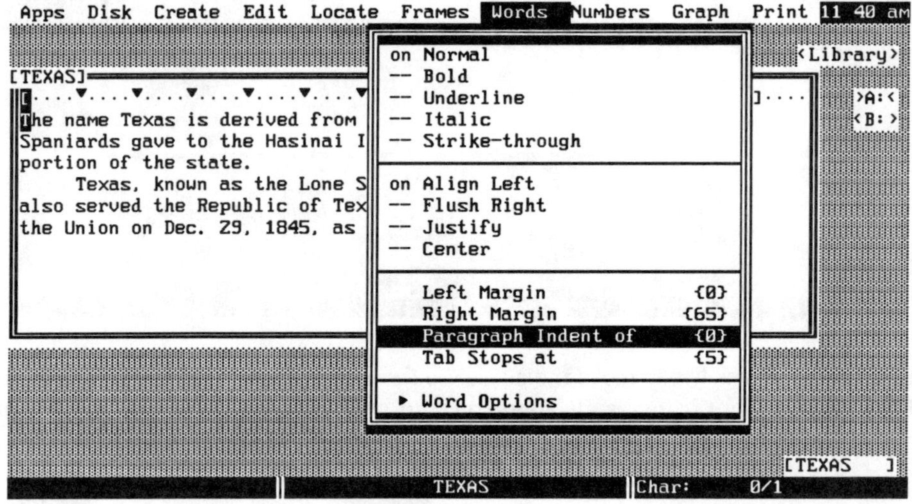

Set the indentation of paragraph's first line, relative to left margin

11. {Press **Ctrl-P**}. With the cursor positioned on the Paragraph Indent option, press **Enter**. The cursor moves to the Message line at the bottom of your screen. Type **5** and press **Enter**. The Words Menu frame disappears. However, your first paragraph is now indented by five spaces.
12. Press **Gray –** to move the cursor to the frame border and then press **Enter**. The frame closes and is put in your desktop tray.
13. {Press **Ctrl-D**}. Press **Ins** to move the cursor to the Main Menu line. Next, press the arrow (cursor) keys until the Disk Menu frame is again open on your desktop.
14. {Press **Ctrl-Q**}. Position the cursor on the QUIT Framework option and press **Enter**. Framework III asks if you want to save the files in your desktop tray. Type **Y** for Yes. You are returned to the DOS prompt.
15. Turn to Module 12 to continue the learning sequence.

Module 66

PAUSE, WAIT FOR EACH PAGE, ALLOW PRINT SPOOLING

DESCRIPTION

There are times when you need to temporarily stop (interrupt) your printer. For example, you need to use the phone or leave the room. Use the Pause option to stop and then restart your printer.

If you use individual sheets of paper instead of continuous computer paper, use the Wait for Each Page option. Use this option to tell Framework III to print a page of the document and then wait until you tell it you're ready to print another page.

Use the Allow Print Spooling option to spool (copy to disk first) your printed output. You can turn this option off to start the printing operation sooner; however, you will not be able to perform any additional work until the printing process is complete.

The Pause, Wait for Each Page, and Allow Print Spooling options are available in the Print Menu frame.

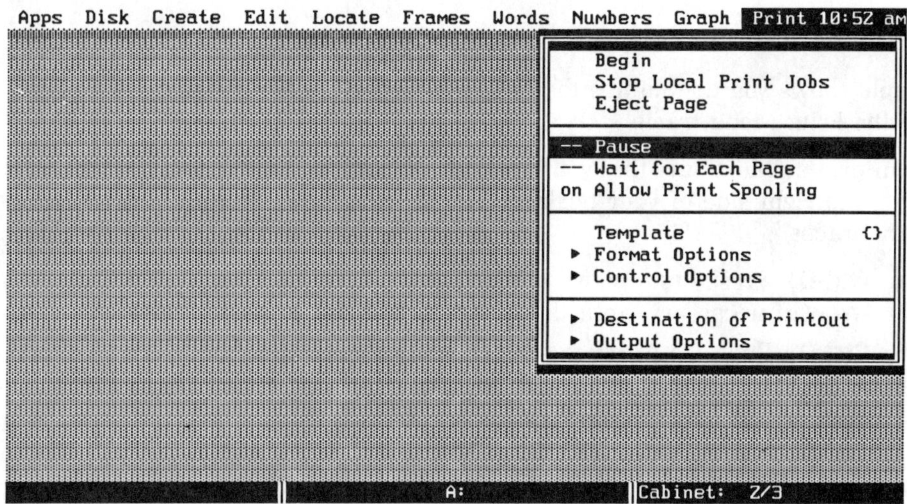

The word "on" is displayed at the left of the option when selected. Otherwise, dashes appear to indicate the option is turned off.

When you select the Pause option to stop the printer, "on" appears next to the option. Selecting it again restarts the printer as though it had never stopped. Use this option after printing has begun.

Select the Wait for Each Page option when you want the printer to stop after printing a page of your document. This option gives you the chance to load each page of paper and print it when you are ready.

Turn the Allow Print Spooling option on to cause Framework III to copy the print file to disk before printing.

First, open the document you want to print. Next, open the Print Menu frame. A message is displayed at the bottom of the screen telling you to press any key to print the first page. Insert the paper, press any key to begin the printing activity. Continue this process until the document is printed, or you can cancel the print operation.

APPLICATIONS

Use the Pause option to tell Framework III to temporarily stop and start the printer. For example, stop the printer when you need to talk to someone without being disturbed by the noise. Later, select this option again to restart the printing activity where you previously stopped it.

Use the Wait for Each Page option to tell Framework III to stop after printing each page of your document. This option gives you the chance to put another page of paper in the printer. When you're ready, press any key to tell Framework III to print another page. Continue this operation until the printed document is complete.

Normally, you would want to leave print spooling on. When the file is copied to disk or a print server on a Local Area Network (LAN), you are free to continue your work.

TYPICAL OPERATION

This example shows you how to use the Pause, Wait for Each Page, and Allow Print Spooling options of the Print Menu frame.

Turn on your printer. Make sure that your desktop is clean and the cursor is positioned on a drive indicator on the right side of your desktop. The shortcut key combinations, if applicable, are enclosed by braces.

1. {Press **Ctrl-D**}. Press **Ins** to move the cursor to the Main Menu line. Press **Left Arrow** or **Right Arrow**, if necessary, until the Disk Menu frame is open on your desktop.
2. {Press **Ctrl-G**}. Press **Up Arrow** to move the cursor to the Get File by Name option and then press **Enter**. The cursor moves to the Message line at the bottom of your desktop.
3. Type **B:BIRTHDAY**. As you type, notice that the braces next to the Get File by Name option fill. When finished, press **Enter**. The disk is read and the frame you specified is opened on your desktop as follows.
4. {Press **Ctrl-P**}. Press **Ins** to move the cursor to the Main Menu line. Press the arrow (cursor) keys until the Print Menu frame is open on your desktop.

5. {Press **Ctrl-B**}. Using the arrow (cursor) keys, position the cursor on the Begin option and press **Enter**. The printer starts printing the document on paper.
6. {Press **Ctrl-P**}. Press **Ins** to move the cursor to the Main Menu line again. The Print Menu frame is again open on your desktop.
7. {Press **Ctrl-P**}. Using the arrow (cursor) keys, position the cursor on the Pause option and press **Enter**. Notice that your printer stops and the word "on" appears next to the Pause option.
8. {Press **Ctrl-P**}. With the cursor still positioned on the Pause option, press **Enter**. Notice that your printer starts again as though it had never stopped and the dashes appear next to the Pause option again.
9. {Press **Ctrl-W**}. Select the Wait for Each Page option so that it is turned on.
10. {Press **Ctrl-B**}. Position the cursor on the Begin option and press **Enter**. Framework III displays a message at the bottom of the screen. It tells you to press any key when ready to print, or press **Esc** to cancel the print operation.
11. Press any key to begin the print. If the document is larger than one page, Framework III prints the first page and asks again for you to press any key when ready to print the next page. Continue this activity until the complete document is printed.
12. {Press **Ctrl-P**}. Position the cursor to the Allow Print Spooling option and press **Enter** to turn print spooling on. Type **B** to print the document again. Notice that your printer doesn't start until the file is copied to disk.
13. {Press **Ctrl-P**}. Position the cursor to the Allow Print Spooling option and press **Enter** to turn print spooling off. Type **B** to print the document again. Notice that your printer starts immediately, but you cannot perform any other work until printing is complete.
14. Press **Del** to remove the document from the desktop.
15. Turn to Module 29 to continue the learning sequence.

Module 67

PRINT LABELS USING { }

DESCRIPTION

Printing mailing labels is easy with Framework III. All you need is a database of names and addresses and a layout frame.

The layout frame is just a word processing frame. You mark where you want the fields from the database printed. Then select the Print Labels using { } option of the Apps Menu frame and provide a database frame name within the braces.

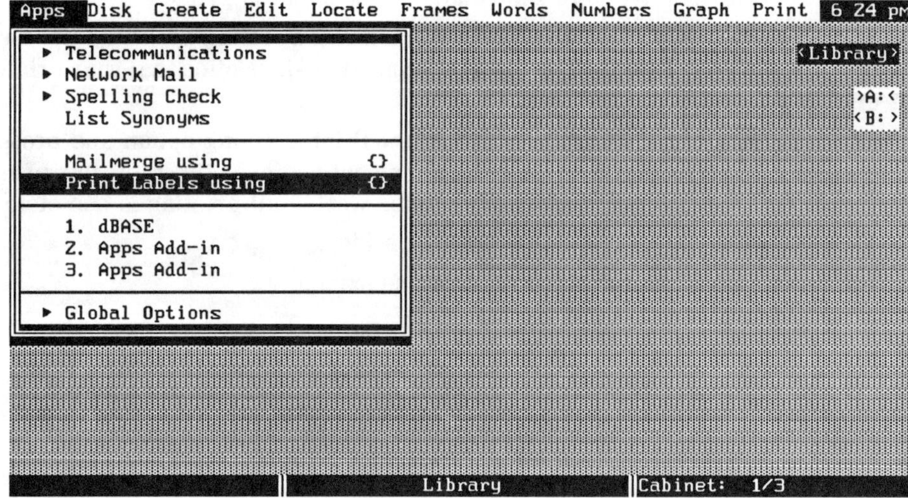

Print mailing labels using specified database and currently selected template

First, read your database from disk to your desktop. Next, open and enter a word processing frame. Type the fieldnames from the database within the open frame and enclose them with angle brackets as in the following example.

Make sure your printer is turned on. Open the Print Menu frame and change the Lines per Page option as well as any other format options. Then open the Apps Menu frame and select the Print Labels Using { } option. Type the database frame name so that it appears within the braces of the option. When finished, press Enter and watch your labels print.

Create a word processing frame for a single row of labels. To print four labels across, create an outline frame with four subframes. Size and drag each subframe until you have them in a row across the open frame border. When finished, begin printing a sample database.

Make adjustments to the size or position, if necessary, and print them again. Continue this adjust and print operation until your sample labels look right. Then, save the frame with the Save and Continue option so that you don't have to do this all over again. Now, you are ready to print the larger databases.

APPLICATIONS

Use this option when you need to print labels or special phone cards for your customer files. Make them as fancy as you want.

For example, print the phone number in boldface type so that it is easy to find. To do this, just highlight the field <PHONE> with the F6 (Extend) key. Then open the Words Menu frame and select the Bold option.

TYPICAL OPERATION

In this illustration, a label model is typed into a frame. It is then used to print phone cards for a card file. Make sure that your desktop is clean, the cursor is positioned on the drive B indicator. The shortcut key combinations, if applicable, are enclosed by braces.

1. {Press **Ctrl-D**}. Press **Ins** to move the cursor to the Main Menu line. Next, press **Left Arrow** or **Right Arrow**, if necessary, until the Disk Menu frame is open on your desktop.
2. {Press **Ctrl-G**}. Press **Up Arrow** to move the cursor to the Get File by Name { } option and then press **Enter**. The cursor moves to the Message line at the bottom of your desktop.

3. Type **PHONE LIST** and press **Enter**. The database frame opens on your desktop.

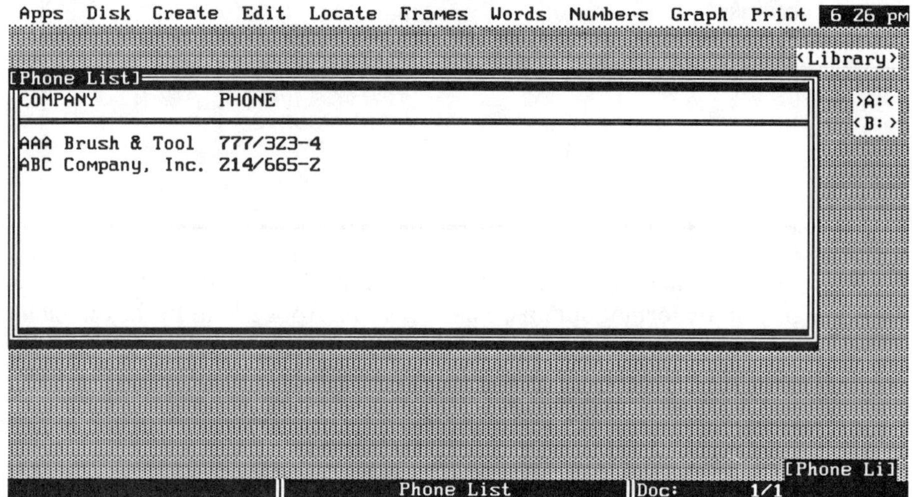

4. {Press **Ctrl-C**}. Press **Ins** to move the cursor to the Main Menu line. Next, press **Right Arrow** until the Create Menu frame is open on your desktop.
5. {Press **Ctrl-E**}. Press **Down Arrow**, if necessary, to move the cursor to the Empty/Word Frame option of the Create Menu frame. Next, press **Enter** to select the option. An empty frame appears on your screen.

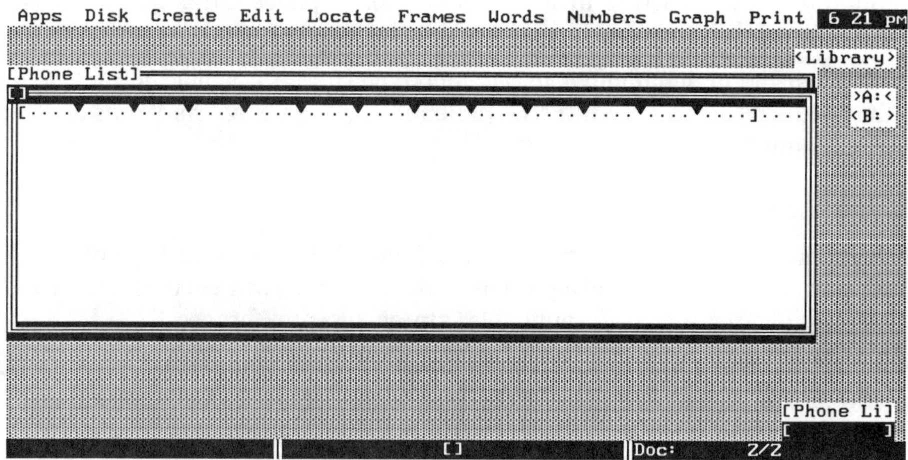

6. The cursor is positioned within the brackets at the top border of the frame. Type **LABELS** and press **Enter**. This is the name of the frame. When it is saved on the disk, it is named LABELS.FW3.

7. Press **Gray +**. Notice that the cursor is now positioned inside your open frame. Press **Enter** twice.
8. Type **<COMPANY>** and press **Enter** twice. Now, the cursor is positioned on the fourth line of your frame.
9. Press **Spacebar** ten times and then type **<PHONE>**. Now, your frame resembles the following display.

10. Press **Gray –** to move the cursor to the frame border.
11. {Press **Ctrl-P**}. Press **Ins** to move the cursor to the Main Menu line. Next, press **Left Arrow** or **Right Arrow** until the Print Menu frame is open on your desktop.
12. {Press **Ctrl-F**}. Press **Down Arrow** to move the cursor to the Format Options option of the Print Menu frame. A submenu also appears on your desktop.
13. {Press **Ctrl-L**}. Press **Down Arrow** to move the cursor to the Lines per Page option of the Print Menu frame and press **Enter**. Type **13** and press **Enter** to see the number within the braces change from 66 to 13. When finished, press **Esc**.

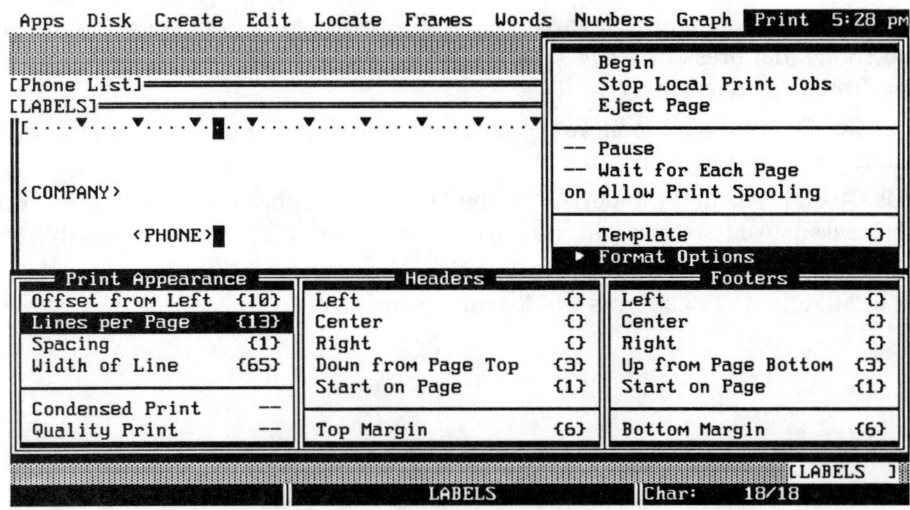

14. {Press **Ctrl-A**}. Press **Ins** to move the cursor to the Main Menu line. Next, press **Left Arrow** or **Right Arrow** until the Apps Menu frame is open on your desktop.

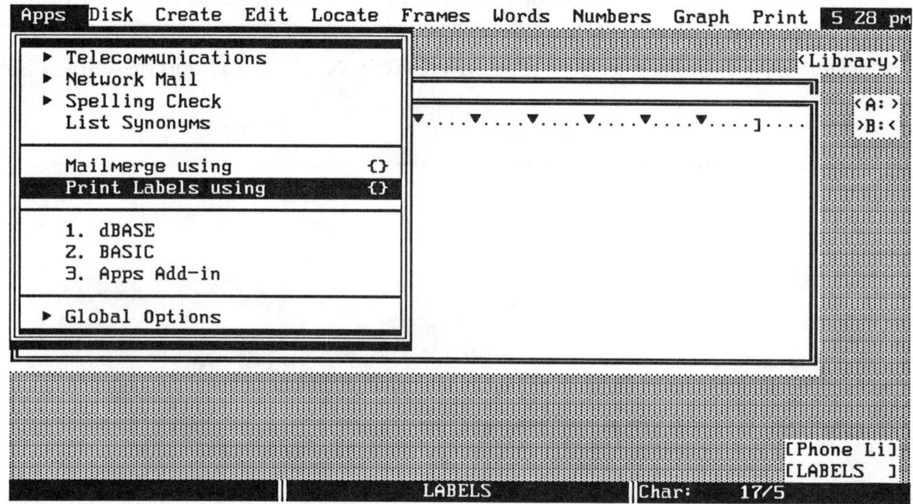

Print mailing labels using specified database and currently selected template

15. {Press **Ctrl-P**}. Press **Down Arrow** to move the cursor to the Print Labels using { } option of the Apps Menu frame and press **Enter**. Type **PHONE LIST**, turn on your printer, and press **Enter**. Your labels begin printing. (Press **Ctrl-Break** to stop the printer.) Press **Gray –** and **Enter** to close the open frame into the desktop tray. Press **Del** to delete the PHONE LIST frame.
16. {Press **Ctrl-D**}. Press **Ins** to move the cursor to the Main Menu line. Next, press **Right Arrow** until the Disk Menu frame is open on your desktop.
17. {Press **Ctrl-P**}. Press **Down Arrow** to move the cursor to the Put Away option of the Disk Menu frame and press **Enter** to save the labels model on disk. Then delete the phone list frame from your desktop.
18. {Press **Ctrl-D**}. Press **Ins** to move the cursor to the Main Menu line. The Disk Menu frame is again open on your desktop.
19. {Press **Ctrl-Q**}. Position the cursor on the QUIT Framework option and press **Enter**. Type **Y** when asked if you are sure you want to quit Framework III. You have ended this Framework III session.
20. Turn to Module 84 to continue the learning sequence.

Module 68

PROTECT FROM EDITING

DESCRIPTION

If you spend hours setting up a spreadsheet model, you don't want it changed accidentally. Use this option to protect some or all of the information (e.g., formulas) within your frame.

This option is available for any type of frame. Access it through the Edit Menu frame.

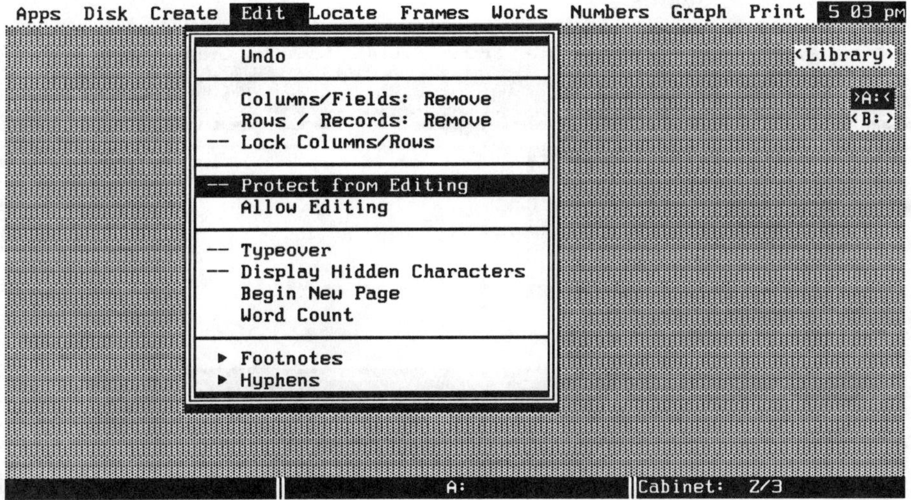

Protect selected frames/cells/fields from changes

To protect spreadsheet cells or database fields, position the cursor on the cell you want to protect. Then open the Edit Menu frame and select the Protect from Editing option. If you need to protect several consecutive cells, use the F6 (Extend) key to expand the highlighted area before selecting the option.

Protect a whole frame by positioning the cursor on the frame border. Then select this option and save the frame on the disk.

APPLICATIONS

The Protect from Editing option is available for any type of frame. For example, protect a cell or field which is calculated. Doing so causes Framework III to remind you that the frame, cell, or field is not to be changed.

If you try to change a protected cell or field, Framework III beeps with each keystroke. Also, a message is displayed at the bottom of the screen telling you that the frame is protected (although it may only be the cell or field).

TYPICAL OPERATION

This example shows you how to use the Protect from Editing option of the Edit Menu frame. Close any open frames on your desktop and position the cursor on your data drive indicator (drive B in this example). The shortcut key combinations, if applicable, are enclosed by braces.

1. {Press **Ctrl-D**}. Press **Ins** to move the cursor to the Main Menu line. Next, press **Left Arrow** or **Right Arrow**, if necessary, until the Disk Menu frame is open on your desktop.
2. {Press **Ctrl-G**}. Press **Up Arrow** to move the cursor to the Get File by Name option and then press **Enter**. The cursor moves to the Message line at the bottom of your desktop.
3. Type **B:CHECKBK**. As you type, notice that the braces next to the Get File by Name option fill. When finished, press **Enter** twice. The disk is read and the frame you specified is opened on your desktop as follows.

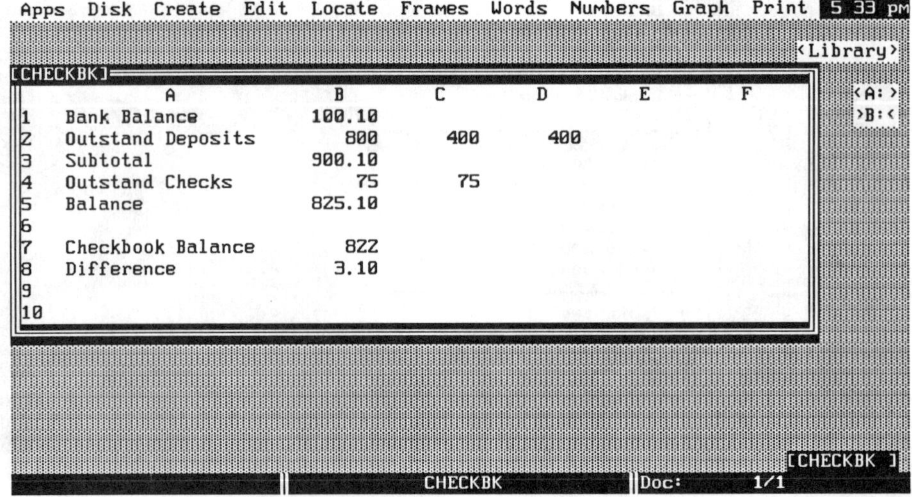

4. Press **Gray +** to move the cursor inside your open frame. Your cursor is positioned after the last change of the document. Press **Up Arrow** so that the cursor is positioned on the "B" in the word "Bank."
5. Press **F6** and notice the message at the bottom of your screen. This message tells you that by pressing the arrow (cursor) keys, you can enlarge the highlighted area. Press **Down Arrow** seven times until the whole A column is included in the highlighted area. Then press **Enter** to tell Framework III you have finished the cursor extension.
6. {Press **Ctrl-E**}. Press **Ins** to move the cursor to the Main Menu line. Next, press **Right Arrow** until the Edit Menu frame is also open on your desktop.

7. {Press **Ctrl-P**}. Press **Down Arrow** until the cursor is positioned on the Protect from Editing option. Press **Enter**. The Edit Menu frame disappears from your desktop. Notice that the Message line reports that Protect from Editing is on for the highlighted areas.

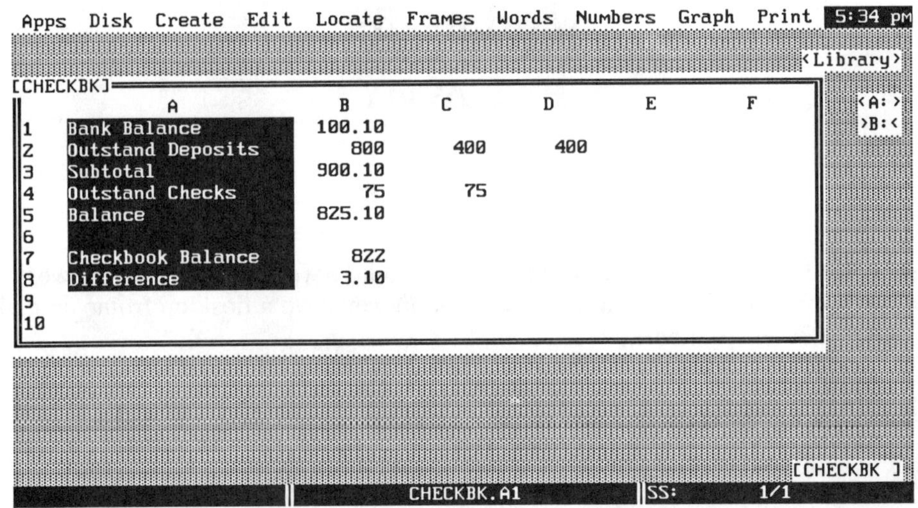

Edit: Protect from Editing on

8. Press **Esc** to return the cursor size to normal. Then press **Right Arrow** and **Down Arrow** until the cursor is positioned on cell B3. Open the Edit Menu and select the Protect from Editing option as you did for column A. Also protect cells B5 and B8.
9. Press **Gray –** to move the cursor to the frame border.
10. {Press **Ctrl-D**}. Press **Ins** to move the cursor to the Main Menu line. Next, press **Left Arrow** until the Disk Menu frame is open on your desktop.
11. {Press **Ctrl-P**}. Press **Down Arrow** to the Put Away option and press **Enter**. This option clears your desktop and saves the file called CHECKBK.FW3 on the data disk.
12. {Press **Ctrl-D**}. Press **Ins** to move the cursor to the Main Menu line. The Disk Menu frame is again open on your desktop.
13. {Press **Ctrl-Q**}. Using the arrow keys again, position the cursor on the QUIT Framework option and press **Enter**. Type **Y** when asked if you are sure you want to quit Framework III. You have ended this Framework III session.
14. Turn to Module 6 to continue the learning sequence.

Module 69

PUT AWAY

DESCRIPTION

Using a computer is supposed to save you time. You should never have to redo any work you have saved on disk. Each time you use the Put Away option, you save a desktop frame on disk so that you don't have to start from scratch again.

In other words, Framework III saves the current desktop version of the frame on disk. Any old version on disk is replaced by the new one.

This option is available through the Disk Menu frame as in the following display.

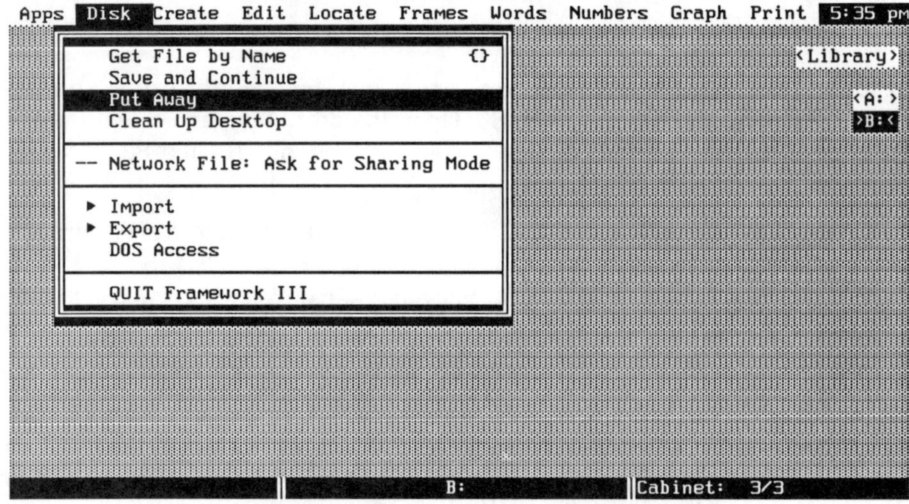

Move document to its home disk and directory

It is a good idea to save your open frame several times as you change it. Use the Save and Continue option when you want to immediately continue working. If you lose power, or some other mishap occurs while you work, at least you can return to the last saved version of your frame.

Another good practice is to save the open frame before leaving the machine — even if it's just to get a drink of water. There's no telling what can happen when you leave a computer unattended. Use the Put Away option when you're finished with the frame and need to go on to other things.

The file is always saved on the disk in the drive which Framework III knows as your data drive. It is normally the last drive listed with your disk drive indicators.

The data drive is preset by the Setup disk. Change it to the drive you prefer by returning to the Framework III Setup disk.

APPLICATIONS

While you work on an open frame, use the Save and Continue option. This saves the open frame on disk and lets you resume your work on that same frame.

When you are ready to open another frame, save the current one by using the Put Away option. This saves the frame on disk and removes it from your desktop. However, if you intend to reopen the frame during the current Framework III session, just move it to your desktop tray and then use the Save and Continue option.

Using the Put Away option takes much less time than having to redo your work. The current version of the frame you see on the screen is saved on disk. When Framework III has completed this save, the frame is removed from your desktop.

TYPICAL OPERATION

This exercise shows you how to tell Framework III to use the Put Away option of the Disk Menu frame. Make sure that your desktop is clear and the cursor is positioned on one of the drive indicators. The shortcut key combinations, if applicable, are enclosed by braces.

1. Type **FW** to load Framework III. {Press **Ctrl-D**}. Press **Ins** to move the cursor to the Main Menu line. Next, press **Left Arrow** or **Right Arrow** until the Disk Menu frame is open on or **Right Arrow** until the Disk Menu frame is open on your desktop.
2. {Press **Ctrl-G**}. Press **Up Arrow** to move the cursor to the Get File by Name option and then press **Enter**. The cursor moves to the Message line at the bottom of your desktop.
3. Type **BIRTHDAY**. As you type, notice that the braces next to the Get File by Name option fill. When finished, press **Enter**. The disk is read and the frame you specified is opened on your desktop.
4. Press **Gray +** to move the cursor inside your open frame. Use the arrow (cursor) keys to position the cursor on the comma of "April 11, 1989." Press **Backspace** twice, then type **1**. Now your frame resembles the following display.

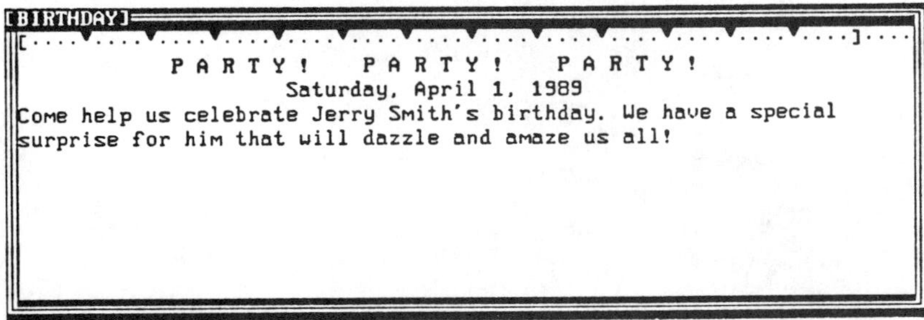

5. {Press **Ctrl-D**}. Press **Ins** to move the cursor to the Main Menu line. The Disk Menu frame is also open on your desktop.
6. {Press **Ctrl-P**}. Using the **Down Arrow** key, position the cursor on the Put Away option and then press **Enter**. The Message line displays the word "SAVING" and the disk drive lights. When finished, the frame name is not on your desktop and the tray disappears.
7. {Press **Ctrl-D**}. Press **Ins** to move the cursor to the Main Menu line. The Disk Menu frame is again open on your desktop.
8. {Press **Ctrl-Q**}. Using the arrow keys again, position the cursor on the QUIT Framework option and press **Enter**. Type **Y** when asked if you are sure you want to quit Framework III. You have ended this Framework III session.
9. Turn to Module 71 to continue the learning sequence.

Module 70

PUT INTO COLUMN

DESCRIPTION

After moving subframes within an open window, this option lets you tell Framework III to move all subframes back to their original position. For example, a frame you want to use for reference is outside the open window. Drag it to the frame on which you want to work. This makes both frames accessible at the same time.

Select the Put into Column option of the Frames Menu frame. Framework III puts everything back into a column. Select this option through the Frames Menu frame.

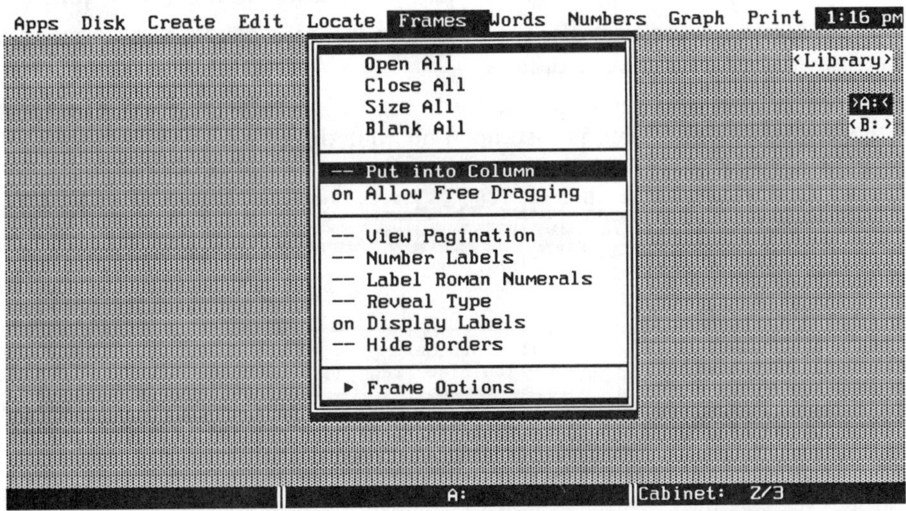

The Put into Column option is turned on and off when selected. If it is turned on, Allow Free Dragging is turned off. When the Allow Free Dragging option is on, the Put into Column option is turned off. When on, the Put into Column option causes all subframes to appear on the left side of the main frame border.

APPLICATIONS

Use this option with any frame which contains subframes which you have rearranged with the Allow Free Dragging option and the F3 (Drag) key. This option lets you put all subframes back at one time rather than having to drag them to their original position.

For example, subtopic 1.1 needs several pieces of the information from subtopic 1.6. Instead of moving the cursor back and forth between the two subframes, just drag subframe 1.6 to an area on your desktop where both are visible.

Select the Put into Column option of the Frames Menu frame so that Framework III handles the clean-up operation. This saves you a lot of time.

TYPICAL OPERATION

This illustration shows you how to use the Put into Column option capabilities of Framework III. Make sure that your desktop is clear and the cursor is positioned on one of the drive indicators. The shortcut key combinations, if applicable, are enclosed by braces.

1. {Press **Ctrl-D**}. Press **Ins** to move the cursor to the Main Menu line. Next, press **Left Arrow** or **Right Arrow**, if necessary, until the Disk Menu frame is open on your desktop.
2. {Press **Ctrl-G**}. Press **Up Arrow** to move the cursor to the Get File by Name { } option and then press **Enter**. The cursor moves to the Message line at the bottom of your desktop.
3. Type **EXERCISE**. As you type, the braces next to the Get File by Name { } option fill. Press **Enter**. The disk is read and the frame you specified is opened on your desktop. If it appears only in the desktop tray with the cursor, just press **Enter** to open it on your desktop.
4. Press **Gray +** to move the cursor to the inside of your open frame. The cursor is positioned on the first major topic of your outline.
5. {Press **Ctrl-F**}. Press **Ins** to move the cursor to the Main Menu line. Next, press **Right Arrow** until the Frames Menu frame is also open on your desktop.

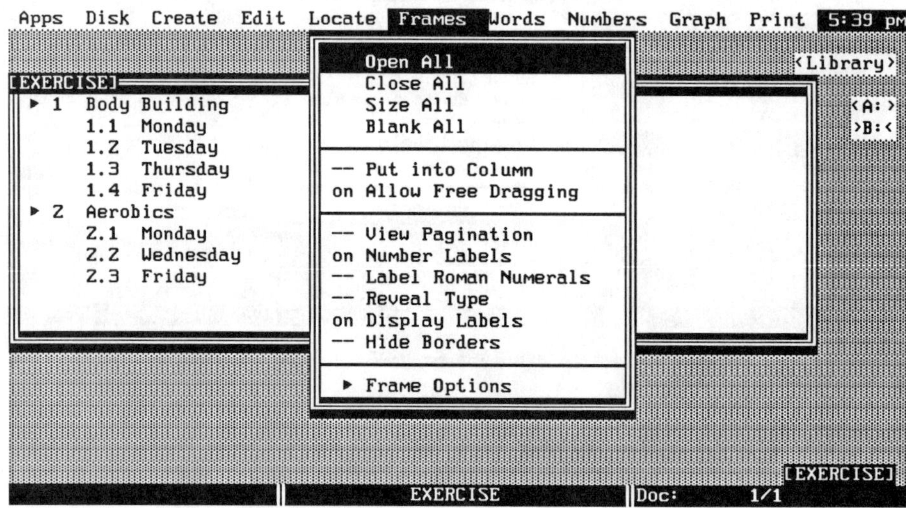

Open the selected frames and all frames within them

6. {Press **Ctrl-O**}. Press **Up Arrow** until the cursor is positioned on the Open All option and press **Enter**. This tells Framework III that you want to see the contents of all subframes.
7. Position the cursor on the major topic line of Body Building. Press **F10** (View) to open the subframe. Then press **F9** (Zoom) to see the following display.

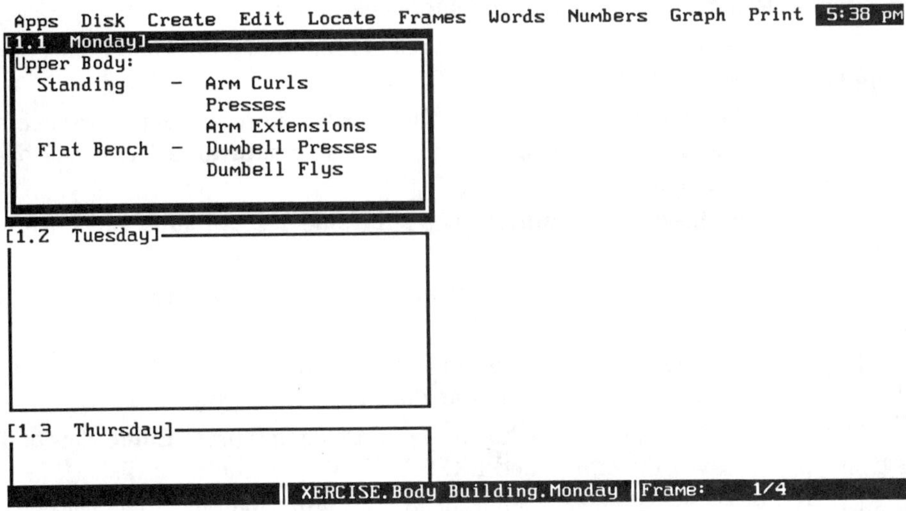

8. Press **Down Arrow** until the cursor is positioned on subframe 1.4.
9. {Press **Ctrl-F**}. Press **Ins** to move the cursor to the Main Menu line. The Frames Menu frame is again open on your desktop.
10. {Press **Ctrl-A**}. Select the Allow Free Dragging option to turn it on.
11. Press **F3** (Drag) and **Right Arrow** to see another border appear and move to the right. Continue this until the new frame is clear of the old border. Next, press **Up Arrow** until subframe 1.4 is even with subframe 1.1 and press **Enter**.
12. Press **Gray +** to move inside subframe 1.4. Type the last two lines of subframe 1.1 until your desktop resembles the following display.

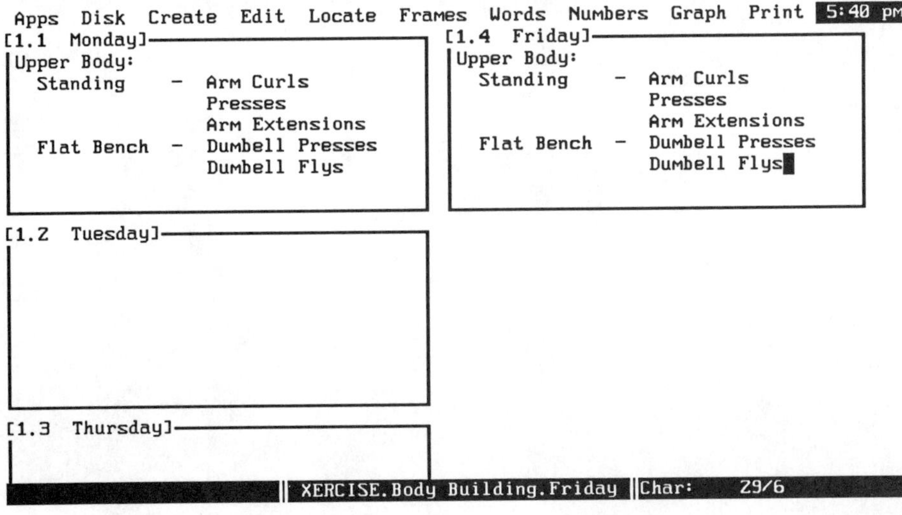

13. Press **Gray –** to move the cursor to the subframe border.
14. {Press **Ctrl-F**}. Press **Ins** to move the cursor to the Main Menu line. The Frames Menu frame is again open on your desktop.
15. {Press **Ctrl-P**}. Select the Put into Column option to turn it on. When the frame disappears, notice that subframe 1.4 is no longer positioned beside subframe 1.1. It has been moved back to where it belongs.
16. Press **Down Arrow** three times until you see subframe 1.4. All subframes are again in a straight line.
17. Press **F10** (View) to return to the outline format. Then press **Gray –** twice to move the cursor to the EXERCISE frame border.
18. {Press **Ctrl-D**}. Press **Ins** to move the cursor to the Main Menu line. Next, press **Left Arrow** until the Disk Menu frame is open on your desktop.
19. {Press **Ctrl-P**}. Press **Down Arrow** to the Put Away option and press **Enter**. This option clears your desktop and saves the file called EXERCISE.FW3 on the data disk.
20. {Press **Ctrl-D**}. Press **Ins** to move the cursor to the Main Menu line. The Disk Menu frame is again open on your desktop.
21. {Press **Ctrl-Q**}. Using the arrow (cursor) keys, position the cursor on the QUIT Framework option and press **Enter**. Type **Y** when Framework III asks if you're sure you want to quit Framework III. The system prompt appears on your screen. This ends this Framework III session.
22. Turn to Module 39 to continue the learning sequence.

Module 71

QUIT FRAMEWORK

DESCRIPTION

Do you just turn off your computer when your work is completed? If so, have you ever lost the work on which you just spent hours? Exiting properly from a program can usually save you a lot of grief. The same is true of Framework III.

Use the QUIT Framework option of the Disk Menu frame to properly end the current Framework III session. The Disk Menu frame is shown in the following display.

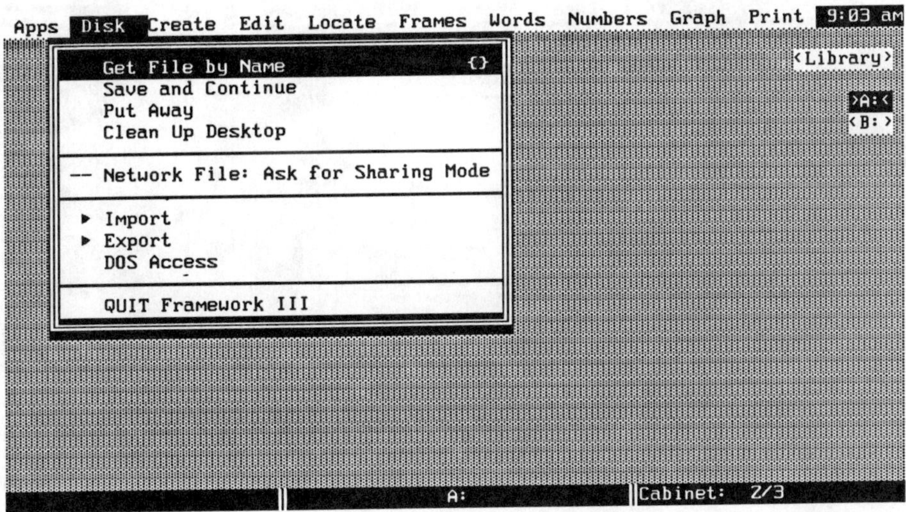

Before Framework III returns the system prompt, it checks all files on the desktop. If one or more have not been saved since their last change, you are asked if you want them saved. When you type Y, Framework III saves the latest version of the files on disk.

When you select the QUIT Framework option and all current versions of the files have been saved, Framework III asks if you are sure you want to quit. Typing Y to that question returns you to the system prompt. Typing N leaves the desktop on your screen.

It's nice to know that all your work is saved on disk before turning off your computer. Framework III can help — if you let it.

APPLICATIONS

Always use this option! It's not required by the computer or Framework III, but it may save you a lot of time some day.

It just makes sense to let Framework III remind you of files that have not been saved on disk since their last change. Just turning off the computer before properly exiting Framework III is likely to bite you when you're tired. After all, slaving away at the computer all day can really cloud your mind.

TYPICAL OPERATION

This exercise shows you how to tell Framework III to use the QUIT Framework option of the Disk Menu frame. Make sure that your desktop is clear and the cursor is positioned on one of the drive indicators. The shortcut key combinations, if applicable, are enclosed by braces.

1. {Press **Ctrl-C**}. Press **Ins** to move the cursor to the Main Menu line. Press **Left Arrow** or **Right Arrow** until the Create Menu frame is open on your desktop. Your screen should resemble the following display.

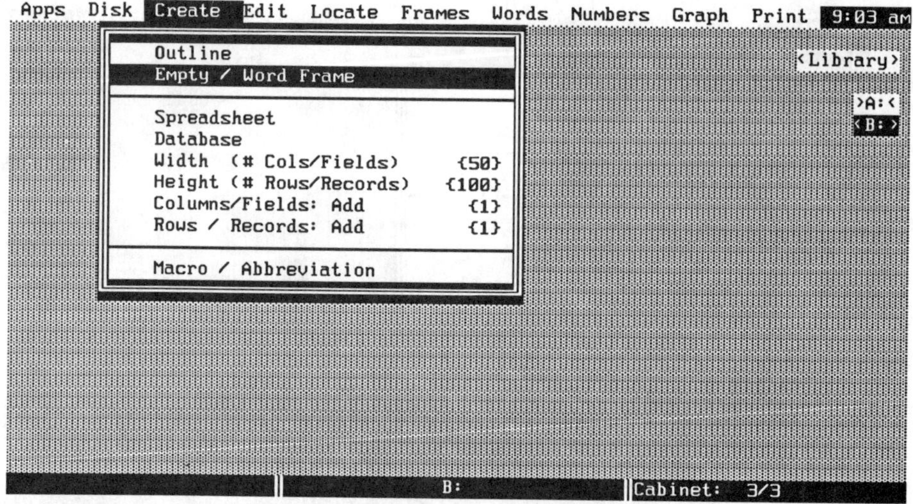

2. {Press **Ctrl-E**}. Press **Down Arrow**, if necessary, to move the cursor to the Empty/Word Frame option of the Create Menu frame. Press **Enter** to select the option. An empty frame appears on your screen.
3. The cursor is positioned within the brackets at the top border of the frame. Type **EMPTY FRAME** and press **Enter**.
4. The cursor is still on the border of the frame. Press **Enter** again to close the frame and put it in your desktop tray.
5. {Press **Ctrl-D**}. Press **Ins** to move the cursor to the Main Menu line. Press **Left Arrow** until the Disk Menu frame is open on your desktop.

6. {Press **Ctrl-Q**}. Using the arrow keys again, position the cursor on the QUIT Framework option and press **Enter**.
7. The computer beeps and the cursor moves to the Message line. The beep is to get your attention. The question asks if you want to save the unsaved file that is on your desktop. Type **N** since it is just an empty frame anyway.
8. The computer beeps again and asks if you are sure you want to quit. Type **Y**. When the system prompt appears on your screen, this Framework III session is ended.
9. Turn to Module 40 to continue the learning sequence.

Module 72

REPLACE { }

DESCRIPTION

Finding repetitive words and phrases or misspelled names is accomplished by the Search { } option of the Locate Menu frame. Use the Replace { } option with the Search { } option to find and replace old text with new text.

This option is available for any type of frame. Access it through the Locate Menu frame.

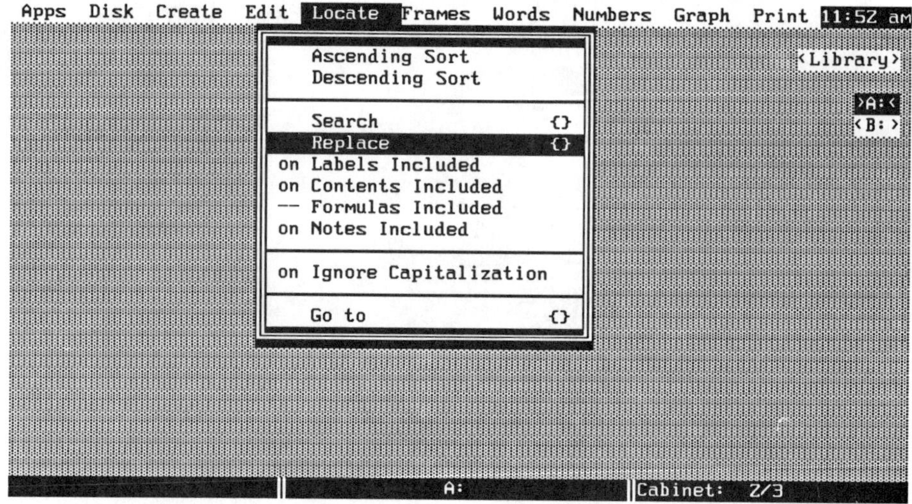

Replace any specified word or phrase with another -- in any type of frame

When you select the Replace { } option, Framework III asks for the text you want to search. As you type, the braces next to the Search { } option fill. Press Enter.

You are then asked to type the replacement text. As you type, the braces next to the Replace { } option fill. Press Enter.

Framework III finds the first occurrence of the specified Search { } text and highlights it with the cursor. Several options appear on the Message line at the bottom of your screen.

By pressing Enter, you tell Framework III that you want to replace the value and find the next occurrence. Down Arrow does not perform the replace but continues the search for the next occurrence.

Pressing Home causes Framework III to replace the current value but does not move the cursor from the current position. By pressing End, you replace all occurrences in the open frame. The Esc key lets you abort the Replace { } option without making any changes.

APPLICATIONS

The Replace { } option is available for any frame type. Use it to find and replace any combination of letters or numbers within an open frame.

For example, if you typed "suprize" instead of "surprise," tell Framework III that you want to search for "suprize" within the open frame and replace each occurrence with "surprise."

TYPICAL OPERATION

This example shows you how to use the Replace { } option of the Locate Menu frame. Close any open frames on your desktop and position the cursor on your data drive indicator (drive B in this example). The shortcut key combinations, if applicable, are enclosed by braces.

1. {Press **Ctrl-D**}. Press **Ins** to move the cursor to the Main Menu line. Next, press **Left Arrow** or **Right Arrow**, if necessary, until the Disk Menu frame is open on your desktop.
2. {Press **Ctrl-G**}. Press **Up Arrow** to move the cursor to the Get File by Name option and then press **Enter**. The cursor moves to the Message line at the bottom of your desktop.
3. Type **B:BIRTHDAY**. As you type, notice that the braces next to the Get File by Name option fill. When finished, press **Enter** twice. The disk is read and the frame you specified is opened on your desktop.
4. Press **Gray +** to move the cursor inside the open frame. The cursor is positioned after the last change of the document. Press **Up Arrow** and **Left Arrow** until the cursor is positioned on the "C" in the word "Come."
5. {Press **Ctrl-L**}. Press **Ins** to move the cursor to the Main Menu line. Next, press **Right Arrow** until the Locate Menu frame is also open on your desktop.

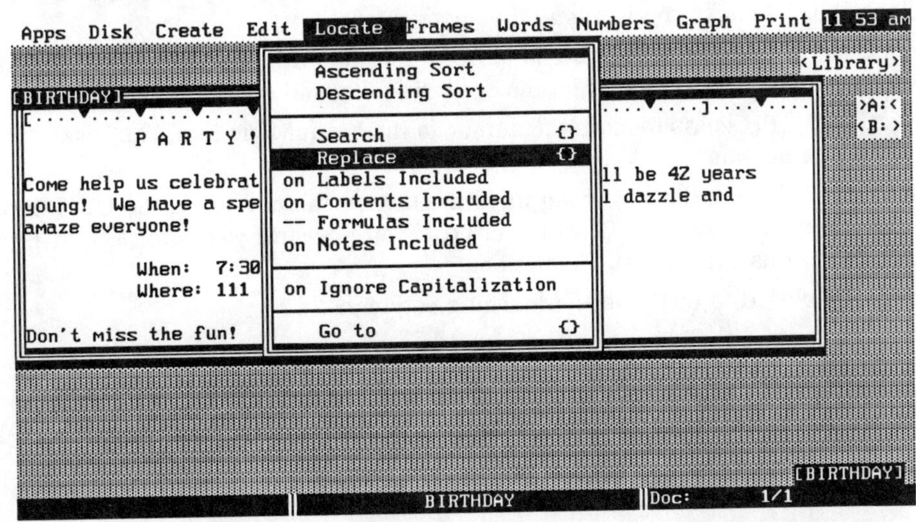

Replace any specified word or phrase with another -- in any type of frame

6. {Press **Ctrl-R**}. Press **Down Arrow**, if necessary, until the cursor is positioned on the Replace { } option and press **Enter**. Type **everyone** and notice the Search { } option braces fill as you type. When finished, press **Enter**.
7. Type **us all** and notice the Replace { } option braces fill as you type. When finished, press **Enter**. The Locate Menu frame disappears but the Message line is filled with several options.
8. Press **Enter** to see the text identified by the cursor change. The computer beeps for your attention. The Message line reports that the text was found only one time. Your screen resembles the following display.

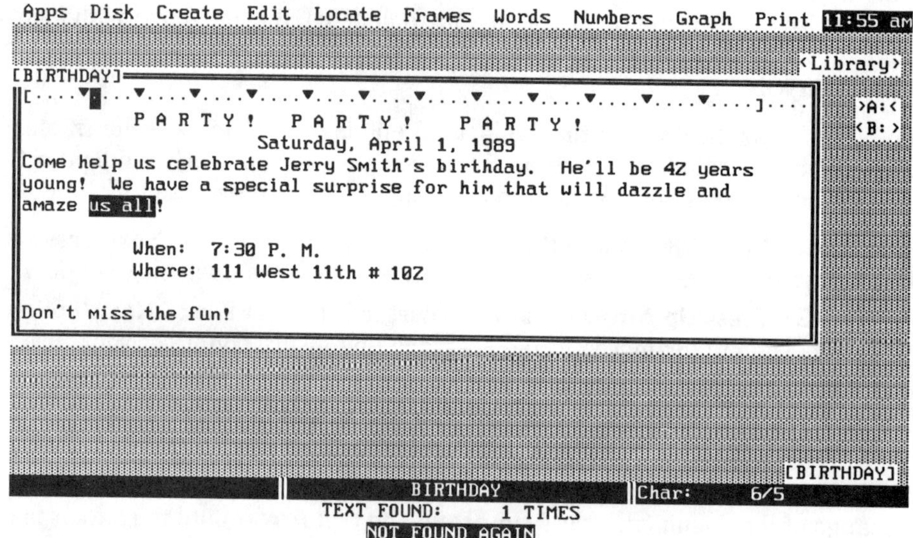

9. Press **Gray –** to move the cursor to the frame border.
10. {Press **Ctrl-D**}. Press **Ins** to move the cursor to the Main Menu line. Next, press **Left Arrow** until the Disk Menu frame is open on your desktop.
11. {Press **Ctrl-P**}. Press **Down Arrow** to move to the Put Away option and press **Enter**. This option saves the changed frame on the data disk. The old one is replaced by this version.
12. {Press **Ctrl-D**}. Press **Ins** to move the cursor to the Main Menu line. The Disk Menu frame is again open on your desktop.
13. {Press **Ctrl-Q**}. Using the arrow keys again, position the cursor on the QUIT Framework option and press **Enter**. Type **Y** when asked if you are sure you want to quit Framework III. This ends this Framework III session.
14. Turn to Module 46 to continue the learning sequence.

Module 73

REVEAL TYPE

DESCRIPTION

Use any type of frame as part of an outline. Word processing frames are usually the main type of frame used for outline documents. However, graphs, spreadsheets, and databases are also eligible.

Use this option to determine at a glance, what type of frames are used. Select this option through the Frames Menu frame.

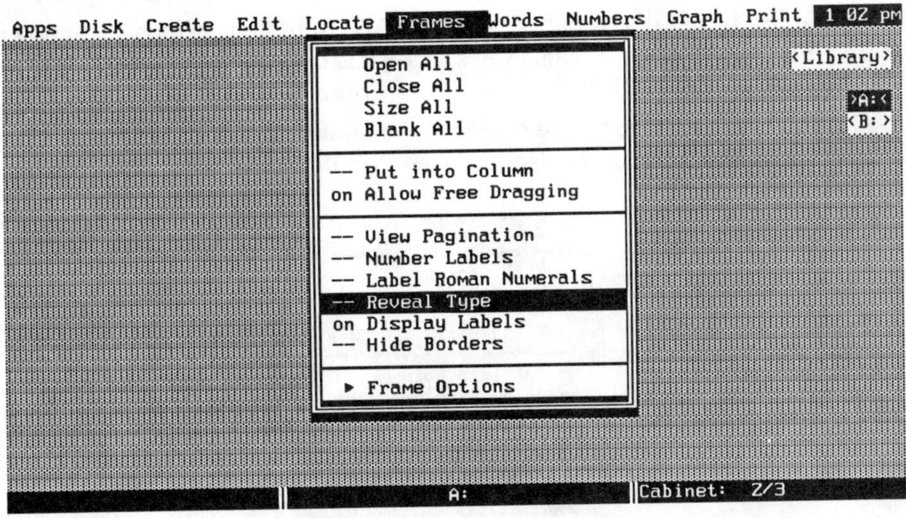

Show the type of the selected frames and all frames within them

The Reveal Type option is turned on and off when selected. Framework III presets this option off so that the frame type is not automatically displayed. Turning this option on causes Framework III to display a letter in parentheses after each subtopic heading as in the following display.

```
EXERCISE
▸ 1  Body Building
     1.1  Monday (W)
     1.2  Tuesday (E)
     1.3  Thursday (E)
     1.4  Friday (W)
▸ 2  Aerobics
     2.1  Monday (E)
     2.2  Wednesday (E)
     2.3  Friday (E)
```

When an (E) is displayed, the frame is empty. A (D) indicates a database frame. When you see a (S), you know it is a spreadsheet. Anytime you see (G) next to the heading, it is a graph frame. Usually, however, the frame is marked with a (W) to indicate it is a word processing frame.

APPLICATIONS

Use this option with any outline frame. It displays the frame type of each frame included in your outline. At a glance, you see which topics are empty and need to be deleted or filled.

TYPICAL OPERATION

This illustration shows you how to use the Reveal Type option of the Frames Menu frame. Make sure that your desktop is clear and the cursor is positioned on one of the drive indicators. The shortcut key combinations, if applicable, are enclosed by braces.

1. {Press **Ctrl-D**}. Press **Ins** to move the cursor to the Main Menu line. Next, press **Left Arrow** or **Right Arrow**, if necessary, until the Disk Menu frame is open on your desktop.
2. {Press **Ctrl-G**}. Press **Up Arrow** to move the cursor to the Get File by Name { } option and then press **Enter**. The cursor moves to the Message line at the bottom of your desktop.
3. Type **EXERCISE**. As you type, the braces next to the Get File by Name { } option fill. Press **Enter**. The disk is read and the frame you specified is opened on your desktop. If it appears only in the desktop tray with the cursor, press **Enter** to open it on your desktop.
4. {Press **Ctrl-F**}. Press **Ins** to move the cursor to the Main Menu line. Next, press **Right Arrow** until the Frames Menu frame is also open on your desktop.

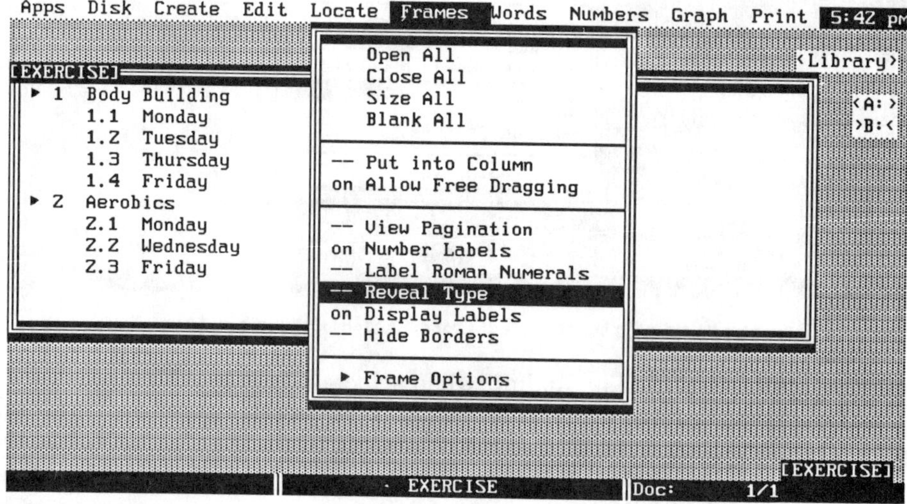

Show the type of the selected frames and all frames within them

5. {Press **Ctrl-R**}. Press **Up Arrow** or **Down Arrow** until the cursor is positioned on the Reveal Type option and press **Enter**. The menu frame disappears and your outline is changed to resemble the following display. Subtopic 1.1 is the only one which contains any work.

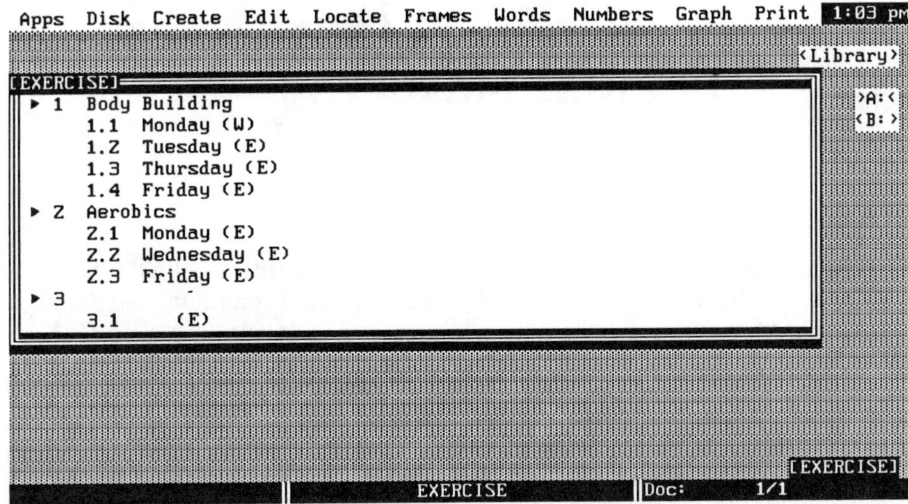

Frames: Reveal Type on

6. The outline on your desktop has not been changed. There is no reason to save it on disk again. Press **Del** to remove the frame from your desktop without saving it.
7. {Press **Ctrl-D**}. Press **Ins** to move the cursor to the Main Menu line. Next, press **Left Arrow** until the Disk Menu frame is open on your desktop.
8. {Press **Ctrl-Q**}. Using the arrow (cursor) keys, position the cursor on the QUIT Framework option and press **Enter**. Type **Y** when Framework III asks if you're sure you want to quit Framework III. The system prompt appears on your screen. This ends this Framework III session.
9. Turn to Module 7 to continue the learning sequence.

Module 74

RIGHT MARGIN { }

DESCRIPTION

When you type a word processing document, Framework III automatically limits the number of spaces for each line. To temporarily change this default (preset) condition, use the Right Margin option of the Words Menu frame.

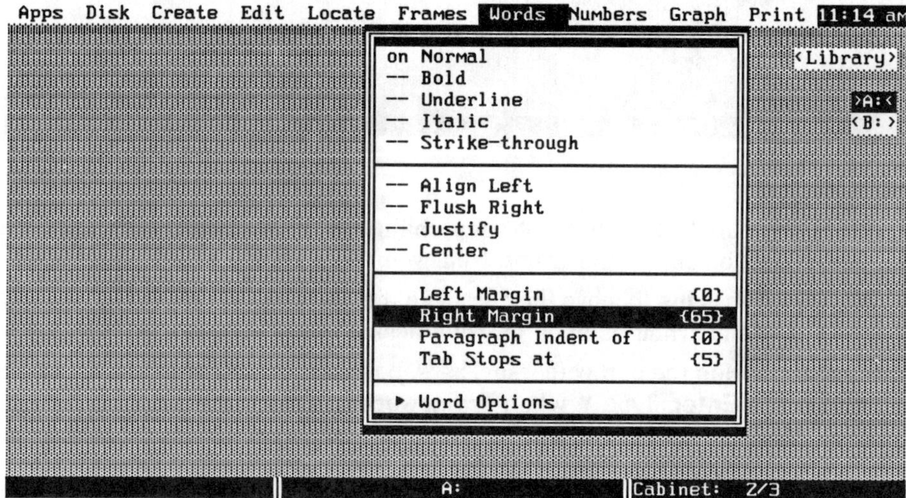

Set a new right margin for selected frames or paragraphs

The Right Margin option is currently set to 65. This means that each line of text is 65 spaces long. Change this number anytime during a word processing activity.

For example, the following party invitation has a right margin setting of 65 spaces.

```
[BIRTHDAY]
              P A R T Y !    P A R T Y !    P A R T Y !
                       Saturday, April 1, 1989
Come help us celebrate Jerry Smith's birthday.  He'll be 42 years
young!  We have a special surprise for him that  will  dazzle and
amaze us all!

          When: 7:30 P. M.
          Where: 111 West 11th # 102

Don't miss the fun!
```

By changing the right margin to 50 and typing the same invitation, the frame resembles the following display.

```
[BIRTHDAY]
[....▼....▼....▼....▼....▼....▼....▼....▼....▼....]....▼....▼....▼....
     P A R T Y !    P A R T Y !    P A R T Y !
              Saturday, April 1, 1989
Come help  us  celebrate  Jerry  Smith's birthday.
He'll  be  42  years  young!  We  have  a  special
surprise for him that  will  dazzle  and  amaze us
all!

          When: 7:30 P. M.
          Where: 111 West 11th # 102
```

Since only 50 spaces per line are allowed, Framework III moves the cursor to the next line sooner than in the previous example. Also, notice that the first line is centered to match the line length.

Even after the invitation is typed with a right margin of 65, a change to 50 affects only the paragraph specified by the cursor. For example, with the cursor positioned on the "C" of "Come," the right margin is set to 50. Notice the invitation now!

```
[BIRTHDAY]
[....▼....▼....▼....▼....▼....▼....▼....▼....▼....]....▼....▼....▼....
            P A R T Y !    P A R T Y !    P A R T Y !
                     Saturday, April 1, 1989
Come help  us  celebrate  Jerry  Smith's birthday.
He'll  be  42  years  young!  We  have  a  special
surprise for him that  will  dazzle  and  amaze us
all!

          When: 7:30 P. M.
          Where: 111 West 11th # 102
```

The paragraph where the cursor is positioned is affected by changing the right margin number. As soon as the value is changed, the paragraph is realigned. The first line is not changed. Its line length is still 65; only the party description has 50 spaces per line.

In short, once a right margin (line length) is set for a line, it remains that length until you reset it by changing the right margin value. You might forget, but Framework III doesn't.

APPLICATIONS

This option is available only for word processing frames — not spreadsheets, databases, or graphs.

Use it and the Left Margin option to tell Framework III where to begin and end each line of your document. Change the option's number when you need to set new limits for the cursor.

Since Framework III automatically moves the cursor to the right margin of the next line when the current one is filled, you don't have to remember to do so. Just type!

TYPICAL OPERATION

This illustration shows you how to change the right margin for a birthday party invitation. Close any open frames on your desktop and position the cursor on your data drive indicator (drive B in this example). The shortcut key combinations, if applicable, are enclosed by braces.

1. With the cursor positioned on the data drive indicator, press **Enter**.
2. Since the cursor is positioned on the border of the open frame, press **Gray +**. Now you're inside the open frame. With the cursor positioned on the filename BIRTHDAY.FW3, press **Enter**. If necessary, press **Enter** again to move the frame from the tray to the desktop.
3. Press **Gray +** to move the cursor from the frame border to the text inside the frame.
4. Use the arrows to move the cursor to the beginning of the paragraph.
5. {Press **Ctrl-W**}. Press **Ins** to move the cursor to the Main Menu line. Next, press **Left Arrow** or **Right Arrow** until the Words Menu frame is also open on your desktop. Notice that the Right Margin option is set to {65} as in the following display.

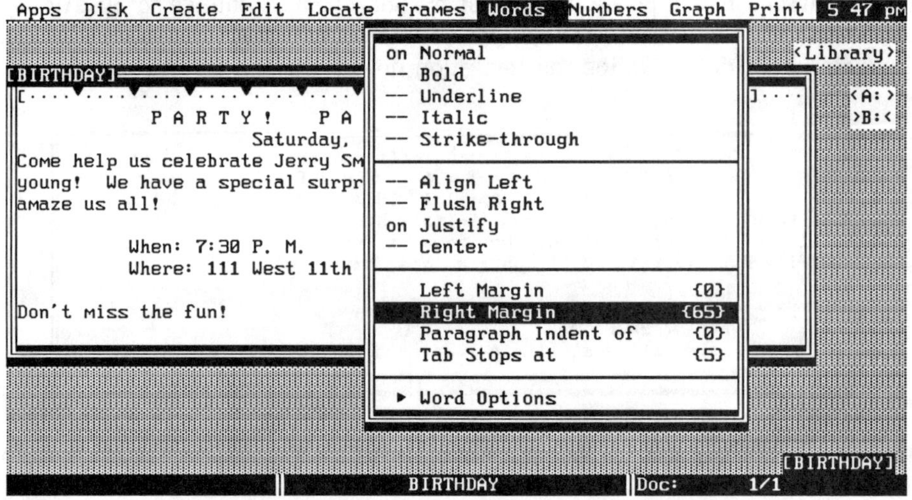

6. {Press **Ctrl-R**}. Press **Down Arrow** until the cursor is positioned on the Right Margin option and then press **Enter**. The cursor moves to the Message line at the bottom of your screen. Type **50** and press **Enter**. The Words Menu frame disappears. However, your current line length is set to 50 instead of 65. Notice the invitation in the following display.

```
[BIRTHDAY]
[....▼....▼....▼....▼....▼....▼....▼....▼....▼....]....▼....▼....▼....
     P A R T Y !   P A R T Y !   P A R T Y !
              Saturday, April 1, 1989
Come help  us  celebrate  Jerry  Smith's birthday.
He'll  be  42  years  young!  We  have  a  special
surprise for him that  will  dazzle  and  amaze us
all!

          When: 7:30 P. M.
          Where: 111 West 11th # 102

MDon't miss the fun!
```

7. Press **Gray** – to move the cursor to the frame border and then press **Enter**. The frame closes and is put in your desktop tray.
8. Press **Del** to delete the invitation from your desktop. By doing this, the changed invitation is not saved on disk.
9. Press **Enter** to close the directory frame.
10. {Press **Ctrl-D**}. Press **Ins** to move the cursor to the Main Menu line. Next, press the arrow (cursor) keys until the Disk Menu frame is again open on your desktop.
11. {Press **Ctrl-Q**}. Position the cursor on the QUIT Framework option and press **Enter**. Type **Y** when asked if you are sure you want to quit Framework III. This ends your Framework III session.
12. Turn to Module 57 to continue the learning sequence.

Module 75

ROW HAS X-AXIS LABELS

DESCRIPTION

Since a spreadsheet is usually a collection of numbers, reserve the first row to describe the information in each column. Also, reserve the first column to describe the information in each row.

Select this option to display the first row of the spreadsheet (descriptions) on the horizontal line (X-axis) of your graph. It is available through the Graph Menu frame displayed below.

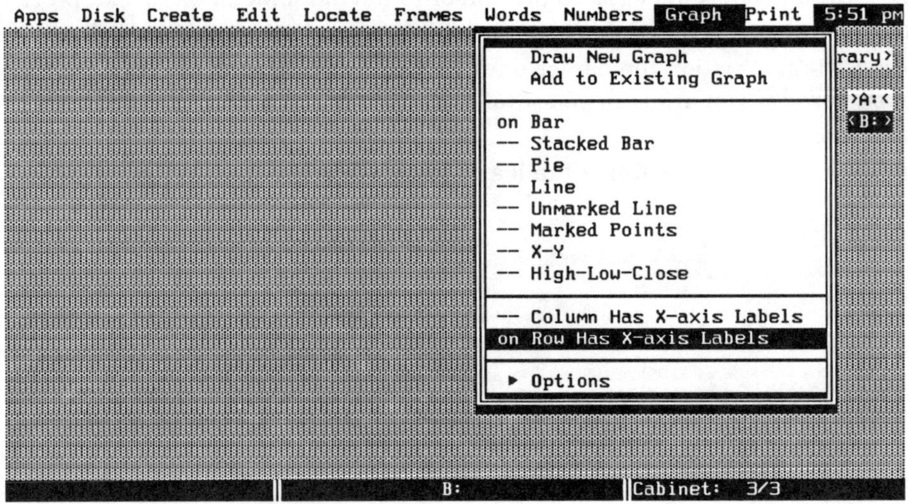

Graph: Row Has X-axis Labels on

When you begin your Framework III session, this option may be on or off. When off, descriptions in the first column are used when the graph is drawn. By opening the Graph Menu and selecting this option, the labels in the first row are used to describe the X-axis of your graph.

For example, notice the following spreadsheet labels.

[SALES]

	A	B	C	D	E	F	G
1		January	February	March	April	May	June
2	J.Sloan	2500	2800	2000			
3	T.Berry	1000	1200	1400			
4	Total	3500	4000	3400			
5							
6							
7							
8							
9							
10							

By using F6 (Extend) to highlight the numbers in rows 2 and 3, column B, you identify the information for your graph. Open the Graph Menu frame, select Row Has X-axis Labels option, and then select the Draw New Graph option. Notice that the names of the months appear on the X-axis.

If the Row Has X-axis Labels is off, the graph is drawn so that the names appear on the X-axis. Choose the way you prefer and then tell Framework III to draw it.

APPLICATIONS

Use the X-axis (horizontal line) of your graph to describe the information drawn. By selecting the Row Has X-axis Labels option, you're telling Framework III to draw the graph so that the labels in row 1 appear under the graph's X-axis.

Be sure that you notice whether this option is on or off before selecting the Draw New Graph option. You might not notice the labels until the graph is drawn and copies are distributed.

TYPICAL OPERATION

This example shows you how to open a spreadsheet, select numbers, and draw a graph so that the row's labels appear on the X-axis. Close any open frames on your desktop and position the cursor on your data drive indicator (drive B in this example). The shortcut key combinations, if applicable, are enclosed by braces.

1. With the cursor positioned on the data drive indicator, press **Enter**.
2. Since the cursor is positioned on the border of the open frame, press **Gray +**. Now you're inside the open frame. Press **Down Arrow** until the cursor is positioned on the filename SALES.FW3 and then press **Enter**.
3. Press **Gray +** to move the cursor from the frame border to the inside of your open frame.
4. The cursor is positioned on cells B4 through D4. Press **Esc** to change the cursor size. Press **Up Arrow** to move the cursor to cell B2.
5. Press **F6** (Extend) to tell Framework III you want to extend the cursor. Next, press **Down Arrow** to see the highlighted area expand to cell B3.
6. {Press **Ctrl-G**}. Press **Ins** to move the cursor to the Main Menu line. Next, press **Right Arrow** until the Graph Menu frame is also open on your desktop.

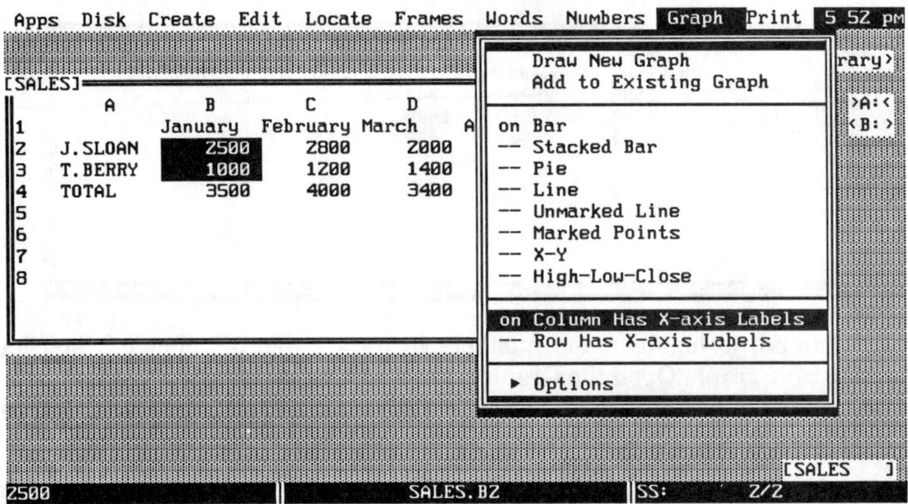

7. Notice whether or not the Row Has X-axis Labels is on. If so, skip this step. {Press **Ctrl-R**}. Using **Down Arrow**, move the cursor to the Row Has X-axis Labels option and press **Enter**.
8. {Press **Ctrl-D**}. Press **Up Arrow** until the cursor highlights the Draw New Graph option and press **Enter**. Framework III asks if you want to draw it in the open frame or a new one. Press **Enter** to use the open frame. The graph should resemble the following display.

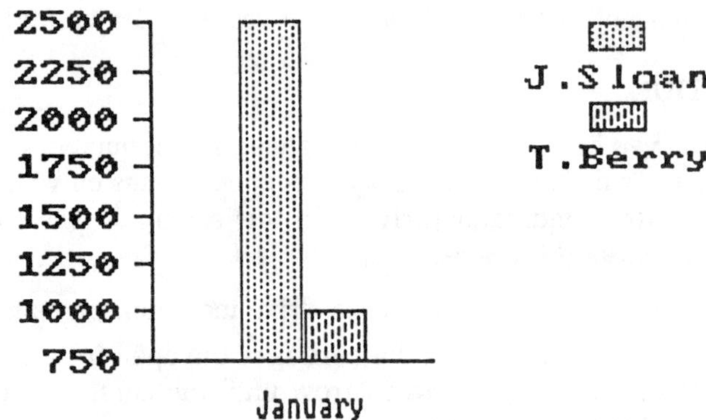

9. Press **Del** to delete the new graph from your desktop without saving it on disk. Press **Del** again to remove the open spreadsheet.
10. {Press **Ctrl-D**}. Press **Ins** to move the cursor to the Main Menu line. Next, press the arrow (cursor) keys until the Disk Menu frame is again open on your desktop.
11. {Press **Ctrl-Q**}. Position the cursor on the QUIT Framework option and press **Enter**. Type **Y** when asked if you are sure you want to quit Framework III. You have ended this Framework III session.
12. Turn to Module 61 to continue the learning sequence.

Module 76

ROWS/RECORDS: ADD { }

DESCRIPTION

When you need a bigger spreadsheet or database file, the Rows/Records: Add option lets you add more space to the file for new information. Use this option to increase the number of rows in your spreadsheet or the number of records in your database.

Remember, the spreadsheet or database file must be open on the desktop and the cursor positioned before selecting this option. It is available from the Create Menu frame as follows.

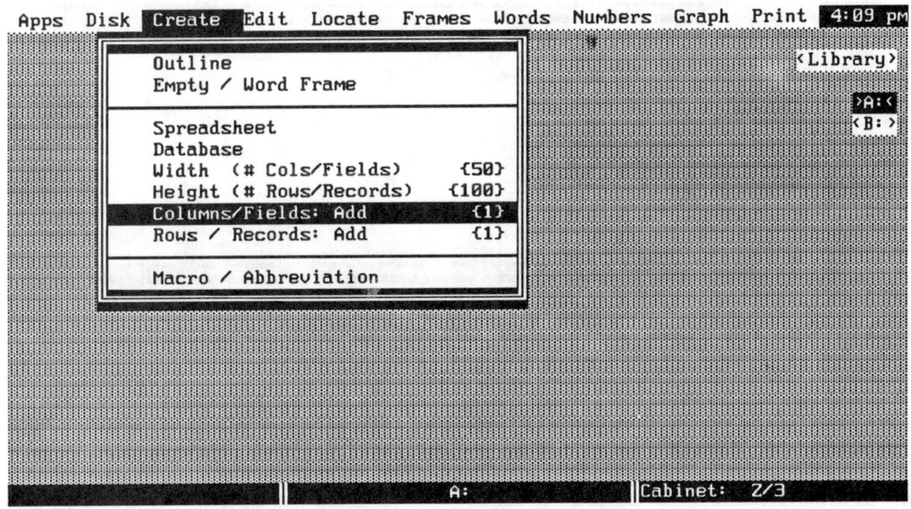

Add specified number of columns/fields after the selected one

Notice the Rows/Records: Add option. The 1 contained within the braces specifies how many new columns or fields are added to the open file. Framework III is currently set to add only one row or record when this option is selected. Before Framework III increases the size of the open spreadsheet or database, you are given the opportunity to change this number.

For example, the following spreadsheet frame has five rows and five columns (A, B, C, D, and E).

```
[Flavors]
        A           B         C         D         E
1              Jeff                Terry
2   Chocolate           5                   2
3   Strawberry          0                   1
4   Vanilla             1                   3
5   Total               6                   6
```

A new flavor of ice cream needs to be added to the spreadsheet. By using the Rows/Records: Add option of the Create Menu, the spreadsheet is increased from five rows to seven rows. Since the fifth row currently has the calculations set up, the new rows are *inserted between* rows 4 and 5.

By positioning the cursor on row 4 of the spreadsheet (column doesn't matter), and using the Rows/Records: Add option, the previous spreadsheet example should resemble the following display.

```
[Flavors]
        A           B         C         D         E
1              Jeff                Terry
2   Chocolate           5                   2
3   Strawberry          0                   1
4   Vanilla             1                   3
5
6
7   Total               6                   6
```

Rows 5 and 6 are the new rows. The Total was on row 5 before the Row/Records: Add option was performed. It is automatically moved down to row number 7 when the two new rows are added.

New rows or records are always inserted below the cursor position. This gives you the choice of where the additional rows or records are added.

This option is also available for database frames. It is used the same way as with spreadsheet frames.

Remember that you can add the new rows or records *anywhere* within the file. Position the cursor within the spreadsheet or database before opening the Create Menu frame. Then select the Rows/Records: Add option, type the number of new rows or records you need, and press Enter. Framework III changes the file within the frame.

If the change meets your needs, save it on disk by using the Save and Continue option of the Disk Menu frame. By saving your open frames at regular intervals (e.g., after you review and approve a major change), power failures and other such "catastrophies" are only bothersome — not a major loss of time and effort.

APPLICATIONS

When you create a new spreadsheet or database, you usually have to guess at the number of rows or records you'll need. As you fill each row or record, you may find your guess was a little short.

The Rows/Records: Add option of the Create Menu frame gives you the ability to increase the number of entries for your spreadsheet or database. New rows or records can be inserted anywhere in the spreadsheet or database by positioning the cursor where you want them added.

Framework III provides the flexibility needed to get your work computerized quickly. If, and when your needs change, the file size can change too. In other words, a quick job can be done for the short-term. Then when time allows, the spreadsheet or database can be enhanced to accommodate your long-term needs.

TYPICAL OPERATION

The following illustration inserts new rows into a spreadsheet. Make sure that your desktop is clean and the cursor is positioned on the data drive indicator. If you have two drives, the data drive is drive B.

1. {Press **Ctrl-D**}. Press **Ins** to move the cursor to the Main Menu line. Next, press the arrow (cursor) keys until the Disk Menu frame is open on your desktop.
2. {Press **Ctrl-G**}. Press **Up Arrow** until the cursor is positioned on the Get File by Name option and press **Enter**. The cursor then moves to the Message line at the bottom of your desktop. Type **FLAVORS** and press **Enter** twice. The spreadsheet opens on your desktop.
3. Press **Gray +** to move the cursor inside the open frame.
4. Press **Down Arrow** and **Left Arrow** to move the cursor to column A, row 3, type **Strawberry**, and press **Enter**. Press **Down Arrow** to move the cursor to row 4, type **Vanilla**, and press **Enter**. Continue changing your spreadsheet until it resembles the following display.

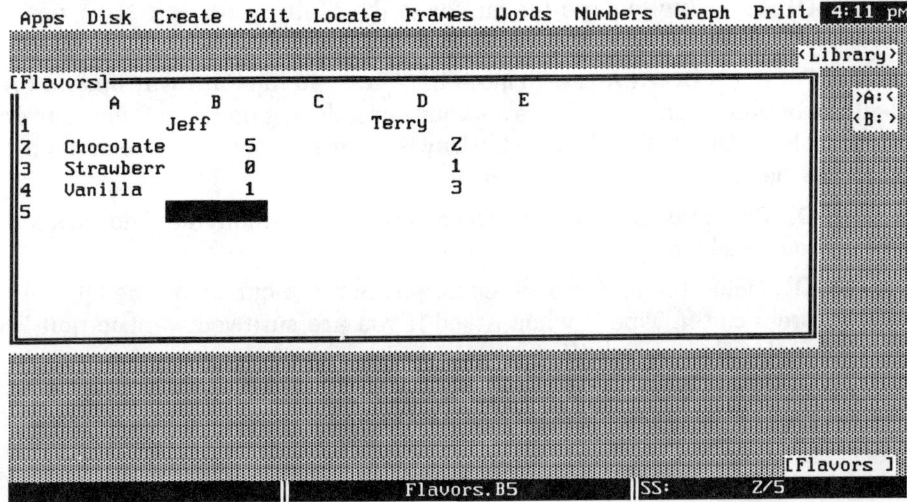

5. Now, it's time to insert two new rows between the rows labeled "Strawberry" and "Vanilla." Position the cursor on row 3, column A, by pressing the arrow (cursor) keys. Press **Ctrl-C** to reopen the Create Menu frame.
6. {Press **Ctrl-R**}. Press **Down Arrow** until the cursor is positioned on the Rows/Records: Add option and press **Enter**. Type **2** and press **Enter**.
7. When the Create Menu frame disappears, notice there are two new rows between "Strawberry" and "Vanilla."

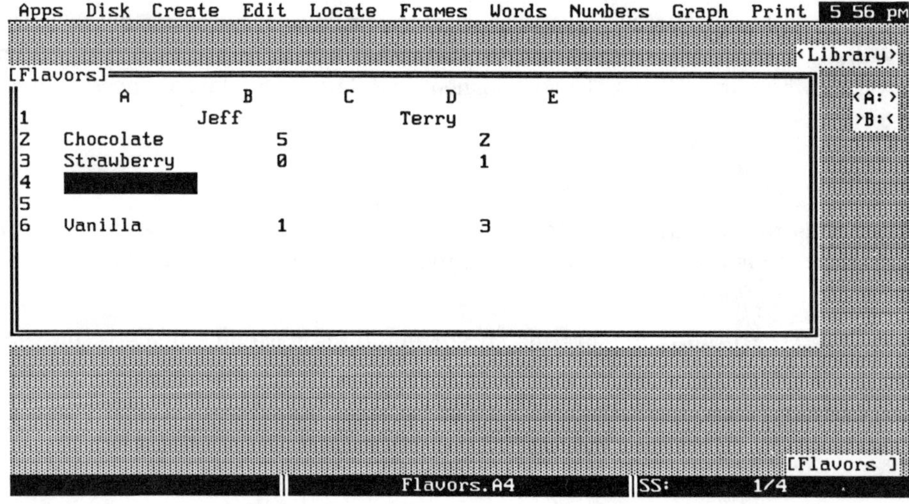

8. Press **Gray –** to move the cursor to the top of the frame border. Press **Enter** to close the open frame. Framework III closes the frame and moves the cursor to the desktop tray.
9. {Press **Ctrl-D**}. Press **Ins** to move the cursor to the Main Menu line. Next, use the arrow (cursor) keys until the Disk Menu frame opens.
10. {Press **Ctrl-P**}. Press **Down Arrow** to move the cursor to the Put Away option. Press **Enter** to select the option. Framework III saves your spreadsheet on drive B (or your data drive) and names it FLAVORS.FW3. The desktop tray is removed from your screen since it is empty. Your file has been "put away" for later use.
11. {Press **Ctrl-D**}. Press **Ins** to move the cursor to the Main Menu line. The Disk Menu frame is open on your desktop.
12. {Press **Ctrl-Q**}. Using the arrow keys again, position the cursor on the QUIT Framework option and press **Enter**. Type **Y** when asked if you are sure you want to quit Framework III. This ends this Framework III session.
13. Turn to Module 77 to continue the learning sequence.

Module 77

ROWS/RECORDS: REMOVE

DESCRIPTION

When you need to make a spreadsheet or database file smaller, the Rows/Records: Remove option lets you take away rows or records. Use this option to decrease the number of rows in your spreadsheet or the number of records in your database.

Remember, the spreadsheet or database file must be open on the desktop and the cursor positioned before selecting this option. It is available from the Edit Menu frame as follows.

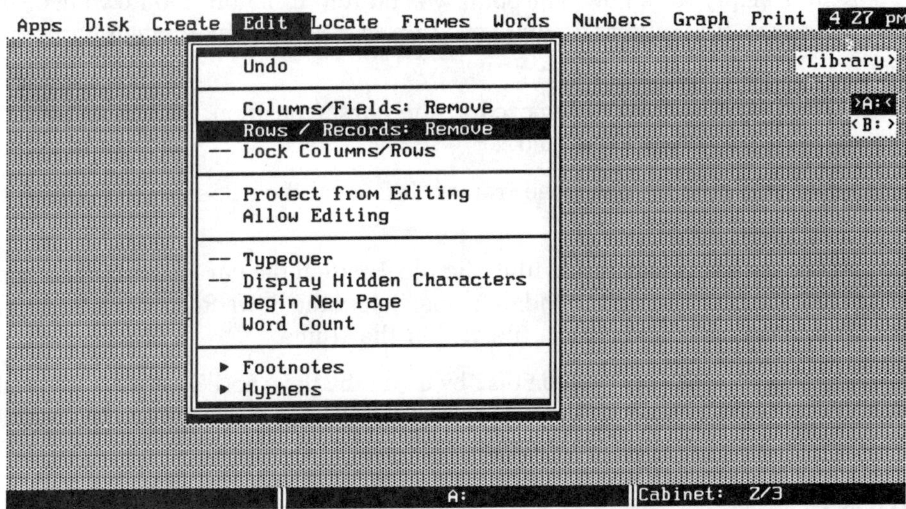

Remove selected rows/records from a spreadsheet/database

Notice the Rows/Records: Remove option. Each time it's selected, a row is deleted. For example, the following spreadsheet frame has 10 rows and four columns (A, B, C, and D).

[Flavors]

	A	B	C	D
1		Jeff	Terry	
2	Chocolate	5	2	
3	Strawberry	0	1	
4	Vanilla	1	3	
5				
6				
7				
8				
9				
10	Total	6	6	

Using the Rows/Records: Remove option of the Create Menu, the spreadsheet is decreased from 10 rows to 9 rows. Since the tenth row currently has the calculations set up, delete one of the empty rows.

By positioning the cursor on row 6 of the spreadsheet (column doesn't matter), and selecting the Rows/Records: Remove option, the previous spreadsheet example resembles the following display.

```
[Flavors]
            A              B         C         D
1                        Jeff      Terry
2   Chocolate              5         2
3   Strawberry             0         1
4   Vanilla                1         3
5
6
7
8
9   Total                  6         6
```

There are only four empty rows now. The Total was on row 10 before the Row/Records: Remove option was performed. It is automatically moved up to row number 9 when one previous row is deleted.

Deleted rows or records are always removed at the cursor position. This gives you the choice of where the rows or records are deleted.

This option is also available for database frames. It is used the same way as with spreadsheet frames.

Remove the rows or records *anywhere* within the file. Position the cursor within the spreadsheet or database before opening the Create Menu frame. Select the Rows/Records: Remove option and press Enter. Framework III changes the file within the frame.

If the change meets your needs, save it on disk by using the Save and Continue option of the Disk Menu frame. By saving your open frames at regular intervals (e.g., after you review and approve a major change), you know your hard work is safe.

APPLICATIONS

When you create a new spreadsheet or database, you usually have to guess at the number of rows or records you'll need. As you fill each row or record, you may find that you overestimated.

The Rows/Records: Remove option of the Create Menu frame gives you the ability to decrease the number of entries in your spreadsheet or database. Remove rows or records anywhere in a spreadsheet or database by positioning the cursor on the row or record you want to delete.

Framework III provides the flexibility needed to get your work computerized quickly. If and when your needs change, the file size can change too. In other words, a quick job can be done for the short-term. Then when time allows, the spreadsheet or database can be changed to accommodate your long-term needs.

TYPICAL OPERATION

The following illustration removes rows from a spreadsheet. Make sure that your desktop is clean and the cursor is positioned on the data drive indicator. If you have two drives, the data drive is drive B. The shortcut key combinations, if applicable, are enclosed by braces.

1. {Press **Ctrl-D**}. Press **Ins** to move the cursor to the Main Menu line. Next, press the arrow (cursor) keys, if necessary, until the Disk Menu frame is open on your desktop.
2. {Press **Ctrl-G**}. Press **Up Arrow** until the cursor is positioned on the Get File by Name option and press **Enter**. The cursor then moves to the Message line at the bottom of your desktop. Type **FLAVORS** and press **Enter** twice. The spreadsheet opens on your desktop.
3. Press **Gray +** to move the cursor inside the open frame.
4. Now, it's time to delete row 4. Position the cursor on row 4 (any column).
5. {Press **Ctrl-E**}. Press **Ins** to move the cursor to the Main Menu line. Next, press **Right Arrow** until the Edit Menu frame is open on your desktop.

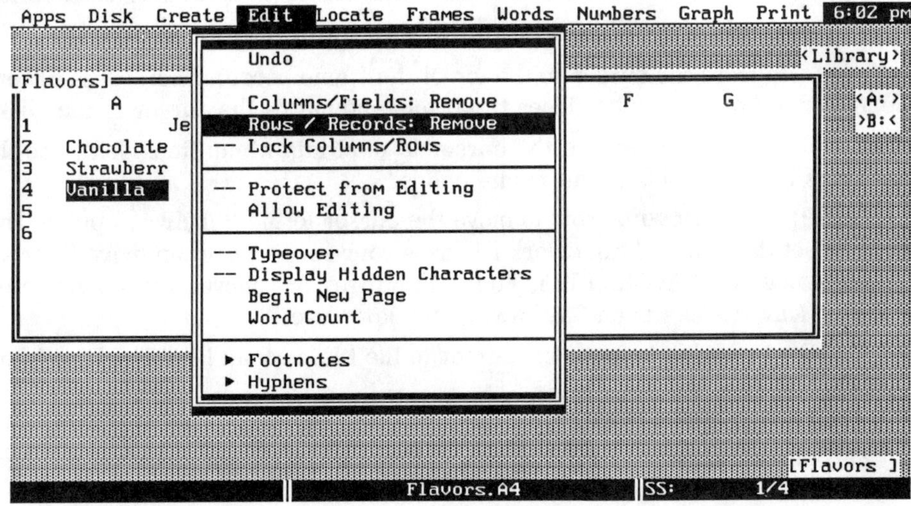

Remove selected rows/records from a spreadsheet/database

6. {Press **Ctrl-R**}. Using the arrow (cursor) keys, position the cursor on the Rows/Records: Remove option and press **Enter**. The computer beeps and tells you that this operation is "undoable." Type **Y** to continue the operation. When the Edit Menu frame disappears, your spreadsheet is changed.

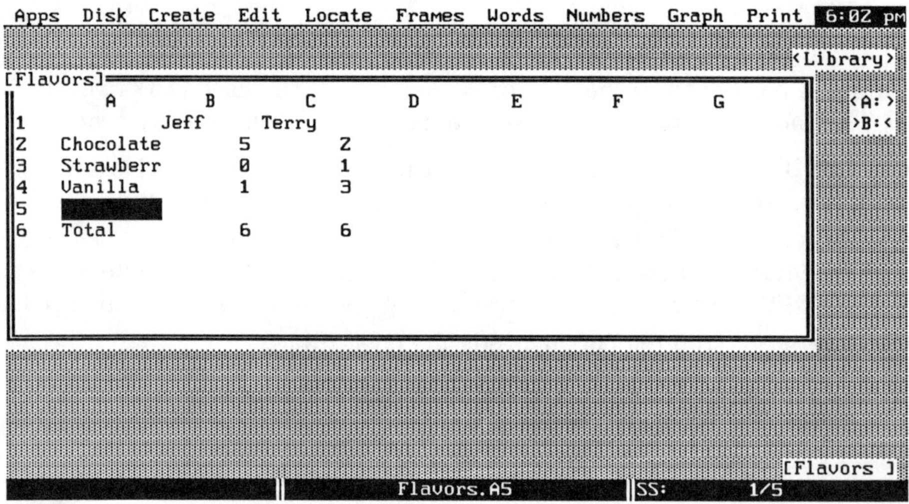

7. Press **Gray –** to move the cursor to the top of the frame border. Then press **Enter** to close the open frame. Framework III closes the frame and moves the cursor to the desktop tray.
8. {Press **Ctrl-D**}. Press **Ins** to move the cursor to the Main Menu line. Next, use the arrow (cursor) keys until the Disk Menu frame opens.
9. {Press **Ctrl-P**}. Press **Down Arrow** to move the cursor to the Put Away option. Then press **Enter** to select the option. Framework III saves your spreadsheet on drive B (or your data drive) and names it FLAVORS.FW3. The desktop tray is removed from your screen since it is empty. Your file has been "put away" for later use.
10. {Press **Ctrl-D**}. Press **Ins** to move the cursor to the Main Menu line. The Disk Menu frame is open on your desktop.
11. {Press **Ctrl-Q**}. Using the arrow keys again, position the cursor on the QUIT Framework option and press **Enter**. Type **Y** when asked if you are sure you want to quit Framework III. This ends this Framework III session.
12. Turn to Module 22 to continue the learning sequence.

Module 78

SAVE AND CONTINUE

DESCRIPTION

Creating a frame full of work is usually a time-consuming activity. Using the Save and Continue option, you save your open frame on disk as you work so you don't have to start from scratch again.

In other words, Framework III saves the current version of the frame on disk without removing it from your desktop. The old version on disk is replaced by the new one.

This option is available through the Disk Menu frame as in the following display.

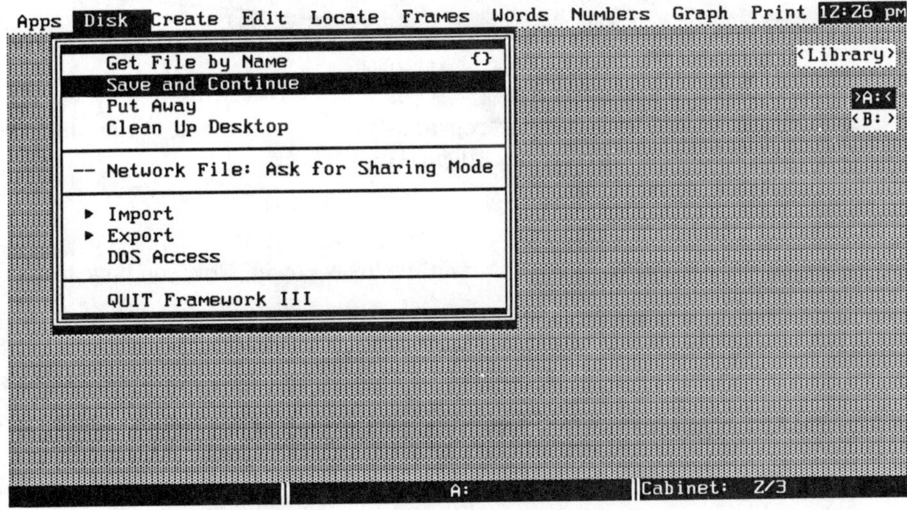

Copy document to its home disk and directory

It is a good idea to save your open frame several times as you change it. If you lose power, or some other mishap occurs while you work, at least you can return to the last saved version of your frame.

Another good practice is to save the open frame before leaving the machine — even if it's just to get a drink of water. There's no telling what can happen when you leave a computer unattended.

The file is always saved on the disk in the drive which Framework III knows as your data drive. It is normally the last drive listed with your disk drive indicators. In the following desktop, the data drive is drive B.

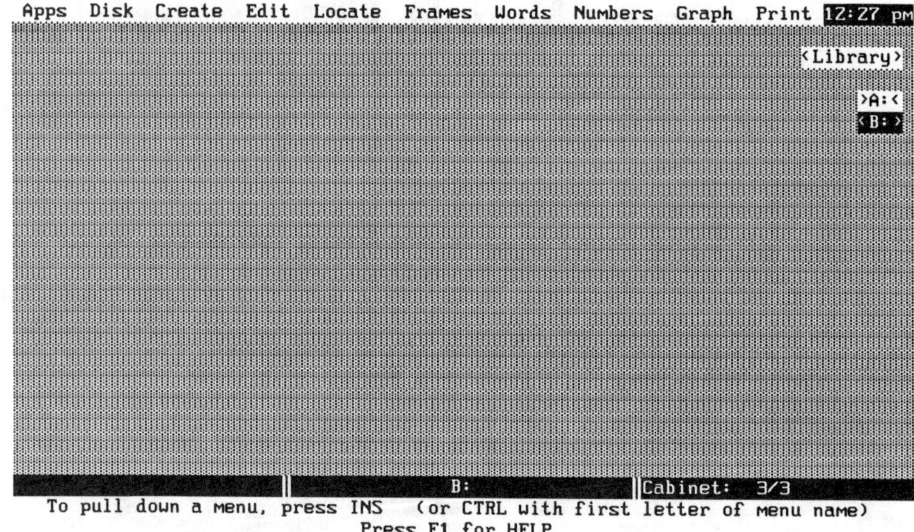

The data drive is preset by the installation program. It can be changed to any drive you prefer by using the Setup disk in your Framework III package.

APPLICATIONS

After typing several pages of a term paper, the building loses power. Now you have to start all over!

The Save and Continue option takes much less time than having to redo your work. The current version of the frame you see on the screen is saved on disk. When Framework III has completed the save, you can return to work at the same point as before the save. What do you have to lose?

Better yet, what do you have to gain?

TYPICAL OPERATION

This exercise shows you how to tell Framework III to use the Save and Continue option of the Disk Menu frame. Make sure that your desktop is clear and the cursor is positioned on one of the drive indicators. The shortcut key combinations, if applicable, are enclosed by braces.

1. {Press **Ctrl-D**}. Press **Ins** to move the cursor to the Main Menu line. Next, press **Left Arrow** or **Right Arrow**, if necessary, until the Disk Menu frame is open on your desktop.
2. {Press **Ctrl-G**}. Press **Up Arrow** to move the cursor to the Get File by Name option and then press **Enter**. The cursor moves to the Message line at the bottom of your desktop.
3. Type **B:BIRTHDAY.FW3**. As you type, the braces next to the Get File by Name option fill. Press **Enter**. The disk is read and the frame you specified is opened on your desktop.

4. Press **Gray +** to move the cursor inside your open frame. Using the arrow keys, move the cursor to the first letter on the top line. Type **P A R T Y !** and press the **Spacebar** four times. Now your frame resembles the following display.

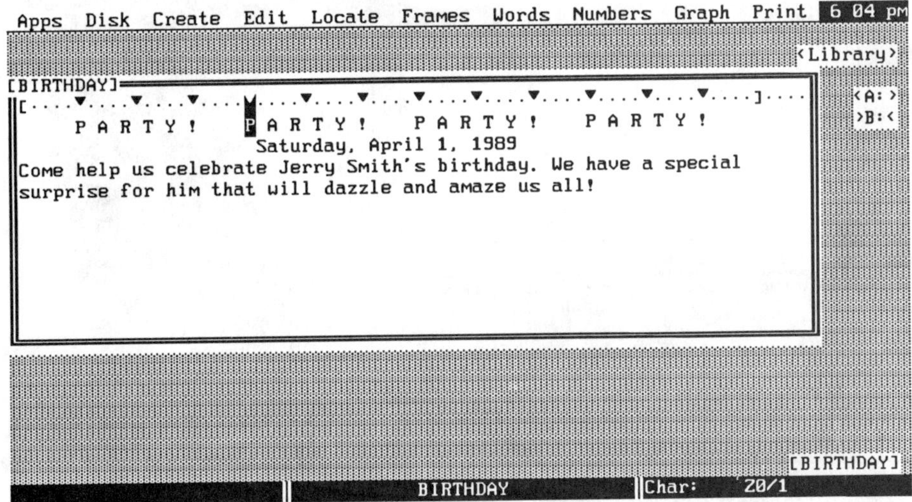

5. {Press **Ctrl-D**}. Press **Ins** to move the cursor to the Main Menu line. The Disk Menu frame is also open on your desktop.
6. {Press **Ctrl-S**}. Using the arrow (cursor) keys, position the cursor on the Save and Continue option and then press **Enter**. The Message line displays the word "SAVING" and the disk drive lights.
7. Press **Gray –** to move the cursor to the frame border.
8. Press **Del** to delete the open frame from the desktop without saving it on disk. The drive did not light.

9. {Press **Ctrl-D**}. Press **Ins** to move the cursor to the Main Menu line. The Disk Menu frame is open on your desktop.

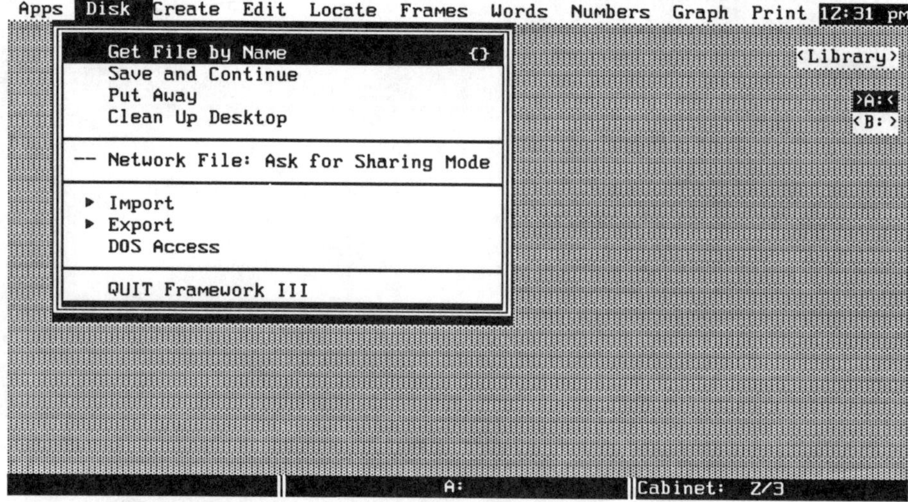

10. {Press **Ctrl-G**}. Press **Up Arrow** to move the cursor to the Get File by Name option and then press **Enter**. The cursor moves to the Message line at the bottom of your desktop.
11. Type **B:BIRTHDAY.FW3**. As you type, notice that the braces next to the Get File by Name option fill. Press **Enter**. The disk is read and the frame you specified is opened on your desktop.
12. Press **Gray +** to move the cursor inside the frame. Use the arrow keys to position the cursor on the "P" of PARTY! in the first line. Then press **Del** until your frame resembles the following display.

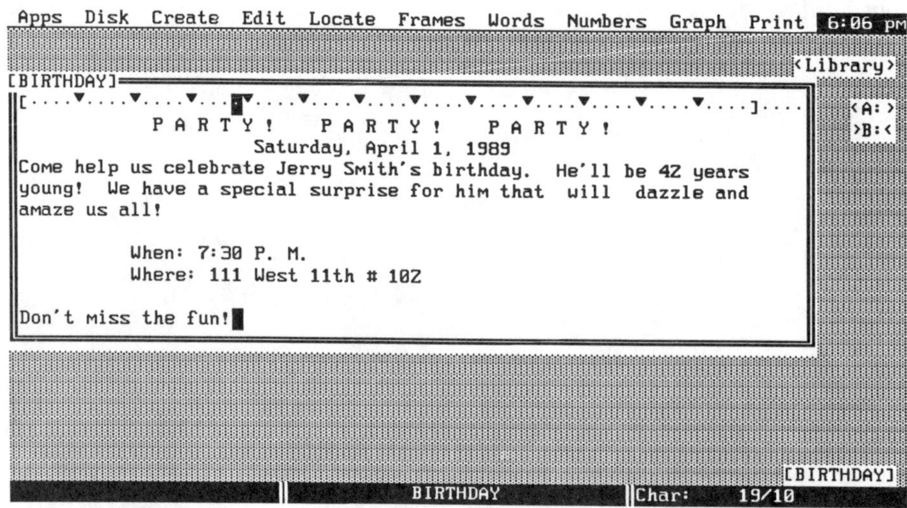

13. Press **Gray –** to move the cursor to the frame border. Then press **Enter** to put the frame in the desktop tray.
14. {Press **Ctrl-D**}. Press **Ins** to move the cursor to the Main Menu line. The Disk Menu frame is open on your desktop.
15. {Press **Ctrl-P**}. Select the Put Away option to save the frame on disk and remove it from the desktop.
16. {Press **Ctrl-D**}. Reopen the Disk Menu frame.
17. {Press **Ctrl-Q**}. Using the arrow keys again, position the cursor on the QUIT Framework option and press **Enter**. Type **Y** when asked if you are sure you want to quit Framework III. This ends this Framework III session.
18. Turn to Module 24 to continue the learning sequence.

Module 79

SEARCH { }

DESCRIPTION

Repeating words and phrases usually makes boring reading. Misspelled names are unforgivable. These are just two good reasons to use the Search { } option of the Locate Menu frame.

This option is available for any type of frame. Access it through the Locate Menu frame.

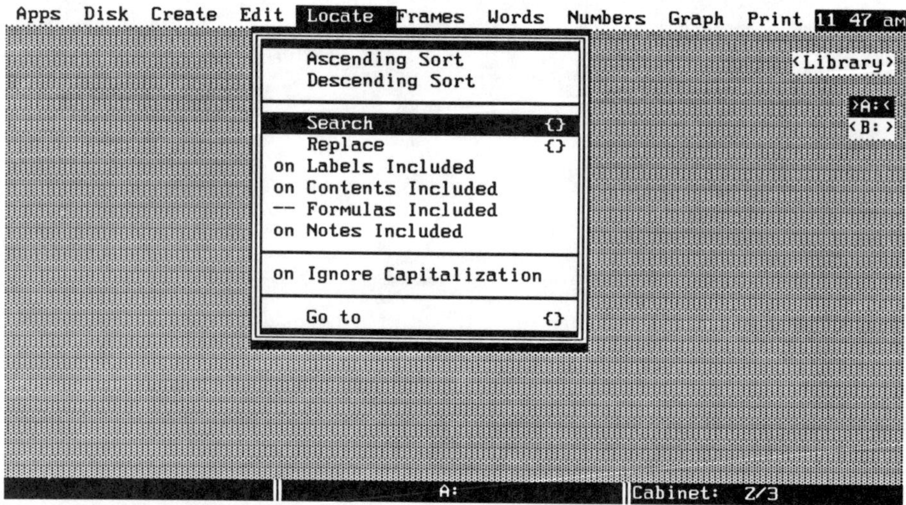

Find any specified word or phrase -- in any type of frame

By selecting this option and typing the word or phrase within the braces, you tell Framework III to find the first occurrence of the specified text. When it is found, Framework III positions the cursor on the word or phrase and awaits your response.

Change it or tell Framework III that you want the next occurrence. If and when another is found, the cursor again identifies it. By pressing Up Arrow or Down Arrow, you have Framework III search for the next or previous occurrence.

APPLICATIONS

The Search { } option is available for any frame type. Use it to find any combination of letters or numbers within an open frame.

For example, if you misspelled "Jerry," tell Framework III that you want to search for "J" (or "Je") within the open frame. If found, the first occurrence of an uppercase "J" is identified by the cursor.

By pressing Down Arrow, you tell Framework III to continue the search. The Up Arrow returns to the previous occurrence. Any other key changes the document.

Use the "?" as a wild card (symbol for telling Framework III that anything is acceptable). For example, to see any word with a "c," fill the braces with "c?". Searching the birthday invitation returns "Come," "celebrate," and "special."

The wild card is as useful a tool in Framework III as the asterisk is to DOS commands.

TYPICAL OPERATION

This example shows you how to use the Search { } option of the Locate Menu frame. Close any open frames on your desktop and position the cursor on your data drive indicator (drive B in this example). The shortcut key combinations, if applicable, are enclosed by braces.

1. {Press **Ctrl-D**}. Press **Ins** to move the cursor to the Main Menu line. Next, press **Left Arrow** or **Right Arrow**, if necessary, until the Disk Menu frame is open on your desktop.
2. {Press **Ctrl-G**}. Press **Up Arrow** to move the cursor to the Get File by Name option and then press **Enter**. The cursor moves to the Message line at the bottom of your desktop.
3. Type **B:BIRTHDAY**. As you type, notice that the braces next to the Get File by Name option fill. Press **Enter** twice. The disk is read and the frame you specified is opened on your desktop.
4. Press **Gray +** to move the cursor inside your open frame. Your cursor is positioned after the last change of the document. Press **Down Arrow** and **Left Arrow** until the cursor is positioned on the "C" in the word "Come."
5. {Press **Ctrl-L**}. Press **Ins** to move the cursor to the Main Menu line. Next, press **Right Arrow** until the Locate Menu frame is also open on your desktop.

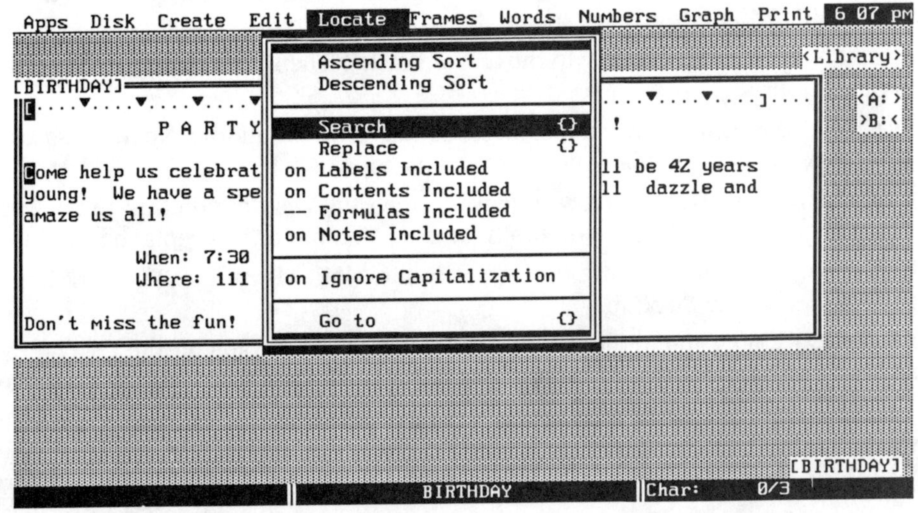

Find any specified word or phrase -- in any type of frame

6. {Press **Ctrl-S**}. Press **Down Arrow**, if necessary, until the cursor is positioned on the Search { } option and press **Enter**. Type **us** and press **Enter**. The Locate Menu frame disappears from your desktop. Notice that the cursor is positioned on the first occurrence of "us."
7. Press **Down Arrow** to see the cursor positioned on the second (last) occurrence of "us." Type **everyone**. Press **Del** six times; your frame resembles the following display.

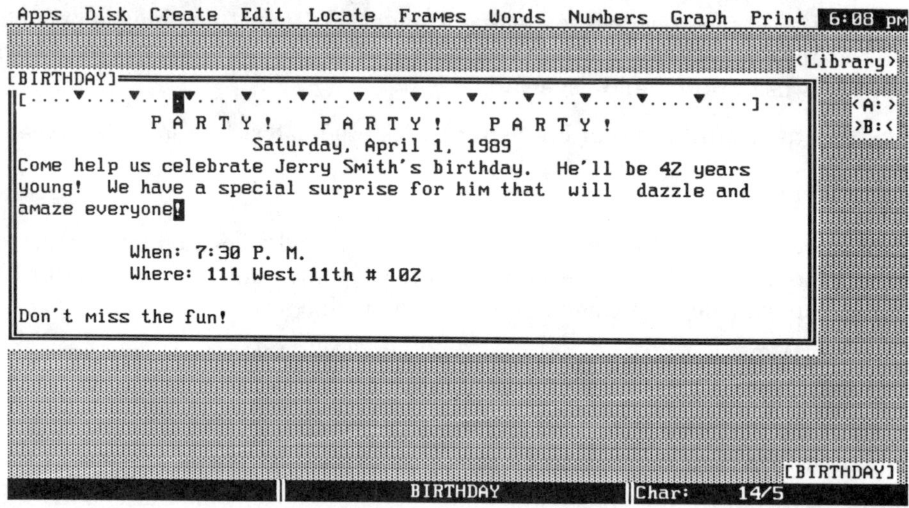

8. {Press **Ctrl-L**}. Press **Ins** to move the cursor to the Main Menu line. The Locate Menu frame is open on your desktop.
9. {Press **Ctrl-S**}. With the cursor still positioned on the Search { } option, press **Enter**. Type **c?** and press **Enter**. The Locate Menu frame disappears from your desktop. The cursor is positioned on the word "Come."
10. Press **Down Arrow** to see the cursor positioned on the word "celebrate." Press **Down Arrow** again to position the cursor on "special."
11. Press **Gray –** to move the cursor to the frame border. Then press **Enter** to close the frame to the desktop tray.
12. {Press **Ctrl-D**}. Press **Ins** to move the cursor to the Main Menu line. Next, press **Left Arrow** until the Disk Menu frame is open on your desktop.
13. {Press **Ctrl-P**}. Press **Down Arrow** to move to the Put Away option and press **Enter**. This option saves the changed frame on the data disk. The old one is replaced by this version.
14. {Press **Ctrl-D**}. Press **Ins** to move the cursor to the Main Menu line. The Disk Menu frame is again open on your desktop.
15. {Press **Ctrl-Q**}. Using the arrow keys again, position the cursor on the QUIT Framework option and press **Enter**. Type **Y** when asked if you are sure you want to quit Framework III. This ends this Framework III session.
16. Turn to Module 72 to continue the learning sequence.

Module 80

SPELLING CHECK

DESCRIPTION

Proofreading every document you write is a time-consuming task. Framework III can help you speed the process. Framework III can use any of the dictionaries you specify before beginning the spelling check operation.

If a word is found which is unfamiliar, Framework III asks if you want suggestions to replace the word, edit the word, add the word to your dictionary, or continue searching the document.

This option is really a submenu within the Apps Menu frame. First, open the Apps Menu frame, position the cursor on the Spelling Check option, and press Enter. Another menu (submenu) opens on your desktop which resembles the following display.

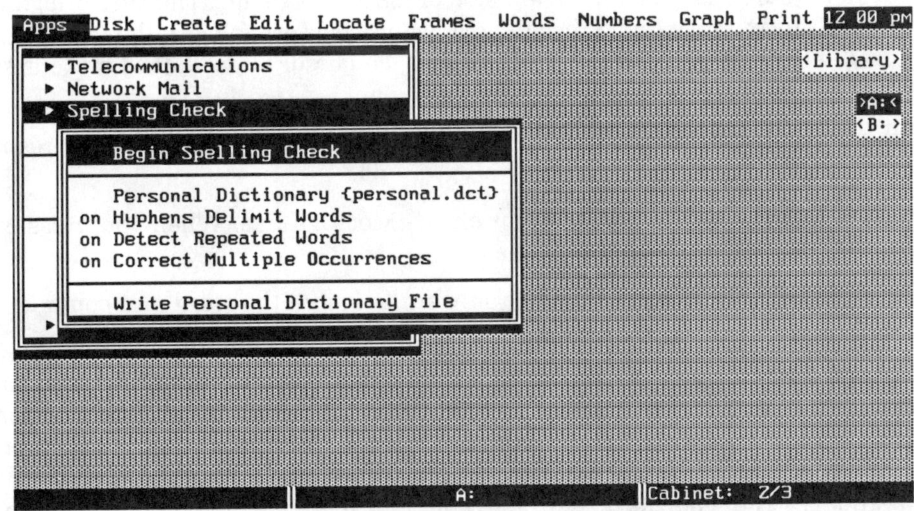

Check the spelling of words within the selection

The Spelling Check option provides several submenu options. Each is described in the order of its position within the submenu frame.

Begin Spelling Check Selecting this option causes Framework III to begin checking the open frame for problems. If you accidentally select this option, press Esc to exit the operation. Otherwise, Framework III displays each unfamiliar word on the Message line for your review. Also, on the

Message line are options from which you tell Framework III what you want to do. Review the following desktop display.

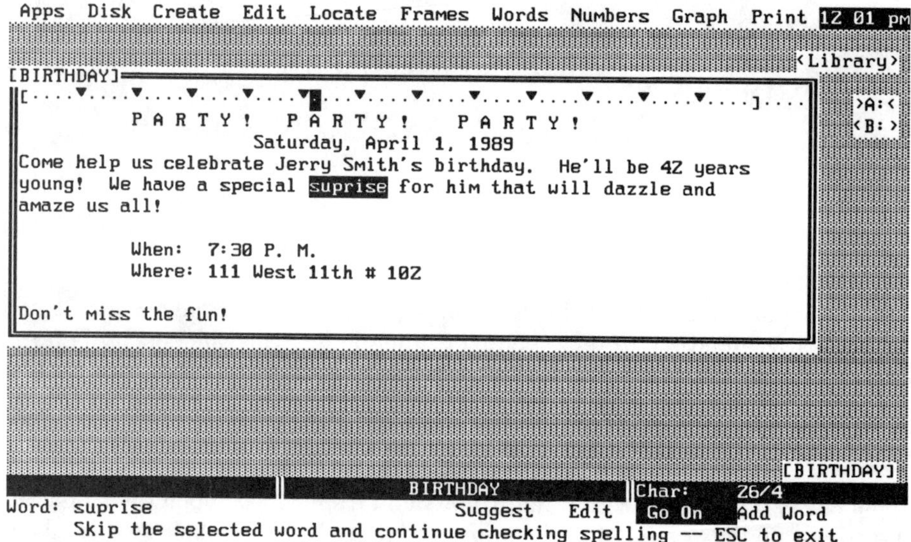

The unfamiliar word is presented on the left side of the Message line. The cursor highlights one of the options on the Message line. Press the arrow (cursor) keys to move the cursor across the Suggest, Edit, Go On, and Add Word options. When the cursor is positioned on your selection, press Enter to tell Framework III which option you want.

Selecting the Suggest option, tells Framework III that you want suggestions for respelling or replacing the unfamiliar word.

The Edit option lets you type a replacement on the Message line. When you press Enter, the replacement is substituted within the document.

The Go On option tells Framework III that you want to ignore the word and continue with the spelling check.

Finally, the Add Word option lets you add the unfamiliar word to your personal dictionary called personal.dct. By doing so, the next time the word is encountered, it is not considered an unfamiliar word.

Personal Dictionary {personal.dct} Use this option to specify which dictionary file you want to use against the open document. Framework III provides the personal.dct, business.dct, and computer.dct dictionary files. It defaults to the personal.dct unless you specify otherwise. If you have written your own dictionaries with the Write Personal Dictionary File option, select this option, type the name of the dictionary file you want to use, and press Enter.

Hyphens Delimit Words This option is turned on or off when you press Enter. If it is on, the spelling checker looks at words like "mother-in-law" as three words instead of just one. When off, this option causes the spelling checker to consider hyphenated words like "mother-in-law" as one word.

Detect Repeated Words This option is turned on or off by pressing Enter. When on, the spelling checker identifies words it has encountered in an earlier part of the document. This helps you keep redundancy out of your document.

Correct Multiple Occurrences This is another on and off option. When it is turned on and a correction is made, the spelling checker looks for the next occurrence of the error.

If one is found, the spelling checker presents the old word and the correction on the left side of the Message line. A *set* of options is presented to you as in the following display.

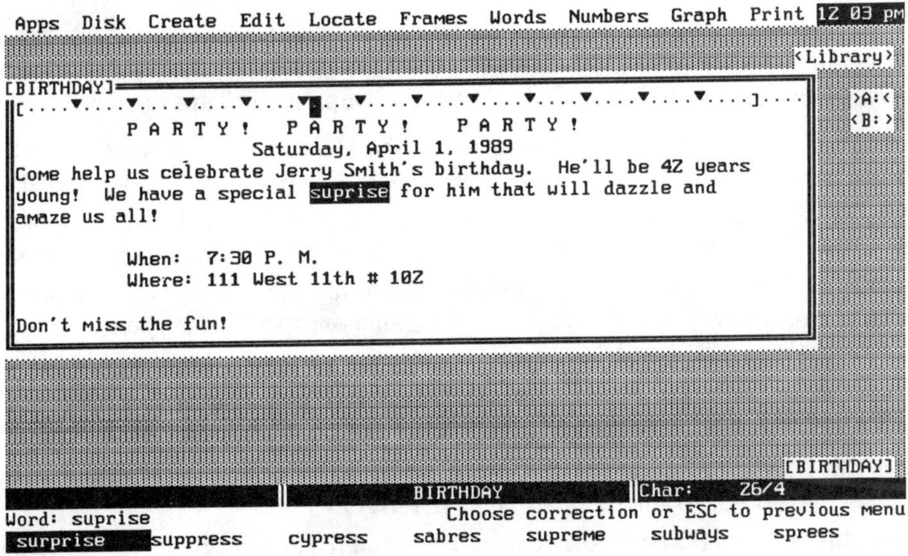

Select the Replace option if you want to replace only this occurrence of the error. Each time the error is encountered, it is presented again.

Auto Replace tells Framework III that you want to replace all other occurrences of the error. Each one is not presented for your review.

Select Edit if you want to change the word to something else. Framework III lets you type whatever you want on the Message line. Press Enter and the new text is substituted within the open frame.

The Go On option tells Framework III that you want to ignore this occurrence of the word and continue with the spelling check.

Write Personal Dictionary File Framework III provides three dictionary files — personal.dct, business.dct, computer.dct. If these don't suit your needs, open a word processing frame, write your own dictionary of words, and then save them on disk. When you're ready to do the Spelling Check option on your open document, specify which dictionary you want to use and then select the Begin Spelling Check option.

When the open frame is checked for spelling or you press Esc, Framework III reports the number of errors found. As soon as you press a key, the error count disappears from the Message line.

APPLICATIONS

Use the Spelling Check option on any type of frame. It reviews each word within the open frame. Although it seems to run a little slow, it's still quicker and more thorough than "eyeballing" it.

First, open the frame you want to check. Select the dictionary and other options you want the spelling checker to use. As the document is checked and errors are found, you are given the chance to add the unfamiliar word to the dictionary or correct it.

TYPICAL OPERATION

In this illustration, an invitation to a birthday party is to be checked for errors. The cursor is positioned on the data drive identifier (drive B if you have two floppy drives). Clear your desktop of any open frames. The shortcut key combinations, if applicable, are enclosed by braces.

1. {Press **Ctrl-D**}. Press **Ins** to move the cursor to the Main Menu line. Next, press **Left Arrow** or **Right Arrow**, if necessary, until the Disk Menu frame is open on your desktop.
2. {Press **Ctrl-G**}. Press **Up Arrow** to move the cursor to the Get File by Name option and then press **Enter**. The cursor moves to the Message line at the bottom of your desktop.
3. Type **B:BIRTHDAY**. As you type, the braces next to the Get File by Name option fill. When finished, press **Enter**. The disk is read and the frame you specified is opened on your desktop.
4. Press **Gray +** to move the cursor inside the frame. Using the arrows, position the cursor on the first "r" of "surprise." Press **Del** so that the word is now "suprise."
5. Press **Gray –** to move the cursor to the frame border.
6. {Press **Ctrl-A**}. Press **Ins** to move the cursor to the Main Menu line. Next, press **Left Arrow** until the Apps Menu frame is open on your desktop.
7. {Press **Ctrl-S**}. Press **Down Arrow**, if necessary, until the cursor highlights the Spelling Check option; then press **Enter**. Your desktop resembles the following display.

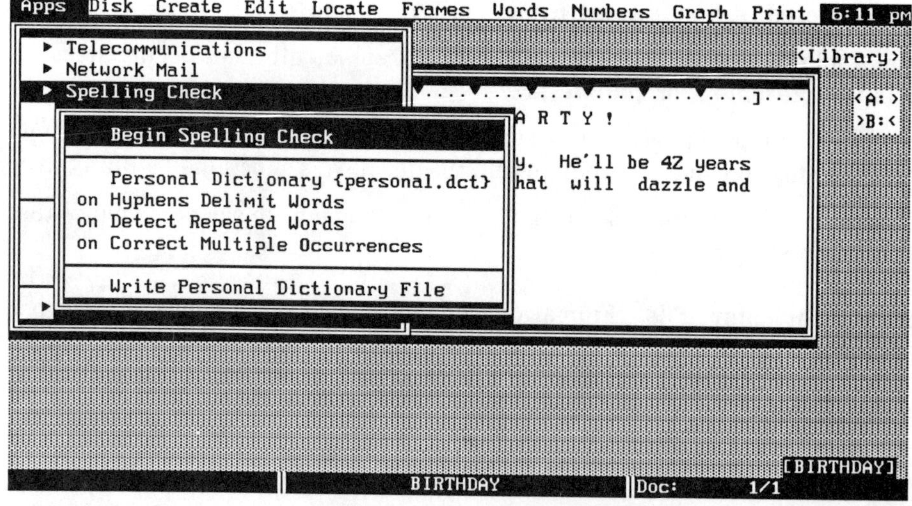

Check the spelling of words within the selection

8. {Press **Ctrl-B**}. With the cursor positioned on the Begin Spelling Check option, press **Enter**. The menus disappear from your desktop. If necessary, insert the Spelling Check Disk in drive A and press **Esc** to continue.
9. The letter "P" is highlighted within the document. The Message line displays the word and several options for your consideration.

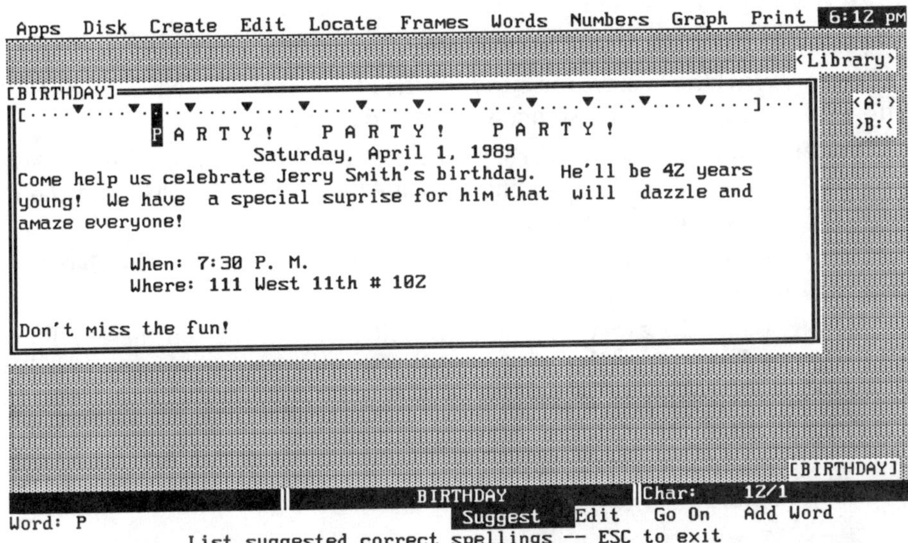

10. {Press **Ctrl-G**}. Press **Right Arrow** or **Left Arrow** until the cursor is positioned on the Go On option and press **Enter**. Continue to bypass the letters in "PARTY" and the word "Jerry."
11. The word "suprise" is highlighted within the document. The Message line displays the word and several options for your consideration.

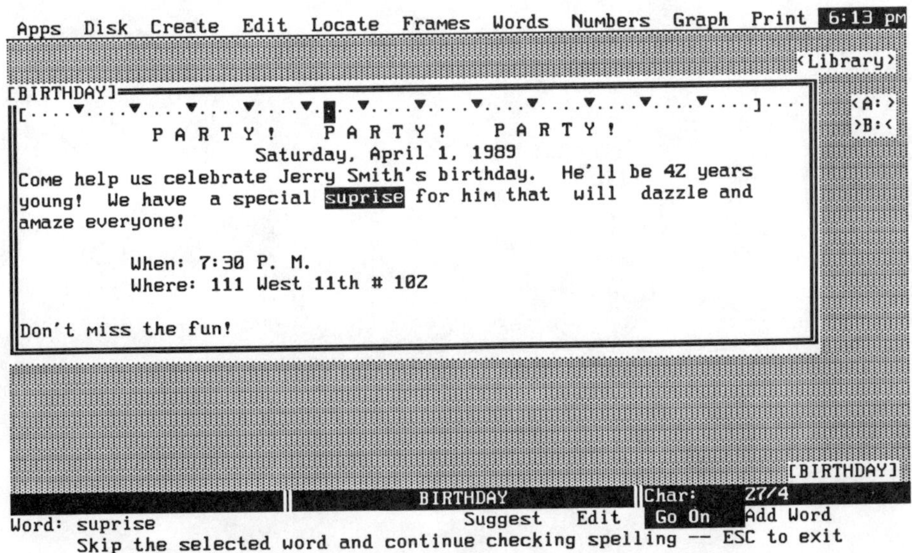

12. {Press **Ctrl-S**}. Using the arrow (cursor) keys, position the cursor on the Suggest option in the Message line and press **Enter**. It is replaced by several words from which you choose one or press **Esc**. Press **Left Arrow**, if necessary, until "surprise" is highlighted and then press **Enter**. Notice that "suprise" is replaced by "surprise."
13. Press **Esc** to discontinue the Spelling Check operation. If necessary, reinsert System Disk 2 in drive A and press **Esc** to continue.
14. Press **Gray –** to move the cursor to the frame border.
15. {Press **Ctrl-D**}. Press **Ins** to move the cursor to the Main Menu line. Next, press **Right Arrow** until the Disk Menu frame is also open on your desktop.
16. {Press **Ctrl-P**}. Using the arrow (cursor) keys, position the cursor on the Put Away option and then press **Enter**. The Message line displays the word "SAVING" and the disk drive lights. When finished, the frame name is not on your desktop.
17. {Press **Ctrl-D**}. Press **Ins** to move the cursor to the Main Menu line. The Disk Menu frame is again open on your desktop.
18. {Press **Ctrl-Q**}. Using the arrow keys again, position the cursor on the QUIT Framework option and press **Enter**. Type **Y** when asked if you are sure you want to quit Framework III. This ends this Framework III session.
19. Turn to Module 85 to continue the learning sequence.

Module 81

SPREADSHEET

DESCRIPTION

A spreadsheet is a thinking tool. It is part calculator, pencil, paper, and eraser. It is much more powerful, however, since you can cause many calculations to occur every time you change a number involved in the formula.

This option is available through the Create Menu frame as displayed on the following desktop.

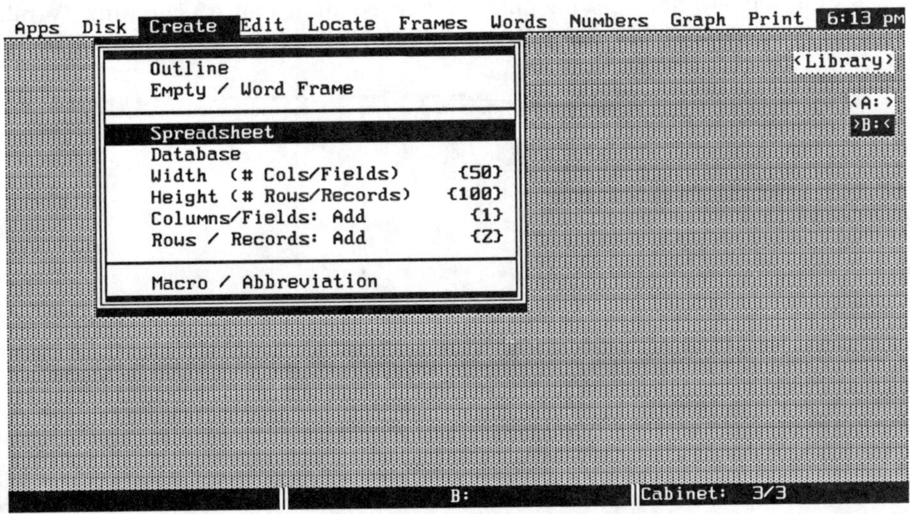

Create a spreadsheet of specified Width and Height

Imagine a blackboard which has horizontal and vertical lines that identify the columns and rows. The first column next to the left margin is where names or descriptions are usually typed. Each row has a different description.

The top row (going across the blackboard) often has names or descriptions which identify people, time, etc. Each area or slot that is created by the lines is called a cell.

For example, you may have three flavors of ice cream listed down the first column, and the name of two people listed across the top row as in the following example.

	A	B	C	D
1		Jeff	Terry	
2	Chocolate	5	2	
3	Vanilla	1	3	
4	Strawberry	0	1	
5	Total	6	6	

Notice that each piece of information is within a cell. Each cell is identified by the letter which appears across the top row and the row number. For example, cell A3 contains "Vanilla" while cell B5 contains 6. The spreadsheet for this example resembles the following display.

```
[Flavors]
      A            B        C       D       E       F       G
1              Jeff     Terry
2  Chocolate          5       2
3  Vanilla            1       3
4  Strawberry         0       1
5  Total              6       6
6
7
8
9
10
```

Remember, however, that the Total line in this illustration can be summed automatically when one of the numbers in the columns change. To accomplish this automation, you must associate a formula with the cell to be calculated. For example, the Total line is the sum of the three numbers in the cells above it. Position the cursor on cell B5 and type +B2+B3+B4. This tells Framework III that you want cells B2, B3, and B4 added together and the sum displayed in cell B5.

The first "+" in the formula is needed to tell Framework III that you are typing a formula. By typing B2+B3+B4, you are telling Framework III that this is a *label* not a *formula*.

Another way to type this same formula is by using a FRED (Framework III's programming language) function. Instead of typing +B2+B3+B4, you must type @sum(B2:B4). This tells Framework III that you want to sum cells B2 through B4 and display that number in the cell where the cursor currently resides.

A calculation within a spreadsheet can be simple addition and subtraction, or a fairly complicated formula. This saves you time, effort, and grief when you have a series of operations which must occur as numbers are introduced or changed.

For example, you can set up a spreadsheet frame to help you verify your bank statement. Since you always perform the same addition and subtraction, you must only provide the changing numbers.

An example of a procedure which helps reconcile your checkbook follows.

Bank Balance	100.00
Outstand Deposits	800.00
Subtotal	900.00
Outstand Checks	75.00
Balance	825.00
Checkbook Balance	822.00
Difference	3.00

Although you could perform this example almost as easily with a calculator, you must first get totals for outstanding checks as well as outstanding deposits. The solution is to make the spreadsheet flexible enough so that you enter each outstanding check and deposit. As each is typed, the spreadsheet adjusts the Subtotal, Balance, and Difference cells.

If the Difference cell is not zero when you finish, you immediately know how much your checkbook is off balance. You do not have to redo the addition and subtraction as you would if you used a calculator. The spreadsheet model can do recalculations automatically or manually (you tell Framework III when to recalculate the cells).

Notice the Width and Height options which are also available in the Create Menu frame. The Width option specifies the number of columns made available across the spreadsheet when it is created. The {50} indicates the number of columns which Framework III defaults on all new spreadsheets.

The Height option specifies the number of lines or rows down the spreadsheet. Framework III allocates 100 as the default number of rows.

Customize your spreadsheet by selecting each of these options and changing the numbers prior to creating it. There is no harm in creating the default size spreadsheet and then adding or deleting columns and rows.

As always, Framework III uses the first eight positions of the name you assign the spreadsheet frame to create the name of the file which is to be saved on the disk. The first eight positions, or whatever you type if it is less than eight, are provided a suffix of .FW3 to develop a filename.

For example, if you type Check 89 within the brackets on the frame border, Framework III saves the spreadsheet as Check_89.FW3. The underline replaces any blank spaces which exist within the name.

Once saved on the disk, you can read it from the disk to your desktop by using the Disk Menu frame. All information and formulas which were saved on disk are available as though they had never left your desktop.

APPLICATIONS

Most people buy a computer to save them time and provide accurate information. The spreadsheet can save a lot of time and work once it's taught what to do.

When using spreadsheets, a series of mathematics can be performed in seconds. Of course, the spreadsheet must be set up originally. However, once done, you only have to type the numbers and let Framework III do the rest.

Spreadsheets are used to balance checkbooks to a bank statement, forecast sales for the year, or layout and maintain budgets (company or personal). Once you begin working with spreadsheets, you find many different uses for this type of frame.

Often it replaces the normal tools you use, like a calculator, paper, pencil, and an eraser. Your spreadsheet allows you to think without having to rework the problem.

TYPICAL OPERATION

This illustration creates a Framework III spreadsheet to reconcile a bank statement. Simple formulas of addition and subtraction are set for automatic recalculation. As the numbers involved in the body of the spreadsheet change, you can see the calculated cells change as a result.

Clear your desktop of all open files and position the cursor on the data drive. Position the cursor on the appropriate drive letter. The shortcut key combinations, if applicable, are enclosed by braces.

1. {Press **Ctrl-C**}. Press **Ins** to move the cursor to the Main Menu line. Next, press the arrow (cursor) keys, if necessary, until the Create Menu frame is open on your desktop.
2. The Width and Height options specify a larger spreadsheet than needed. {Press **Ctrl-W**}. Press **Down Arrow** until the cursor is positioned on the Width option and press **Enter**. The cursor then moves to the Message line at the bottom of your desktop. Type **30** and press **Enter**. Notice that the number within the braces is now 30.

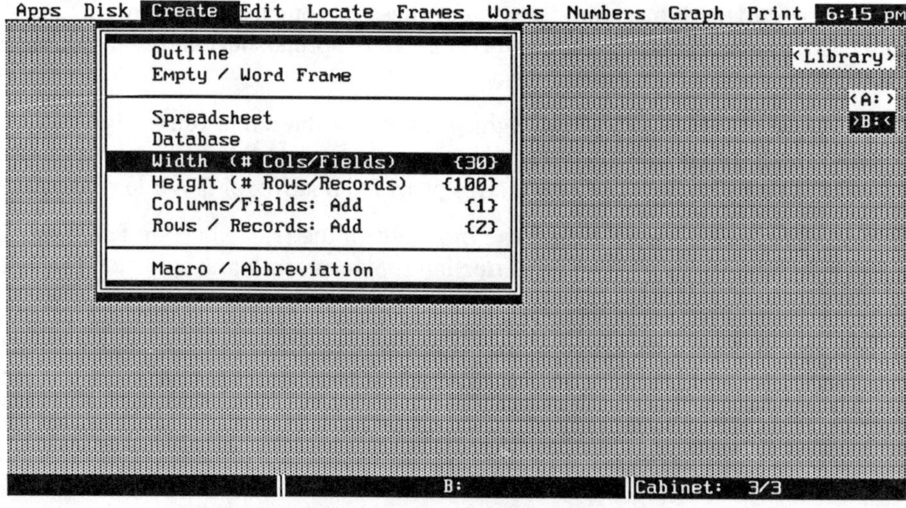

Create: Width (# Cols/Fields) {30}

3. {Press **Ctrl-H**}. Press **Down Arrow** until the cursor is positioned on the Height option and press **Enter**. The cursor then moves to the Message line at the bottom of your desktop. Type **8** and press **Enter**. Notice that the number within the braces is now 8.
4. {Press **Ctrl-S**}. Press **Up Arrow** to position the cursor on the Spreadsheet option and press **Enter**. An empty spreadsheet frame opens on your desktop. Only eight rows appear within your open frame. All 30 of your columns are available; however, the size of the frame hides them. When you move the cursor toward the right edge of the frame, the other columns appear as needed.

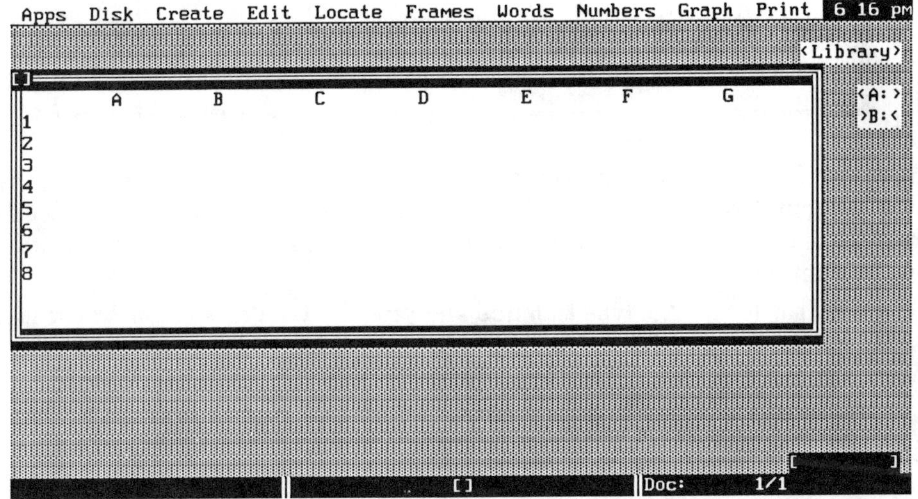

5. The cursor is positioned at the top border of the frame within the brackets. Type **CHECKBK** within the brackets and press **Enter**. The name of the file, when saved on the disk, is CHECKBK.FW3.
6. Press **Gray +** to move the cursor to the inside of your open spreadsheet frame. The cursor appears in column A of row 1 (cell A1). Press **F4** (Size) and then press **Right Arrow** ten times to increase the size of each cell in column A. Press **Enter** when finished.
7. Type **Bank Balance** and press **Enter**. Press **Right Arrow** to move the cursor to the second column of the same row (cell B1). Type **100.10** and press **Enter**.
8. Press **Down Arrow** and **Left Arrow** to move the cursor to column A of row 2. Type **Outstand Deposits** and press **Enter**. Move the cursor to cell B2. Type **@SUM(C2:N2)** and press **Enter**. This formula tells Framework III to add the numbers, if any, which appear in columns C through N of row 2.
9. Move the cursor to column C in row 2. Type **400** and press **Enter**. Press **Right Arrow** to cell D2, type **400**, and press **Enter**. Notice that the total automatically appears in cell B2.

10. Move the cursor to cell A3, type **Subtotal** and press **Enter**. Press **Right Arrow** to move the cursor to column B and type @**SUM(B1:B2)** and press **Enter**. This tells Framework III that cells B1 and B2 are added and the total is placed in cell B3.

```
[CHECKBK]
            A                  B          C          D          E          F
1   Bank Balance            100.10
2   Outstand Deposits          800        400        400
3   Subtotal                900.10
4
5
6
7
8
```

11. Using the arrow keys, move the cursor to cell A4, type **Outstand Checks** and press **Enter**. Move to column B, type @**sum(C4:N4)**, and press **Enter**. Press **Right Arrow** to cell C4, type **75**, and press **Enter**. The same number appears in cell B4 since it is an automatic addition of cells C4 through N4.
12. Move the cursor to cell A5, type **Balance** and press **Enter**. Press **Right Arrow** to move the cursor to column B, type **+B3–B4**, and press **Enter**. Your spreadsheet resembles the following display.

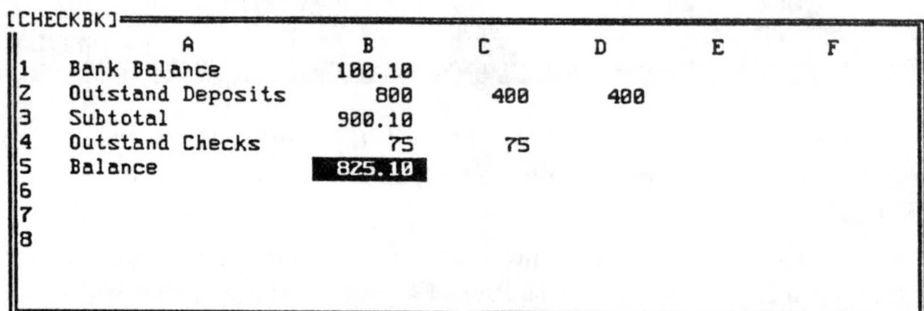

```
[CHECKBK]
            A                  B          C          D          E          F
1   Bank Balance            100.10
2   Outstand Deposits          800        400        400
3   Subtotal                900.10
4   Outstand Checks             75         75
5   Balance                 825.10
6
7
8
```

13. Press **Left Arrow** once and **Down Arrow** twice to move the cursor to cell A7, type **Checkbook Balance**, and press **Enter**. Move the cursor to B7, type **822.00** and press **Enter**.
14. Move the cursor to cell A8, type **Difference** and press **Enter**. Finally, move the cursor to cell B8, type **+B5–B7** and press **Enter**. Notice that the checkbook balance does not reconcile with the bank balance since the difference is not zero. There is a $3.10 error in your checkbook.
15. {Press **Ctrl-D**}. After all this work, you want to save the spreadsheet so that it is available next month. Press **Ins** to move the cursor to the Main Menu line. Press the arrow (cursor) keys until the Disk Menu frame is open on your desktop.

16. {Press **Ctrl-P**}. Using the **Down Arrow** or **Up Arrow** key, position the cursor on the Put Away option and press **Enter**. This saves the spreadsheet on the disk and removes it from your desktop.
17. {Press **Ctrl-D**}. Press **Ins** again to move the cursor the Main Menu line. The Disk Menu frame is open on your desktop.
18. {Press **Ctrl-Q**}. Position the cursor on the QUIT Framework option and press **Enter**. When asked if you really want to quit Framework III, type **Y**. This Framework III session is complete.
19. Turn to Module 43 to continue the learning sequence.

Module 82

TAB STOPS AT { }

DESCRIPTION

When you type a word processing document, there are times you need to arrange information into columns. The Tab key and this option are used to make your job easier by letting you set tab stops. Each time you press Tab, the cursor moves to the next tab stop.

The Tab Stops at option is available in the Words Menu frame.

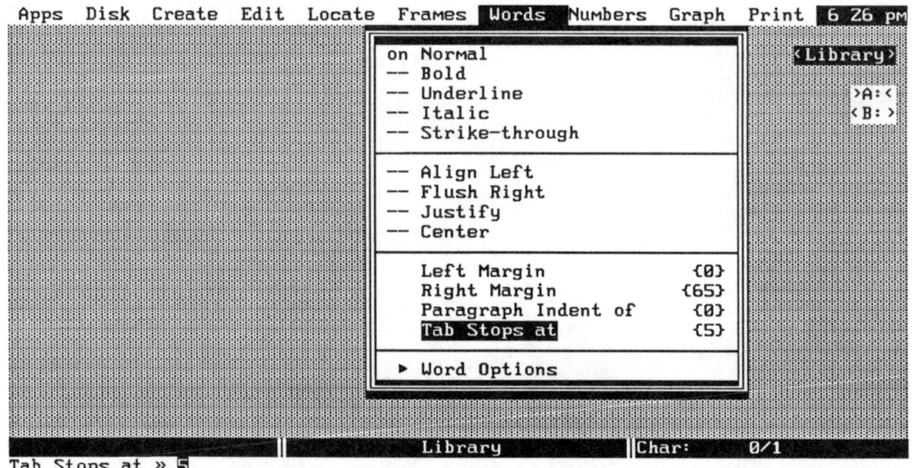

Notice that the Tab Stops at option is currently set to 5. This means that each tab stop is five spaces apart — 6, 11, 16, 21, 26, 31, etc.

If you type past a tab stop, the next press of Tab moves the cursor to the next available tab stop. Change the value of this option anytime during a word processing activity.

For example, the following list has been typed with the Tab Stops at option set to 5.

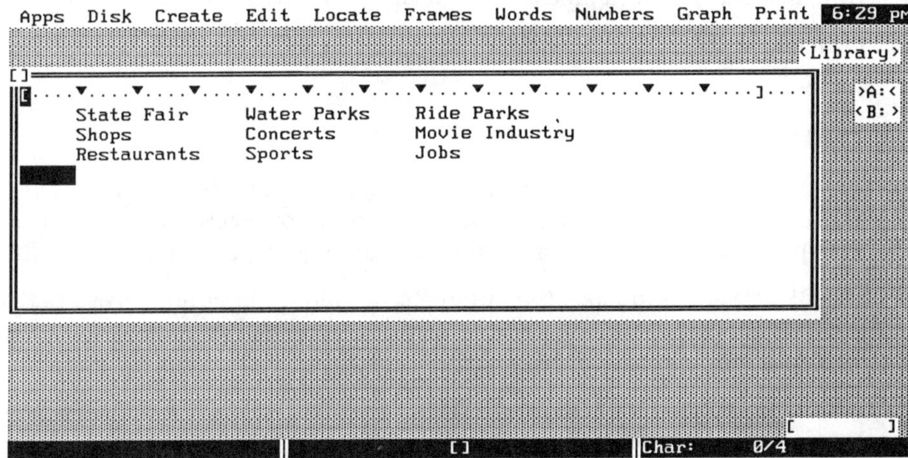

By changing the option to 10 before typing the list, each column is farther apart. The list looks like the following display.

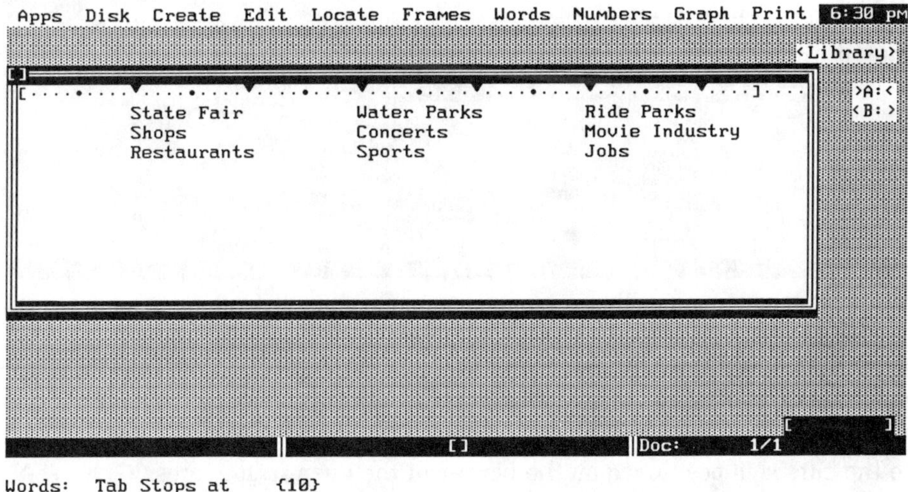

If the document already exists, position the cursor on the word you want to move to the right. Then open the Words Menu frame to select and set the Tab Size option. The line where you positioned the cursor is moved to the new tab stop.

Once this option is changed, every press of the Tab key moves the cursor to the next available tab stop. Each line of all columns must be tabbed until everything is arranged in proper columns.

APPLICATIONS

This option is available only for word processing frames — not spreadsheets, databases, or graphs.

Use it to tell Framework III how many spaces you want for each tab stop. Change the option's number when you want.

TYPICAL OPERATION

This illustration shows you how to change the Tab Stops at option for typing a columnar list. Close any open frames on your desktop and position the cursor on your data drive indicator (drive B in this example). The shortcut key combinations, if applicable, are enclosed by braces.

1. {Press **Ctrl-C**}. Press **Ins** to move the cursor to the Main Menu line. Press **Left Arrow** or **Right Arrow**, if necessary, until the Create Menu frame is open on your desktop. Your screen should resemble the following display.

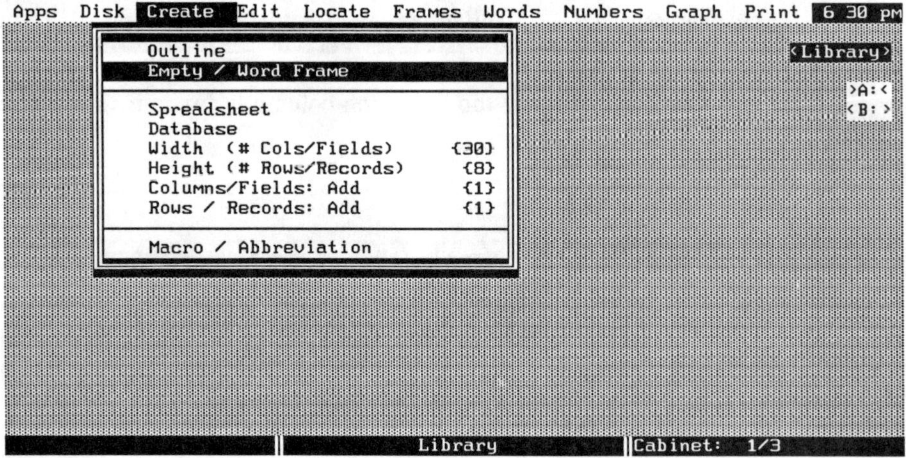

2. {Press **Ctrl-E**}. Press **Down Arrow**, if necessary, to move the cursor to the Empty/Word Frame option of the Create Menu frame. Press **Enter** to select the option. An empty frame appears on your screen.
3. Since the cursor is positioned on the border of the open frame, press **Gray +**. Now you're inside the open frame.

4. Press **Tab** once. Type **State Fair** and press **Tab** again. Type **Water Parks** and press **Tab**. Then type **Ride Parks** and press **Enter**. Your desktop should resemble the following display.

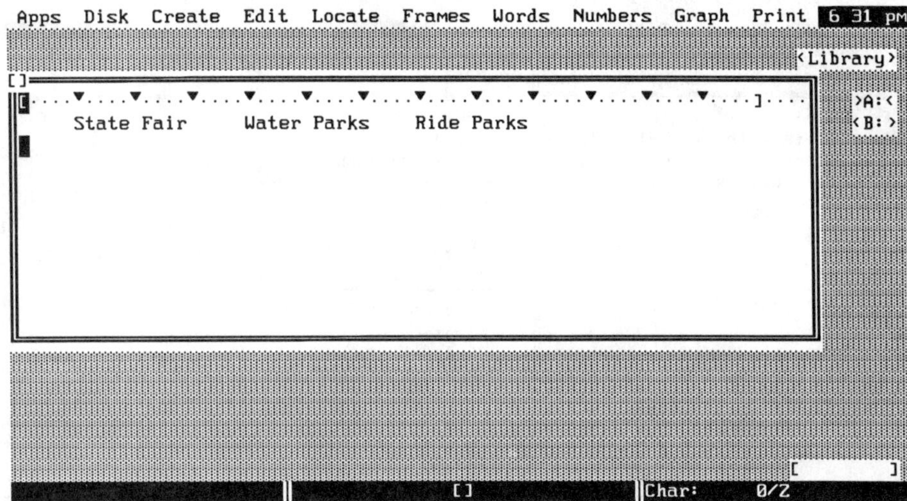

5. Press **Tab** once. Type **Shops** and press **Tab** twice. Type **Concerts** and press **Tab** twice. Type **Movie Industry** and press **Enter**.
6. Press **Tab** once. Type **Restaurants** and press **Tab** again. Type **Sports** and press **Tab** twice. Type **Jobs** and press **Enter**. Your desktop should now resemble the following display.

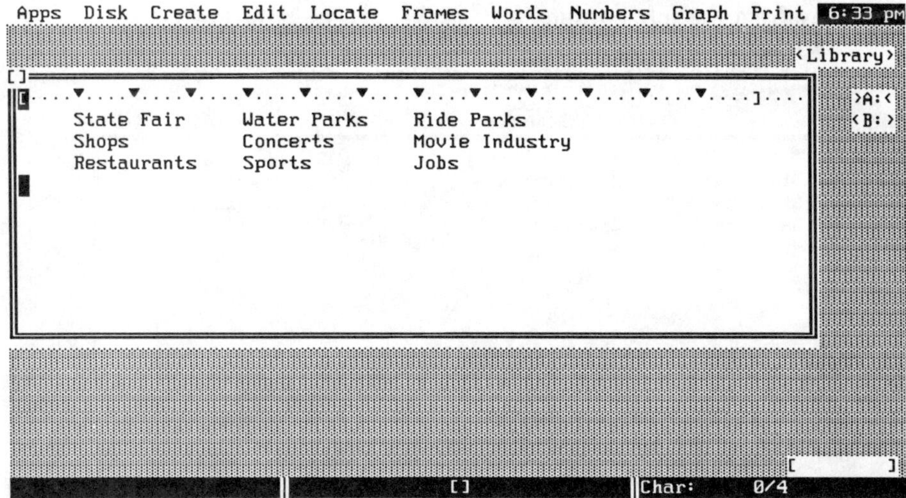

7. Press **Up Arrow** and **Right Arrow** until the cursor is positioned on the "S" of the word "Shops."

8. {Press **Ctrl-W**}. Press **Ins** to move the cursor to the Main Menu line. Next, press **Right Arrow** until the Words Menu frame is also open on your desktop. Notice that the Tab Stop is set to 5 as in the following display.

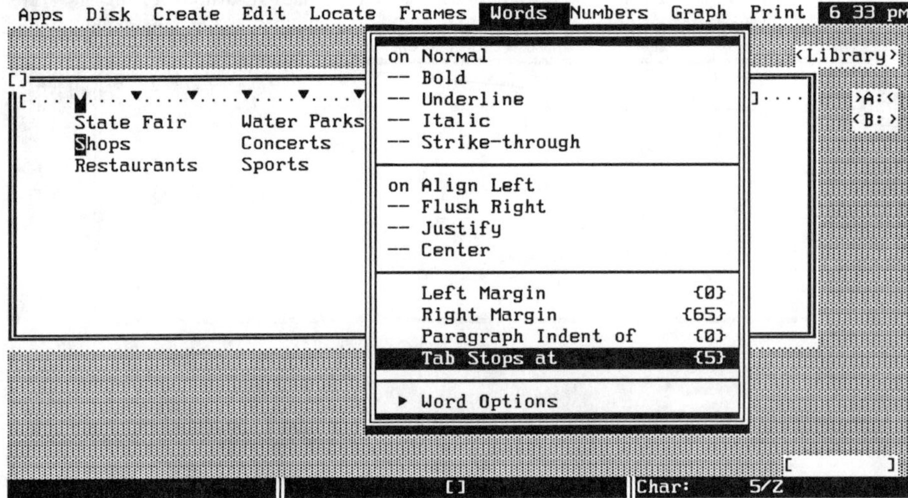

9. {Press **Ctrl-T**}. Press **Down Arrow** until the cursor is positioned on the Tab Stops at option and then press **Enter**. The cursor moves to the Message line at the bottom of your screen. Type **8** and press **Enter**. The Words Menu frame disappears. The cursor line has moved farther away from the left border.

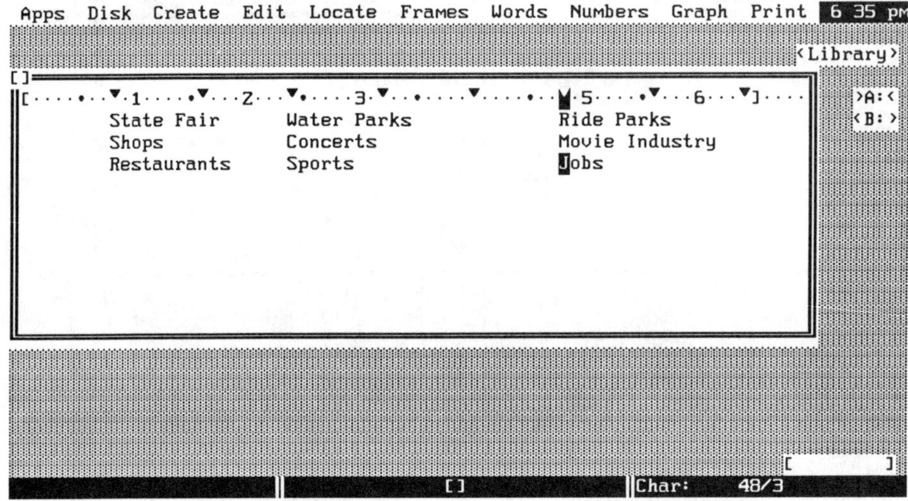

10. Use the Right Arrow (cursor) key to move "Concerts" and press **Tab**. When finished, compare your desktop to the following screen display. Notice that each column is farther apart.

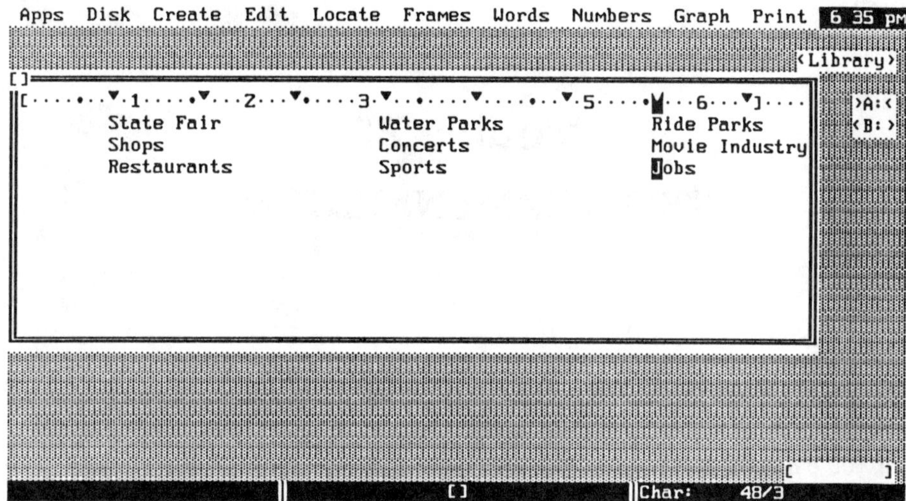

11. Press **Gray** – to move the cursor to the frame border.
12. If you want to save this frame on disk, refer to the Put Away option of the Disk Menu frame. Otherwise, delete this frame from your desktop. Since the cursor is positioned on the border of the frame, press **Del** to delete the open frame from your desktop.
13. {Press **Ctrl-D**}. Press **Ins** to move the cursor to the Main Menu line. Using the arrow (cursor) keys, move the cursor to the Disk option. The following menu frame appears on your desktop.

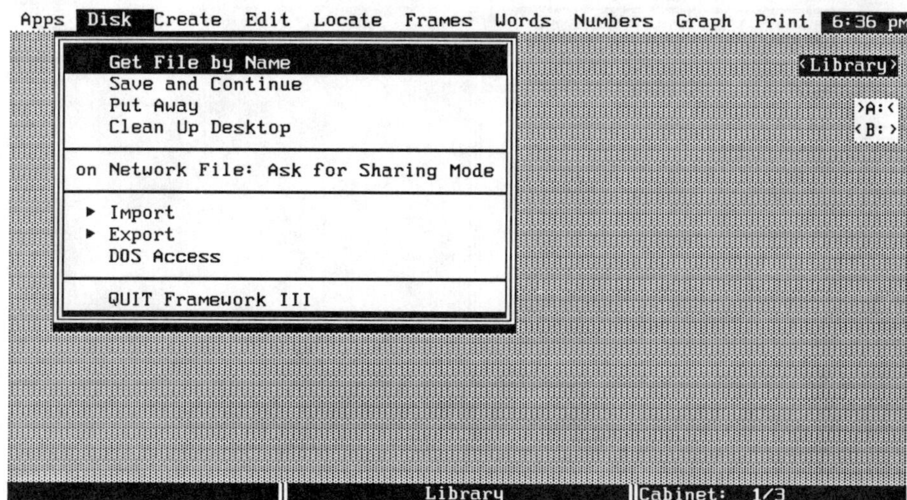

Bring specified file from disk and place beneath selected frame

14. {Press **Ctrl-Q**}. Position the cursor on the QUIT Framework option and press **Enter**. Type **Y** when asked if you are sure you want to quit Framework III. This ends this Framework III session.
15. Turn to Module 78 to continue the learning sequence.

Module 83

TELECOMMUNICATIONS

DESCRIPTION

There are many computers (and their users) that you can talk to through your computer and Framework III. All you need is a telephone line and a phone modem.

For example, you can talk to a fellow computer owner via computer. Although slower than voice communication, it's a good way to begin your telecommunications experience.

Once you learn, call some of the bulletin boards (they're all over the nation), or a service like Dow Jones or The Source. Although some require a membership fee and/or charge for computer time, they are good sources of news, public domain software, and stock quotes.

Use the Telecommunications option of the Apps Menu frame. When this option is selected, a submenu of options is also opened on your desktop as in the following display.

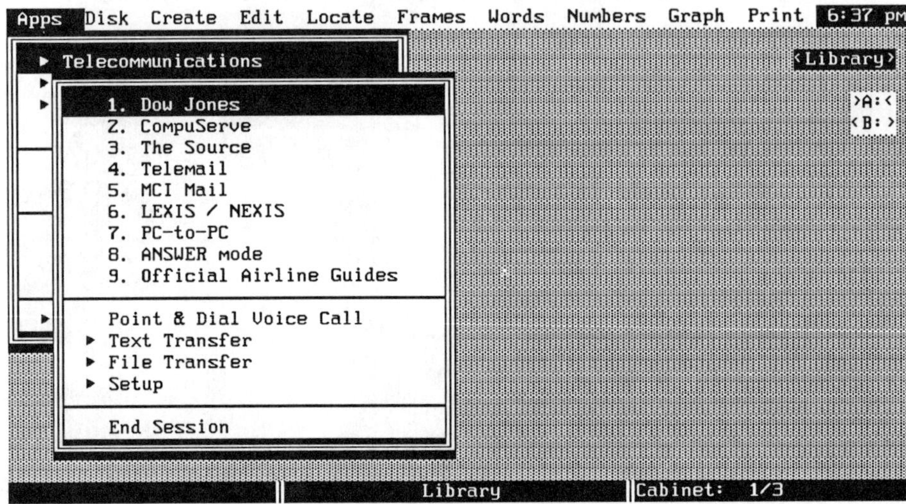

Dial first service for quick access (install your own service in Setup program)

The options with pointers on the left side of the option indicate submenu frames which you open by selecting the option. There are several submenus available for your review. Select each submenu option until you open the last one. Press Esc to close all open menu frames.

For example, selecting the Text Transfer submenu option adds another submenu to your desktop of open menu frames. Just select the options you want to change or press Esc to close the menu frames unchanged.

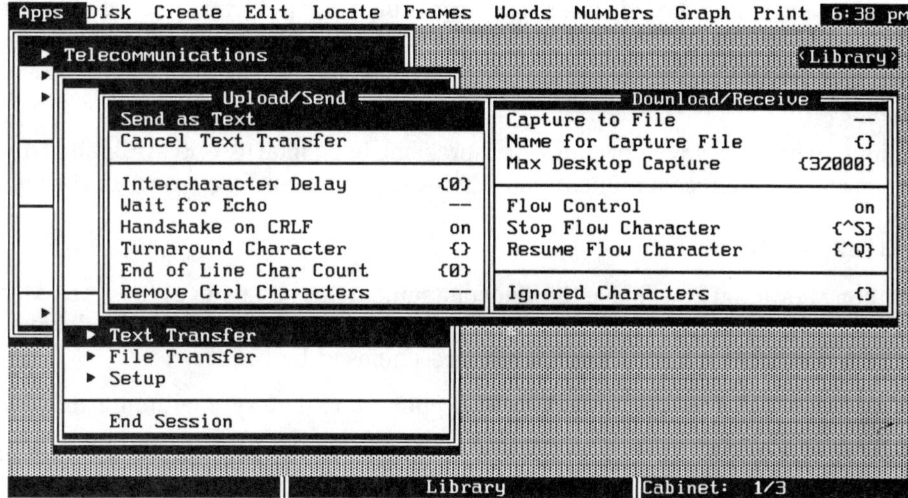

Send the entire current selection, as text, to the remote system

To begin a telecommunications session, select one of the eight preset options. Framework III opens a Telecommunications (Telecomm) frame and positions the cursor inside that frame. As long as it is considered active, the frame cannot be deleted from your desktop. You must select the End Session option of the Apps Menu frame to discontinue the active session.

Use the telecommunications options to transfer word processing, spreadsheet, or database files to or from other computers over the phone lines or directly connected by an RS-232 cable. Send or receive the information as characters, as blocks of characters, or as a file of characters.

When transferring text character by character, or as a block of information, work on other Framework III frames as the transfer continues. If you transfer a file, you must remain in the Telecomm frame until the transfer is complete. You must transfer information as a file when it contains nontextual characters such as borders, underlines, and margin settings.

APPLICATIONS

Use the Telecommunications submenu when you want to connect your computer to another for transferring information. Sending and receiving information via computer provides several advantages.

For example, sending a letter or report to another computer gets the information to your destination within just a few minutes. It can then be printed, if desired, and circulated per your instructions.

Transferring a file of information from one computer to another keeps errors to a minimum. Also, the data does not have to be typed more than once.

For example, call one of the stock quote services and retrieve the information directly to your disk. Disconnect your computer from the service and review, at your leisure, the information you collected. This cuts down your phone and connection charges.

Reviewing computer bulletin boards is a good way of collecting public domain software (programs contributed for general use). If you have a problem with your computer or its software, report it on an appropriate bulletin board. There is usually someone who is willing to provide a solution or helpful suggestion for your problem.

Linking computers and sharing information is increasing in popularity and availability. By learning to use Framework III's telecommunications abilities, you expand your own horizons.

TYPICAL OPERATION

This illustration shows you how to use the Telecommunications submenu of the Apps Menu frame. Make sure that your desktop is clear and the cursor is positioned on one of the drive indicators. The shortcut key combinations, if applicable, are enclosed by braces.

Connect your computer and phone modem to a phone jack before continuing this exercise.

1. {Press **Ctrl-A** and then **Ctrl-T**}. Press **Ins** to move the cursor to the Main Menu line. Next, press **Left Arrow** until the Apps Menu frame is open on your desktop. Use **Up Arrow** to position the cursor on the Telecommunications option and press **Enter**. The submenu also opens on your desktop.

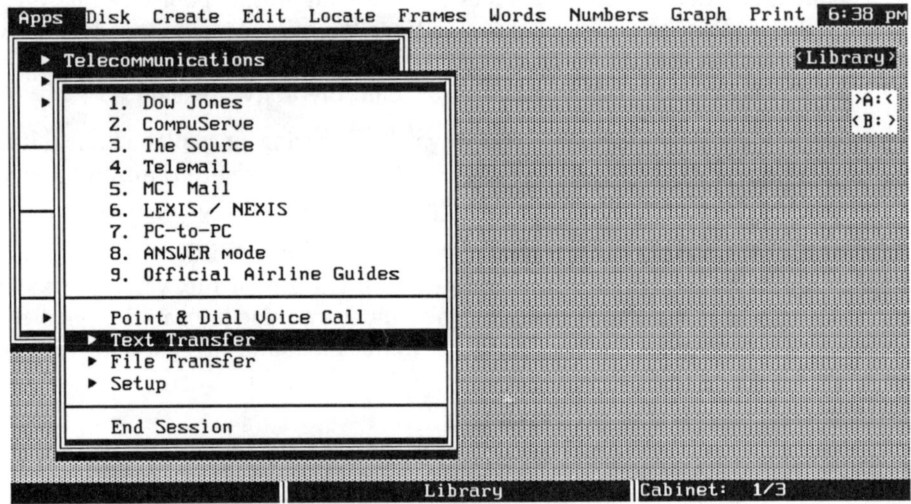

Send (upload) text and receive (download) text

2. {Type **1**}. Position the cursor on the Dow Jones option and press **Enter**. Framework III opens a Telecommunications frame and positions the cursor inside it. Messages appear at the bottom of the screen to tell you what Framework III is doing.
3. If you do not hear the dial tone and the number being dialed, there is a problem with the modem hookup or the setup values. Press **Ctrl-Break** to discontinue the dialing attempts.

4. {Press **Ctrl-A** and **Ctrl-T**}. Reopen the Apps Menu frame and select the Telecommunications submenu option.
5. {Press **Ctrl-E**}. Use the arrow (cursor) keys to position the cursor on the End Session option and press **Enter**. Now the message says that the Telecomm frame is inactive.
6. Press **Gray –** to move the cursor to the frame border. Then press **Del** to remove the frame from your desktop.
7. {Press **Ctrl-A** and then **Ctrl-T**}. Reopen the Apps Menu frame and the Telecommunications submenu.
8. {Press **Ctrl-S**}. Select the Setup submenu option. Framework III opens another submenu on your desktop.

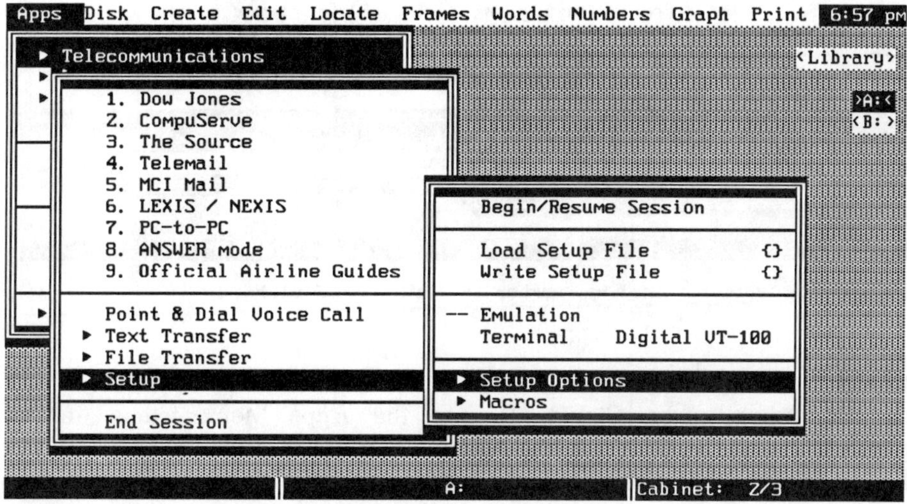

9. {Press **Ctrl-S**}. Select Setup Options from the Setup Menu. Now a fourth frame of options is also opened on your desktop.

10. Use the arrow (cursor) keys to change the options for your computer modem configuration. Select the Number to Dial option and type **4955616** or a phone number you want to dial, and press **Return**. Your screen now resembles the following display.

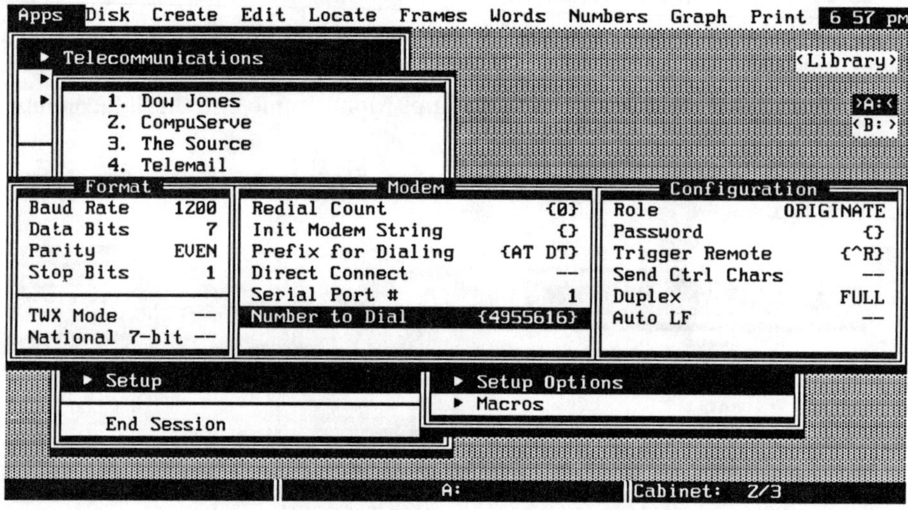

11. Press **Esc** to close all the open menu frames.
12. {Press **Ctrl-A** and then **Ctrl-T**}. Reopen the Apps Menu frame and select the Telecommunications submenu option again.
13. {Press **Ctrl-S**}. Reopen the Setup submenu and position the cursor on the Begin/Resume Session options. When ready, press **Enter**. When the connection is successful, the cursor begins to move and text appears within the open frame. If you still haven't made a good connection, the Setup Options probably need other changes. Review your modem manual for the proper settings.
14. Type **Y**. It then asks for your name, address, and other information. Just type the answers and select the options you want. Then exit the system on which you are logged. There is usually an exit option for you to select. The other computer acknowledges your exit and your Telecomm frame is changed to inactive status.
15. Press **Gray –** to move the cursor to the Telecomm frame border. Then press **Del** to remove the frame from your desktop.
16. {Press **Ctrl-D**}. Press **Ins** to move the cursor to the Main Menu line. Next, press **Right Arrow** until the Disk Menu frame is open on your desktop.

17. {Press **Ctrl-Q**}. Using the arrow keys, position the cursor on the QUIT Framework option. Press **Enter**. When asked if you really want to quit Framework III, type **Y**. Your session is now complete.
18. Turn to Module 8 to continue the learning sequence.

Module 84

TEMPLATE { }

DESCRIPTION

A template is like a model or pattern. Create a template when you need to assign certain values, formulas, or print format options to a frame.

For example, create a template of your check reconciliation spreadsheet. Enter the information that doesn't change as well as any formulas needed. Save the template on disk as you do for any frame you want to keep for later use.

Each month put the template on your desktop with the Get File by Name { } option of the Disk Menu frame. Type a new name on the frame border. Then start entering the values for the current month's statement. When finished, print it or save it on disk for later reference.

The Template { } option is used to assign a set of print values to the open document frame. Create a template to set the frame's format options. For example, if you have several sizes of paper, create a template for each size.

This option is available through the Print Menu frame.

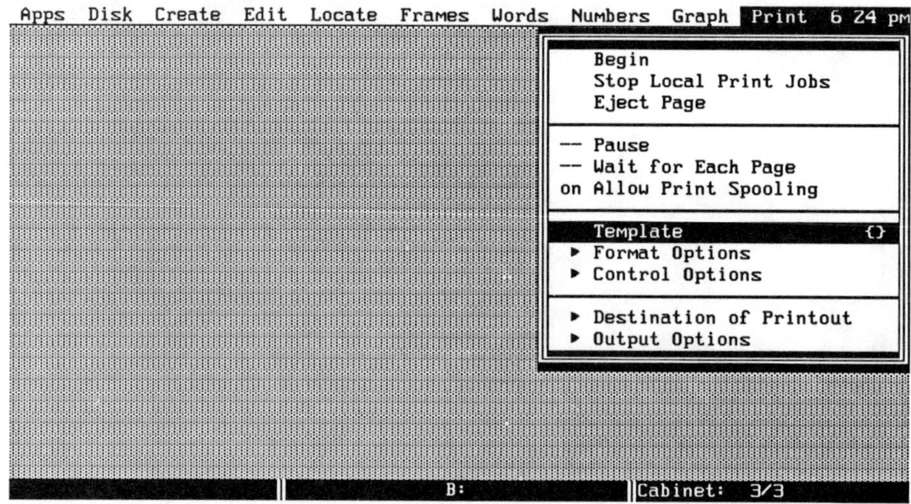

First, create a printing template by just opening a word processing frame on your desktop. Type a name within the brackets on the open frame. Next, open the Print Menu frame and select the Format Options menu. A submenu of formatting options is also opened on your desktop. Change any of the option's values so that most documents fit the paper dimensions.

Press Esc to close the open Print Menu frames. Save the template on disk as you do all frames you want to use later.

When ready to print, make sure the document which you want to print as well as the print format template are both on the desktop. Position the cursor on the document to be printed. Then open the Print Menu frame and select the Template { } option.

The cursor moves to the Edit line. Type the name of the print format template and press Enter. A message at the bottom of the screen tells you that the template has been used on the open document. It now has the same print format options as the template.

Finally, print the document. If necessary, change some of the Format Options until the printout is the way you want it. Then save the document on disk. The print format is also saved. Every time it is printed, it looks the same.

APPLICATIONS

A template just helps you save time. Instead of setting all the format options for each document, you use a template which has already been properly set.

When you create a new document, the print format is preset by Framework III. Either change the print format options yourself or use a template to assign a pre-selected format. Create as many templates as you need and save them on disk or put them in the Print Format area of the Library for later use.

For example, all business letters are printed on 66 lines per page in letter-quality print. Create and save an empty template with those print settings. Then create another frame for your letter.

Another example is a wide spreadsheet. It needs condensed print for 220 characters across the page. Create and save another template for that type of document.

Unless the template is already in the Library, make sure that the document you want to print as well as the template frame are both on the desktop when you're ready to print.

TYPICAL OPERATION

In this illustration, a template is created to print three documents on one page of paper. It is then used to print the birthday party invitation. Make sure that your desktop is clean and the cursor is positioned on the drive B indicator. The shortcut key combinations, if applicable, are enclosed by braces.

1. {Press **Ctrl-C**}. Press **Ins** to move the cursor to the Main Menu line. Next, press **Left Arrow**, if necessary, until the Create Menu frame is open on your desktop.
2. {Press **Ctrl-E**}. Using the arrow (cursor) keys, position the cursor on the Empty/Word Frame option and press **Enter**. An empty frame opens on your desktop.

3. Type **INVITATIONS** and press **Enter**. This is the name of the template. When it's saved on disk, Framework III knows it as INVITATI.FW3.
4. {Press **Ctrl-P**}. Press **Ins** again to move the cursor to the Main Menu line.
5. {Press **Ctrl-F**}. Use the arrow keys to move the cursor to the Print Menu and select Format Options. A submenu of options opens on your desktop.
6. {Press **Ctrl-L**}. Press **Down Arrow** until the cursor is positioned on the Lines per Page option and press **Enter**. The cursor moves to the edit line. Type **22** and press **Enter**.
7. {Press **Ctrl-Q**}. Next, select the Quality Print option and press **Enter**. Your desktop now resembles the following display.

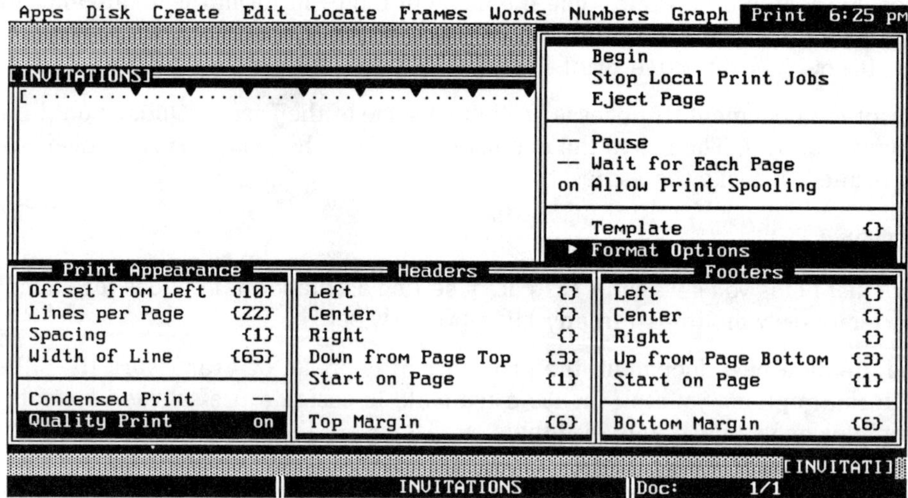

8. Press **Esc** to close the Print Menu frame.
9. {Press **Ctrl-D**}. Press **Ins** to move the cursor to the Main Menu line. Next, press **Left Arrow** or **Right Arrow** until the Disk Menu frame is open on your desktop.
10. {Press **Ctrl-S**}. Select the Save and Continue option and press **Enter**. The template is now saved on disk.
11. {Press **Ctrl-D** and then **Ctrl-G**}. Open the Disk Menu frame again. This time select the Get File by Name { } option.
12. Type **BIRTHDAY** and press **Enter**. The frame is opened on the desktop on top of the open template.

```
[BIRTHDAY]
[....▼....▼....▼....▼....▼....▼....▼....▼....▼....▼....▼....▼....]....
              P A R T Y !    P A R T Y !    P A R T Y !
                      Saturday, April 1, 1989
Come help us celebrate Jerry Smith's birthday. He'll be 42 years
young! We have a special surprise for him that will dazzle and
amaze us all!

          When: 7:30 P. M.
          Where: 111 West 11th # 102

Don't miss the fun!
```

13. {Press **Ctrl-P** and then **Ctrl-F**}. Open the Print Menu frame and select Format Options. Notice that the Lines per Page option is 66 and the Quality Print option is turned off.
14. Press **Esc** to get out of the submenu.
15. {Press **Ctrl-P** and then **Ctrl-T**}. Reopen the Print Menu frame and select the Template { } option. When you press **Enter**, the cursor moves to the edit line. Type **INVITATIONS** and press **Enter**. The braces fill as you type.
16. {Press **Ctrl-P** and then **Ctrl-F**}. Open the Format Options submenu again. Notice that now, the BIRTHDAY frame is set for 22 lines per page and letter-quality print.
17. Press **Esc** to close the submenu again.
18. {Press **Ctrl-P** and then **Ctrl-B**}. Now, reopen the Print Menu frame and select the Begin option. The printing begins. When the printer stops, the paper is not advanced the 66 lines per page. Also, the letters are in the letter-quality print font.
19. Press **Enter**, **Up Arrow**, **Enter** to close the open frames and put them in the desktop tray. Position the cursor on the INVITAT frame and press **Del** to remove the template from the desktop tray.
20. {Press **Ctrl-D**}. Press **Ins** to move the cursor to the Main Menu line. Next, press **Left Arrow** or **Right Arrow** until the Disk Menu frame is again open on your desktop.
21. {Press **Ctrl-P**}. Select the Put Away option. When you press **Enter**, the BIRTHDAY frame and its new print format settings are saved on disk.
22. {Press **Ctrl-D**}. Reopen the Disk Menu frame.
23. {Press **Ctrl-Q**}. Position the cursor on the QUIT Framework option and press **Enter**. Type **Y** when asked if you are sure you want to quit Framework III. This ends this Framework III session.
24. Turn to Module 25 to continue the learning sequence.

Module 85

TYPEOVER

DESCRIPTION

When typing text in an open frame, Framework III inserts the new letter in front of the cursor and moves all others to the right. This is not always the type of change you intended to make to the text. The Typeover option, when turned on allows you to type over, or actually replace existing letters with the new ones. It is available through the Edit Menu as displayed below.

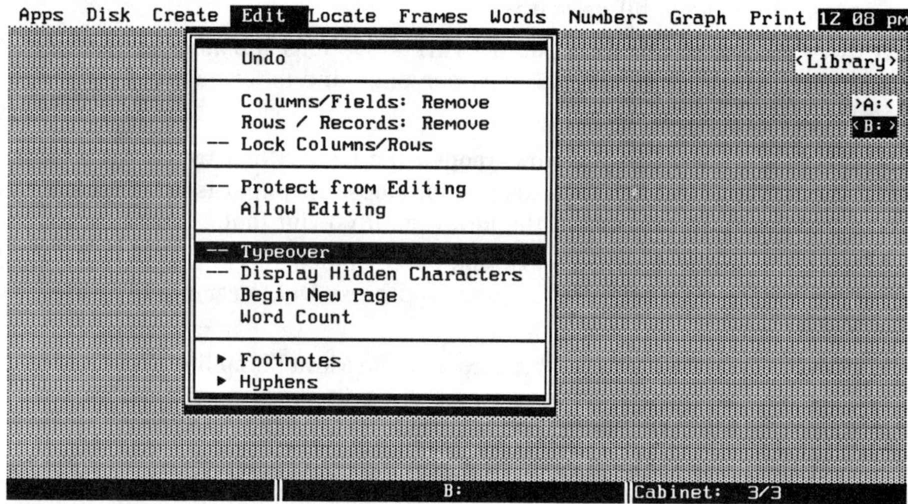

If ON, typing replaces existing characters; if OFF, new characters are inserted

For example, if the line you need to change is "Now is hte itme," position the cursor on the "h" of "hte." If the Typeover option is off when you begin typing the correction, Framework III inserts the new text. Now you have "Now is the timehte itme." The "hte itme" must then be deleted.

If you select the Typeover option so that it is turned on, you can type "the ti" and see the line corrected. It says "Now is the time." Framework III's normal insertion of text did not take place.

APPLICATIONS

Select this option at any time during your Framework III session. It stays set during the current Framework III session. Each new session begins with the Typeover option turned off.

TYPICAL OPERATION

This example shows you how to use the Typeover option of the Edit Menu frame. Make sure that your desktop is clear and the cursor is positioned on one of the drive indicators. The shortcut key combinations, if applicable, are enclosed by braces.

1. {Press **Ctrl-C**}. Press **Ins** to move the cursor to the Main Menu line. Next, press **Left Arrow** or **Right Arrow**, if necessary, until the Create Menu frame is open on your desktop.
2. {Press **Ctrl-E**}. Press **Down Arrow**, if necessary, to move the cursor to the Empty/Word Frame option of the Create Menu frame. Next, press **Enter** to select the option. An empty frame appears on your screen.
3. The cursor is positioned within the brackets at the top border of the frame. Press **Gray +** to move the cursor inside the frame. Type **Now is the time for all good men to come to the aid of their peoprl.** Your desktop should resemble the following display.

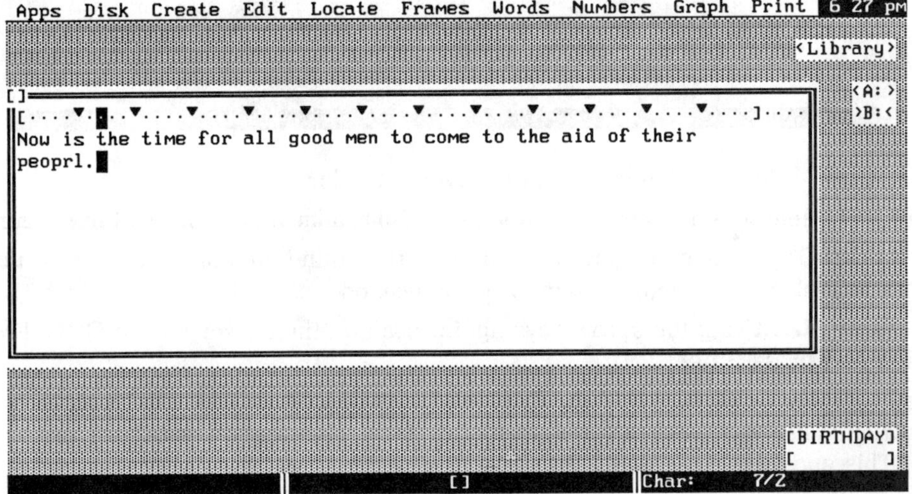

4. Press **Left Arrow** until the cursor is positioned on the "r" of "peoprl." Type **le**. The word is now "peoplerl." Framework III has inserted the "le" instead of letting you type over the error.
5. Press **Backspace** twice to delete the inserted letters.
6. {Press **Ctrl-E**}. Press **Ins** to move the cursor to the Main Menu line. Then press **Right Arrow** until the Edit Menu frame is open on your desktop.
7. {Press **Ctrl-T**}. The "--" next to the Typeover option indicates that it is currently off. Press **Down Arrow** until the cursor is positioned on the Typeover option, then press **Enter**. This option is now turned on so that inserting isn't allowed. When you pressed **Enter**, the menu frame disappeared from your desktop.

8. Type **le** as in the previous step. Notice that the word is spelled correctly and insertion did not take place. Your desktop should resemble the following display.

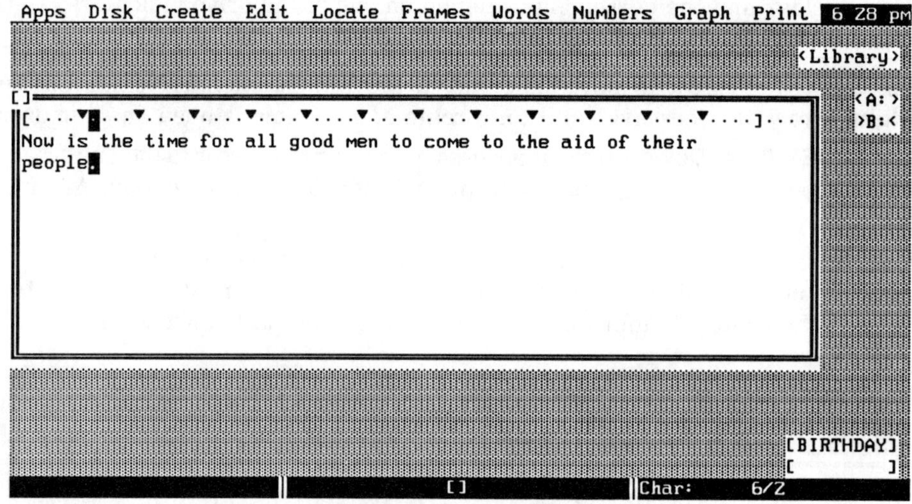

9. Press **Gray** – to move the cursor to the frame border.
10. Since this frame does not need to be kept, press **Del** to immediately delete it from your desktop.
11. {Press **Ctrl-D**}. Press **Ins** to move the cursor to the Main Menu line. Next, press **Left Arrow** until the Disk Menu frame is open on your desktop.
12. {Press **Ctrl-Q**}. Using the arrow keys again, position the cursor on the QUIT Framework option and press **Enter**.
13. The computer beeps and the cursor moves to the Message line. The beep is to get your attention to ask you if you really want to quit this Framework III session. Type **Y** to answer Yes. This ends this Framework III session.
14. Turn to Module 86 to continue the learning sequence.

Module 86

UNDO

DESCRIPTION

"Woops! I didn't mean to do that!"

Errors happen to everyone, but some of them can be "undone." Use this option to undo your last Framework III selection. Although you can't use this option for everything, it can save you time if you select the Undo option immediately after the error occurs.

This option is available for any type of frame. Access it through the Edit Menu frame.

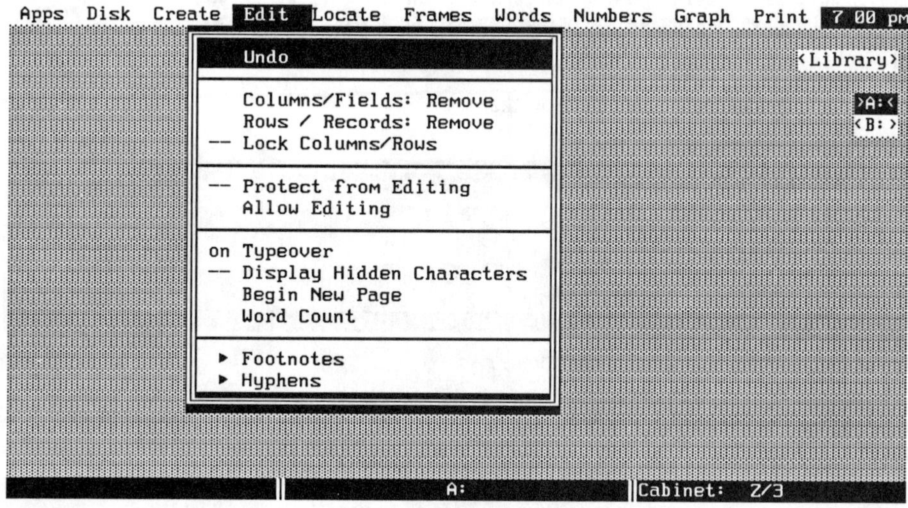

Undo the last action taken that can be undone

When you make a selection or change in error, immediately open the Edit Menu frame and select the Undo option. If possible, Framework III returns the text to its original status before the deletion or edit. Undo each activity as soon as possible if you make a mistake.

APPLICATIONS

This option is available for any frame type. However, it cannot be used to undo all Framework III operations.

Select this option immediately after you have just made an error. If possible, Framework III reverses the effect of the last operation.

TYPICAL OPERATION

This example shows you how to use the Undo option of the Edit Menu frame. Close any open frames on your desktop and position the cursor on your data drive indicator (drive B in this example). The shortcut key combinations, if applicable, are enclosed by braces.

1. {Press **Ctrl-D**}. Press **Ins** to move the cursor to the Main Menu line. Next, press **Left Arrow** or **Right Arrow**, if necessary until the Disk Menu frame is open on your desktop.
2. {Press **Ctrl-G**}. Press **Up Arrow** to move the cursor to the Get File by Name option and then press **Enter**. The cursor moves to the Message line at the bottom of your desktop.
3. Type **B:BIRTHDAY**. As you type, notice that the braces next to the Get File by Name option fill. When finished, press **Enter**. The disk is read and the frame you specified is opened on your desktop as follows.

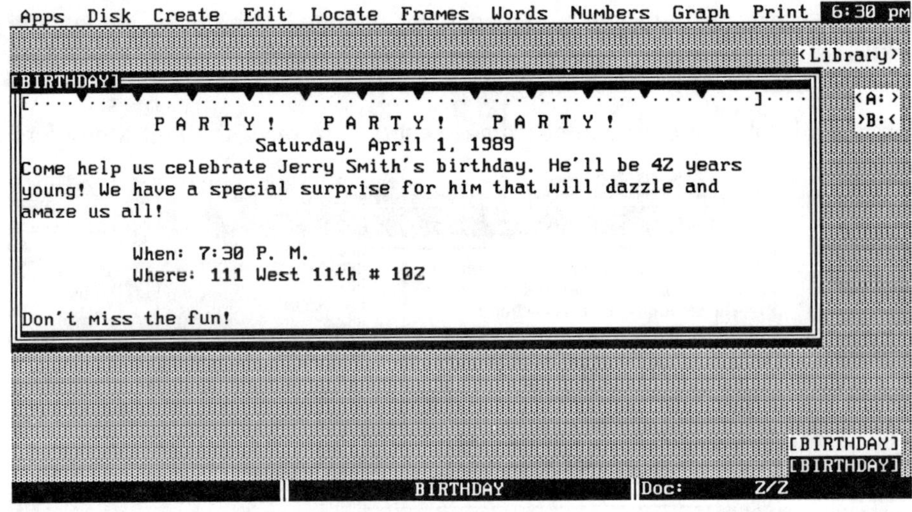

4. Press **Gray +** to move the cursor inside your open frame. Your cursor is positioned after the last change of the document. Press **Up Arrow** and **Left Arrow** until the cursor is positioned on the "A" in the word "April."
5. Press **F6**, then press **Right Arrow** four times until the whole word is included in the highlighted area. Press **Enter** to tell Framework III you have finished the selection.

6. Press **Del** to delete the highlighted text. Now, your invitation resembles the following display.

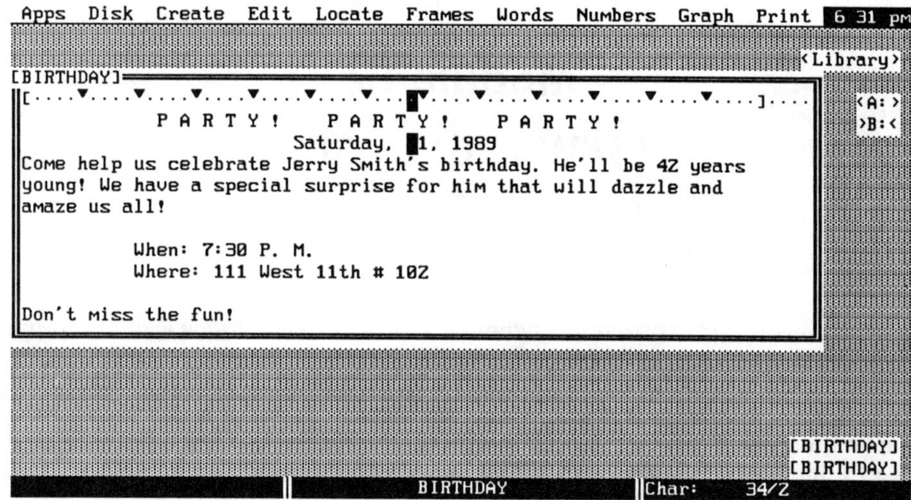

7. {Press **Ctrl-E**}. Press **Ins** to move the cursor to the Main Menu line. Next, press **Left Arrow** or **Right Arrow** until the Edit Menu frame is also open on your desktop.
8. {Press **Ctrl-U**}. Press **Up Arrow** or **Down Arrow**, if necessary, until the cursor is positioned on the Undo option. Press **Enter**. The Edit Menu frame disappears from your desktop. Notice that the word you just deleted has now reappeared. The deletion was undone. By selecting the Undo option again, the word disappears again. The next Undo option brings it back into your open frame.
9. Press **Gray –** to move the cursor to the frame border. Then press **Del** to delete the frame from your desktop without saving it on disk.
10. {Press **Ctrl-D**}. Press **Ins** to move the cursor to the Main Menu line. Next, press **Left Arrow** until the Disk Menu frame is open on your desktop.
11. {Press **Ctrl-Q**}. Using the arrow keys again, position the cursor on the QUIT Framework option and press **Enter**. Type **Y** when asked if you are sure you want to quit Framework III. This ends this Framework III session.
12. Turn to Module 87 to continue the learning sequence.

Module 87

VIEW PAGINATION

DESCRIPTION

The View Pagination option is accessible anytime a word processing frame is open on your desktop. The cursor may be positioned on the frame border or within the open frame when you select this option. At that time, it is turned on until you close and save the open frame.

The number of lines per page is set through the Print Menu frame. When Framework III counts that number of lines, it displays a dashed line between the pages. The number in the middle of the line is the page number for the previous page.

As you type within the open frame, the page designators are being recalculated. There is no need to worry about a page getting too long or too short.

This option is available only for word processing frames. Access it through the Frames Menu frame.

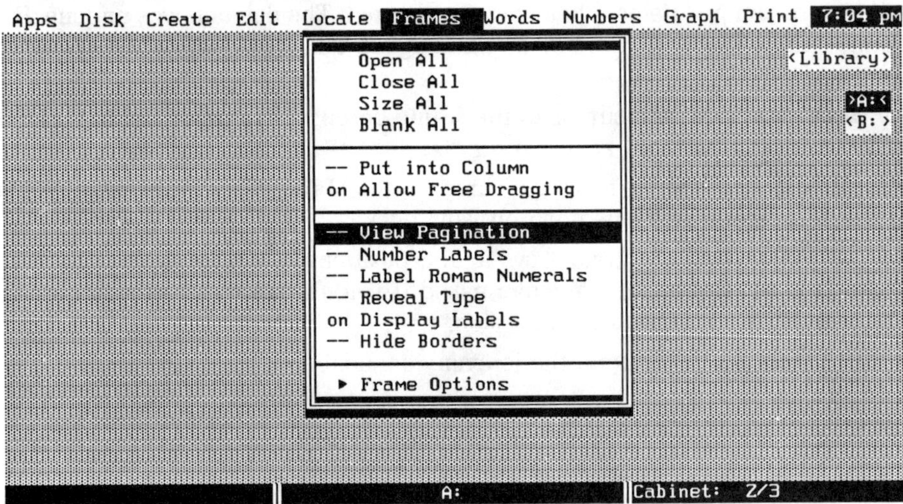

When you begin a Framework III session, pagination is turned off. Selecting View Pagination causes the word "on" to appear on the left side of the option. The Frames menu frame disappears and each page of your document is separated by the dashed line and page number.

APPLICATIONS

The option is available for word processing frames. Instead of printing the document to see how many pages exist within the open frame, select View Pagination.

When you're supposed to write a five-page essay, use this option to tell Framework III that you want the page numbers displayed within the open document. Each page is identified by a dashed line with the page number in the middle of the line.

TYPICAL OPERATION

This example shows you how to use the View Pagination option of the Frames Menu frame. Close any open frames on your desktop and position the cursor on your data drive indicator (drive B in this example). The shortcut key combinations, if applicable, are enclosed by braces.

1. {Press **Ctrl-D**}. Press **Ins** to move the cursor to the Main Menu line. Next, press **Left Arrow** or **Right Arrow**, if necessary, until the Disk Menu frame is open on your desktop.
2. {Press **Ctrl-G**}. Press **Up Arrow** to move the cursor to the Get File by Name option and then press **Enter**. The cursor moves to the Message line at the bottom of your desktop.
3. Type **B:BIRTHDAY**. As you type, notice that the braces next to the Get File by Name option fill. When finished, press **Enter**. The disk is read and the frame you specified is opened on your desktop as follows.

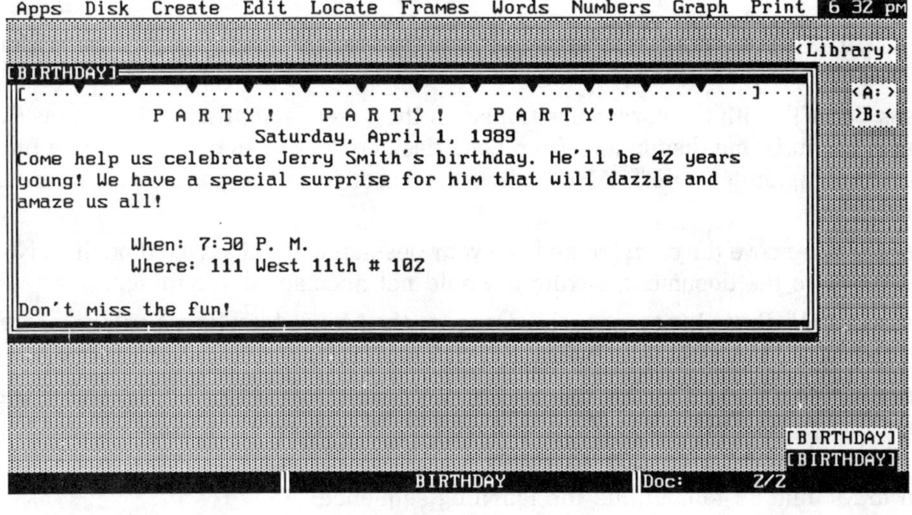

4. {Press **Ctrl-F**}. Press **Ins** to move the cursor to the Main Menu line. Next, press **Right Arrow** until the Frames Menu frame is also open on your desktop.

5. {Press **Ctrl-V**}. Press **Down Arrow** until the cursor is positioned on the View Pagination option. Press **Enter**. The Frames Menu frame disappears from your desktop. Notice that the Message line reports that Framework III is calculating page numbers. The page designator appears within your open frame.

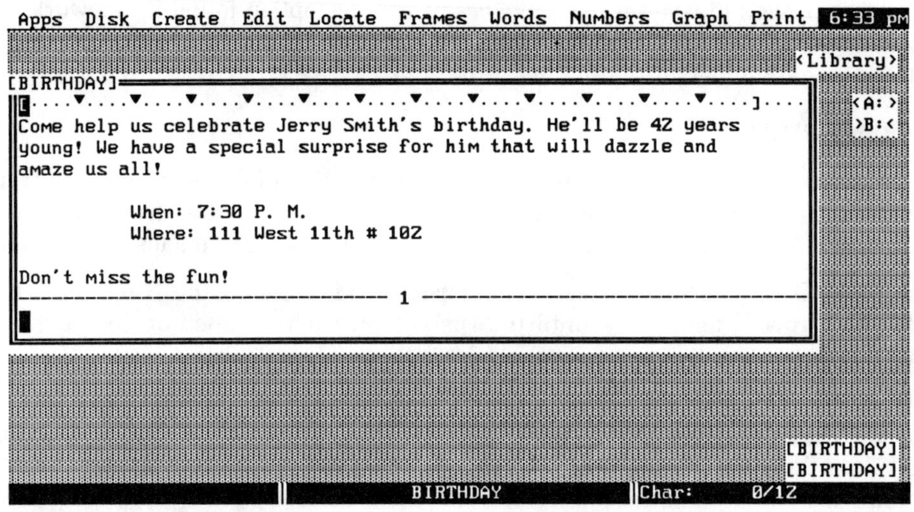

Frames: View Pagination on

6. {Press **Ctrl-F**}. Press **Ins** to move the cursor to the Main Menu line. The Frames Menu frame is also open on your desktop.
7. {Press **Ctrl-V**}. With the cursor positioned on the View Pagination option, press **Enter**. The Frames Menu frame disappears from your desktop. Notice that the Message line reports that View Pagination is off. Also, notice the absence of the page designator within the open frame.
8. Press **Del** to remove the open frame from your desktop without saving it on disk. No changes were made to the document; saving it would not accomplish anything.
9. {Press **Ctrl-D**}. Press **Ins** to move the cursor to the Main Menu line. Next, press **Left Arrow** until the Disk Menu frame is open on your desktop.
10. {Press **Ctrl-Q**}. Using the arrow keys again, position the cursor on the QUIT Framework option and press **Enter**. Type **Y** when asked if you are sure you want to quit Framework III. This ends this Framework III session.
11. Turn to Module 89 to continue the learning sequence.

Module 88

WIDTH (# COLS/FIELDS) { }

DESCRIPTION

Before creating a new spreadsheet or database frame, use this option to set the number of columns you want across your sheet of paper. The vertical rows of a spreadsheet are called *columns*. Within a database, each column is called a *field*.

If you use the {50} which is provided by Framework III, your file contains 50 columns. By changing the number to 20, you can create a narrower file.

The Width option allows you to create a new spreadsheet or database which can hold more or fewer columns of information. Outlines and word processing frames are not affected by selecting and changing the number.

This option is available from the Create Menu frame which appears in the following display.

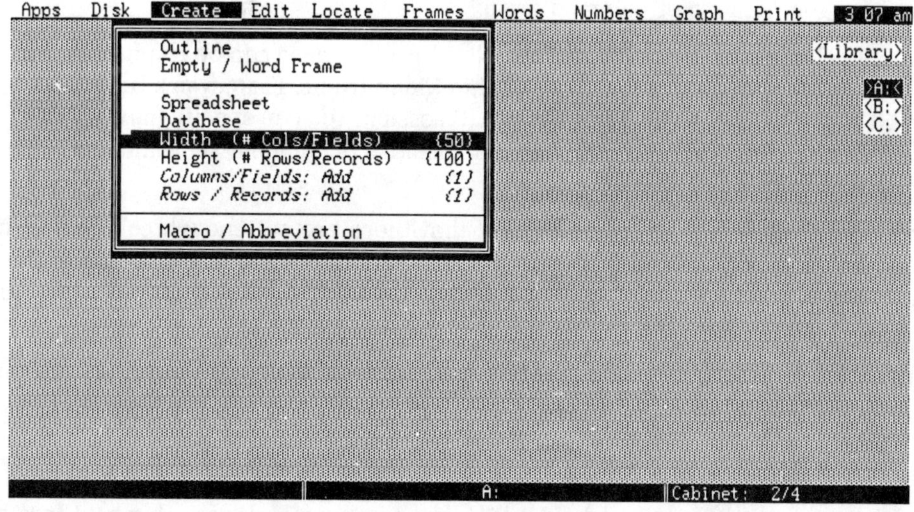

Set the number of columns/fields for a new spreadsheet/database

Evaluate this option before creating a new spreadsheet or database since it determines the original size of your new file. For example, you have five names of people and their phone numbers to store in a database. The 50 columns which Framework III automatically provides are too many for the information.

First, select the Width option and change the 50, which is the Framework III default (preset number), to 2. This provides one field (column) for the name and the second for the phone number. Next, select the Spreadsheet or Database option to actually create your new file.

Remember that using this option does not affect the size of the frame on your desktop. The Width option only controls the number of columns or fields a new spreadsheet or database has when you create it.

The frame size can be adjusted by F4 (Size) or F9 (Zoom). By changing the size of the frame, you can see more of your file through the window. Each of the columns across your file is available to you when you scroll (move left and right) within your open frame.

If you create a new spreadsheet or database which is not big enough for your information, you can either create it again or add new columns to the existing one. Your choice should be based on whether or not the current file is still empty.

To recreate it, first, delete the current one on your desktop by pressing Del. Next, select the Width option and change the number. Then create your new spreadsheet or database file. If you have already entered data into your file, the next choice is a better one.

To add new columns to your file, use the Columns/Fields: Add option of the Create Menu frame. This option is covered in another module in this book.

APPLICATIONS

When you create a new spreadsheet or database, the size of the file is set at that time. The Width option specifies the number of columns or fields for your new sheet of paper.

The number of columns for a spreadsheet or fields for a database can be changed before selecting the Spreadsheet or Database option of the Create Menu frame. Framework III presets the Width number to 50 each time you begin a Framework III session. You can specify the number of columns you need by selecting the Width option, changing the 50 to the number you want, and then creating your new spreadsheet or database.

As you work with your new file, you may find that there are not enough columns or fields for the information you need to keep. If this is the case, add new columns or fields to the existing file. The new areas are added or inserted where needed by using the Columns/Fields: Add option of the Create Menu frame.

The Width option is used only when creating new spreadsheets and databases. It is available by opening the Create Menu frame.

TYPICAL OPERATION

This example creates a new spreadsheet which has ten rows and two columns. Close any open frames on your desktop and position the cursor on one of the drive indicators. The shortcut key combinations, if applicable, are enclosed by braces.

1. {Press **Ctrl-C**}. Press **Ins** to move the cursor to the Main Menu line. Next, press **Left Arrow** or **Right Arrow**, if necessary, until the Create Menu frame is open on your desktop. Notice the Width and Height options.

2. Since the new spreadsheet is to have two columns, you need to change the number specified by the Width option. {Press **Ctrl-W**}. Move the cursor to the Width option by pressing **Down Arrow**. Press **Enter**. The cursor moves to the Message line at the bottom of the desktop.
3. Type **2** and press **Enter**. The 50 in the Create Menu frame has changed to 2.
4. Since the new spreadsheet is to have ten rows, change the number specified by the Height option. {Press **Ctrl-H**}. Move the cursor to the Height option by pressing **Down Arrow**. Press **Enter**. The cursor moves to the Message line.
5. Type **10** and press **Enter**. The 100 in the Create Menu frame has changed to 10 as in the following display.

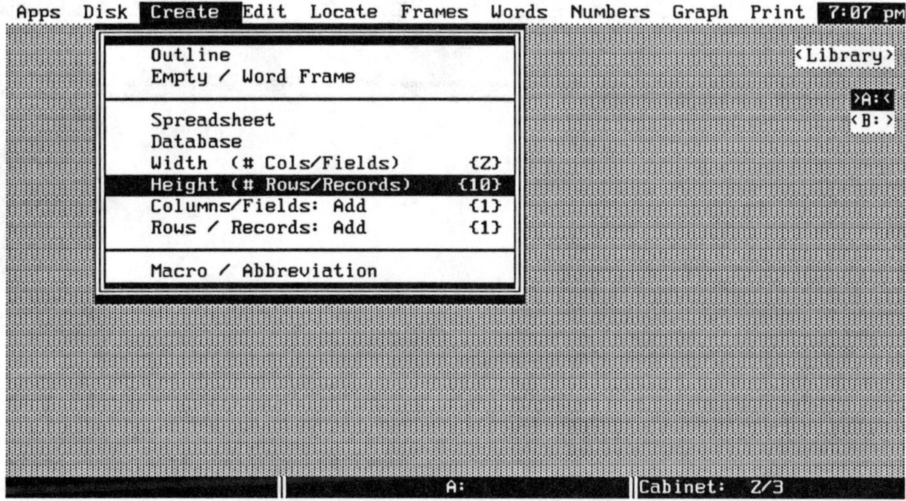

6. {Press **Ctrl-S**}. Press **Up Arrow** to position the cursor on the Spreadsheet option. Next, press **Enter** to open the new spreadsheet frame on your desktop. Notice that there are only two columns in your new spreadsheet (A and B) and only ten rows.

7. Since the cursor is positioned on the border of the frame, press **Del** to delete the open frame from your desktop.

8. {Press **Ctrl-C** and then **Ctrl-W**}. To create a new spreadsheet which has five columns, you need to change the number specified by the Width option. Press **Ins** to move the cursor to the Main Menu line. Now the Create Menu frame is open on your desktop. Move the cursor to the Width option by pressing **Down Arrow**, then press **Enter**. The cursor moves to the Message line.
9. Type **5** and press **Enter**. The 2 in the Create Menu frame has changed to 5.
10. {Press **Ctrl-S**}. Now it's time to create your new spreadsheet. Press **Up Arrow** to position the cursor on the Spreadsheet option. Next, press **Enter** to open the spreadsheet frame on your desktop. Notice that there are now five columns and ten rows in your open spreadsheet.

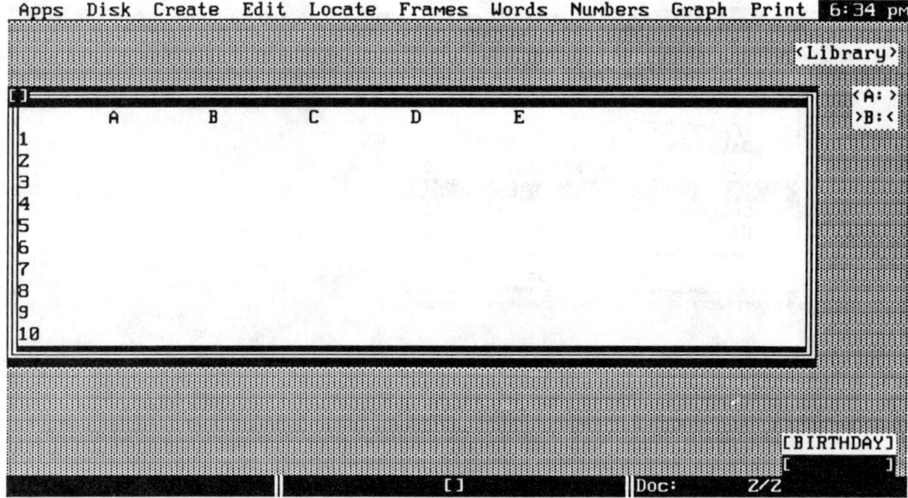

Create: Spreadsheet

11. If you want to save this spreadsheet on disk, refer to the Spreadsheet or Database module. Otherwise, delete this frame from your desktop. Since the cursor is positioned on the border of the frame, press **Del** to delete the open frame from your desktop.
12. {Press **Ctrl-D**}. Press **Ins** to move the cursor to the Main Menu line. Using the arrow (cursor) keys, move the cursor to the Disk option.
13. {Press **Ctrl-Q**}. Press **Down Arrow** until you position the cursor on the QUIT Framework option and press **Enter**. Framework III asks if you are sure you want to end this session. Type **Y** to agree. The system prompt reappears on your screen. This Framework III session is complete.
14. Turn to Module 16 to continue the learning sequence.

Module 89

WORD COUNT

DESCRIPTION

When you're supposed to write a 1500 word essay, don't count the number of words! Open the frame, position the cursor on the frame border, and tell Framework III you want a word count.

This option is available for any word processing frame. Access it through the Edit Menu frame.

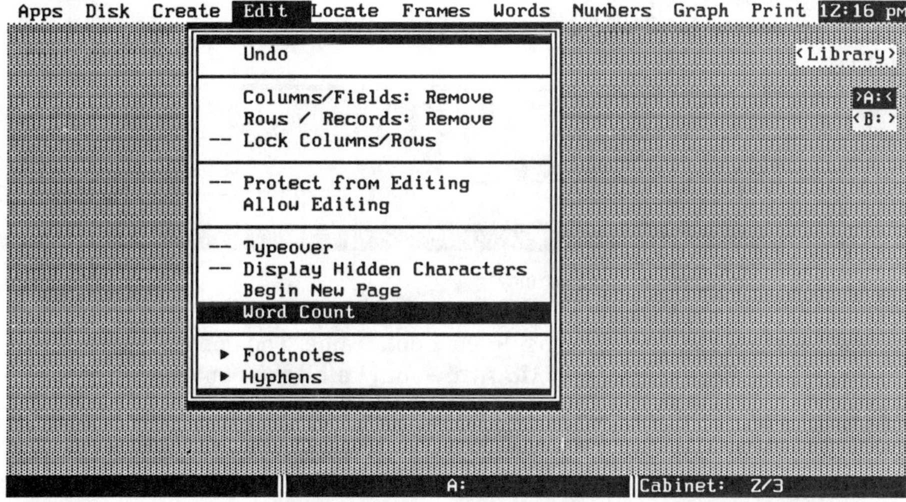

Count the words in the currently selected frames or text

To have Framework III count the number of words in a paragraph, highlight the paragraph by pressing F6 (Extend) and Down Arrow. Once the paragraph is completely highlighted, select the Word Count option of the Edit Menu frame.

APPLICATIONS

The option is available for word processing frames. Use it to count the number of words in the open frame or highlighted area.

TYPICAL OPERATION

This example shows you how to use the Word Count option of the Edit Menu frame. Close any open frames on your desktop and position the cursor on your data drive indicator (drive B in this example). The shortcut key combinations, if applicable, are enclosed by braces.

1. {Press **Ctrl-D**}. Press **Ins** to move the cursor to the Main Menu line. Next, press **Left Arrow** or **Right Arrow**, if necessary, until the Disk Menu frame is open on your desktop.
2. {Press **Ctrl-G**}. Press **Up Arrow** to move the cursor to the Get File by Name option and then press **Enter**. The cursor moves to the Message line at the bottom of your desktop.
3. Type **B:BIRTHDAY**. As you type, notice that the braces next to the Get File by Name option fill. When finished, press **Enter**. The disk is read and the frame you specified is opened on your desktop as follows.

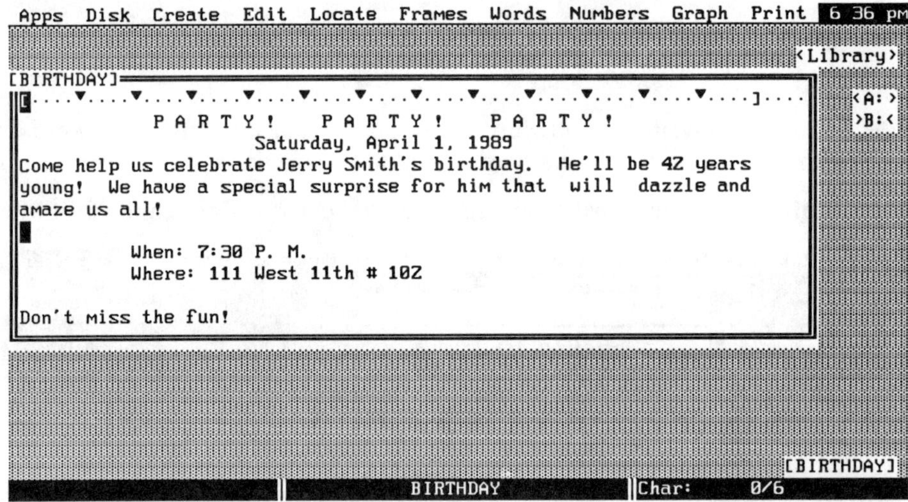

Disk: Get File by Name {BIRTHDAY}

4. Press **Gray +** to move the cursor inside the open frame. The cursor is positioned after the last change of the document. Press **Up Arrow** and **Left Arrow** until the cursor is positioned on the "C" in the word "Come."
5. Press **F6** (Extend) and notice the message at the bottom of your screen. Press **Down Arrow** three times until the whole paragraph is included in the highlighted area. Then, press **Enter** to tell Framework III you have finished.
6. {Press **Ctrl-E**}. Press **Ins** to move the cursor to the Main Menu line. Next, press **Right Arrow** until the Edit Menu frame is also open on your desktop.
7. {Press **Ctrl-W**}. Press **Down Arrow** until the cursor is positioned on the Word Count option. Press **Enter**. The Edit Menu frame disappears from your desktop. Notice that the Message line reports 26 words were counted in the highlighted area.
8. Press **Gray –** to move the cursor to the frame border.
9. {Press **Ctrl-E**}. Press **Ins** to move the cursor to the Main Menu line. The Edit Menu frame is also open on your desktop.

10. {Press **Ctrl-W**}. With the cursor positioned on the Word Count option, press **Enter**. The Edit Menu frame disappears from your desktop. Notice that the Message line reports 60 words were counted in the open frame.

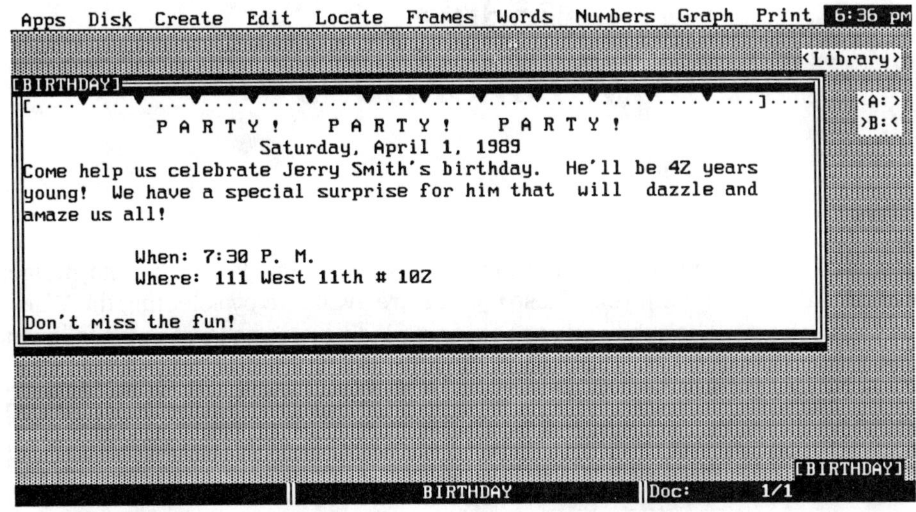

60 words

11. Press **Del** to remove the unchanged frame from your desktop.
12. {Press **Ctrl-D**}. Press **Ins** to move the cursor to the Main Menu line. Next, press **Left Arrow** until the Disk Menu frame is open on your desktop.
13. {Press **Ctrl-Q**}. Using the arrow keys again, position the cursor on the QUIT Framework option and press **Enter**. Type **Y** when asked if you are sure you want to quit Framework III. This ends this Framework III session.
14. Turn to Module 82 to continue the learning sequence.

Module 90

WORD OPTIONS

DESCRIPTION

Modifying a word frame is usually a time-consuming process. The Word Options submenu frame provides features that might help you. These options are available by selecting the Words Options in the Words Menu frame. The submenu appears on your desktop as shown in the following display.

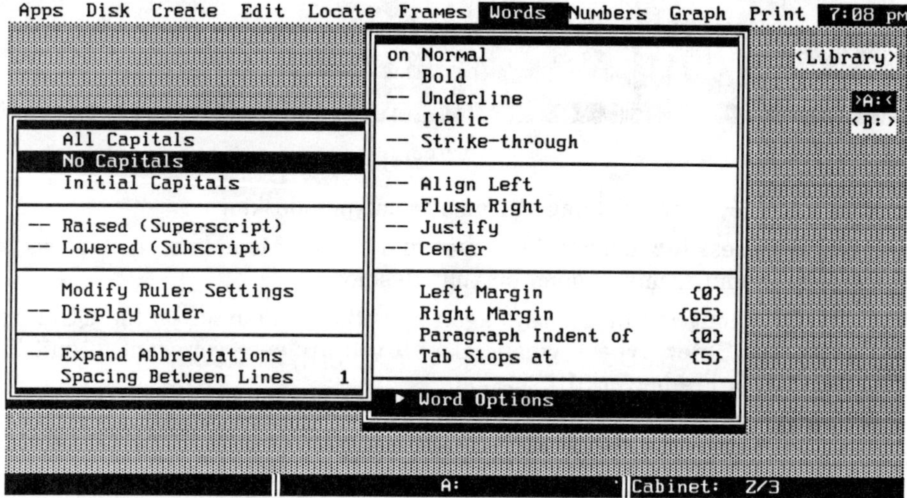

Reduce all selected text to lower case

Before opening the submenu, you must open the frame on your desktop and position the cursor on the text to be modified. Then press Ctrl-C to open the Words Menu and select Word Options. Use the Up and Down Arrow keys to position the cursor on the option to be applied to the highlighted text and press Enter.

Select the All Capitals, No Capitals, or Initial Capitals option to change the case of the highlighted text. Remember to use the F6 (Extend) key to highlight more than one character of the text.

Use the Raised (Superscript) or Lowered (Subscript) option to move the highlighted text up or down one-half line on the screen as well as on paper. Use the F6 (Extend) key to highlight more than one character of the text.

The Modify Ruler Settings option lets you set tabs, clear tabs, set right margins, set left margins, and set the number of spaces for indention.

Turn the Ruler on or off by selecting the Display Ruler option. When this option is turned on, the ruler appears in the open frame. Dashes next to the option tells you that the ruler is turned off.

Use the Expand Abbreviations option to turn the feature on or off. When turned on, Framework III immediately replaces abbreviations with the expanded words that you specified through the Macro/Abbreviations option of the Create Menu.

Provide single, double, or triple spacing for word frames by selecting the Spacing Between Lines option. The number changes each time you press Enter while the cursor is positioned on this option. When the desired number is displayed to the right of the option, press the Esc key. The selected line spacing remains in effect until you change it or end the current session.

APPLICATIONS

This menu of options is available for word frames. Use the Word Options submenu frame to handle case, subscripts, rulers, abbreviations, and line spacing.

TYPICAL OPERATION

This example shows you how to use the Word Options submenu of the Words Menu frame.

Make sure that your desktop is clean and the cursor is positioned on a drive indicator on the right side of your desktop. The shortcut key combinations, if applicable, are enclosed by braces.

1. {Press **Ctrl-D**}. Press **Ins** to move the cursor to the Main Menu line. Press **Left Arrow** or **Right Arrow**, if necessary, until the Disk Menu frame is open on your desktop.
2. {Press **Ctrl-G**}. Press **Up Arrow** to move the cursor to the Get File by Name option and then press **Enter**. The cursor moves to the Message line at the bottom of your desktop.
3. Type **B:BIRTHDAY**. As you type, notice that the braces next to the Get File by Name option fill. When finished, press **Enter**. The disk is read and the frame you specified is opened on your desktop as follows.

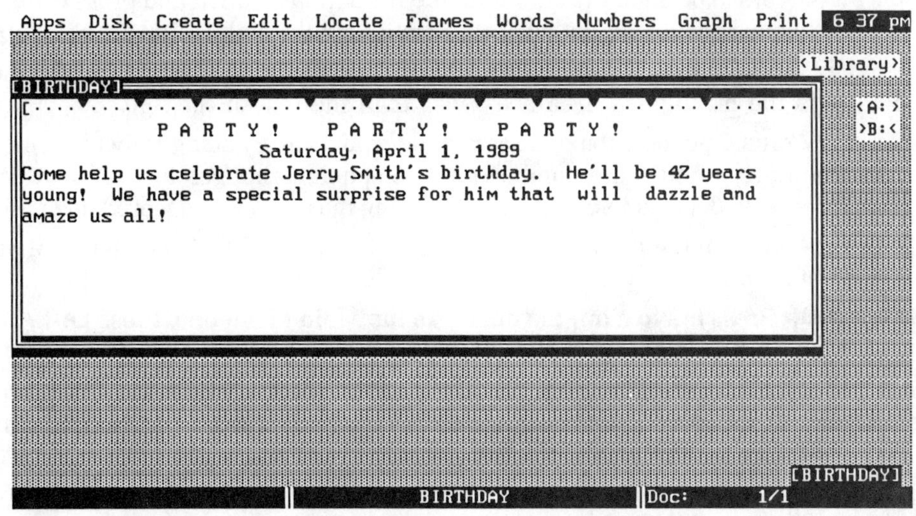

Disk: Get File by Name {BIRTHDAY}

4. Press **Gray +** to move the cursor inside the open word frame.
5. Use the arrow keys to move the cursor to the "J" of Jerry. Press **F6** (Extend) to tell Framework III you want to extend or stretch the cursor. The message at the bottom tells you to start stretching.
6. Press **Right Arrow** until "Jerry Smith's" is included in the highlighted area. Press **Enter** to stop the stretching.
7. {Press **Ctrl-W**}. Press **Ins** to move the cursor to the Main Menu line. Press **Left Arrow** until the Words Menu frame is also open on your desktop.
8. Press **Down Arrow** until the cursor is positioned on Word Options. Press **Enter** to select the option. Your screen resembles the following display.

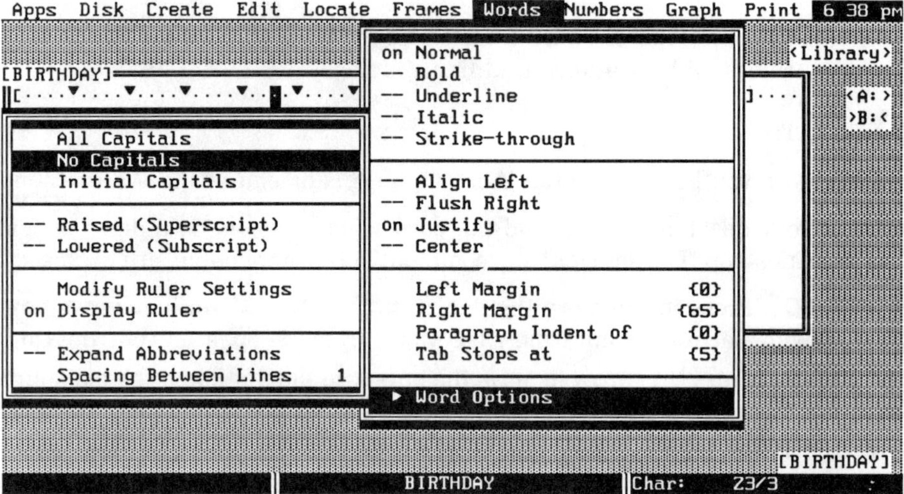

9. Use the arrow keys to position the cursor on the All Capitals option and press **Enter** to select it. When the menus disappear, notice that the letters in the highlighted area are uppercase.
10. Reopen the Words Options submenu frame. This time select the Lowered (Subscript) option. The letters in the highlighted area are lower than the rest of the line.
11. Reopen the Words Options submenu frame and select the Spacing Between Lines option. Each time you press **Enter**, the number for line spacing changes to 1, 2, or 3. When the line spacing is set to 3, press **Esc**. The lines following the cursor have moved down three lines.
12. Press **Gray –** to move the cursor to the border. Then press **Del**. When asked if you really want to delete the frame, type **Y**.
13. {Press **Ctrl-D**}. Press **Ins** to move the cursor to the Main Menu line. Press **Left Arrow** until the Disk Menu frame is open on your desktop.
14. {Press **Ctrl-Q**}. Using the arrow keys again, position the cursor on the QUIT Framework III option and press **Enter**. Type **Y** when asked if you are sure you want to quit Framework III. This ends this Framework III session.
15. Turn to Module 11 to continue the learning sequence.

Module 91

WORDS LEFT/#s RIGHT, LEFT, RIGHT, MIDDLE

DESCRIPTION

When you use a spreadsheet or database, cells or fields containing words are left-justified, while numbers are right-justified. This is how Framework III is preset when your session begins.

Use these options to control the position of the values or numbers in cells or fields. These options are available through the Numbers Menu frame.

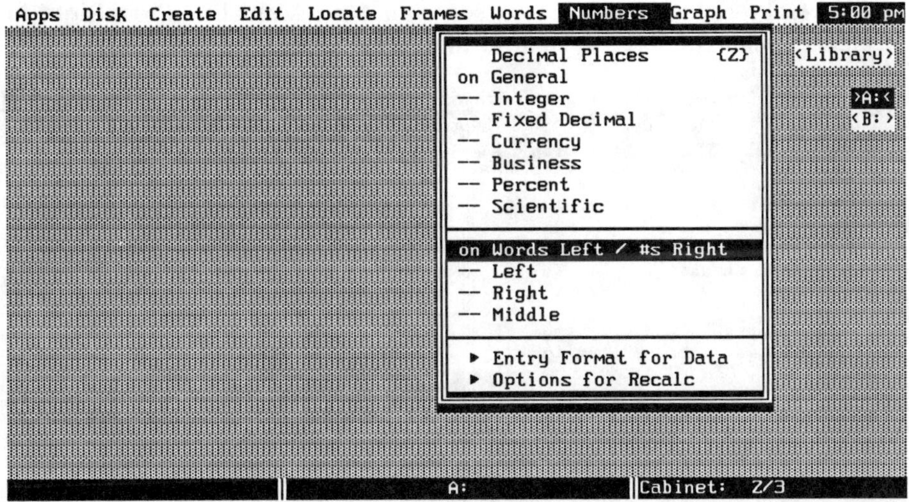

In a spreadsheet or database, align numbers to the right, words to the left

The selected option is turned on and all other positioning options in the Numbers Menu frame are turned off. The word "on" appears to the left of the selected option while all others have dashes.

First, position the cursor on the frame border (for all) or on the specific cells or fields you want to be affected. When the cursor identifies your selections, open the Numbers Menu frame. Position the cursor on the option you want and press Enter. Any value you type within the specified cells or fields is automatically positioned as you type.

APPLICATIONS

Use these options for spreadsheet or database frames only. Each option tells Framework III how to position the value within the cell or field. Each session begins with the Words Left/#s Right option turned on.

Select the Left option to left-justify the value within the cell or field. The Right option right-justifies the value. Use the Middle option to center the value in the cell or field.

TYPICAL OPERATION

This illustration shows you the differences in a spreadsheet when the positioning options of the Numbers Menu frame are used. Make sure that your desktop is clear and the cursor is positioned on one of the drive indicators. The shortcut key combinations, if applicable, are enclosed by braces.

1. {Press **Ctrl-D**}. Press **Ins** to move the cursor to the Main Menu line. Next, press **Left Arrow** or **Right Arrow**, if necessary, until the Disk Menu frame is open on your desktop.
2. {Press **Ctrl-G**}. Press **Up Arrow** to move the cursor to the Get File by Name { } option and then press **Enter**. The cursor moves to the Message line at the bottom of your desktop.
3. Type **CHECKBK**. As you type, notice that the braces next to the Get File by Name { } option fill. When finished, press **Enter**. The disk is read and the frame you specified is opened on your desktop. If it appears only in the desktop tray with the cursor, press **Enter** to open it on your desktop. The cursor is positioned on the frame border.
4. {Press **Ctrl-N**}. Press **Ins** to move the cursor to the Main Menu line. Press **Right Arrow** until the Numbers Menu frame is opened on your desktop.

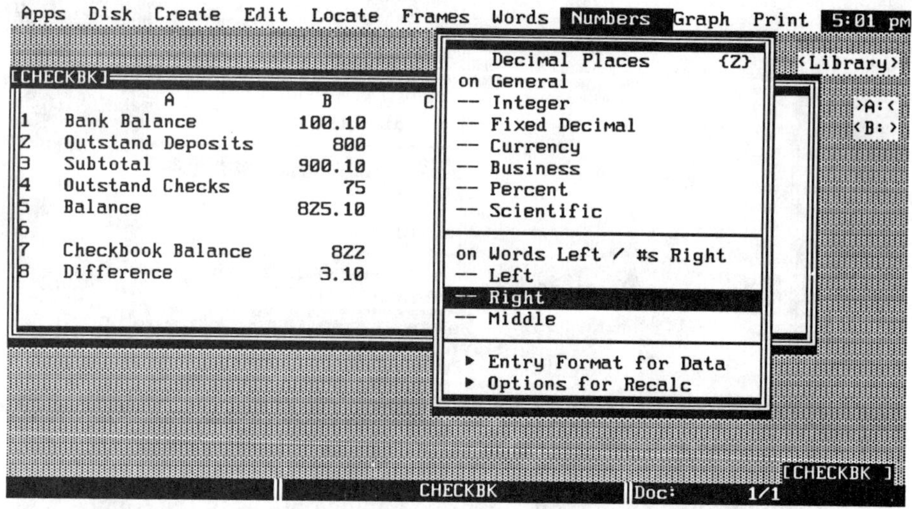

Align numbers and words to the right in a spreadsheet or database

5. {Press **Ctrl-R**}. Position the cursor on the Right option and press **Enter**. Now, all values are right-justified within each cell.
6. {Press **Ctrl-N** and then **Ctrl-L**}. Reopen the Numbers Menu frame and select the Left option. Now, all values are left-justified as in the following display.

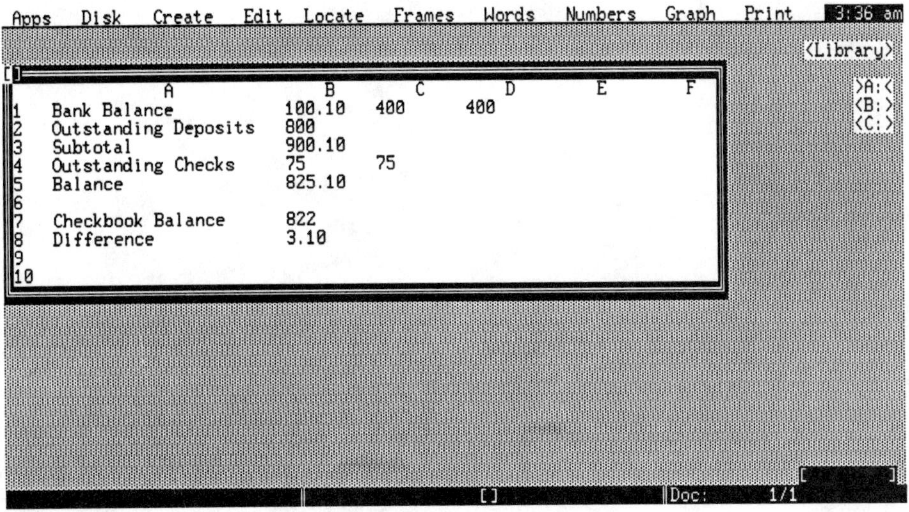

7. {Press **Ctrl-N** and then **Ctrl-M**}. Reopen the Numbers Menu frame and select the Middle option. Now, all values are centered.
8. {Press **Ctrl-N** and then **Ctrl-W**}. Reopen the Numbers Menu frame and select the Words Left/#s Right option. Now, all values are changed back to the original positions.
9. Press **Gray +** to move the cursor inside the open frame. Use the cursor keys to position the cursor on cell A8.
10. {Press **Ctrl-N** and then **Ctrl-M**}. Reopen the Numbers Menu frame and select the Middle option. Now, the text of that cell is again centered.
11. Press **Gray –** to move the cursor to the frame border. Press **Del** to remove the frame from your desktop.
12. {Press **Ctrl-D**}. Press **Ins** to move the cursor to the Main Menu line. The Disk Menu frame is open on your desktop.
13. {Press **Ctrl-Q**}. Position the cursor on the QUIT Framework option and press **Enter**. When asked if you really want to quit Framework III, type **Y**. This Framework III session is complete.
14. Turn to Module 68 to continue the learning sequence.

Appendix A

TERMS AND DEFINITIONS

Term	*Definition*
Access	The manner used by the computer to reference files on disk.
Alphanumeric Character	A letter (A through Z), number (0 through 9), or special character (@, %, $, (,), etc.)
Application	A set of procedures used to perform a task.
Arithmetic Expression	A formula containing a combination of data names and numeric literals joined together by one or more arithmetic operators (+, −, *, /) to calculate a number.
Block	Computers can handle a group of characters or records at one time. It moves each group into and out of the computer memory instead of one record at a time.
Border	The edge of an open frame which contains a label in the top left corner.
Byte	An area of memory which can hold one letter, number, or special character.
Cell	A data area in a spreadsheet where the row and column cross. It contains one piece of information (like a field in a database).
Column	A vertical arrangement of data from the top to the bottom of a frame.
Comment	A note included in a program. This note identifies or describes a program and/or its function. It is ignored when the program is executed.
Compiler	A program which translates a program written in a higher level language into a lower machine language object program.
Conditional Statement	A comparison which is evaluated for a true or false situation.
Data Item	A unit of information that can be identified by a symbolic name or by a combination of names and subscripts.
Data Name	A name assigned by the programmer to an area of memory. The name must contain at least one alphabetic letter.
Database	Information that is organized and saved on the computer for later retrieval. The type and amount of information you keep, as well as the way it is organized is up to you. For example, a class of students and their grades could be kept in a database.
Edit Line	The line at the bottom of the desktop where you enter a heading, a formula, or an answer Framework III needs to continue.
Execution	The computer performs each statement of a program. This processing is called program execution.

Term	Definition
Field	A unit of information that can be identified by a symbolic name or by a combination of names and subscripts. These areas are described in the DATA DIVISION. A data item is often called a "data item."
Filename	A name assigned to a set of input data or output data. A filename can only be eight positions in length and must include at least one letter.
Frame	A window for the work on your desktop (like a sheet of paper on your desk).
Function	A combination of the @ symbol and a word string to tell Framework III what you want provided. These special combinations make up the FRED programming language. For example, @date provides the current date and time to your open frame.
Key	One or more data items used to order or sequence the data in the file.
Key Word	A reserved word which is essential to the meaning and structure of a Framework III formula.
Literal	A character string whose value is obvious. For example, "DALLAS," "John Davis," 832, and 21.444 are called literals.
Manual Calculation	Telling Framework III when you want all formulas within the current frame reworked.
Message Line	The area at the bottom center of your desktop where Framework III tells you what is happening.
Process	Any operation or combination of operations upon data.
Program	A collection of Framework III functions that is kept and performed consecutively by the computer.
Record	By combining related fields of information, you create a record. For example, a person's name, address, and phone number fields is called a record.
Row	The horizontal arrangement of data from the left to the right sides of the open frame.
Spreadsheet	A frame containing cells of information arranged in rows and columns. A spreadsheet is used for drawing graphs.

Appendix B

FRAMEWORK III FUNCTIONS

Function	Description
@abs	Absolute Value
@acos	Arc Cosine
@alarm	Alarm
@and	And
@asin	Arc Sine
@atan	Arc Tangent
@atan2	Four-quadrant Arc Tangent
@avg	Average
@beep	Beep
@bm	Bottom Margin
@bop	Beginning of Paragraph
@business	Business
@ceiling	Ceiling
@choose	Choose
@chr	Character
@col	Current Column
@cos	Cosine
@count	Count Items
@currency	Currency
@date	Date (yy,mm,dd)
@date1	Date Format 1 (mm dd, yyyy)
@date2	Date Format 2 (mm yyyy)
@date3	Date Format 3 (mm dd)
@date4	Date Format 4 (mm dd, yyyy)
datetime	Date and Time
@dbasefilter	dBASE File Filter
@dblookup	Database Lookup
@decimal	Decimal
@delete	Delete a frame or a region
@diffdate	Date Subtraction
@display	Display
@dollar	Dollar
@draw	Draw a Picture
@drawgraph	Draw a Graph
@echo	Echo
@eraseprompt	Erase Prompt
@exact	Values Match Exactly
@execute	Execute
@exp	Exponent

Function	Description
@fc	Footer Center
@fill	Fille
@fl	Footer Left
@floor	Floor
@fp	Footer Position
@fr	Footer Right
@frametype	Type of Frame (number)
@frameview	Frame View Type
@fv	Future Value
@get	Get
@getenv	Get Environment
@getformula	Get Formula
@hc	Header Center
@hf	Headers/footers Start
@hide	Hide
@hl	Header Left
@hlookup	Horizontal Lookup
@hp	Header Position
@hr	Header Right
@if	If
@inputline	Input Line
@int	Integer
@integer	Integer
@irr	Internal Rate of Return
@isabend	Is Abnormal End
@isalpha	Is Alphabetic
@isbop	Tests for Beginning of Paragraph
@iscapslock	Tests Caps Lock key for on or off
@isdocument	Tests if document is at desktop level
@iserr	Is Error Value
@isna	Is Not Available
@isnumeric	Is Numeric
@isnumlock	Tests Num Lock key for on or off
@item	Parameter Passing
@item1	First Parameter Passed (1 to 16 allowed)
@itemcount	Item Count
@key	Key
@keyfilter	Key Filter
@keyname	Key Name
@kp	Keep on Same Page
@len	Length
@list	List
@ll	Line Length
@ln	Natural Logarithm
@local	Local Variables
@log	Logarithm
@max	Maximum Value
@memavail	Memory Available
@menu	Menu
@mid	Middle
@milli	Milli Format
@min	Minimum Value

Function	*Description*
@mirr	Modified Internal Rate of Return
@mod	Modulus
@nationalize	Nationalize
@next	Next
@nextkey	Next Key
@not	Not
@np	New Page
@npv	Net Present Value
@or	Or
@panel1	Return left element of status panel coordinates
@panel2	Return right element of status panel coordinates
@performkeys	Perform Keys
@pi	Pi
@pk	Perform string as if typed at keyboard
@pl	Page Length
@pmt	Payment
@pn	Page Number
@po	Page Offset
@position	Sizes and positions frame on desktop or within frame
@pound	Pound
@pr	Group Printing Functions
@print	Print from Program
@printreturn	Print Return
@prompt	Prompt
@put	Put
@pv	Present Value
@quitmenu	Quit Menu
@rand	Random Number
@rept	Repeat
@reset	Reset
@result	Result
@resume	Resume program processing
@return	Return
@round	Round
@row	Current row
@run	Run
@scan	Returns position of value
@scientific	Scientific
@screeninfo	Return attributes of Framework III screen
@select	Select
@sense	Return value of menu options
@set	Set
@setdirectory	Set Directory
@setdrive	Set Drive
@setformula	Provide formula to an area of a database
@setmacro	Set Macro
@setselection	Set Selection
@sign	Sign
@sin	Sine
@sk	Skip Lines
@sort	Sort a database field or spreadsheet column
@sp	Spacing

Function	Description
@sqrt	Square Root
@st	Printer Setup
@std	Standard Deviation
@Stdbias	Standard Deviation with bias
@sum	Sum
@sumdate	Date Addition
@suspend	Suspend execution of program
@tan	Tangent
@tchr	Wait for next character
@textselection	Text Selection
@thousands	Thousands Format
@time	Time
@time1	Time Format 1
@time2	Time Format 2
@time3	Time Format 3
@time4	Time Format 4
@tlimit	Restricts telecomm processing
@tline	Wait for next line from remote computer
@tm	Top Margin
@today	Current Date and Time
@trace	Trace
@twait	Wait for a specified string from remote computer
@unhide	Unhide
@unit	Unit
@value	Numeric Value
@var	Variance
@vlookup	Vertical Lookup
@while	While
@wordcount	Number of words from selected frame
@writeframefile	Write Frame File
@writetextfile	Write Text File
@yen	Yen
#AFTER	#NO
#BAR	#NULL
#BEFORE	#NUM!
#BOTH	#ODD
#COLUMN	#OFF
#DIV/0!	#ON
#EVEN	#PICTURE
#FALSE	#PIE
#FILTER	#REF
#FUNCTION	#ROW
#GRAPH	#STAKEDBAR
#HIGHLOW	#TBD!
#KEY	#TRUE
#LINE	#UNMARKEDLINES
#MACRO	#VALUE
#MARKEDPOINT	#XY
#N/A!	#YES
#NAME	

Appendix C

FRAMEWORK III EXERCISES

1. About This Book
   a. Name the company which is responsible for Framework III.
   b. List five Main Menu options that appear on the desktop.
   c. What hardware is necessary to run Framework III?

2. An Overview of Framework III
   a. List three types of software packages that are replaced by using Framework III.
   b. Briefly describe Framework III operation.

3. Game Rules
   a. List four items on the Framework III desktop.
   b. Which Main Menu frame is used to read from and write on disk?
   c. Briefly describe the uses of the Graph Menu frame.
   d. Which Main Menu frame is used to sort data?
   e. List five Framework III special keys.
   f. Briefly describe the results of pressing F4.

4. Add to Existing Graph
   a. When is the Add to Existing Graph option used?
   b. Briefly describe the process of using the Add to Existing Graph option.
   c. Which graph forms are available for this option?

5. Align Left
   a. For which frame type is this option available?
   b. Briefly describe what happens when you select the Align Left option.
   c. Is this option turned on or off when you begin your Framework III session?

6. Allow Editing
   a. Why is the Allow Editing option necessary?
   b. In which Main Menu frame does this option appear?
   c. This option is available for which type of frame?

7. Allow Free Dragging
   a. What frame type is affected by this option?
   b. The Allow Free Dragging option is available through which Main Menu frame?
   c. Which function key is used for dragging?
   d. What happens when the Allow Free Dragging option is turned off?

8. Apps Add-in
   a. Briefly describe this option.
   b. Which application is preinstalled in the Apps Menu frame?
9. Ascending Sort
   a. For which frame types is this option used?
   b. Which other option in the Locate Menu frame affects the sequence of the information when this option is used?
   c. What is the data sort sequence used when this option is selected?
10. Bar, Stacked Bar, Pie, Line, Unmarked Line, Marked Points, X-Y, High-Low-Close
    a. Briefly describe each graph form.
    b. How do you choose one graph form instead of another?
11. Begin, Stop Local Print Jobs
    a. How are these two options used?
    b. Describe the procedure necessary to print a document.
12. Begin New Page
    a. When is this option useful?
    b. Which Main Menu frame contains this option?
13. Center
    a. What happens when this option is selected while you are working a word processing frame?
    b. After this option is turned on, where is the cursor positioned?
    c. Is this option available for all frame types?
14. Clean Up Desktop
    a. When is this option used?
    b. Does this option save files on disk?
    c. What must be done if this option is not used?
15. Column Has X-axis Labels
    a. In which menu and/or submenu is this option located?
    b. What happens to your graph when this option is turned off?
    c. Which column is used for labeling your graph when this option is turned on?
16. Columns/Fields: Add { }
    a. For which frame types is this option useful?
    b. What is the preset number of columns or fields added?
    c. How do you tell Framework III where to add the new columns or fields?
    d. Which Main Menu includes this option?
17. Columns/Fields: Remove
    a. Briefly describe the procedure for using this option.
    b. By selecting this option, does Framework III affect the height or width of your file?
    c. Do empty columns and fields reserve space on the disk?

18. Contents Included
    a. What happens when this option is turned off during a search operation?
    b. For which frame types is this option useful?
19. Control Options
    a. List four options of this submenu.
    b. Briefly describe the four options listed.
    c. Describe the use of control codes for the printer.
20. Database
    a. Describe a database and give an example of how one is used.
    b. What options control the size of your database?
    c. Can a database contain calculated fields?
    d. What happens if the data for a field is longer than the field on the desktop?
21. dBASE
    a. What happens when this option is selected?
    b. How much computer memory must be available to run dBASE?
    c. Which Main Menu frame includes this option?
22. Decimal Places { }, General, Integer, Fixed Decimal, Currency, Business, Percent, Scientific
    a. List examples of each of the numeric forms.
    b. Which numeric forms use the Decimal Places { } option?
    c. Describe the method used to set a column of a spreadsheet so that the Currency format is used.
23. Descending Sort
    a. For which frame types is this option used?
    b. Which other option in the Locate Menu frame affects the sequence of the information when this option is used?
    c. What is the data sort sequence used when this option is selected?
24. Destination of Printout
    a. Which submenu option in the Print Menu includes this option?
    b. Describe using the DOS File option.
25. DOS Access
    a. How is this option used?
    b. What happens to open frames on your desktop when this option is selected?
    c. List four DOS commands.
26. Display Hidden Characters
    a. Why is this option helpful?
    b. What happens when this option is turned on?
27. Display Labels
    a. Which Main Menu frame includes this option?
    b. What happens when this option is turned off?
    c. Framework III presets this option to which status?

28. Draw New Graph
    a. For which frame types is this option useful?
    b. Briefly describe the procedure to draw a graph.
    c. Why use this option?

29. Eject Page
    a. What happens when this option is used?
    b. Does a frame have to be open on the desktop before using this option?
    c. Which Main Menu frame includes this option?

30. Empty/Word Frame
    a. Briefly describe this frame type.
    b. List three uses for the frame created by this option.

31. Entry Format for Data
    a. Briefly describe the effect of selecting options from this submenu.
    b. List five valid data formats.
    c. List three valid date data formats.

32. Export
    a. When is this option useful?
    b. List four preset formats for exporting a file.
    c. Briefly describe the procedure for using this option.

33. Flush Right
    a. Describe the effects of using this option.
    b. For which frame type is this option useful?
    c. How is this option turned off?

34. Footnotes
    a. Briefly describe the effect of setting options in this submenu.
    b. List three of the options included in the Footnotes submenu.

35. Format Options (Footers)
    a. List four options included within the Footers section of this submenu frame and describe each.
    b. When the Format Options submenu opens, which keys must be pressed to move the cursor to the Footers section?
    c. Briefly describe the procedure to print a footer on the left side of the page.

36. Format Options (Headers)
    a. List four options included within the Headers section of this submenu frame and describe each.
    b. When the Format Options submenu opens, which keys must be pressed to move the cursor to the Headers section?
    c. Briefly describe the procedure to print a heading in the center of the page.

37. Format Options (Print Appearance)
    a. List four options included within the Print Appearance section of this submenu frame and describe each.
    b. When the Format Options submenu opens, which keys must be pressed to move the cursor to the Print Appearance section?
    c. Briefly describe the procedure to increase the left margin of a page without changing the document.

38. Formulas Included
    a. When is this option useful?
    b. Which Main Menu frame includes this option?
    c. Which other option must be turned on when using the Formulas Included option?
    d. List the frame types for which this option is used.

39. Frame Options
    a. Which Main Menu frame includes this submenu?
    b. List five valid options available in this submenu.
    c. What happens when you select the Snaked Columns option?

40. Get File by Name { }
    a. Describe the use of this option.
    b. Which Main Menu frame includes the Get File by Name { } option?
    c. What other method is used to accomplish the same thing as using this option?

41. Global Options
    a. Which Main Menu frame includes this option?
    b. List the three options available in the Global Options submenu.
    c. Briefly describe the effect of selecting the Safety option.

42. Go to { }
    a. Which Main Menu frame includes the Go to { } option?
    b. Briefly describe the procedure for using this option.
    c. For which frame types is this option used?
    d. What value must be typed within the braces?

43. Height (# Rows/Records) { }
    a. When is this option useful?
    b. Which Main Menu frame includes this option?
    c. What is the difference between this option and the Width (# Cols/Fields) { } option?

44. Hide Borders
    a. Which Main Menu frame includes this option?
    b. What happens when the Hide Borders option is turned on?
    c. Does this option affect the printed output?

45. Hyphens
    a. Describe the difference between a hard and soft hyphen.
    b. When this option is used, what is the only way to see if it was successful?
    c. Which Main Menu frame includes this option?

46. Ignore Capitalization
    a. Which Main Menu frame includes this option?
    b. When this option is turned off, what is the result of a Search { } operation?
    c. Is "dot" the same as "Dot" to the computer?

47. Import
    a. Which Main Menu includes the Import option?
    b. When is this option useful?
    c. List four preset formats for importing a file.
    d. Briefly describe the procedure for using this option.

48. Justify
    a. What happens to a document when this option is used?
    b. Which Main Menu frame includes the Justify option?
    c. How is this option turned off?

49. Label Roman Numerals
    a. Which Main Menu frame includes this option?
    b. For which frame types is the Label Roman Numerals option used?
    c. Briefly describe the effects of using this option.

50. Labels Included
    a. When is this option useful?
    b. Which Main Menu frame includes the Labels Included option?
    c. List the frame types for which this option is used.

51. Left Margin { }
    a. What value is typed within the braces of this option?
    b. Which Main Menu frame includes the Left Margin { } option?
    c. Briefly describe using this option.

52. Lock Columns/Rows
    a. Which Main Menu frame includes this option?
    b. For which frames is the Lock First Column/Row option useful?
    c. Describe what happens when this option is used.

53. Macro/Abbreviation
    a. Briefly describe the use of this submenu.
    b. Which cabinet is accessed when the options in this submenu are selected?
    c. List five preset macros available through this submenu frame.
    d. Describe the procedure for adding new abbreviations.

54. Mailmerge Using { }
    a. Which Main Menu frame includes this option?
    b. Briefly describe the procedure necessary for using the Mailmerge Using { } option.
    c. What value is typed within the braces of this option?

55. Network File
    a. Which Main Menu frame includes this option?
    b. Describe the effect of turning this option on and off.

56. Network Mail
    a. List three options available in this submenu.
    b. Why would you select the Use ASCII Text Format option?

57. Normal, Bold, Underline, Italic, Strike-through
    a. Describe the uses of these options.
    b. Which Main Menu frame includes these options?
    c. Which font is Framework III preset to use?
    d. Is it possible to use more than one of these print fonts for a word?

58. Notes Included
    a. Briefly describe the effect of turning on this option.
    b. Which Main Menu frame includes this option?

59. Number Labels
    a. Which Main Menu frame includes this option?
    b. For which frame types is the Number Labels useful?
    c. What type of numbering system is used?

60. Open All, Close All, Size All, Blank All
    a. Briefly describe each of these options.
    b. Which Main Menu frame includes these options?
    c. When should the Close All option be used?

61. Options (for Graph)
    a. List five options available through the Options submenu frame.
    b. When are these options useful?
    c. Which Main Menu frame includes these submenu options?

62. Options for Recalc
    a. List two options available through this submenu frame.
    b. Briefly describe the use of the two options.
    c. For which frame types is the Options for Recalc submenu useful?
    d. When is using the Row-wise option a problem?

63. Outline
    a. Which Main Menu frame includes this option?
    b. When is this frame type useful?
    c. Which numbering systems are used for outline frames?

64. Output Options
    a. List four options available through the Output Options submenu.
    b. Describe each of the four options.
    c. Which Main Menu frame includes these options?

65. Paragraph Indent of { }
    a. How is this option useful?
    b. Which Main Menu frame includes this option?
    c. What value is typed within the braces of the Paragraph Indent { } option?

66. Pause, Wait for Each Page, Allow Print Spooling
    a. Describe the use of each of these options.
    b. Which Main Menu frame includes these options?
    c. What is the difference between these two options?

67. Print Labels Using { }
    a. Which Main Menu frame includes this option?
    b. Briefly describe the procedure necessary for using the Print Labels Using { } option.
    c. What value is typed within the braces of this option?

68. Protect from Editing
    a. Which Main Menu frame includes this option?
    b. Briefly describe the use of this option.
    c. For which frame types is this option available?

69. Put away
    a. Describe what happens to your desktop when this option is selected.
    b. Which Main Menu includes this option?

70. Put into Column
    a. For which frame type is this option useful?
    b. What happens when this option is selected after dragging frames on your desktop?
    c. Which Main Menu frame includes this option?

71. QUIT Framework
    a. What happens when this option is selected?
    b. Which Main Menu frame includes this option?

72. Replace { }
    a. Briefly describe the use of this option.
    b. What value is typed within the braces of the Replace { } option?
    c. Which Main Menu frame includes this option?

73. Reveal Type
    a. What happens when this option is selected?
    b. For which frame type is this option useful?
    c. Which Main Menu frame includes this option?

74. Right Margin { }
    a. What is the effect of using this option?
    b. What value is typed within the braces of this option?
    c. Which Main Menu frame includes this option?

75. Row Has X-axis Labels
    a. In which menu and/or submenu is this option located?
    b. What happens to your graph when this option is turned off?
    c. Which row is used for labeling your graph when this option is turned on?

76. Rows/Records: Add { }
    a. Which Main Menu frame includes this option?
    b. Briefly describe the effects of using this option.
    c. For which frame type is this option useful?

77. Rows/Records: Remove
    a. Which Main Menu frame includes this option?
    b. Briefly describe the effects of using this option.
    c. For which frame type is this option useful?

78. Save and Continue
    a. Describe what happens to your desktop when this option is selected.
    b. Which Main Menu frame includes this option?

79. Search { }
    a. Briefly describe the use of this option.
    b. What value is typed within the braces of the Search { } option?
    c. Which Main Menu frame includes this option?

80. Spelling Check
    a. Briefly describe the use of this option.
    b. Which Main Menu frame includes this option?
    c. For which frame types is the spelling checker used?

81. Spreadsheet
    a. Which Main Menu frame includes this option?
    b. List three uses of a spreadsheet frame.
    c. Briefly describe how information is typed into the spreadsheet.

82. Tab Stops at { }
    a. What is the effect of using this option?
    b. What value is typed within the braces of this option?
    c. Which Main Menu frame includes this option?

83. Telecommunications
    a. Briefly describe the use of the options within this submenu frame.
    b. Which Main Menu frame includes these options?
    c. List four options available through this submenu frame.
    d. Why is a telecommunications ability useful?

84. Template { }
    a. Which Main Menu frame includes this option?
    b. What value is typed within the braces of the Template { } option?
    c. Briefly describe the use of a template.

85. Typeover
    a. Which Main Menu frame includes this option?
    b. What happens when the Typeover option is selected?
    c. For which frame types is this option available?

86. Undo
    a. Which Main Menu frame includes this option?
    b. What happens when the Undo option is successful?
    c. For which frame types is this option available?

87. View Pagination
    a. Which Main Menu frame includes this option?
    b. What happens when the View Pagination option is turned on?
    c. For which frame types is this option available?

88. Width (# Cols/Fields) { }
    a. When is this option useful?
    b. Which Main Menu frame includes this option?
    c. What is the difference between this option and the Height (# Rows/Records) { } option?

89. Word Count
    a. Which Main Menu frame includes this option?
    b. What happens when the Word Count option is used?
    c. For which frame types is this option available?

90. Word Options
    a. List six options available in this submenu.
    b. Which Main Menu frame includes this option?
    c. For which frame types is this option available?

91. Words Left/#s Right, Left, Right, Middle
    a. Briefly describe the use of each option.
    b. Which Main Menu frame includes these options?

Index